SAVING GRACES

SAVING GRACES

FINDING SOLACE AND STRENGTH
FROM FRIENDS AND STRANGERS

ELIZABETH EDWARDS

LARGE PRINT PRESS

An imprint of Thomson Gale, a part of The Thomson Corporation

THOMSON

™

GALE

Detroit • New York • San Francisco • New Haven, Conn. • Waterville, Maine • London

LIBRARY OF CONGRESS CATALOGING-IN-PUBLICATION DATA

Edwards, Elizabeth, 1949–
    Saving graces : finding solace and strength from friends and strangers / by Elizabeth Edwards.
      p. cm. — (Thorndike Press large print biography)
    ISBN-13: 978-0-7862-9167-0 (hardcover : alk. paper)
    ISBN-10: 0-7862-9167-2 (hardcover : alk. paper)
    1. Edwards, Elizabeth, 1949– 2. Edwards, Elizabeth, 1949– — Philosophy. 3. Legislators' spouses — United States — Biography. 4. Cancer — Patients — United States — Biography. 5. Lawyers' spouses — North Carolina — Biography. 6. Edwards, John, 1953 June 10– 7. Edwards, John, 1953 June 10– — Family. 8. North Carolina — Biography. 9. Large type books. I. Title.
    E840.8.E29E24 2007
    973.931092—dc22
    [B]

                                                 2006031151

ISBN-13: 978-1-59413-232-2 (softcover : alk. paper)
ISBN-10: 1-59413-232-1 (softcover : alk. paper)

Published in 2007 by arrangement with Broadway Books,
a division of Random House, Inc.

Printed in the United States of America on permanent paper
10 9 8 7 6 5 4 3 2 1

For Wade, Cate, Emma Claire, and Jack

This is a small offering, for no mother has ever been more blessed.

CONTENTS

CHAPTER 1
KENOSHA

October 21, 2004

My face was tilted toward the stream of water from the showerhead. Water spilled from the corners of my closed eyes as my fingers outlined the unfamiliar lump in my right breast. Around and around again, I traced its edges. Try as I might, it wouldn't go away. How could I have missed something this size when I showered yesterday? Or the day before? Or . . . but it didn't matter. I'd found it today, this lump, firm and big on the side of my breast. I kept my eyes closed and finished rinsing my hair.

Until that moment — until the lump — October 21, 2004, was meant to be an ordinary day, if such a thing can exist on a campaign trail two weeks before a presidential election. An 11:00 A.M. town hall meeting at the Kenosha United Auto Workers hall. A rally later that day in Erie, Pennsylvania. Scranton in time for dinner, and

Maine by sunrise the next morning. I would speak to at least two thousand people, prepare to tape a segment for *Good Morning America,* discuss Medicare premiums with senior citizens, talk college tuition with parents, and, if it was a very good day, influence at least a few undecided voters. Just another ordinary day.

But I had learned long ago that it was typically the most ordinary days that the careful pieces of life can break away and shatter. As I climbed out of the shower, I heard the door to my hotel room click shut. I knew instantly who it was, and I was relieved. "Hargrave," I called out from the bathroom, wrapping myself in a towel, "come feel this." Hargrave McElroy was my dear friend of twenty-three years, my daughter Cate's godmother, a teacher at the high school my children had attended, and now my assistant and companion on the road. She had agreed to travel with me after John had been named the Democratic vice presidential nominee. I had previously chased away a couple of well-intentioned young assistants who aroused my desire to parent them instead of letting them take care of me, which was wearing me out. I needed a grown-up, and I asked Hargrave to join me. She had no experience on campaigns, but she was a teacher and what's more, the mother of three boys. That's enough experience to handle any job. Choosing Hargrave was one of the best decisions I would make. She instinctively knew when to buy more cough drops, when to hand me a fresh Diet Coke, and, I now hoped, what to do after one discovers a lump in her breast.

Hargrave pressed her fingers against the bulge on my right breast, which felt as smooth and firm as a plum. She pressed her lips together and looked at me directly and gently, just like she was listening to a student in one of her classes give the wrong answer. "Hmmm," she said, calmly meeting my eyes. "When was your last mammogram?"

I hated to admit it, but it had been too long, much too long. For years, I had made all the excuses women make for not taking care of these things — the two young children I was raising, the house I was running. We had moved to Washington four years earlier, and I had never found a doctor there. Life just always seemed to get in the way. All lousy excuses, I knew, for not taking care of myself.

"We better get that checked out as soon as we can," Hargrave said.

I had a feeling she meant that very morning, but that was not going to be possible. We had less than two weeks before the election. Undoubtedly people had already gathered in the union hall to listen to the speakers scheduled before me, and there were young volunteers setting up for a town hall in Erie, and — as the King of Siam said in the musical — "et cetera, et cetera, et cetera." My lump would have to wait; the ordinary day would go on as scheduled. Except for one thing. Today, I planned to go shopping.

The previous evening, I had spotted an outlet mall on our way to the hotel. We had spent the night in a Radisson — a fact I discovered that morning when I read the soap in the bathroom. Since I started campaigning, it had been a different hotel in a different city each night. We would arrive late, traveling after it was too late to campaign, and we would enter and exit most hotels through the same back door used to take out the trash. Unless the trash dumpster bore the name of the hotel, I'd figure out where we were only if I remembered to look at the soap in the bathroom.

As soon as we spotted the outlets, Hargrave, Karen Finney — my press secretary — and I started calculating. The stores would open at ten, and it was a ten-minute drive to the UAW hall. That left about forty-five minutes to shop. It wasn't a lot of time, but for three women who hadn't been shopping in months, it was a gracious plenty. Despite the lump and everything it might mean, I had no intention of changing our plan. We had all been looking forward to the unprecedented time devoted to something as mindless, frivolous, and selfish as shopping. The clothes I had in my suitcase that day were basically the same ones I had packed when I left Washington in early July, and it was now nearing November in Wisconsin. It was cold, I was sick of my clothes, and, to be honest, I wasn't particularly concerned about the lump. This had happened before, about ten years earlier. I had found what turned out to be a harmless fibrous cyst. I had it removed, and there were no problems. Granted, this lump was clearly larger than the other, but as I felt its smooth contour, I was convinced this had to be another cyst. I wasn't going to allow myself to think it could be anything else.

In the backseat of the Suburban, I told Hargrave how to reach Wells Edmundson, my doctor in Raleigh. With the phone pressed to her ear, she asked me for the details. No, the skin on my breast wasn't puckered. Yes, I had found a small lump before.

At the Dana Buchman outlet, I looked through the blazers as Hargrave stood nearby, still on the phone to Wells. I spotted a terrific red jacket, and I waved to Hargrave for her opinion. "The lump was really pretty big," she said into the phone while giving me a thumbs-up on the blazer. There we were, two women, surrounded by men with earpieces, whispering about lumps and flipping through the sales rack. The saleswomen huddled, their eyes darting from the Secret Service agents to the few customers in the store. Then they huddled again. Neither of us looked like someone who warranted special protection — certainly not me, flipping through the racks at manic speed, watching the clock tick toward 10:30. Whatever worry I had felt earlier, Hargrave had taken on. She had made the phone calls; she had heard the urgent voices on the other end. She would worry, and she would let me be the naive optimist. And I was grateful for that.

She hung up the phone. "Are you sure you want to keep going?" she asked me, pointing out that our schedule during the remaining eleven days until the election entailed stops in thirty-five cities. "It could be exhausting." Stopping wasn't going to make the lump go away, and exhaustion was a word I had long ago banished from my vocabulary.

"I'm fine," I said. "And I'm getting this red blazer."

"You're braver than I am," she told me. "From now on, I will always think of that blazer as the Courage Jacket." Within minutes, she was back on the phone with Kathleen McGlynn, our scheduler in D.C., who could make even impossible schedules work, telling her only that we needed some free time the next Friday for a private appointment.

While I bought a suit and that red jacket, Hargrave set up an appointment with Dr. Edmundson for the next week, when we were scheduled to return to Raleigh. Through the phone calls and despite her worry, she still found a pale pink jacket that suited her gentle nature perfectly. All the plans to deal with the lump were made, and the appointments were days away. I wanted to push it all aside, and thanks to Hargrave and the thirty-five cities in my near future, I could. We gathered Karen and headed out for that ordinary day.

The town hall meeting went well — except at one point I reversed the names of George

Bush and John Kerry in a line I had delivered a hundred times, a mistake I had never made before and never made after. "While John Kerry protects the bank accounts of pharmaceutical companies by banning the safe reimportation of prescription drugs, George Bush wants to protect your bank account. . . ." I got no further, as the crowd groaned, and one old man in the front good-naturedly shouted out that I'd gotten it backwards. "Oops." I said it again, right this time, and we had a good laugh. I looked at Hargrave and rolled my eyes. Was this how it would be for the next week? Fortunately, it was not. We flew to an icy Pennsylvania, where the two town halls went well enough, or at least without event. I had my legs again. And then on to Maine for the following day.

I could tell by the look on the technician's face that it was bad news. Hargrave and I — and the Secret Service agents — had ridden to Dr. Edmundson's office as soon as we landed back in Raleigh the following week, just four days before the election. I had told Karen and Ryan Montoya, my trip director on the road, about the lump, and the Secret Service agents knew what was going on because they were always there, though they never mentioned a word about it to me or to anyone else. Ryan had quietly disappeared to my house in Raleigh, and the Secret Service agents respectfully kept a greater distance as Hargrave led me inside. I was lucky because Wells Edmundson was not only my doctor, he was our friend. His daughter Erin had played soccer with our daughter Cate on one of the teams that John coached over the years. His nurse, Cindy, met me at the back door and led me to Wells' office, dotted with pictures of his children.

"I don't have the equipment here to tell you anything for certain," Wells said after examining the lump. Ever the optimist, he agreed that the smooth contour I felt could be a cyst, and ever the cautious doctor, he ordered an immediate mammogram. His attitude seemed so very positive, I was more buoyed than worried. As Hargrave and I rode to a nearby radiology lab for the test, I felt fine. One thing I had learned over the years: hope is precious, and there's no reason to give it up until you absolutely have to.

This is where the story changes, of course. The ultrasound, which followed the mammogram that day, looked terrible. The bump may have felt smooth to my touch, but on the other side — on the inside — it had grown tentacles, now glowing a slippery green on the computer screen. The technician called in the radiologist. Time moved like molasses as I lay in the cold examining room. I grew more worried, and then came the words that by this point seemed inevitable: "This is very serious." The radiologist's face was a portrait of gloom.

I dressed and walked back out as I had walked in, through a darkened staff lounge toward a back door where the Secret Service car and Hargrave waited for me. I was alone in the dark, and I felt frightened and vulnerable. This was the darkest moment, the moment it really hit me. I had cancer. As the weight of it sank in, I slowed my step and the tears pushed against my eyes. I pushed back. Not now. Now I had to walk back into that sunlight, that beautiful Carolina day, to the Secret Service and to Hargrave, who would be watching my face for clues just as I had watched the image on the ultrasound monitor.

"It's bad," was all I could manage to Hargrave.

As the Secret Service backed out onto the road for home, Hargrave rubbed my shoulder and silent tears snuck across my cheeks. I had to call John, and I couldn't do that until I could speak without crying. The thing I wanted to do most was talk to him, and the thing I wanted to do least was tell him this news.

I had mentioned nothing to John earlier, although I spoke to him several times a day during the campaign, as we had for our entire marriage. I couldn't let him worry when he was so far away. And I had hoped there would be nothing to tell him. Certainly not this. I had promised myself he would never have to hear bad news again. He — and Cate, our older daughter — had suffered too much already. Our son Wade had been killed in an auto accident eight years earlier, and we had all been through the worst life could deal us. I never wanted to see either of them experience one more moment of sadness. And, after almost thirty years of marriage, I knew exactly how John would respond. As soon as he heard, he would insist that we drop everything and take care of the problem.

Sitting in the car, I dialed John's number. Lexi Bar, who had been with us for years and was like family, answered. I skipped our usual banter and asked to speak to John. He had just landed in Raleigh — we had both come home to vote and to attend a large rally where the rock star Jon Bon Jovi

19

was scheduled to perform.

He got on the phone, and I started slowly. "Sweetie," I began. It's how I always began. And then came the difference: I couldn't speak. Tears were there, panic was there, need was there, but not words. He knew, of course, when I couldn't speak that something was wrong.

"Just tell me what's wrong," he insisted.

I explained that I had found the lump, had it checked out by Wells, and now needed to have a needle biopsy. "I'm sure it's nothing," I assured him and told him that I wanted to wait until after the election to have the biopsy. He said he'd come right home, and I went there to wait for him.

Hargrave and I got there first. I opened my back door to the smell of clean laundry. As much as I truly enjoyed traveling the country campaigning, there's nothing like walking into your own house warm with fresh laundry. Ryan appeared in the kitchen, clean socks in his hands. It was often impossible to do laundry on the road, and everyone knew that our house in Raleigh was there for their use whenever they needed it. When he saw Hargrave's face, Ryan simply gave me a hug. I sent them all home — Ryan to his hotel, Hargrave to her house around the corner — and I sat in the study looking out at the basketball goal where I had watched Wade play so often, and in my perfectly still house I waited for John.

I have always loved my house. John and I had bought the lot more than twenty years earlier, when Wade was a baby and I was pregnant with Cate. It had taken every penny we had at the time to build it, but it had always been worth it. We designed it to be built in stages. It started as a simple house for a young couple with two infants and had since grown to be so much more. It had been a home brimming with teenage enthusiasm, a cradle for a family in grief, and a playroom for babies nearly twenty years apart.

It was where we had raised our two oldest children, watching them grow to young adults. There was the big kitchen, its barstools accustomed to the weight of teenage boys. There was the playroom above it that the children had decorated as a fifties diner, with old metal advertising signs on the walls. What was once the garage had been transformed into a small bedroom for our youngest children, Emma Claire, then six, and Jack, who was four. Upstairs was Cate's room, for her visits home from college, and Wade's room, unchanged, his book bag beside his bureau, still filled with his papers and eleventh-grade textbooks.

I heard John's Secret Service caravan pull into the driveway, and I went to the door. He got out alone. He walked through the gate as I came through the door. His eyes, narrow and focused, filled with tears when he looked up at me, and his face, which had been set with purpose, softened. We didn't say anything. We just held each other. The Secret Service didn't exist; the neighbors, the house, the beautiful day all melted away. We held on and made the pact we wish we could have made to save Wade. "Nothing can happen to you," he whispered in my ear. "Nothing is going to happen to you."

"It will be fine. I will be fine."

John had called Wells on the way to the house, and he didn't think it would be fine. Wells had told him what he hadn't told me, that it was likely breast cancer. When John asked if we should stop campaigning and take care of this right away, Wells had responded, "I don't think that will help." John was stricken. His good friend had just told him that nothing could help, that the cancer was too advanced to save me. Though John didn't know it at the time, it wasn't what Wells had meant at all. He simply meant that a few more days didn't matter. John had to talk to another doctor

— Cliff Hudis, a specialist at Memorial Sloan-Kettering in New York who had been recommended by Peter Scher, his chief of staff — before he could be convinced that he had misunderstood. As he waited to speak to the specialist, he told me that he wanted to stop campaigning and immediately do whatever was needed to make me well. "I'll cancel my schedule," he said to me.

We couldn't let that happen. Without talking to a doctor, I believed it would do no harm if I chose to wait the four days until the election to do the biopsy and begin treatment — whatever that was going to mean. I had already waited more than a week.

But there was another reason.

During the months I spent campaigning, I had gotten to know so many people around the country, and I don't mean "know" them like I spent twenty minutes talking to them from a stage. I mean that they shared their deepest fears with me. A day didn't pass that someone didn't cry in my arms: their son was getting ready to leave for Iraq and they were trying to buy him body armor from the Internet, their company was moving to Korea and the place they had worked for thirty years was closing, their health insurance company had increased their premiums so much that insurance was now out of reach, Medicare premiums, gas prices, college costs, all going up when their wages were going down, and the list went on and on. I couldn't even think about stopping or letting John stop. Those faces — the parents in Manchester, the wife in Sandusky, the father in Detroit — were with me, and they were why John and I got up each morning, week after week, month after month. We couldn't stop. Lump or no lump, cancer or not, I had to continue to talk to as many people as possible, debate whatever issue needed debating, and do what I could for those people, and more importantly, John had to do the same. The rest we'd take care of after the election.

We could do it. It was only four more days. We had to do it. We only had four more days.

But first, there were people to tell. Cate was coming home for the concert, but before she got there, John called John Kerry, who, like my husband, was terrific. Whatever you need to do, he said. He said it to John, then he said it to me. We told him that we'd decided to keep going. John Kerry can be a great cheerleader, arm around your shoulder, flattering you and urging you on, and that is what he was that day, a sincere and compassionate cheerleader. We won't ever forget it.

Cate was the hard one. I had called my parents and told my mother — my father had a stroke in 1990 and doesn't talk on the phone much — that I had found a lump but that I wasn't worried and neither should she be. I tried the same nonchalance on Cate, but — unbeknownst to me — John later told her that it was more serious than I was letting on, which was as hard for her to hear as I had feared. I didn't know he'd done that or I wouldn't have let her leave my side for the rest of the campaign. But she did leave. By the next morning we were in West Virginia, about to scatter across the country for the last push.

A day or two later, I was in Cleveland Heights. We ate a terrific breakfast at a restaurant called the Inn on Coventry. It was a wonderful local favorite, crafted of oak and chrome and vinyl and filled with customers who knew the waitresses by name. We ate and shook hands, spoke to the crew in the kitchen, and worked our way to the bright outdoors. The Secret Service detail always attracted a crowd long before people knew whom to expect, and there was the usual crowd outside the Inn. Most stood back and waved or shouted good luck, but two women came over to say hello. One had short, sparse hair growing in patches on her head; the other wore a wide scarf. They handed me a pink ribbon pin, symbolizing the fight against breast cancer. "Are you a survivor?" one of them asked me. I was caught off guard. I had done a good job of pushing thoughts of my ultrasound aside for the last few days, and now I found I didn't know how to respond. So I just hugged each of them tightly and thanked them. For exactly what, I wasn't yet sure.

I held it together until Election Day. That morning — November 2, 2004 — I woke up alone in my hotel room in Des Moines, Iowa, and discovered blood in my urine. Nothing like that had ever happened before, and with that discovery came all of the thoughts that I had been pushing aside the four days since seeing the technician's face. I was pretty certain I had cancer, but there was still so much I didn't know. Like how long the lump had been there — it could have been years — or what it was doing to me on the inside. Had it metastasized? Did the blood mean it had spread? I hadn't allowed myself to visit that possibility before, but I knew that my chances of survival were much less if the cancer had spread. *Stop thinking about this,* I told myself. *Get through this day. John and Cate and the children are at the end of this day. But what if . . .* My mind played out the debate back and forth as I dressed.

The knock on the door and Hargrave's happy "Ready?" interrupted the debate. We hurried to meet Christie Vilsack, the Governor's wife. We stopped at a local bakery and bought dozens of bagels to deliver to volunteers working get-out-the-vote drives. There was a slow cold rain as we stood on a downtown street corner thanking voters and handing out bagels. Then it was Des Moines and the Governor and a few dozen people who were once important supporters but were now even more — we had become friends during the two years I had been visiting Iowa. It seemed like the perfect way to close the campaigning — in the company of friends. By the time we got back in the car, my hair had gotten wet in the rain. I looked rough.

Of course, I was headed to a television studio to do remote television interviews. I would sit in a room with an earpiece hidden in my ear and talk to the voice in the earpiece while looking at the camera in front of me in the darkened room, and I would be on television in Reno and Las Cruces and St. Louis, wherever. It was like talking on the telephone with a camera on you, so you couldn't scratch your nose or fool with your hair or squirm because you were tired of the same chair.

My rain-wet hair looked terrible. Typically, I did my own hair and makeup, but today, the campaign had found a young local woman to do my hair. As she worked, I tried to think of nothing — not of cancer or metastasis or what I would find out the next day at the doctor's office in Boston. I asked her about herself, and as she talked, I watched her small pretty face. What I didn't watch was what she was doing to my hair. By the time I did notice, it was too late. I looked awful. It would have been a darling hairdo on someone young and tiny, like she was. On me, it was dreadful. And so, bless this woman's heart, I started to cry. Little tears at first, as I tried to say what was wrong with the style, then sobbing that stopped me from speaking at all.

"Oh my God," was all she could say, the hairbrush frozen in midair as she looked at me, stricken.

I tried to respond but couldn't speak through the tears. She put the brush down and struggled to speak herself. "Mrs. Edwards," she said, tears filling her own eyes, "I'm so sorry. You don't like it?"

I just shook my head and got out of the chair. I walked into the hall, where I knew Hargrave was waiting. When she saw the state I was in, she came over and hugged me.

"Is this not the worst hair you've ever seen in your life?" I asked her, pulling away.

"Oh, Elizabeth," she said, "it's just a little flat. We just need to pouf it up a bit."

I started to cry harder and sank into Hargrave's arms. "This is not about your hair," she said, stating what I already knew. "But listen to me. You are going to be fine."

The young woman came out into the hall and saw us both crying. Then her own tears started, as hard as ours. "I am so sorry," she said again, her words breaking apart between the sobs. "I can't tell you what today meant for me, Mrs. Edwards. It was such an honor to be asked to do your hair, and you're probably about to become the wife of the vice president of the United States, and all week I couldn't wait to meet you, and I can't believe how much you hate your hair."

That just made me feel worse. "I'm not upset," I tried to say, too upset to say it.

She cried harder, and I noticed others looking with embarrassment at the scene we had created in the hall. I grabbed the young woman's hand, led her to the bathroom, and locked the door behind us.

"I'm going to tell you something," I said to her, her hands in mine, "but it's a secret." I could have made up something, kept my secret from this stranger, and I thought about it, but I knew I couldn't be convincing. And so I told this young woman the news that most people in my family still did not know. "I have breast cancer. And I am afraid, because for all I know right now, it could be even worse." I could see both her grief and her relief that she hadn't caused this breakdown. We cried some more and hugged each other. When our eyes finally dried, my face streaked with fresh mascara, we went back to the chair, and — with Hargrave's instructions — she fixed my hair. Ryan came in and asked me if I needed anything. Typically I would ask for a Diet Coke and some sliced green peppers — it was nearly impossible not to gain weight on a campaign, and I was doing what I could to watch what I ate — but that worry had lost its importance. I described the mint meringue cookies they sell in large plastic tubs at Target. "See if you can find those," I asked him. Within an hour, the entire staff and all the makeup people were full on green cookies.

When we left Iowa in the late afternoon, we thought we had won the election. Throughout the afternoon, the campaign staff was jubilant. Exit polls were showing heavily in our favor, and many pollsters were declaring Kerry-Edwards the winners. Ryan and Karen were glued to their BlackBerrys, checking their e-mail and communicating with campaign workers across the country and at the headquarters in Washington, D.C. John was spending most of the day in Florida, and we had planned to meet Cate, Emma Claire, and Jack in Boston around 8 P.M. that night. As we flew to Boston, thinking the election was won, we were celebrating the end of the campaign, mourning the impending breakup of our traveling family, which included Brett Karpy, a young pilot who had stayed on past his scheduled vacation to see this to the end, and anticipating the ventures and challenges the electoral victory would bring. Someone opened a bottle of champagne, and we all talked of foolish things and laughed and enjoyed each other in those last naive hours. Ryan was explaining that thousands of Kerry-Edwards supporters were waiting in Boston's Copley Square, but the people I most wanted to see would be waiting in the quiet of my hotel room. I needed to hug John and Cate and sit with Emma Claire and Jack before we went out to celebrate.

But as soon as our plane touched down at a small airstrip in Boston, I could see that the mood had changed. Someone was there to meet us with a car, and they instructed us to leave our luggage and hurry. I was driven immediately to the hotel, where more satellite interviews had been scheduled. I would do mine and some that John Kerry — who had already spent hours in the remote chair — had been scheduled to do. Ted Koppel, the ABC news anchor, was leaving the makeshift studio in the hotel when I walked in, and we talked a minute while they readied the hookup for the first interview. I was told the first one would be with a station in Hawaii.

"Hawaii?" I asked, incredulous, but not too much so, since Ted Koppel was still within earshot. Hawaii was supposed to be a comfortable win.

I got back in the satellite chair at the hotel and put in my best effort until finally, at about 9:45 P.M., I was asked to do an interview with a local station in New

Mexico. "When do the polls close there?" I asked.

"In fifteen minutes," someone answered.

"What in the world do you want me to say? Wherever you are, run as quickly as possible to the polls and hope you get there before they lock the door." It was the only time I didn't do what I was asked to do. Instead, I took out my earpiece and went downstairs to my room. Cate and Emma Claire and Jack were there with my brother, Jay, my sister, Nancy, and their families, who had come to Boston to be with us for election night. The children talked excitedly about their trip to the New England Aquarium that day and laid out the souvenirs they had collected. After they left to get ready for bed, I told Cate, and then my brother and my sister, what I suspected would be confirmed by needle biopsy the next day. We sat together quietly for a while, overlooking the crowd in Copley Square, the television pundits calling states behind us.

Finally, around 10:00 P.M., John called. He had spent a long day in Florida and had just gotten to Boston. "It doesn't look good," I told him as he headed to our hotel. He'd had the same experience I had. When he left Florida, it appeared that their ticket had won, so he joked with the staff and the traveling press corps on the plane and slept lightly but easily, preparing for the night's celebrations. When he got to Boston, it was another story.

John arrived at the hotel, and we had only a minute to ourselves before his staff — mostly people who had been with us for years — gathered in our suite. With a backdrop of music from Copley Square, John sat down with the pollster he respected and was told that it was going to come down to Ohio, and though we were down now, there was still a long shot. We wouldn't know anything tonight. John called John Kerry, and I left him to talk while I got ready for bed. Although I was exhausted, I couldn't sleep. John came in around 1 A.M. and told me the campaign had heard that George Bush was preparing to declare victory. They wanted John to go out and speak to the crowd in Copley Square — and the television audience — before Bush went on the air.

"Just you?" I asked.

"Just me," he said. Senator Kerry was at his Boston home. He had also spent the day thinking he had won, and the night had been hard on him. John agreed to do it. Hundreds, maybe thousands of supporters still stood outside in Copley Square, where it was cold and raining, and they deserved to hear from the ticket.

Finally, around 2 A.M. Peter Scher and John's other closest advisors came to our room with the speech someone in the campaign had written and the invisible "they" in some other room wanted John to deliver. I heard them in the next room. He couldn't give that speech, John said. It was too close to a concession, making it easier, not harder, for George Bush to declare victory while there were votes yet to be counted in Ohio. I listened from my bed as they tried to rearrange the existing words into something accurate and strong. Finally, unencumbered by the suggested speech they were trying to edit, I yelled out from the bedroom: "We've waited this long. We can wait a little bit longer."

John scribbled a note to himself, pulled up his tie, and headed out. I heard the roar from Copley Square as he came onstage ten floors below me. "We've waited this long," he told the somber crowd. "We can wait a little bit longer."

I woke up early the next morning. John and Cate and I had a few minutes alone to talk about all that had happened the night before and what would happen later that day, when we would all meet the Boston doctor who would later be my surgeon. I went to dress as John's staff and other members of my family started trickling in. I showered, and as I put on pants and a sweater I listened to John in the other room, arguing into a speakerphone that we could not concede until the votes were counted. "We promised," he said. "We told these people that if they stood in line and fought for their right to vote, we would fight to have them counted. We promised."

He was giving no room, but I could see that he was losing this argument to unnamed voices on the other end of the line. Someone would recite the latest numbers from Ohio, and John would counter. But he was alone, and the fight was lost. John's staff sat silently, glumly, at the table around him. Jay and Cate were eating breakfast, watching the muted television and listening to the phone conversation behind them. I kissed Cate, then John, and I wandered out into the hall, still barefoot. I checked on the children, who were happily eating breakfast in their room and watching cartoons on television, then I headed back to the hallway.

The hotel was strangely silent. "Do you know where my staff has gathered?" I asked the Secret Service agent guarding our room.

He pointed to the room of Lori Denham, my chief of staff. Inside, Ryan, Hargrave, Kathleen, and all the others who formed our little family were gathered. The campaign had originally budgeted the vice presidential candidate's spouse for no staff whatsoever, and I had always considered them the miracle staff. The team had been pulled together on a moment's notice, staffed with people who'd thought they would sit this one out or wouldn't be tapped for the campaign. Like many an accidental family, we had lashed ourselves to one another so we couldn't and wouldn't be torn apart. These women — except for Ryan, they were all women — had had more contact with me in the last months than I did with my own family, and now here they sat, spread out on the beds and floor of Lori's room, around the telephone. Mary Beth Cahill, the Kerry-Edwards campaign manager, was already on the speakerphone. She had organized a conference call to tell everyone that the election was over and we were conceding.

Mary Beth's voice broke as she trailed to a close, and Kathleen reached over and hung up the phone. There were tears, but no one said a word. I broke the silence.

I told them that they had my admiration,

my appreciation, and my affection. No one had a staff smarter, or more dedicated, or harder-working than I did. They had given up their lives and jobs and families at the drop of a hat to join this staff, but they were more than that — they had become like family. "And, like family, I want to tell you something first that I will talk about publicly later." I explained that I had found the lump in Kenosha, that it was almost certainly breast cancer, and that immediately following Kerry's speech at Faneuil Hall I was going to the Dana-Farber Cancer Institute in Boston to meet with a surgeon for a biopsy and, if it was positive, as I suspected it would be, to decide on a strategy for treatment.

The room immediately dissolved once more, and although I had managed to hold it together since Des Moines, I could feel my eyes fill up again. I didn't know how much these young people knew before I talked to them, but for the last four months they had fed me and briefed me and planned for me and awakened with me and slept only after I slept, and I felt terrible for them. This time yesterday, we'd been winning the election and I'd been healthy. Today, we had lost and I had breast cancer. Someone had yanked a giant brake somewhere, and their lives had come to a jolting stop. I couldn't diminish the importance of the loss; I had no way to make it better, so I simply went to each of them and hugged each one tightly. And though these women were all a group and in some sense I was at the center of it, I was also the absent center. They had functioned together without the physical me among them for months, and I knew that without me now they would still be a complete cloth because of their bonds with one another, whatever happened to me. So after a little bit I left them to be together and went back to my room.

As I walked to my room, I wiped away my tears. There would be plenty of times in the days and months to come when I would need John; now it was his time to need me, and I couldn't be in tears.

Even though I was afraid of what breast cancer would mean to my family, and even though I didn't want my parents or my children to have to hear that I had cancer, I really was at peace about the disease. I have sometimes talked about the strange gift that comes with the awful tragedy of losing a child. I had already been through the worst, I believed; we all had, and I had the gift of knowing that nothing will ever be as bad as that. The worst day of my life had already come. And I knew too that I had a chance to beat this, a chance my son never had, a chance we never had to save him. Wade was dead by the time an EMT came to the side of his car to help him just seconds after his accident, and there was nothing I could have done in that moment to save him, no matter how many nights I had spent begging God for the opportunity to go back and give us the chance to try. But this was different. I had a chance. I was resolved, not defeated.

And I sensed that I had a few people who would be pulling for me, maybe speaking to God for me. Those women I had just left, who had stood with me in the last months, I thought they would be there — and they were. The people I had met as I campaigned, people who had told me they counted on me, I thought I could count on them, too — and it turned out I could. Those two spirited women in Cleveland Heights who asked if I was a survivor. I knew I wasn't walking alone.

I went back to my room. John and Cate were waiting to meet me, to tackle all that still lay ahead of us that day. I pulled on what Hargrave called my Courage Jacket, and we went out to Faneuil Hall.

CHAPTER 2
JACKSONVILLE

Many people grow up in one house, and there they learn the stories of most of their neighbors and of their town. Their home phone number is one they will have for twenty years or sometimes much longer than that. Decades later they take their children back to their old neighborhood and point out the places that marked the events of their lives. I always wanted that, but, like every child who grew up in a military family, it was not to be. For me, it's not one place. Sure, I could drive through Alexandria, Virginia, and show my children where the Topps Drive-In once stood, where its aging posts with mounted menus touting Sirloiners have been replaced by a shiny Lexus dealership. I could circle Hemming Park in Jacksonville, Florida, and ride past the old May Cohen windows that had delighted me at Christmas when I was seven. There I could show my children the

41

Morrison's Cafeteria where we ate after Sunday school, beckoned by the enveloping intonations of James, the doorman, whose warm, "Come on in, no waiting in the Carriage Room" drifted across the park and invited us in. I could, and did, fill my children with the stories of Pistol Pete Maravich when we passed by his high school on the way to basketball at the YMCA in Raleigh, how he'd averaged thirty-two points a game and no one could stop him.

But the truth is, I was in those places, but they weren't in me, not like a hometown is. I didn't watch them change as I grew, and I cannot measure the changes in my life by the evolution of a place. When I date an event, I don't ask, "Was the new high school built then?" but rather, "Where were we stationed?" Things happened in a place, but eventually I moved away, and one place was replaced by another and then another. James in front of Morrison's was replaced by the wooden backstop at Bandy Field in Atsugi, Japan, which was replaced by the red metal roof of the Topps Drive-In. My life is measured by which air station, which town, which country I lived in. And the cast of characters changed with each move. I don't have a house that was always home or neighbors I have known all my life. My only constant is my family. And for me, describing them is like describing my hometown: it's where I come from.

My father spent his career as a pilot in the U.S. Navy. It was a dream for my dad and his family. Although Dad was born in America, his parents had both been born in Italy. The Navy meant that you were really part of this country, the credential of a real American that no one could dispute. But it didn't come easily.

The one-hundred-year-old, three-story home in Brownsville, Pennsylvania, in which my father grew up might have been grand had it not also been the factory where his father, Flores, made and sold his potions and ointments and where his mother, Mary, made soaps in the kitchen. The neighborhood was all that way: family homes and family businesses under one roof. Next door the Silvers ran a dry-goods and novelties business from their house. All the houses are gone now, lost to the cloverleaf for the Lane-Bane Bridge that solved a lot of traffic problems in Brownsville but took histories, and my family's history, with it. Still, that house on Market Street, from which he could look down on the Monongahela River, was probably the grandest house my father ever lived in, even if the upper floors were rented to roomers. It was there that my grandfather, Dr. Flores Anania, supported his growing family as a pharmacist and chemist, and from there, in 1931, he left to be sworn in as an American citizen.

At Brownsville High School, my father was as dapper as his father, but taller. Sports consumed the time left over after he helped his father or worked the several jobs he had in high school. When I look at the pictures of my father from those days, I can imagine him serving dinner in a supper club he had once described, where his wealthiest customer tipped only on the dinner but never on the drinks that kept my father running to the bar throughout the evening. In photographs, I see him dressed in a double-breasted suit, with thick wavy hair and an open handsome face, and I can imagine the girls swooning over him, as two lovely eighty-year-old twins told me they had, sixty-plus years before, when I met them on a campaign visit to Brownsville in 2004.

And although I never met my grandfather, I can picture him as the Italian father in control. He died before my parents even met, but I've heard the stories all my life. How he would sell one of his formulas to a company, make a small fortune, and spend it on fancy clothes, or an automobile. It may even explain that grand house on Market Street. Then times would be lean again, and my grandmother — Nana, we called her — would be in the basement making soap in a dress that had been custom-ordered from France. One of our favorite stories, told enough times that it might even be true, concerns a new automobile he purchased when my father was about sixteen. He took the family to New York City in the car to see his brother Joseph, who lived on Long Island and broadcast a radio show from Radio City Music Hall. While negotiating the streets in New York, my grandfather's new car stalled in the middle of an intersection. Traffic was being directed by a large barrel-chested Irish policeman who ordered that he move the car. My grandfather tried to start the engine and failed, the policeman bellowed, and the scene repeated itself. Finally, my grandfather, exasperated and unused to being yelled at, told my father to take "the women" — that is, his mother and sisters — to the sidewalk nearby. When he turned back around at the curb, my father saw this short, well-dressed Italian man, his own father, opening the hand of the policeman who towered over him, slamming the keys into his hand, and stomping off, yelling over his shoulder, "You move it. It's your car now."

After a year at the University of Pittsburgh, my father got the long-sought-after appointment to the U.S. Naval Academy in Annapolis, Maryland. At six feet three inches, he had broad shoulders accentuated by the navy blue uniform, and with his mother's thick black hair and his father's soft eyes, he was a model of a robust young American. He stayed that way even when he started losing enough hair that his classmates called him Baldie. When I was in seventh grade and living at the Naval Academy, I went to the library and looked up my father's placement in his graduating class. I was disappointed that it wasn't high. But that was just his academic placement; he was made a commander in his company when he was a first-classman, which is a senior; he was a more than reliable football player and an All-American lacrosse player in a world where athletic success was valued at least as much as academic success; and he was — and remains to this day — beloved by those men who graduated above and those few who graduated below him in the Class of 1945, which because of World War II graduated in three years, in 1944.

When he graduated from the Naval Academy, his orders came to report immediately to the USS *Quincy,* a heavy cruiser, "the biggest ship you could ever imagine seeing," as he wrote home. On January 23, 1945, when the *Quincy* and my father set sail from Newport News, Virginia, President Franklin D. Roosevelt himself was aboard, destined for the Black Sea in the Soviet Crimea, where Roosevelt met with Churchill and Stalin at what became known as the Yalta Conference.

In early March 1945, after the President had been returned home, the *Quincy* and my father sailed for the Pacific theater, to fight the war with Japan. The *Quincy* took part in the first bombardments of the Japanese mainland at Kamaishi, north of Tokyo, and survived a severe typhoon that flooded my father's bunkroom and swept, he complained, his gray worsted trousers out to sea. His letters home were censored, of course, so after the *Quincy* bombed a factory in Hamamatsu, he wrote about how thrilled he was to hear that his older sister had finally become serious with a boy. "Hope she will be leaving home soon," he wrote. "At last, more room for me. Besides, she always stayed in the bathroom too long." After the first atomic bomb was dropped on Hiroshima, he wrote his mother that "life out here is still wonderful. Thanks for the brownies. They were very good, though a little hard by the time they reached us. One boy asked if they were left over from my high school graduation party." World War II, the Korean War, Vietnam, he was in those places, but he always talked as he did in his censored letters home, keeping everything cheery. He lived through a terrible great war, and two more to follow, but you would never know it from talking to him.

In October 1945, after Germany was defeated and Japan had surrendered, my father returned home. He went to Navy flight school, where he spent his nights in a classroom and his days in a cockpit. My father loved flying and swore he'd never get out of a plane. He never minded the danger, but he did mind the unrelenting heat of Corpus Christi and the intense schedule. "I still have a lot to learn," he told his mother as his training program came to a close. "We have to know everything about this plane except how to make it talk." That left little time, he complained, for the more important things, like football and girls. But all that was about to change.

In a letter home to his mother, my father slipped in the name of my mother — and his plan to marry her — between the notice that he had taken $135 from his bank account and a reminder that his Plymouth was due for a free checkup. "Believe me," he wrote, "this is it. She is tall, shapely, light brown hair — fairly attractive. Hope you will like her."

My mother was born Mary Elizabeth Thweatt, the daughter of a Navy pilot and a Mississippi farm girl. Her father, Troy, had courted my grandmother Mary in letters from the front as part of the first Navy Air Corps during World War I. While in France, he wrote her a sweet letter about how much he adored and missed her. He always started his letters "Dearest Girl," and that is how this one started. On the outside of the letter he wrote that if the letter wasn't welcome, she needn't keep it. She could send it back, and he would send it to another girl. My grandmother wrote back that she liked the letter fine and believed she would keep it, but she would always wonder who had gotten it before she did. He knew then he had to marry her.

My mother never knew a hometown any more than I did. There was land in Hazelhurst, Mississippi, that her mother's family owned, land she and her siblings still own today, but it was no more home to her than my grandparents' houses in Pittsburgh or Pensacola were to me. She too had grown up on naval bases around the country, moving every few years, with her elementary school days in Norfolk, her junior prom at California's famous Hotel Del Coronado, and graduation from high school at Punahou in Hawaii, as if in a prequel to my own life.

After Pearl Harbor, Liz, as my mother was known, left college to work at the air station in Kingsville, Texas, where her father was stationed, and there, through a friend, she met a young pilot from Illinois, Carl Hallen. When he was transferred to Hanford, Washington, she traveled by train — with a wedding dress and veil — to marry him under crossed swords, surrounded by near-strangers, since neither her family nor her friends could afford to travel in wartime. She moved to San Diego when his squadron moved and went home to her family — then in Pensacola, Florida — when the squadron was deployed to the Pacific theater.

It was there that she was living when she got a telegram that Carl's plane had lost its positioning and flown nose-down into the Pacific. No body was recovered; there was no funeral to attend. Mother accepted the news with the same silent strength she had seen women draw on to accept similar news her whole life; her grief would be private. Mother simply went back to college, this time to Florida State College for Women in Tallahassee. This time as Mary Elizabeth Hallen, widow.

I suppose every little girl grows up thinking her mother is beautiful. When I was eight I drew a picture of a woman's face with X's at the corners of the mouth — my mother had just had surgery to remove cysts on her chin — and I labeled it "Beautiful Woman," so I was no exception to the rule. But as I look back at photographs of my mother, I can see now that she really was a great beauty, long-legged and lean — she had been named "Best-Placed Protoplasm" in high school, a title my brother and sister and I found hilarious. She had soft brown curls and clear blue eyes above Rita Hayworth cheekbones. She said Carl Hallen fell for her when he saw her in jodhpurs and boots, with beads of sweat running down her cotton blouse, after she'd been out horseback riding in Kingsville. My father fell for her when he saw her dressed in layers of organdy. I've seen pictures of her in Esther Williams-style bathing suits, in short shorts, in gowns, and in suits; I've seen pictures of her with her hair in pigtails and in long curls and in bobs. It never mattered: she was always the most splendid girl in the crowd. Of course my father fell for her, as had a long line of young men before him.

They met at a wedding rehearsal dinner. My grandfather, a great sports fan, had spotted my father, whom he recognized as that terrific end on the flight school football team, and he cornered him to talk football. On the ride home, my grandfather asked Mother if she'd met Vince Anania. No, she said, who was he? The tall, dark-haired young man at dinner. No, she didn't remember him. Granddaddy went on so excitedly that at the wedding Mother did seek him out. Well, he was tall, dark, and pretty good-looking, she thought. When she turned him down for a date a few weeks later because of a planned family trip to Mobile, my grandfather was beside himself. From that point on, her family could not have been more helpful to the courtship.

It was not as easy on the other side of the family. The fact that my mother had been married before was a source of tension for my father's mother. In addition, Nana took her Catholicism very seriously, and my mother was a Methodist. And . . . well, there was probably an endless list. Not long before the wedding, my mother wrote to Mary Anania in Pittsburgh: "I am sorry for the circumstances that make me not exactly what you wanted for your son, but I shall try to make up for that in other ways. Please believe me — no one could love him more or be more interested in his happiness." I believe that from then on, my mother never spoke to anyone of her life as Liz Hallen, and it wasn't until I was an adult that I even knew of my mother's first marriage. Although I had seen my parents' wedding invitation when I was snooping around as an eighth grader, I had just assumed that she was keeping it because of the novelty of the printer's error, having printed some other bride's name, Hallen, instead of Thweatt.

They were married on December 30, 1947, in my grandparents' house in a simple nondenominational ceremony. My father had to report to the Naval Air Station Jacksonville in early January. Jacksonville was followed by the Naval Air Station at Quonset Point, in Rhode Island, followed by a deployment to Europe. When he returned to the States, my father discovered he was being stationed back in Jacksonville, and my mother discovered she was pregnant. I was born in the hospital at the

Jacksonville Naval Air Station on July 3, 1949. I was named Mary Elizabeth, after my mother — although I was called Mary Beth, and my brother, born a year later at the Bethesda Naval Hospital in Maryland, was named for my father, although he was called Jay. My sister, born a year after that, was named Nancy, after my mother's sister; with no competition in the immediate family, she was called Nancy. As my mother left the hospital with Nancy, the doctor — who had also delivered Jay fifty-three weeks earlier — cheerfully bid Mother farewell, saying, "I'll see you next year." My mother, her baby in her arms and two toddlers waiting at home, just looked at him and replied, "Don't count on it."

We outgrew the Washington, D.C., apartment my parents first rented, so my parents bought a tiny bungalow — a dollhouse, my mother always said — in Falls Church, Virginia. Mother promptly filled the yard with trees and signed up to be the neighborhood military wives' liaison. And just as promptly, Dad got transferred again, this time to Japan. But first he had temporary duty in Korea, which was still at war. Mother packed up the dollhouse alone and drove us to Pensacola. When Dad wrote that he was ready for us, my mother took a train across the country and boarded a military transport ship for a thirty-day trip across the Pacific with three toddlers. If you have ever been on a cruise and are imagining its bright staterooms and open corridors, you are not imagining a military transport ship. Imagine instead everything painted battle-ship gray and the hallways periodically interrupted by raised hatch doorways that — while they undoubtedly provided a measure of safety had we been hit by a torpedo — were a tremendous hurdle to climb over, and over, and over for children not quite two, three, and four. Every time I feel overwhelmed as a mother, I try to remind myself of what this first trip with three young children must have been like for my mother.

The hardest part was keeping track of us. Mother bought each of us new outfits for the trip: matching navy blue coats and hats, just like real sailors. Afraid, however, that we would fall overboard and she would arrive in Japan with fewer children than she had when she left, she also bought each of us a harness that went around our chests and attached to a leash. While it meant we were always no more than a leash's length away from her for the thirty-day voyage, it also meant that she could never be more than a leash's length away from three toddlers for thirty days. When the ship finally prepared to dock at Yokohama, my mother dressed us in matching outfits. When we were ready, she took a few minutes in the outer section of the stateroom to make herself look as good as possible for the husband she hadn't seen in months. When she returned, wearing a fresh dress and smelling of perfume, she found us sitting quietly on the floor, me with a pair of scissors in my hand and most of the hair from the right side of my head on the floor beside me. With barely a word, she pulled my sailor hat over the mess I had made, clipped on the harnesses, and led us toward our new life in Japan.

Because my father was a junior officer, we didn't qualify immediately for base housing. Dad had rented a small Japanese version of an American house in Minami Rinkin, a village tucked in a valley near the Atsugi Naval Air Station where he worked, on a road filled with bicycles, oxcarts, and mud. We had a round-faced Japanese cleaning lady — as did all the military families at the time — named Koko-san, who saved my brother's life after he scooped kerosene from the heater that warmed the living room and drank it, and who taught my sister to speak

English — with a Japanese accent that she had until she was a teenager. We would walk with Koko-san into the little town to shop, and when we did, we drew a crowd — that is, if my sister was with us. Jay and I had dark, nearly black hair, and if you looked across a group of Japanese children, you wouldn't pick us out unless our round blue eyes were fixed on you. But Nancy had sunshine yellow hair, and wherever we went, Japanese children in their school uniforms would follow her like she was the Pied Piper, jostling to be closest to her, reaching their hands out to stroke her unimaginably beautiful hair. Nancy has always been pretty and has always garnered her share of attention, but never again like it was in Minami Rinkin. I've often thought that a lesser person than Nancy might have found life to be a disappointment after that opening act.

Dad eventually qualified for on-base housing — a one-story, three-bedroom stucco house that looked like every other one-story, three-bedroom stucco house in the Army housing area at Sagamihara. The houses looked the same on the outside, and they were all the same on the inside. Not just the same floor plan — living room in front, dining room to the left, bedrooms back to the right — but all painted the same, too. In the military, you didn't choose your wall colors. The military painted the walls an eggshell color, and when you moved out and another family moved in, they painted them eggshell again, and the houses perpetually smelled of fresh paint. We lived there for two years, and Koko-san — now a part of the family — came with us.

Just as we had begun to settle into our lives and I had started first grade at the base school, it was again time for my mother to pack up the house. My father got word he was being stationed back in Jacksonville. I was leaving the fifth house I had lived in during my six years, but that didn't bother me. I was already used to that. What did bother me was that I was leaving Koko-san. She was plain and sturdy and warm, and Jay, Nancy, and I loved her completely. It was the first time I had to say goodbye to someone I thought — rightly, it turns out — I would never see again. Although my mother had my father to help her cross the Pacific this time, now she had three young crying children, grieving the loss of Koko-san. It may have been an easier crossing than the first, but only marginally so.

When we moved back to Jacksonville, Florida, it was the middle of the 1950s and we were the prototype for the 1950s family. In Japan, we only found out about the changes in American fashion or American music or even American restaurants when magazines — consistently two months late — arrived at the Navy Exchange or when there was a revealing section in the News of the Day reel that preceded each movie at the station theater. The result was that what we thought was fashionable might be unrealistic, as if aliens had dressed for school by looking at old *Vogue* magazines and what the First Lady was wearing as she greeted a visiting head of state. That's how it came to be that the Anania family arrived at the first community picnic at the Naval Air Station Jacksonville in matching outfits. My mother had gotten some blue and white Japanese cotton, and she had a Japanese seamstress Koko-san knew make jumpsuits — little shorts with attached blouses — for Nancy and me, and button-up skirts that went over the shorts. That part was cute. My mother had a shirtwaist dress of the same material, and maybe that was cute, too. But then Jay had shorts and a shirt, and it didn't end there; my father had a matching shirt. After the reception we got at that first picnic — hoots as if we had dressed that way as a prank — my father never wore the shirt again.

Not that he wouldn't wear ridiculous outfits. He wore a revealing wrapped skirt to a luau on the base. He wore a truly ludicrous plaid suit and a matching plaid oversize hat and "played" a guitar, gyrating like Elvis, at the officers' club talent show. He and a few other brave men wore pink bikini tops and matching skirts and did a Rockette-ish routine — hairy legs and all — at another club event. And that was all just while we were in Jacksonville. It wasn't complicated; my father liked to make people laugh. Absolutely nothing embarrassed him. And when I was seven, nothing he did embarrassed me — although that would change over the next few years. At this point, though, I was a child living in the circus. Other children went to watch *Peter Pan?* Well, Dad was in it, and so my brother and I got to be Lost Boys. Then he was Captain "Ironsides" Brackett in Jacksonville's Starlight Theatre production of *South Pacific.* And then he was Harry Brock in *Born Yesterday.* But he didn't need a play — anywhere was a stage to him.

It never occurred to me that there could be people who were shy or reclusive. We certainly weren't; we couldn't be. Believe me, once you have seen your father dancing in a pink bikini, walking into a new school or playing a boy in green tights onstage is a piece of cake. So suburban Venezia Elementary School, my new school, was just a new school, and I made new friends, fell for a civilian boy — Steve Alston, who chased me on the playground, which I think means he fell for me, too — and had my first of a series of teachers who enchanted me.

The summer I turned eight my father got orders to return to Japan, this time to the Marine Corps Air Facility in Iwakuni. But first Dad would be in survival training in California for several months, so the remaining four of us moved in with my grandparents in Pensacola. Not every place has a smell you can remember, but my grandparents' house did, and it was the smell of starched and ironed linens, fresh starched linens in those days, and later, when the bedrooms of their house were no longer regularly filled with family, the smell of stale starched linens. Anyone who has been in a Southern home where the heat collects in every fold of cloth or skin and undoes every sweet odor in time knows the difference.

There we played with cousins and — for the first time — really got to know our grandparents. Grandmother Thweatt would spend her days in the kitchen, while my grandfather sat in his leather chair in the living room playing solitaire or Scrabble. The grandchildren would gather around him and watch him play. Every once in a while, someone with a short memory would ask him what a word he had put down on the Scrabble board meant. Then, as he did anytime he thought we didn't know the definition of a word, he would send us to the back hall, where the *Webster's Third Unabridged Dictionary* stood on a tall stand. None of us was tall enough to reach it, and we had to pull a stool from the kitchen to read the words at the top of the page. When my grandmother died, nearly thirty years after her husband, that dictionary stand and *Webster's Third* were all I wanted. They sit in my house today, and I play the role of my grandfather.

CHAPTER 3
IWAKUNI, JAPAN

When I complained to my mother that I was called Maleficent after a base theater showing of *Sleeping Beauty* featuring the evil witch of that name and that some of the children had thrown stones at me, she promptly cut my long straight black hair into a boyish cut. Based on the photographs of me at the time, it is safe to say that she cut it rather than she had it cut. When it grew out, I got my first Toni, as we called all permanents, and my hair looked more like Jacqueline Kennedy's than any witch's.

Mother was there to solve that problem. Harder to solve was the smart-girl dilemma. It wasn't that I was so smart; it was just that the base in Iwakuni, Japan, was a very, very small pond. I had only one real competitor in the classroom, a pretty waif named Daryl Mayer, but more often than not, I bested her by a little, which made me feel good when Mrs. Defenderfer handed out the papers but didn't serve me well when we were released to the playground. In fourth grade, when I won out over fifth and sixth graders in art and poetry contests, my fate was sealed: I was a square, what my children now call a nerd. And looking back over the years that followed, I was always a square, or at best on the edge of it. I made many of my own clothes when I was in graduate school, for crying out loud. Roll that image back to a fourth grader, and you get a pretty clear picture of me.

Despite all that, and except for the rock-throwing incident, I don't think of that time as unhappy. In fact, quite the opposite. Even if I wasn't the popular Noony Bemis or the blonde and beautiful Christine Rodgers, they were my friends. There were so few people with whom you could play tetherball or bike along the edge of the seawall that everyone, even squares, was included in the fun. We all were Girl Scouts; we all sang in the choir. What else was there to do?

It was 1959. I was nine years old, wearing dresses ordered from the Montgomery Ward catalog and riding my bike around our new base. I spent the greater part of my days in the Matthew C. Perry School or on the playground with other children whose fathers also wore the Navy uniform, most of them pilots, many of them reconnaissance pilots. My father was an aviator trained in intelligence, and his squadron, VQ-1, patrolled the borders of North Korea and what we then called Red China. Though he never talked about what he did as a reconnaissance pilot, not then, not ever, that was the first time I thought I understood his job. It didn't occur to me, however, that what he did for a living was extraordinarily courageous, even though I had warnings, as when the screen at the base theater would go black during a showing and a message would appear telling all military personnel to go immediately to the terminals. Single men would don their hats, fathers would bend over and kiss their children, the aisles would fill for a few minutes and then be still, and the movie would start again. Or I might have guessed about the danger when Dad said he would be back by Jay's baseball game on Saturday and he wasn't, but the newspaper was full of stories of violence in Laos that erupted Friday — maybe Dad was there. In my world, fathers did dangerous work. It wasn't that they had more courage. It was simply what fathers did. As far as I knew, every nine-year-old American girl lived exactly the same way. As far as I knew, all their fathers — the fathers of every nine-year-old girl, the fathers of every girl — got in a plane and flew away and didn't come back for days or weeks or even months, and sometimes didn't come back at all.

And that is what happened to April Decker.

Just before Memorial Day 1959, a plane from my father's squadron stalled on its approach to the Iwakuni runway and crashed into the Sea of Japan. Four men — one of them April's father, Lieutenant Commander Ben Decker, who had been a classmate of my father's at the Naval Academy — were dead.

Within hours of the plane's tumble, my mother was at the Decker home, breaking the terrible news to April's mother, Helen. It was news Mother had heard herself before, when she was told that Carl Hallen had died, so she knew what to do and what to say, and what not to say. Mother took April, then only two, to our house, and returned to help Helen dismantle the life her family had shared in Japan. Helen's parents and Ben's were half a world away, and the Iwakuni military community that had become her family in the last year would soon be far away. She had to move, quickly. The protections of the military overseas extended to wives but not to widows. Helen needed to pack up what she could of her life in Japan, literally and figuratively, and begin to prepare for the unknown life she and April now faced. But, for the time, she wasn't alone. She had my mother by her side.

Helen and April stayed with us that first night, and then April stayed on with us for the next week while Helen went home to pack. Mother stayed with her each day until Helen slept and tried to arrive in the morning before she awoke. When some other wife would spell her, Mother would rush home to check on April and on us. She was so tired she could hardly move, but she never thought of stopping.

Oblivious to the pain in her own home, April was happy with the new adventure with our family. She slept with my sister and me in our small bedroom. She went to the pool with us in the day. She ate dinner with our family. Each night one of us would bang an antique Japanese gong to call the family to our happy dinner. April shared the side of the table my brother usually had to himself. When everyone was at the table, one of us children would say grace. It was all a delightful mystery to a young only child.

One night, April said, "I want to say it."

"What?" my mother asked.

"Grace."

"That's fine, hon," then, turning to us, "April is saying grace tonight."

The table got quiet. Everyone folded their hands. April, with a resoluteness she would need in life, took over. She had never said grace before. It was quiet a bit too long, and my brother squirmed. Finally it came. One word.

"Grace."

April unfolded her hands and picked up her fork.

We all opened our eyes over our folded hands and looked to my mother for guidance. Mother gave the unmistakable signal that we were to treat April's version as a real blessing. Because, of course, it was.

It was impossible at nine to understand the reach of April's blessing. The terrible, heartbreaking circumstance that brought her to us was in impossible juxtaposition with the completely open happy way in which she accepted our embrace, as if we were her closest cousins.

We knew, she didn't. Every spoken word — even for seven-, eight-, and nine-year-old children — was burdened with double meaning. But we each played our parts. The natural way that my mother had of taking this child and, for as long as we were needed, pulling her into our family was probably learned from her mother, also the wife of a Navy pilot. Wherever she learned it, Mother taught it to each of us the way all real lessons are taught, by simply doing it: when you are needed, you step up, and you don't step up reluctantly or self-importantly. I was blessed to learn this lesson at nine. I have needed it over the last forty-eight years, for in this life I have been my mother, and sadly I have been April.

Maybe the examples were there all the time, but I was too young to absorb the lessons until they had a name — April's name. From that day on, I knew that I too had a community around me that would be there for me if I fell from my bike, or if my father's plane fell from the sky.

As far as bases in Japan went, the Marine Corps Air Station at Iwakuni was remote. And it was small. The high school graduating class of 1959 had three seniors. My class that year, the fourth grade, was one of the classes that didn't share a room with another grade, but then we had the school library at the back of the room. Fortunately, we had Edna Defenderfer at the front of the room.

Teachers in the overseas schools run by the Department of Defense come from all over the country. Mrs. Defenderfer came from Green Bay, Wisconsin, a hometown she loved and shared with us in details we found fascinating, as when she told us about contests they had when she was young to guess when the winter ice would melt. A class of nine-year-old nomads, we were warmed by her tales of a hometown, even such an icy hometown. In the Democratic primary race in 2004, I visited Green Bay for the first time, campaigning for my husband. I spoke at a county Democratic dinner. I looked out at wholesome Wisconsin faces and felt right at home. And I told them why.

"All my life," I started, "I have wanted to come to Green Bay." I told them about Edna Defenderfer and how she had shared Green Bay with a room full of nine-year-olds, forty-five years before, and how I knew that if she loved Green Bay, I loved Green Bay. When I stepped down from speaking, a man came up to me and said that Mrs. Defenderfer had been his teacher in Green Bay, and he knew her daughter. That night, I spoke to her daughter, and the next day, I spoke to Mrs. Defenderfer herself, then in a nursing home, and listened to her recount moments in that classroom decades and continents away. She remembered me as "Mary Beth" — the name by which I was known until college. All the affection I felt at nine came flooding back, and — honestly — it comes flooding back now, as I type.

That classroom was magical to me, and although the building is no longer there — on the Internet I have seen the sparkling school that replaced it — in my mind I can walk through that old school. Our room was second on the right down the main hall, and I sat in the second row, midway back, and listened to the best teacher I ever had.

I had junior choir and Girl Scouts. My brother, Jay, had the baseball field, and my sister, Nancy, had her bicycle and then, when the hula hoop hit Japan, she had that. She'd walk to school spinning a hula hoop around her waist, stopping traffic as she stepped down from the curb, spinning and talking to friends. She would turn and wave to Mother without slowing the hoop's speed.

It always amazes me that such different children can grow up in precisely the same soil. My mother found the perfect way to describe the differences when she wrote to her mother, "From now until eight tonight

I lose all personal identity — I'm Mary Beth's 'Mother' — very dignified — Nancy's 'Mommie,' and, since last week — horrors — I'm Jay's 'Mama Guitar.' " Different as we were then, and are now, what binds us is family and years of being each other's most constant friends — and, until we were adults, each other's most constant enemies as well.

The summer that I was between fourth and fifth grades, we had a base-wide war between the boys and the girls. We were all enemies. There were no malls, and there was no television — unless you wanted to watch sumo wrestling or *I Love Lucy* in Japanese (which, frankly, everyone should see at least once, just to hear Ricky Ricardo dubbed in Japanese). So fifty military children of all ages did what you might expect: we waged a war. My parents had had a piece of furniture delivered that spring, and the empty crate sat in the backyard. The garbagemen ignored it, so I asked my mother if the girls could have it for a fort. Of course, every day the boys would take it over by force, and every day Nancy or I would march home to complain, and Mother would come out and tell the boys that the prized crate was ours.

The movie theater. The pool. And the war. That was Iwakuni.

Or it was Iwakuni inside the air station gates. Outside was Japan, a Japan almost untouched by Western culture. The roads were usually dirt with *benjo* ditches running along the side and separating rice paddies or other fields from the road. The Japanese had an efficient, if fragrant, way of dealing with human waste. Receptacles in the houses emptied into open wide ditches along the road. Every road. Periodically, a man with a wooden bucket would walk beside the *benjo* ditches and scoop out the floating waste, which he then put in his wagon — which we called a honey wagon — and carried it to a version of a compost heap to later be used as fertilizer. As hard as it is to believe, it wasn't difficult at all to get accustomed to the unrelenting odor. On our second and third trips to Japan, we arrived, took a deep breath, and said, "Ah! The smell of home."

Directly behind our house was a stone seawall that formed the border of the base and the retaining wall for a river that ran to the inland sea. From my brother's windows or from the cliffs right outside the gate, we would watch as the Japanese celebrated

Obon, a summer festival honoring the dead, its last day marked by a moving and beautiful ceremony. The Buddhists believe that at death the spirits cross the river to the other side, but that once a year they return silently and, for the several days of Obon, visit the living. To guide the dead back across the water, Japanese families would use tiny straw boats, and in the bow they would place a candle to light the way. To entice the dead into their boats, the living leave messages and elaborate treats. That last night of Obon the little boats would be set out on the river, and the landscape would gleam with the tiny flames and then gleam again with reflection of those flames in the water and on the white paper sails of some of the boats. The beauty and the glory of this image never left me, not just of the image but of the sense that all these souls, thousands of them, were being led by the delicacies their families had prepared and by the lights in their bows glistening above the black water, and that all of the souls were traveling together to be on the other side of the river, together. Even if in life they may not have known each other, these souls crossing back across the river formed a great and glorious, even a joyous, community. It was like the title of Mark Yakich's book of poetry, *Unrelated Individuals Forming a Group Waiting To Cross.* Although I am Christian, this Buddhist tradition made it easier for me when we sat in the base chapel for the memorials when Lieutenant Commander Decker and three others died in May 1959, and when in November another VQ-1 plane crashed and again four men died, and again we all sat in the chapel, with our friends and their mothers, some beaten, some stoic, all filled with grief, alone in the front pew. I would stare at the still backs of the necks of my now fatherless schoolmates and imagine them bent over their boats and pushing them out to sea, sending the souls of their fathers home — until the next year. For children who were used to their fathers being gone, it was almost enough.

I nearly had to test the redemptive power of that image with my own father.

One night in June 1959, only a few weeks after April had left our house, my father didn't come home. We didn't worry. It was not unusual. The pilots and crew of VQ-1 could never tell their families when they were leaving for a reconnaissance flight or how long they would be gone. If Dad didn't come home for dinner, we knew he was in the air somewhere. We could sometimes tell where he had been, or at least where he had refueled, by what he brought back to us. If he brought home bananas, he had been to Taiwan; a piece of jewelry for my mother, we decided, was Thailand. If he had landed at Midway, it was the best treat of all — pictures and stories about the gooney birds, heavy waddling albatrosses. Dad would delight us mimicking a gooney bird's outstretched neck and graceless dance. We made a game of guessing.

But on this mission, something went wrong. My father and Commander Donald Mayer, Daryl's father, were piloting a P4 Mercator along the coast of North Korea. A large, heavy four-propeller bomber, built for nine men, with a gun turret in the back, it was holding fourteen men, and most of the guns had been replaced with cameras and surveillance equipment. My father was piloting the plane. As the Mercator made her maneuvers trying to set off — and thereby expose the location of — communist radar stations, two MiG jet fighters with red stars emblazoned on them made a pass. Dad and Commander Mayer weren't surprised to see them. Chinese or Korean jets often flew close to watch the maneuvers near their coastlines, perhaps to intimidate.

But this time they weren't just watching.

This time they were shooting.

As the MiGs passed the converted Navy bomber, the sharp report of gunfire tore through my father's plane. The crew scrambled, while the MiGs circled back to make another pass. The Navy gunner, Donald Corder, rushed to his only gun, but he never even got a shot off. In their second pass the MiGs blew out the gun turret, wounding him. They continued to make passes, six in all, riddling the helpless plane, which had nowhere to hide, no way to shoot back. It seemed they had no way to save the plane or themselves.

Through fifteen hits on the plane, through fire and deafening noise, the fourteen men on the Mercator instinctively acted as one. Covered in blood, his flight suit on fire, Corder managed to crawl out of the mangled turret. Lieutenant Owen Farley knocked out the flames, and an ordnance man named Richard Nelson bandaged Corder. Bullets continued to shower the plane, and Nelson draped his larger frame over Corder's body to protect his injured friend.

My father was piloting a plane that was now rudderless, with both engines on the starboard side knocked out or on fire. The hydraulic system was out, and the holes in the plane created even more instability. A plane in this condition is almost impossible to fly, but keeping it aloft was not all he had to do. He had to fly it with enough precision to avoid the continued passes by the MiGs and dodge the incoming tracers. If he couldn't do that, they wouldn't survive. To limit the maneuvering room of the MiG jets, he decided to force the plane down from seven thousand feet above the water to fifty feet. The plane shook as it dived, four thousand, two thousand, five hundred feet. Then came the real test: Dad had to use his considerable strength to bring the plane level again — the water just five stories below them — and hold it there. One of the men on board said my father's unflinching arms looked like they had been chiseled in marble, for nearly two hours flexed and unchanging.

The dive worked, and the MiGs disappeared into the clouds, but the plane still had a lot of water to cross before it was out of harm's way. When the crew was sure that the MiGs were gone, Dad brought them back up to a safer sixteen hundred feet. Then one of the two port engines started to go, and it was hard to keep aloft the now one-engine rudderless plane. It dropped back to three hundred feet. Even my father's strength might not be enough to save the plane. Commander Mayer radioed that they were thirty miles out from a small landing field at Miho, Japan, and that they had begun to jettison the plane's nonessential equipment to lighten the load. It worked. The plane maintained three hundred feet until landing. President Eisenhower was notified what happened immediately. We found out half a day later.

It seemed everyone on base knew before we did. But all our next-door neighbor Bob Greenwood told Mother was that Dad's plane had had a flat tire and that he had landed at Miho, a couple of hundred miles from Iwakuni. Commander Greenwood got Dad on the phone, and Dad simply told Mother he was fine and he would join her at a dinner party that night. At the dinner, Commodore Staley came in late and told Mother that Dad was delayed talking to investigators. Investigators, she asked, for a flat tire? Mother knew something more was wrong, and she turned to Commodore Staley and asked, "Don't I deserve to know what's going on?" "Yes," he said and took her to the next room and told her what had happened, that Corder had survived and that Dad was all right and was a hero in fact. Finally, hours later than expected, Dad walked in, still dressed in his flight suit. He took one look at the assembled guests, and the first thing he said was, "Holy smokes, Liz, you told me this was a party. It looks more like a wake to me. Let's play charades!"

One night at home was followed by a long debriefing at the Seventh Fleet command in Yokosuka. The first news stories said that the Mercator hadn't shot back because the guns jammed. Dad and the crew went to Washington to testify first about nonexistent jammed guns and then about actual surveillance activities. All the while, we read about it in our only news source, the *Stars and Stripes,* but we later heard from friends in the States that the crew was on every news program, on television and radio, in every newspaper, in *Life* and *Time,* on front pages, on covers, and in conversations across the country.

Finally he was back from Yokosuka and Washington and was again with us in Iwakuni. Commander Mayer and my father were each awarded the Distinguished Flying Cross, the highest medal a pilot can earn outside of wartime. Then life was quiet again, or at least quiet in our way, for things had returned to our version of normal. Dad was coming home for dinner, and then sometimes not coming home.

I never had any doubt that my father had saved himself and the thirteen others aboard that plane, and apparently I was not alone. When my father was seventy-five years old — about five years after he had a massive stroke that doctors said might have killed another man and crippled him — he got a letter from one of the Mercator crew, writing from California, where he and his family and grandchildren lived. He wrote that he had a full life, and he just wanted to thank Dad for it. What the man said in his letter was a great gift to my father.

All these years later, I still feel connected to the military, especially when incidents like the one involving my father occur. In 2001, after a collision with a pursuing Chinese fighter, a reconnaissance plane from that same squadron, VQ-1, was forced down in Hainan, China. The Chinese accused the plane of flying in their airspace and refused to give up the crew or the plane, which, like my father's planes, had an electronic surveillance system aboard it. The crew came back in April 2001, and the plane came back a few months later. During the ordeal, I felt as if the men and women on board were my military family. I had to remind myself how young they were, that they were not my father's age, that they were not even my age. Yet I felt the connection. When Shane Osborne, the pilot of that EP-3 plane, was awarded the Distinguished Flying Cross, I felt a satisfaction and pride that a family member might feel. I was fifty-one with no present connection to the Navy; it made no sense except that the bonds built in the military community are strong enough to last a lifetime.

Now, some who have grown up in military families will tell you a story of scars left by a largely absent father and an oppressive warrior mentality. For some that is undoubtedly true. There were fathers I won't name who drank too much; there were mothers who were lonely and depressed, even suicidal in this nomadic life. I know that it did happen. It just didn't happen to me.

The common image of a military pilot is the father in Pat Conroy's brilliant and heartbreaking *The Great Santini,* but my own father was as far from Bull Meecham as any military man could be. Oh, sometimes he would wake us up with a bugle — because he thought it was funny. Sometimes he would "inspect" our rooms — but I never remember anything awful happening, and believe me, the condition of my side of the room I always shared with my very neat sister would have justified memorable punishment. Dad clearly expected more from his son than from his daughters, just as his Italian father had from him. My brother was never allowed to have his hands in his pockets. Of course, he put his hands in his pockets anyway — there are dozens of family photos that attest to that — but when my father spotted it, the bellowing would begin. I thought about it later and realized that John Kennedy's natural easy pose with his hands in his pockets was never, absolutely never, repeated by anyone in uniform.

At the same time that he was hard on Jay, Dad would give him every spare minute. That my brother loved baseball is an understatement, for as far as Jay was concerned, the hidden meaning of life was found on a baseball diamond. So the year before my brother was eligible, my father signed up as the head of the Iwakuni Little League, and he decided that, to round out the teams, the age limit would be dropped a year — just this once. The whole family joined in — my sister and I, and other sisters on Jay's team, dressed up in plaid — what were we thinking, plaid? — cheerleading uniforms, chanting cheers like "*Iki masho,* let's go!" which translates to "Let's go, let's go." Dad's decision to allow cheerleaders may have generated some complaints, but his decision to lower the age limit never did. Jay was a spectacular baseball player, pitching and hitting well that first year and leading the league with a staggering .750 average the next year. My grandfather, who died that year, would have been proud: the next generation of athletes and sports fans was born.

My mother arranged activities for Nancy and me. She found Toshiko, a lovely woman in her mid-thirties, to teach us Japanese dance and music. Toshiko had trained intensively to be a geisha, and before going to Tokyo to begin her esteemed career, she returned home for a last visit with her family — in Hiroshima. While she was home the atomic bomb fell on her town. Seventy thousand were killed that day, her chest was blown off, and her life was blown apart.

No longer a vision of perfection, she could not be a geisha. Instead here she was, in our living room, imparting her life's learning to two awkward American girls, the daughters of a Navy pilot, the symbolic daughters of the men who had taken away her chance to practice it herself. She dressed in a *yukata,* a plain cotton kimono, and a woven obi, and at the V of her neckline we could see the scars on her chest. Each week she would show me where to put my hands, how to angle my legs for the most grace, how, with a single touch, to close a fan. She sat with me, a samisen in my lap and the oversize ivory pick in my hand, and taught me the notes to the songs that, because they had no written music, could only be handed down from a mistress to an initiate. She would wrap her small scarred arms around me as I knelt with the instrument across my lap, showing me just where my fingers should be for each note and where they should be when I rested.

Although there was never a moment of unguarded laughter or joy during the lessons, there also was never a moment of resentment in the two years that she came every week. She was not resigned in any way that was marked by bitterness or defeat. She had realigned her expectations, a sad moment undoubtedly, and from that time on, she moved with all the grace and serenity that her new station would allow. There was a part of that serenity that could break your heart, but in it, too, was the indomitable:

some things cannot be taken away.

Serene Sundays were spent on the sacred island of Miyajima. It was much changed from a century before, when — because they could not walk on the holy soil — Japanese worshippers would enter on boats through the huge *torii* that appeared to be floating in the water and make their way on docks and bridges to the temples. By the 1950s, American children could and did hike in the foothills around Mt. Misen, climb wizened trees, and hope to catch sight of the sacred god-deer. We would roam and play while my mother sketched, and when she was through, we would pull her to the red-painted stall outside the five-story pagoda where we would buy oats for what we believed was the Emperor's white horse, and maybe it even was. I have seen a picture of that stall as it stands today, in which a statue commemorating the white horse now stands. If you had had the good fortune to feed the stout, square-muzzled horse we knew as children, you would be hard-pressed — even in that same stall — to recognize the sleek rendition. I hope to be remembered as favorably.

We would add new places to our list of

weekend haunts as Mother would discover them, and she discovered many as she drove throughout southern Honshu. Mother had a secret list of junk stores and antique stores where she knew all the shopkeepers, their wives, and their children by name. And in those shops she spent her time and her money, shopping for herself and for the Red Door.

The Red Door had been a charity project of the base wives. They collected and sold used children's clothing, but once, when my mother was back in the States at my grandfather's funeral, the wives donated the entire inventory to local Japanese families who had been devastated by a typhoon. In 1959 the Red Door reopened, but instead of selling used clothes to raise money, it sold Japanese antiques, and Mother was one of the buyers. Twice a week or more, Mother and another base wife, Peggy Boettcher, would leave the air station in our Ford station wagon and head to Hiroshima or Kure or Yanai or just some rural store Mother had heard about. Or out to see a farmer who had a few things he was willing to sell stored in the treasure room behind his house. Mother and Mrs. Boettcher would be back — at first to unload at the Red Door and then home with the things she'd bought for herself. She brought home so many antiques that my sister was convinced we were terribly poor. All Mother ever bought were old used things.

Mother became such friends with one shopkeeper that when we left Iwakuni in 1960, she gave him a number of prized American items, including — for his daughters — the dress clothes Nancy and I had outgrown. The family came to see us off, and in a gesture of appreciation, the daughters were wearing some of what we had given them. You would think that with a father who would dance in a pink bikini nothing would embarrass us, but let me assure you that Nancy and I wanted to melt into the sidewalk when the girls arrived wearing, as sundresses, our white cotton slips.

Mother would drive us everywhere in search of Japan for us and, for her and the Red Door, more antiques. She would pile Jay, Nancy, and me into the backseat of a terrifically ugly two-tone flesh and white station wagon and compete for road space with bicycles and oxcarts. During our sojourns and treasure hunts, we would drive by women squatting in the rice paddies, wearing flat straw hats, their kimonos pulled up around their thighs as they worked. We'd see silk drying in the fields after being dyed, huge banners of blues and reds billowing from enormous racks. Crowded into the rear-facing seat, we watched a lot of Japan through that back window. Jay would spot Japanese children playing in the streets and yell to them, "Baseball, *ne?*" Baseball was enormously popular in Japan, and the children would always scream back, "Baseball! Baseball!" and wave excitedly and chase the car a few hundred feet. Jay was just beginning to do something our parents had taught us. He was reaching out and making connections with everyone around him, even those children we only passed on a dusty road, using as connective tissue what they had in common.

My mother would sit and talk with a Japanese farmer, or the Admiral's wife, or the maid Toyo-san, and her demeanor was never different. She once told me that if I could talk about the news, about soap operas (when in the States, of course), and about sports, there were very few people with whom I could not have a conversation. It has turned out to be true.

My father didn't even need that. He would reach for the hands of strangers. He would corral teenagers at a table and ask them what they liked. He would tell the nurses in the clinic how pretty they were. Every little girl he passed he'd say, "Could she be? Well, she must be. Here's a princess. Imagine that, a princess, right here in the mall!" He would chat with cashiers as if he knew them, complimenting them on their hair or their eyes or the speed with which they worked. By the time they left, my father would know the life stories of the family in the next lane at the bowling alley. Why not pass the time with the cashier? You're not doing anything anyway. Why not make friends with the bowling family? Hey, we were a bowling family, too.

My father was doing something most of us do or want to do — reaching for connections. Now, he was, and still is, an extreme example. And, probably as a consequence, so am I. I'm not likely to change either, because the connections I have made have enriched and sustained me; they have strengthened me by holding me up when I needed it, and they have strengthened me by letting me hold up my end when it was needed. My life is immeasurably better because I know that although we may say grace differently, or not know how to say it all, we still need one another.

Because of the way I grew up, because

time and again I had to walk into a class-room where everyone else knew one an-other, I had to find a way to make enough connections to make my life work. I under-stood early in life that I needed them. So I thrust my hand out. Like my father had taught me. And I found out what they liked and talked about that. Like my mother had taught me. We just had to recognize the sameness among us and build on that for our community. We didn't have to be the same; we just had to recognize what a great blessing we could be to one another. Like April taught me.

In the summer of 1960, Dad's squadron moved to Atsugi Naval Air Station, in the region nearer Tokyo, where my father had been stationed on our first tour in Japan. We were moving to a much larger place, with many more children, but for once the whole squadron, all of VQ-1, nearly my whole class, moved at once. That meant there was not enough housing on the air station at Atsugi for all of the families, so we moved to the large American complex in Yokohama, on the bluffs above the high school. Not knowing any better, going from Iwakuni to Yokohama seemed like moving from a Japanese community to an American one. Sure, in Yokohama we went shopping in the cramped stores on narrow Motoma-chi Street, and we still rumbled down dirt back roads, my brother shouting "Baseball, *ne?*" the whole way. We took lessons in *sumi* — ink drawing — and *ikebana* — flower arranging. But to us, Yokohama might as well have been America. It had a complex that resembled a strip mall, where the Navy Exchange, a snack bar, the theater, the bowling alley, even places I didn't need like the package store and the Teen Club, were located all together with a big mall-like parking lot in front. When we weren't at the Officers' Club having the best chocolate sundaes made, we were getting hot dogs at the snack bar and walking back to the baseball field behind the package store. Our daily dose of Japan was paying the Japanese vendor in front of the Navy Exchange a hundred yen — then less than thirty cents — to open an oyster we picked from his pail. He would take the chosen oyster, push his wooden-handled knife deep into it, and twist until the shell popped open. If there was a pearl in it, he would hand it to us, tossing the shell into a cotton bag. If there was no pearl, we could reach into the pail and pick out another oyster, but they were cultured, so there was always a pearl.

When a submarine came into port, many families would travel to Yokosuka just to see it, and we would crowd the second-floor roller rink on the base. We gathered for Yo-Hi football games or bowling league, but by far the best-attended community events were when we had to turn in our MPC. MPC were Military Payment Certificates, pastel paper money about the size of Monopoly money on which there were drawings of regal and beautiful women. We had MPC for every denomination of bill and coin except pennies. Periodically, everyone had to turn in their MPC so that their aqua-colored fifty-cent papers could be exchanged for light green fifty-cent papers. I am sure there must have been some convenient place for soldiers and sailors to convert their MPC, but not for dependents. The windows where we exchanged MPC for yen would have long lines of wives and children on the day of the exchange. The day was always a surprise, and after that date the aqua-colored fifty-cent papers would be worthless. The day was celebrated in our house in the same way it was celebrated in the quarters around us: we turned every pants pocket inside out, emptied every purse, and scrambled through every junk drawer in search of dying MPC. MPC and reconstituted milk were the reminders that despite the roller rink and the movie theater, despite the mall-like parking lot and the football games, this was still Japan.

It was 1960, and my sixth-grade class ran a mock election for the elementary school between Richard Nixon and John F. Kennedy. One side of the class was assigned to be the campaign staff for each candidate, and as it turned out, I was assigned to campaign for Richard Nixon. Kennedy's Catholicism was as big an issue to the military — if judged by the letters in the overseas military newspaper, *Stars and Stripes* — as my mother's Methodism was to Nana. But the usual argument that Kennedy's allegiance would be to papal decrees instead of the Constitution was not going to win over fourth and fifth graders to Nixon. We needed something concrete. Thinking about the Catholic schools at the time, the Nixon side of the room found just the opening we needed. Donald Segretti, Nixon's later dirty-tricks guru, was not in our class, but he might as well have been. The campaign for Nixon consisted of a few posters in the hallways and a calculated, oft-repeated rumor — in which I was as culpable as every other student on my side of the class — that, as a Catholic president and commander in chief over our dependents' schools, John Kennedy would send us all to school on Saturdays. Nixon won the mock election at Kinnick Elementary School by a landslide.

Normally a tour of duty is over in the summer, but my father got assigned to a six-month tour at the Armed Forces Staff College in Norfolk beginning in January 1961. We were leaving Japan early. And we were leaving three days after Christmas. Mother had to plan Christmas for fourth, fifth, and sixth graders, go to Christmas parties and school and church pageants, pack all our belongings — some marked for storage, some for use in our smaller Norfolk quarters — pack traveling clothes for all five of us for a seven-thousand-mile trip, and be ready to leave by ship on December 28th. It was a testament to the flexibility of the military family, or at least the military mother. We had a tree decorated entirely with paper ornaments we made. It had the advantage of being entirely disposable — we tossed it out, still fully decorated, after Christmas — and while my brother and sister and I were making ornaments, it allowed Mother uninterrupted time to pack. Somehow she got everything done. And on December 28th, the five of us went aboard ship and headed back to the States.

It wasn't until a couple of days later that Mother realized she hadn't gotten everything done and, in fact, had forgotten something important. On December 30th, my father gave her a lovely pearl pin for their thirteenth wedding anniversary. Their wedding anniversary? She looked so forlorn that my sister and I went to the tiny ship store and bought some handkerchiefs and thread. We spent the rest of the day embroidering my father's initials on her only gift to him. She gave it to him, and he acted pleased. The next morning Mother awoke, certain she had nothing left to be done. Except that we had crossed the International Date Line, and it was December 30th again. My father had figured this out before the trip, so on their second thirteenth anniversary in as many days, he gave her a mink stole. My sister and I went again to the ship store and again bought and sewed. And again he acted pleased. Maybe he was, but one thing I am certain of is that my mother was relieved to wake up the next morning with no extravagant gifts awaiting her.

CHAPTER 4
ZAMA

Once when my older children were in school, they asked me to show them on the globe all the places I had lived when their grandfather was a pilot. I traced my history with my finger: a single line that crisscrossed the Pacific, back and forth, back and forth, and back and forth again. It seemed so simple, but with each reversal of direction, our family's lives had changed. In the winter of 1961, when I was eleven, the line took us from Japan to Norfolk, Virginia, to a new school and new quarters, and by the summer of 1962, it had taken us from Norfolk to Annapolis, Maryland, Annapolis Junior High School, and grand quarters on the parade grounds at the Naval Academy.

By the fall of 1962, Wednesday parades became a feature of our lives, a line of junior high school girls sitting on the top row of the bleachers, pointing at — and in our imaginations choosing from — the four thousand college boys marching in front of us. With Wednesday parades came Wednesday tourists who walked our streets, peered in our windows, and sometimes even came in and sat down in our living room. Mother would find them running their fingers across the spines of books on our shelves or lifting a frame to look closer at a photograph of my grandfather in his Navy uniform walking with Eleanor Roosevelt in Trinidad. Sometimes they would be nice, and sometimes Mother would even talk to them a bit, asking where they were from as she gently led them back out to the porch. Some, however, were not so malleable. When we would ask the most unpleasant visitors to leave, they would stomp out, muttering something about their tax dollars paying for the house. It was good for a laugh — and good training, too, for years later, when John and I were staying in a private home during a retreat on Nantucket for senators and I arrived back in our room to find a fully dressed man who, mistaking the house for his guest cottage, had stretched out on our bed, his shoes neatly tucked under the footboard, his jacket hung on the desk chair. I simply tiptoed in, retrieved my book, and went downstairs to the parlor to read there until the man's nap was over.

Our host was terrifically embarrassed, but it honestly didn't bother me at all. At least the sleeping man hadn't yelled at me. I figure I have those tourists in Annapolis to thank for my mellowness that day.

Life inside the yard, as the Naval Academy grounds are called, was idyllic.

And we imagined life on the parade field at Annapolis was just like life in any other American neighborhood. Jay played Little League again, and warm summer nights would find all of us piled in the Ford station wagon and then in the bleachers of a dusty field to watch Jay pitch and hit. When we got to Annapolis, he heard about a terrific Pony League team, but he would have to try out for it. The coach was an Annapolis native in the construction business, and the tryouts and practices were in a large field his business owned. Jay showed up to try out and found out there weren't really any places. Last year's team had returned in full. The coach asked for his name and phone number in case the situation changed, which was probably his nice way of shuffling Jay off the field. He even started to write it down.

"Jay," my brother said, waiting to say and, he knew, spell his last name.

"Jay." The coach wrote.

"Anania," Jay said. "A-N —"

The coach looked up. "Are you Vince Anania's boy?"

This man was a few years younger than Dad and had watched Dad when he was a midshipman. It wasn't just that Dad had been a great athlete, which was true enough. It was that Dad had been great to the boys who hung out at the sides of the practice field every day. He'd learned their names and teased them about their girlfriends. And he'd made a friend and admirer of a boy who would later grow up and own a construction company. The end of the story tells itself — though that won't stop me. Jay made the team, and the coach was not disappointed, not by the boy on the field or by the man in the bleachers.

By the next year, it was time for orders again. And again it was Japan. So in the late summer of 1963, we were headed back to Atsugi Naval Air Station, where Dad had been stationed when we were two, three, and four. But now we were twelve, thirteen, and fourteen, and this time Dad had command of a squadron, VU-5. We had changed, and so had Japan. The oxcarts that had slowed our travel in 1953 and the bicycles that had clogged the roads in 1958 had been replaced by kamikaze trucks. There were still *benjo* ditches and expanses of rice pad-dies, but Japan was becoming Westernized. Beautiful kimonos gave way to pleated skirts and shirtwaist dresses on the streets of Tokyo. Shopkeepers still watered the dirt in front of their small storefronts. But *A Hard Day's Night* played at a movie theater on the Ginza in Tokyo. It was the Japan of the early 1960s, a Japan that existed for a few years, then disappeared. The awkward, forgettable teenage years of a country in transition as old traditions and ways yielded uneasily to modernity.

My father, who had been the circus father up until then, suddenly set out dozens of rules for his teenagers facing physical maturity. I couldn't be outside the house after dusk alone, and whomever I was with had to be acceptable to Dad. I couldn't go to the snack bar unless I was with my parents or my brother. I could not do more than nod in greeting to an enlisted man. Dad overreacted, but it hadn't been so long since he had written his mother about the wilder girls at the air station in Pensacola when he was single. He needn't have wor-ried about me, though. I was deciding whether to quit Girl Scouts — I had already gotten to Curved Bar and there wasn't anything like Eagle Scout for which to shoot — not deciding which sailor to date. Besides, we all knew that we had to behave — for Dad's career.

Each officer in the military had regular evaluations, called Fitness Reports, completed by a superior officer; they rated the officer's performance and conduct. On the Fitness Report forms, there was a place to comment on the conduct of the officer's family. Everything we did was watched and recorded, and if it was unbefitting an officer, it could hurt Dad's chance for promotion. That same thing was true in every house, in every service, on every base. When a teenager did something bad enough to be mentioned on the Fitness Report and a family was sent back to the States, we all had an unforgettable lesson in cause and effect. No one talked about it, but everyone knew it. We all had as our first allegiance the professional reputations of our fathers. If someone's mother was drunk at the Officers' Club, if a teenager had a fight at the Teen Club, if someone's daughter got pregnant, all the things that might be talked about for a few days in the States, but here meant a ruined career, a shortened tour of duty, a life spoiled by an indiscretion.

My father didn't need to have a single

rule. We had them for ourselves, and so did our neighbors and our classmates. We knew that getting caught doing something "unbefitting" had consequences beyond being grounded. It didn't mean anything to us when we were younger, but now that we were in high school, it was different. Alcohol could be — and was — purchased outside the gate or at a thousand places in Tokyo, a short trip by train. We had boyfriends and girlfriends and lots of time on our hands. Those who broke the rules went to extraordinary lengths to make sure they weren't caught, and no one turned them in because we all appreciated and feared the very real consequences. The result of this shared fear was that, without thinking about it, we developed an intimacy, an alliance, with the people we protected, who protected us. And it wasn't just the children; it was the mothers, too. One mother used to call our house at least weekly, drunk and crying. My voice sounded like my mother's on the telephone, and often she would be well into a sobbing rant to Mother before I managed to tell her my mother was not home. Sometimes I didn't bother; I just listened sympathetically. I never told anyone except my mother. And my mother never told anyone at all.

When I was in college taking a journalism

class on reviewing, a fellow named Todd Cohen wrote a review of a soap opera, writing about how, in every scene, someone was drinking coffee — coffee, coffee, coffee. When we lived in Japan, the story of our lives could have been centered on military buses — buses, buses, buses. When I think about what made us so cohesive, what stuck us together in such a way that years and distance and different lives haven't torn us apart, I think of the Fitness Reports and buses. The bus was more than a means of transportation; it was a meeting place. It was like the bedroom where we told our best friends our dearest secrets, or like the back row of the theater where we would kiss a special boy, or like a pep rally, or a song-fest, or a giant sleeping bag at the end of a long trip. I suppose everyone who grew up in a small town can imagine it to some degree — the closeness, the intimacy, the innocence — but what is harder to imagine is that we were never ever apart. We didn't have summers at the beach or Christmas at our grandparents' house. And although it was theoretically possible to go to the next town on a Friday night, or in our case the next base, we didn't do it much because there wasn't any easy transportation. No one stayed home and played video games;

there weren't any. No one stayed home and watched television; there wasn't any.

What we missed also bound us. We missed the trends in fashions, and we missed teenage music. I remember sitting in geometry my freshman year of high school and reading a letter from Linda Stuntz from Annapolis. The Beatles had performed in Washington, D.C., and Linda wrote that Susan Schwartz had passed out at the concert. I leaned over to the next desk and pointed to a word in the letter.

"Can you read that? What is that word?"

"It's Beatles, I think."

"With an *a?* Is that right?"

Then from another desk, "Yeah, they're a new band from England."

Susan Schwartz was passing out, and I hadn't even heard of them, couldn't even spell their name. And so it went.

We recovered from the missed music. We were spared the missed shopping malls. But we missed big events in America. We shared our through-the-keyhole, everything-at-a-distance look at them, but always with a difference. My dad was the officer of the day on the day President Kennedy was shot. The job of officer of the day, who is responsible for order and security on base, rotates among various officers. News such as the

106

death of the commander in chief would come first to the OOD. So the news of the assassination of the President came first to our house, by telephone, in the middle of the night.

Everyone woke to the ring. We could hear Dad hurry down the hall to the only phone. We could hear him moan Oh my God. And then we were all up, all crying. What is it? It couldn't be. The crying had to stop so Dad could make the calls he needed to make, and then he dressed and left, and we could only turn on the radio and listen for details. There was mourning in our community, but for us, the President's death was accompanied by an eerie ghost-town-like feeling on base as fathers involved in intelligence disappeared for weeks and by a heightened degree of alert whenever we stepped off our base.

If it wasn't enough that we all had the same code of conduct, that we all wore clothes from the narrow selection at the exchange, that we went to the same theater, the same teen club, the same school, there were still other things that bound us together. At sunset, the flags on base would come down, the sound of Evening Colors would roll across the station, and the world would come to a halt. The baseball game would stop. Mother would stop the car, and we would all get out. No one would speak. The world inside our gates, inside our world, would be completely quiet save for that single bugle. And we would all face the sound of it and the flag, even if we could not possibly see it. When Evening Colors was over, and the All Clear sounded, life would begin again as quickly as it had stopped. The Pledge of Allegiance in school assemblies, the National Anthem before every movie, and the shared knowledge that when our fathers were buried, we would have to stand, backs straight and jaws set, as the most mournful call of all, a lone bugle playing Taps, said goodbye to a soldier, a sailor, an airman.

It is not like we were little cut-outs of the same people. Far from it. Guy Decker wore white all the time; we thought he played tennis, but he thought he just looked best in white. He turned down a singing career in Japan when he was eighteen. Gayle Steele, pretty and affable, spent a lifetime trying to replicate the close community of Zama and finally found it in a Minnesota town. Jim Little played Big Ten football. Paul Bolinger carved Christmas ornaments while his brother Jan flew airplanes. We produced our fair share of lawyers — Eddie Northwood and Martha Hartmann and me — and a few nurses, Barbara Bradford and Glenn Tart. Keith Carmack is a doctor. My brother is a filmmaker. Jean Freeman teaches college. Misty Draz teaches elementary school. Barry Doyle went to Dartmouth, Kele McDonough to Sofia University in Tokyo. A lot of us went into the military ourselves or, like Donna Grounds, married into the military. The world was wide open to us.

And there were extraordinary things, too, such as the 1964 Olympics. There was a lottery on base for tickets, but tickets could also be purchased in Tokyo, so nearly everyone went to one event or more. My dad and Jay walked into a USA basketball game by simply following the Soviet team into the arena. Benny Graeff and Dan Doherty were mistaken for athletes on the New Zealand team by the gate attendant, misled by the Zs on their letter jackets, and they enjoyed the Olympics from prime athletes-only seats. Tina Morgan was down near the finish line when Bob Hayes won the gold in the one hundred meters. Barbara Bradford made her way to a chair on the field of the track and field events. When an official tried to chase her off, Don Schollander, the swimming sensation, told the official she could stay, she was his sister. (Yes, she is very pretty.) And I was with my dad trying to buy tickets in the lobby of the Tokyo Hilton when my father did his typical bellowing "Hey! Great to see you," and reached his hand out to a muscular older man. Dad pulled him toward us when their hands met. "Jesse," he said, in that intimate way he had of talking to everyone, "I want to introduce you to my daughter." Did he know absolutely everyone? I wondered. "Mary Beth, this is Jesse Owens." The great American Olympic star who taught Hitler that the black man could compete. It was an extraordinary time.

My junior year I was a cheerleader. My sister, Nancy, had tried out for junior varsity and I had tried out for varsity cheerleading on the same day, and my mother sat home praying, both or neither, both or neither. It was both. And I was cheering at the Chofu v. Zama football game the day my father left for Vietnam. A year's tour of duty. I said goodbye to him as halftime started and cried all the way through the second half. We lost the game — we didn't win a game that season — and the Chofu fans thought I was the worst sport they had ever seen.

I had never been afraid before, never worried, even when there had been reason to worry about Dad. But this was different, this was war. Many of the wounded were coming to the military hospital near us, so it was a war we saw up close. Even though we got no music from the States, even though the magazines and movies came late, we did get news about Vietnam. In fact, we got it constantly over Armed Forces Radio and in the *Stars and Stripes.* We didn't know anything about the Smothers Brothers, but we knew about Prime Minister Ky.

My mother was worried, too, and she did something then I had never seen her do — she pulled herself in. She piddled in the house, she wrote in her journals, she read constantly, but she didn't answer the telephone. Her busy life engaged in her community, to which we had become accustomed over the years, was over. She was just waiting, waiting for Dad to come home. Everything was Vietnam. When the news of the war came on the radio, all conversation stopped. When Mother had the chance, she invited an injured soldier — we didn't even know him — who had been sent to Japan to recuperate before returning to war, to spend Thanksgiving with us. And when Dad would get leave, even a day, the world would stop. If it was just a day, we would drive to Tokyo and meet him there. Oddly, I don't think war changed my father as much as worrying about war changed my mother. When I campaigned in 2004, I would often say what I knew to be true about the families of soldiers and Marines in Iraq and Afghanistan: they could not listen to the news, and they could not stop listening to the news. It was the paradox that made the waiting unbearable. And there was no escape, no relief. Not then, not now.

Dad lived in the Hotel Rex in Saigon, and while he was there, it was bombed nearly nightly. We would hear it had been bombed before we would hear whether there had been any casualties, and those hours before the all-clear were a lonely, miserable time. After eight were killed and more than one hundred were wounded in a December bombing, he moved out. We were relieved, for he was going to Tan Son Nhut air base, which was secure, or so we thought until April when it was bombed and 140 died.

When in 1966 I was the overseas winner of a Veterans of Foreign Wars speech contest, I think it is safe to say that I was the only contestant whose father was then engaged in a foreign war. Thirty years later, to the week, our son Wade was one of the winners in a similar national essay contest sponsored by Voice of America. In my case, and later in his, all the winners were to gather in Washington. Arrangements were made for me to fly from Haneda International Airport in Tokyo. There was terrible weather the day I was to depart. My mother and I stood in long lines after my flight was canceled, trying to get me on one of the few departing flights. Finally I was put on a flight to the States that was boarding right away. Mother watched from the observation windows as, in the dark rain, I walked up the steps and onto my flight. But just as I stepped into the cabin, behind the plane the sky lit up, as, on the incoming runway a Canadian Pacific flight from Hong Kong was cartwheeling in flames. There had been a plane crash four weeks earlier when a commercial flight fell into Tokyo Bay, and pilots and their families all believe, or at least fear, that crashes come in threes. And now this was crash number two. Mother found someone who found someone who got me off the plane, and, her hands shaking the whole way, Mother walked me past the waiting families of the Canadian Pacific flight as they stood in shock and grief. She drove me home, promising we would try again in the morning, when the weather would be better.

The weather was only marginally better

the next day, and the airport was chaotic. Four days earlier, a fiery Argentinian named Horacio Accavallo had won the flyweight boxing title in Tokyo. In addition to two days' worth of passengers trying to leave Haneda at once, Accavallo and his entourage were an impenetrable knot of yelling and exaggerated hand gestures, and as I tried to make my way into the lounge for outgoing passengers, I was stuck on the wrong side of this juggernaut. Two businessmen rescued this helpless-looking sixteen-year-old, took me around the edges of the dangerously vigorous crowd to the lounge where we all waited for our flights to be announced, bought me a soda, and asked about my trip. Their flight was announced first, we said goodbye, and mine followed shortly after. Mother watched again as I climbed onto my plane, and she went to her car for the hour drive back to Camp Zama. She had been in the car only minutes when, over Armed Forces Radio, they announced that a plane that had just taken off from Haneda had crashed into Mt. Fuji. The third crash. She was the daughter and wife of pilots — how could she have let me fly? She could hardly drive. She turned for Tokyo, to get to the American embassy or somewhere, anywhere, they could tell her what plane it was.

I spoke to her next nearly a full day later when I was in Washington. "It wasn't your plane," she said, telling me the obvious. "It took off at the same time yours did, but it was headed to Hong Kong." Hong Kong? The businessmen, my rescuers, had been going to Hong Kong. I never knew their names; I had no one to tell how they had spent their last minutes helping me. No one to thank, no way to thank anyone, except maybe now, maybe here.

Chapter 5
Chapel Hill

When I was in eighth grade, I sat one rainy day under the covered review platform on the Naval Academy parade grounds and talked to one of the younger Navy wives from our street. She was pretty, in white capris and a blue sleeveless shirt. I adored my mother, but she was, well, a mother, with shirtwaist dresses and a perfect French twist. This woman had wispy short hair, not done at all, and she sat on the cement platform and talked to me like I was a friend. And, as a friend, she said that when the time came, I should go to college where she had gone, Mary Washington College. I hadn't heard of it, but if she liked it, I liked it, and I carried this flimsy notion with me throughout high school. During my senior year of high school — now back in the States, in Alexandria, Virginia — when it came time to apply to college, I applied to Mary Washington College, the women's college of the University of Virginia, in Fredericksburg. And when I was accepted, I went. I went at the end of an era, the tail end of what I refer to as the Franny and Zooey years, after the novel by J. D. Salinger.

There was a time in the late 1960s when a world that had existed for decades ended. The world of men's colleges, muscular and intense, and women's colleges, serene and pastoral, and the weekend trips from one to the other. A time of hard-sided suitcases carried by well-dressed young women onto local trains, and then by sport-coated young men to the grand old houses of widows where bedrooms had been transformed into bunk rooms for visiting girls. I wasn't Franny Glass, but like Franny, I took the train to the men's college, in my case, the University of Virginia in Charlottesville, for weekends. Like Franny, my date met me at the station and we walked to whatever approved guesthouse he had found for me for the weekend, where I would room with girls from Hollins and Sweet Briar and Randolph-Macon, and I would admire their elegant clothes and their shiny blonde hair and gold jewelry, and then later, like Franny, I would make fun of all that I had envied, drawing amusing caricatures of the other colleges to a date more intent on getting me drunk than being amused by me. It was the very last minutes of this era, and I was glad to be there, glad to have slipped in before the door shut forever.

The point of a women's college, or so I had always thought, is that young women, uninhibited and unintimidated by young men, would blossom and find their rightful place in communities, and they would take that sense of confidence and sometimes entitlement with them into the world. You would have to ask someone who was inhibited or intimidated whether it worked. I was neither. I had been president of my class; I had been brash enough to get kicked off the cheerleading squad for talking back to a teacher. I am pretty certain I didn't need to feel less inhibited, less intimidated. In the first weeks, still wearing my freshman beanie (yes, we really had to wear them), I was already flexing a robust independence. Asked in freshman English to write an essay that started "I began to become an individual when . . . ," I did not write the recipe-style essay (add a pinch of fun, bake for eighteen years) that won the best grade. Instead I wrote an essay about the abortion conflict and got one of the worst grades. And it was fine with me.

There is a camaraderie at a women's college that is intellectual and social and political. This is not to suggest we were made out of one cloth. The student referendum on whether to allow us to wear pants to class, rather than dresses, failed, for Pete's sake . . . in 1968. A fellow student turned me in one time when, after getting out of physical education late, I wore my shorts — under my buttoned raincoat — to class in violation of that dress rule. (She should know, if she reads this, that I could name her but choose not to.) We dated fraternity men who wore sports coats and Marines from Quantico who wore uniforms. We acted or danced or — in my case — wrote, or we did none of these. We were not all friends, but within that larger body, we worked out communities, often more than one, which met our needs and allowed us to find essential parts of the adults we would become.

As a freshman at Mary Washington, I had a junior roommate. While my parents tried to figure out how to pay for college, the freshman dorms filled up, and I found myself in a grand old dormitory rooming with Christine Cole from Warren, Ohio — her blonde hair shaved like a boy's, her paintings of nudes propped along every wall of our room, her expensive clothes hanging,

119

tags still attached, on every door frame. Other than my younger sister, she was my first roommate, and I wasn't sure my parents were going to let me — dressed head to toe in a peach Villager outfit, except for my red beanie — stay in a room with this . . . grown-up. But they did. I stayed, and Christine tried, unsuccessfully, to introduce me to coffee and cigarettes and, successfully, to bridge and to her circle of literary friends — Christina Askounis, as beautiful as she was eloquent, Linda Burton, sexy and mysterious, Susan Forbes, daffy and adorable and brilliant, and Ann Chatterton, maternal and warm. They were sophisticated; I was naive but smart enough to sit silently on the sidelines, learning as I was listening, the sponge all mothers hope their children will be — although I suspect this was not what my mother hoped I would absorb. I hoped I could, by osmosis, acquire their ease with words, with professors, with men. With the girls my own age — with Nancy Bolish and Karen Adlam, Ernie Kent, Debbie Oja — it was easy, weekdays of work and weekends of fun, fraternity houses and trips home, boys like Kellam Hooper and Toby Summerour, and vegetable soup in Ann Carter Lee Hall.

I wanted to be grown and sophisticated.

And I wanted to be young and carefree. I succeeded at neither. I was still a girl, used to boundaries and rules, struggling with a complex world, made more complex by war. I tried to push aside the Vietnam War, which had dominated my life — and not in a positive way. But I could not, and not simply because it was still in the news but because it was still in my house. My father was in charge of all the Navy ROTC units across the country, and when I would call or come home, he would complain about "those college students" who had fire-bombed an NROTC unit at one school or were staging a sit-in at another. I was two people then — the carefree college student, hanging on to what I thought was a normal American life, and a military daughter. My political opinions were forming, but I was quiet. Or quiet at home. I was in Washington, in Georgetown at the Tombs, a watering hole frequented by Georgetown University students, when the word went out in March 1968 that Lyndon Johnson was withdrawing from the race for the Democratic nomination for President. The place exploded into celebration.

In the State of the Union address in 1966 Johnson had beautifully expressed his angst about this war. "Yet, finally, war is always the same. It is young men dying in the fullness of their promise. It is trying to kill a man that you do not even know well enough to hate . . . therefore, to know war is to know that there is still madness in this world." But since 1966, he had become a symbol to young people of intransigent commitment, a commitment that was written in their young blood. So the strangers in the Tombs, and I suppose in places like it across the country, linked arms and sang protest songs and celebrated, years too early, the success of protest. The next month, April 1968, brought the blood of Martin Luther King, Jr., followed by the blood of Robert Kennedy in June. Johnson had been right, and not just about the war: there was still madness in this world. Men of purpose were dying. Men of greatness and men whose names we'd never know. I wanted to do something, but not the something I saw that summer on the streets of Chicago. I didn't want to throw a rock or burn a flag, certainly. But what could we do that would make a difference when men who might have made a difference were being killed?

The war and the protests were still going on in the fall of 1969. My father was assigned to the NROTC unit at the University of North Carolina at Chapel Hill, and I transferred there with him. There was no one there to watch me, no one who might put my protests on my father's fitness reports, but I was still self-editing, still taking care not to do anything that might hurt my father. My attendance at campus protests was just that: the almost invisible protester. Even on December 1, 1969, as we sat in the student union watching as blue capsules were pulled, like bingo balls, and the dates on them read, in the first Selective Service lottery since 1942, I sat silently at one of the tables with friends. I don't remember any noise at all until the first date, September 14, was posted on the board, and a fist slammed on a table behind me. With each ball, a new boy was placed in a symbolic draft line; the first dates called marked the first to be drafted. We were all there together, hoping together, but this fist was my reminder that we were mostly hoping individually, hoping for ourselves or our brothers or our boyfriends. I know because I still know my brother's lottery number, 116. 116. He was safe; he could continue college. The crowd at the student union dwindled at the end, the lucky and the unlucky both now knowing their places, if not their fates. The sense of unrest renewed itself after Christmas, after exams, but life on a Southern campus — even one known for civil rights and free speech and workers' rights protests in the past — was still primarily life on a Southern campus.

But on May 4, 1970, at a protest at Kent State University in Ohio, four students were killed by young National Guardsmen who had been ordered there by Governor Rhoades. Campuses across the country caught fire, and Southern campuses, which had so far been relatively tame, caught fire as well. There was an article in one of the early issues of *Ms.* magazine that I remember as being titled "Click!" written by Jane O'Reilly. She writes about the moment you realize you might be a feminist. The example I remember is that your husband agrees to pick up the laundry at the dry cleaner, but — *click!* — you are the one who has to remember that it needs to be picked up. I had a click moment, a moment when I pushed aside my impotence. When I heard about the killings at Kent State, I ran into the common room to tell other students in my dormitory what had happened. One boy just looked up from his hand of cards and said, "They probably deserved it."

Click! Who was this boy, who spent his afternoons playing cards, to say such a thing? He would do nothing to protest, and if I did nothing, I would — for all of history — be just like him. I might as well play cards or fiddle if this did not move me to action. Maybe I had stewed silently in the past, maybe because of my father or because of the faces of wounded soldiers I had seen in the hospital in Japan; maybe I was understandably conflicted about the tone of protests against our military instead of against our policies, whatever my reasons for inaction. But this was different. And in that moment I was different. I watched Allison Krause's father on television, his face flat and sad and helpless. *Why did they shoot her? Why did they shoot my daughter?* You couldn't hear that, I thought, and not be different.

That night we gathered, radicals and liberals and people who were simply leveled by what had happened in Ohio. There were a hundred, maybe more, filling the room. I stood against the wall and listened. The first to speak were voices of unrestrained anger — ugly rhetoric and talk of violence. The diatribes continued, each one besting the last. At times they didn't even seem to be talking about Kent State at all. The Chicago Seven, Bobby Seale, everything was part of the rant. One fellow even pounded his fist against the wall and screamed, *What about Albania?* Albania? I edged toward the door. I wanted to do something, but maybe this was not where I needed to be. Then Forrest Read, an English professor, spoke. We were talking about Kent State, he said, and we needed to listen to the new voices in the room. The diatribes stopped or at least slowed. The nonviolent coalition prevailed, and I set to work. Going to meetings, putting up posters, handing out fliers, I was a worker bee doing whatever was needed. And in what seemed like minutes, the war protests that had been at the edge of campus life were now almost all there was of campus life. When the consensus was to boycott the remainder of classes in the semester — a protest, fortunately, approved later that month by the Faculty Council — I went on strike with everyone else. I did continue going to one class. The great professor Hugh Holman had agreed to teach one undergraduate class, definitely the first he had taught in years and probably the last he ever taught, and, because there was an imposing reading list, there were only about ten undergraduates in his American Novel survey. But it was worth it to hear him talk with such fluidity about the literature, the art, the social fabric of each novel. I kept going to his class — but I went with a tape recorder, and I taped his lectures, which he gave to the two of us who still came. Then I typed the transcript of the lectures onto mimeo sheets and printed them, smelly and purple, and handed them out to Todd Cohen and Fenner Urquhart and the others who were not in class. I didn't know them well, but I knew what they were missing, what they were paying for this statement of principle, and I was trying to help. One day when I was packing up my tape recorder, Professor Holman asked me why we were striking. "It is useless, you know," he told me. "They don't hear you in Washington." "We know that," I said, "but we can't do nothing."

And so it was. We were part of something bigger, something that in time, years later, could have shaped a national resolve, but as much as I wanted to change the policies of the government, I participated because I had to, for me. Even if I was spitting in the wind, at least I had to try to spit. And it was so much easier to get up each morning and prepare for the march on South Building or hand out fliers for another rally in the Pit, because we were all trying together to let our outrage, our sadness, our vision be heard. I can tell you that I worked with Grady Ballenger or Charlie Dean, or that I took orders from John Rosenthal, or that I marched behind Rich Leonard, and all that would be true, but what would also be true is that I worked and marched and chanted alongside students whose names I did not know, but I knew we were joined in a cause.

Sometimes I would have to step back. At one evening rally, there was a call to march to President Friday's house. The University provided Bill and Ida Friday with a lovely home on Chapel Hill's main street, Franklin Street. The University also rented the house next door to the Fridays to the head of the Naval Science Department, the commanding officer of NROTC — my father. As soon as the call went out to march to President Friday's, I took off running. Breathless, I flew in the front door, turned off the television in the front room, and told my mother and father to stay indoors. Did anyone even know the head of NROTC was in the next house? I wasn't sure, but I didn't want these worlds colliding. Mother, Dad, and I talked in the kitchen while the protesters gathered, unaware, next door.

In terms of national policy, Hugh Holman was right. Nothing we had done had changed the government's policies. But we had been part of changing the national mind. By fall many of us who took multiple incompletes in courses the previous spring had to put away the protest signs and finish our classes for the fall semester and the previous semester, too. But we had changed things. Despite Jesse Helms' television commentaries about the "communists in Chapel Hill," opposition to the war was not just at coffee houses and SDS meetings anymore. It was at fraternities and in student government, who sponsored one of the largest protests, in the football stadium. Even Dad took some of the armaments that had surrounded the NROTC down in order to do his job without interruption or protest.

After all this, English graduate school seemed like another world, but I wanted to teach, particularly to teach young people to love literature as I did, so this was where I wanted to be, or so I thought at the time. English graduate schools in the early 1970s were dismal places. The learning was quite fine, the students came full of purpose and with a genuine love of literature, but there was nowhere to go, there were no jobs at the end of three years or four or five, for some it was now six and seven. It might have made a more aggressive group cutthroat and competitive, but not UNC English graduate students. We were complacent in the way that gentlemen are complacent — not in any way lazy, but civil to the point of inaction sometimes. And some were content that our bleak prospects allowed us entry into high emotion, even if the high emotion was despair. We had all been children of promise, and now we found ourselves imprisoned in a lovely garden of a town from which we could find no exit. So we didn't really try to exit; we tried to create for ourselves a place of civility and purpose, which was, I think now, really always out of our reach. But maybe the reaching for it taught us how to create that decency when we did finally manage to — and this is too harsh a word — escape.

I started graduate school at UNC in 1971 in a program in which I would go straight to a doctorate, bypassing a master's degree. It sounds more prestigious than it was. For me it was economics. I was borrowing money all the time to pay for school, and I didn't want to slow down to write a master's thesis. After our first year, we played the most erudite games of charades ever played as some studied for the master's writtens.

We even had to come up with a special hand gesture to designate that we were acting out the name of a poem. There were "conversations" in which every word spoken was a line from a different Shakespearean play. We did it because we could, but the intellectual pursuit, which meant so much to each of us, was tainted for me by the manic effort to make this lovely treading water seem important. It was like a mockery of gaiety, like a mockery of life. We all knew, but we had no choice.

I decided I had a choice. I didn't want to keep piecing together loans and tips from waitressing so that I could keep working on a degree that would never result in the job I wanted. In some ways, waitressing itself was more satisfactory. "Mom" of Mom's and Pop's Restaurant told me I was a born waitress, certain, I am sure, that this was encouragement to an English graduate student. At the Pines, where I waitressed next, Leroy Merritt had quite a different idea about waitresses. He saw us as an elegant waitstaff, never hurried, never really in need of tips — which drove the women who were trying to live on tips to distraction. For all the menial parts of waitressing, it was — unlike the Shakespearean conversations of graduate school — real in a way that graduate school might have been real had it been for more of us a path to the profession we had hoped it would be. In waitressing, what I saw is what I got. Work hard six hours, then go home tired with a pocketful of quarters. Unlike graduate school, if I did my part, it did not disappoint.

By the end of my second year, I'd made the decision to go to law school. My mother had always wanted me to go; she said I was argumentative. I don't think that distinguished me as a daughter, but I decided to follow her advice nonetheless. The transition was easy, for I wasn't leaving the lovely garden. I would go to law school in Chapel Hill. My friend Errol wrote of Chapel Hill that everything smells of life and the air is abuzz as if it had just sifted down from heaven. Nothing quite like it.

Law school was not, as I had expected and hoped, real life. People talked more about what was happening around us than they had in graduate school. But with the exception of a table of veterans who played cards together in the student lounge, there was pretty much unanimity about the war, about equal rights for women — starting, it turned out, with trying to find space for an adequate women's bathroom on the main floor. The small contingent of women law students started a group called Women in Law, to address issues such as bathrooms and matters of more importance, such as equal employment opportunities. The veterans countered with Veterans in Law. But it was not as contentious as it sounds. The conflicts were generally pedestrian. The biggest disagreement occurred when Susan Sabre changed the channel on the lounge television from an afternoon ACC basketball tournament game to *Sesame Street* so that her children could watch while she studied. She lost that fight.

The male law students bonded immediately. Men who had been strangers the week before went out from the law school in packs, slapping each other on the shoulder as they walked to the Tin Can to play pickup basketball. The women, on the other hand, sat uneasily on the steps of the brick courtyard and complained about bathrooms and interviews with yet another all-male firm. It created a bond, but a negative one. Men, I thought, had sports, and we did not. The only sports for women at my high school in Japan had been cheerleading and tennis. We played half-court basketball, three girls on each side of the court, the way Iowa girls played long after the rest of the country liberalized the rules, and even that was only in physical education and an annual upperclassmen-versus-underclassmen game. I was, believe it or not, the second-fastest girl in my high school, but the fastest girl, Sandy Choate, was faster than most of the boys. In another two decades, Sandy would have gone to college on that speed. But this was a different era. I could see that sports were good for boys, and they were good for those new male law students, so why, I wondered, could they not be good for us, too?

In nearly every intramural sport over three years of law school, I entered a women's law school team. Volleyball, basketball, softball. And I want to be clear: we were terrible. In every sport. But no team had as much fun. Mary Norris Preyer getting fifteen volleyball serves straight to her corner and missing them fifteen straight times and apologizing sweetly each time. We laugh about it still. Margo Freeman showing up to play softball in bare feet. No, she couldn't play shortstop like that; she'd at least have to go to the outfield. Donna Triptow dribbling the ball eight inches off the floor into the corner of the court and being trapped there. We were truly terrible. And yet year after year, I could still get women to sign up because we were getting to do what seemed a birthright to men: we were teammates, and then we were companions, and finally we were friends.

My dear friend Glenn Bergenfield, whom I met that first year, will tell you that I was a meddler, making people talk to one another, passing out those intramural sign-up sheets, gathering people for dinner, introducing people I didn't know, but the truth is that it is Glenn who was the go-between. It was Glenn who said I should go out with John. John Edwards? He was a textiles major from a small town, wasn't he? And wasn't he the one who had had a date to a football game with a majorette? I did not think this match would work. But Glenn kept after me, and finally I agreed that I would go out with him.

John picked me up in his red Duster. It was a flood car; he and his dad had cleaned out the mud, and the black and white checked interior gleamed. He wore a bow tie — I have never seen him wear one since — and a sweater vest — also not a staple of his current wardrobe. He took me to the Holiday Inn to dance to a disc jockey under a disco ball. I could hardly hear a word he said for hours. As he drove me home, I decided that Glenn would hear from me what a waste of time this was. And then, at my door, John leaned over and kissed me on the forehead, said goodnight and walked to his car. In an era of fast-forward sexual relationships, I was used to the fight at the door, or worse, in my apartment. And then this, this sweet and tender gesture. I suppose if he hadn't turned out to be the sweet and tender man that gesture promised, I might not be writing of this at all, but he was, and is. And so when years later I talked to our son Wade about his first kiss, I told him not to underestimate the power of a gentle kiss. It had won me over that first date. I never went out with anyone else again.

At first John was cautious. He didn't use any words that might be construed as suggesting any permanence to this relationship. When he abandoned that, he started talking as if we had already agreed to get married. There were lots of signs of that. In one real-life gift-of-the-Magi experience, I got a job in Greensboro to be close to where his family lived in Robbins, and he got a job in Washington to be close to where my family lived in Alexandria. And then he actually lived with my family, eating breakfasts my mother made, taking the bus to his job at the Securities and Exchange Commission, then eating dinners my father made, followed by dull-as-dishwater evenings in front of my parents' television set watching the Pirates — whose best years were behind them — play baseball. "Do you like Washington?" I asked him hopefully. His response: "I don't know about a place where the punch lines to jokes are in French."

In so many ways, John and I were different. I had traveled the world; he had never left the South. I had studied literature in order to teach college; he had studied textiles in order to run the mills in which his father had worked. But we had each moved from place to place, following our fathers' jobs. We had each lived in company housing — military bases for me, mill villages for John. Neither of us had a chance to be rooted in a place, so we were each rooted in family and faith, the things we took with us. In the essential ways, we were not different at all. By our third year, it was clear we would marry.

The North Carolina State Bar Exam was July 25th, 26th, and 27th in Raleigh. Most of our friends had leases that would run out on July 31st, the end of the month. So we decided to get married on July 30th. It would be hectic, but it would be a grand party. I went home to Alexandria to buy a wedding dress. My mother and I found just the dress I wanted in a small Old Town bridal store, and the owner, his white shirt buttons pulled tight and a tape measure around his neck, looked me over and said he could size it perfectly, I didn't need to try anything on. I should have known from that shirt that he didn't have that great an eye. On the Saturday morning before the bar exam started on Monday, my dress arrived. I knew I didn't need to pass the exam for my job — I would be working for a federal district judge the next year — so I could afford the luxury of being excited rather than just nervous, and I was . . . until I tried the dress on. Two of me could have worn it. Even alterations couldn't fix this. In North Carolina in 1977, stores closed at 5:00 P.M. on Saturdays and did not open at all on Sundays. And Monday morning when they reopened, I would be sitting in Memorial Auditorium in Raleigh taking the first portion of the bar exam. I took it just as quickly as I could, and when I rushed out after an hour, the poor fellow at my table, who had already snapped two pencils in frustration, was beside himself. I spent my now-extended lunch hour looking in the downtown stores — at the time, Belk's and Montaldo's — but I found nothing. After the exam, John and I drove back to Chapel Hill and I drove to a Durham bridal store. Still nothing. The second day of the exam, I did the same thing, only I went to Crabtree Valley Mall, where I found a dress — not the dress I dreamed of, not even a dress I liked that much, but it fit and I didn't hate it. It was four days before the wedding. I hadn't remembered to bring my shoes, but the women at Belk's said that if I brought them back the next day at lunch, they would hem and then press the dress during the last afternoon session of the bar exam. So lunch on Wednesday was the same as lunch on Monday and Tuesday, but on the ride home on Wednesday afternoon, a wedding dress lay between us.

My wedding, as many weddings, was a picture of my life. In the wedding party my sister, Nancy, and her oldest daughter, Laura, and John's sister, Kathy, were joined by Martha Hartmann from Japan, Maggie Ketchum from English graduate school, and Bonnie Weyher from law school. My brother, Jay, who went on to be an accomplished filmmaker, took the video; it is not, he would admit, his best work. My mother's best friend, Hazel Greenwood, who had lived next door to us in Iwakuni and who never got to manage a wedding for her son Bobby because he died in law school of cancer, was a second mother to me for my wedding. After it was over we drove away from our friends and family on our way to a one-night honeymoon in Williamsburg, and I started work at the federal court in Norfolk the next day.

Neither John nor I had ever been in a law office prior to law school. We went to our first jobs — each clerking for federal judges — with only one summer's legal experience each behind us. And during our judicial clerkships we applied for permanent jobs by writing letters to law firms across the country, many in places we'd never seen. It was not a focused evaluation of what was right for either of us. We were simply doing what the map to success suggested: law school, law review, federal clerkship, corporate law firm. None of it was bad for us. In fact, we learned a lot. Among the things we learned, though, was that this wasn't what we wanted. We ended up in Nashville, practicing law with people we enjoyed immensely. We had a beautiful home, two cocker spaniels, and a station wagon. A picture-postcard life, really. We had good friends, friends as close to us as family in George Masterson and Sol Miller, young lawyers who, like us, had been transplanted to Tennessee.

We were not all that young, but it seems now, from this vantage point, that we must have been. Working at our first real jobs, painting the rooms of our first house. George was our best friend, a best friend to both of us. When George wanted to buy a place for himself, we looked with him, the three of us checking the bathrooms and the view. No wonder George did not marry then; he was nearly married to us. It was George we first called when the doctor told us we were listening to our "daughter's" heartbeat. We learned to mimic the sound: I would do the *sh-sea* and John would do the *pa-tum, pa-tum.* My sister's home Drano test said we were having a girl as well. So my mother gave all the girl baby clothes to us and all the boy baby clothes to my sister, who was having a baby a month later. Only the Korean man who worked in the parking garage in my building disagreed. "Korean saying," he said. "A woman having a boy baby look rough. You having a boy."

I had not been asleep long. Awaking, I knew I was in labor. I got up and took a shower, thinking, correctly, I might not get another shower for a day or two. Then I got John up, and we went to Baptist Hospital.

There my labor progressed, slowly but surely through the night and into the morning, until it didn't progress anymore. The resident spoke in whispered tones to someone about what he should do. He needn't have whispered; in the next room a woman was delivering a baby she already knew to be stillborn, and her wail was all any mother on the maternity ward heard. For hours. Finally my obstetrician came, looked at the X-ray they had taken, and started preparing me for a cesarean section. As was the practice then, I left John at the operating room door. As the anesthesiologist leaned over me, I could hear my obstetrician talking through each step. And then I heard him say, "It's dead." "What did he say?" I asked the anesthesiologist. Had he really said the baby was dead? I was frantic. "Don't worry about anything," the anesthesiologist said, "the baby is fine." But all I could think about was the mother of the stillborn baby and her pitiful wail. "Tell me what is happening," I insisted, speaking loudly enough for the obstetrician on the other side of the curtain to hear me, but only the anesthesiologist answered: "Be still. It will be fine." When, seconds or minutes or hours later — I was too frightened to calculate anything — they showed me our son, I didn't count his fingers or toes. I simply saw the contorted face and heard the beautiful scream, and I cried. It turned out that what was "dead" was the power to the cauterizing machine, and you can just imagine what I said to the obstetrician later about his choice of words. In the recovery room, I didn't tell John about the scare, and he didn't tell me that Wade's head — having been stuck in the birth canal for hours — was shaped like a cone. We were just happy.

There was another problem. Wade's blood and mine were not compatible. It was a problem each baby I had would suffer. And his liver was having problems because of it. For days he was under a lamp, his eyes covered with patches, his bare bottom high above his tucked legs. And during those days, we tried to find a boy's name. Catharine Wade Edwards would not do. If only we had listened to the Korean garage attendant. Each day the nurse would come in and ask, Does he have a name yet? Not yet. He needs a name. Yes, we know. Finally, when he was four days old, we settled on Lucius Wade Edwards, Wade from John's mother's maiden name and a family name on my side of the family, and his first name from a nearly forgotten Lucius from my mother's Mississippi roots. Wade he would be. And although spelling Lucius was a trial for him at first, it was a name he liked. Even when substitute teachers called him Lucius, he liked it. When his friends said it, or changed it to Bubblucius, he recognized it as affectionate teasing. It is a strong and gentle name, a Southern name without any foolishness about it.

Those three years in Nashville are, for me, a collection of unrelated remembrances, I suppose because I was learning to become a lawyer and, more importantly, learning to become a mother, and there wasn't much room for anything else. I remember that the hardest part of leaving Nashville was taking Wade away from Shirley Mayberry, who worked at the child care center Wade attended in a big old home on a park-like lot near our house. We never went by when Wade wasn't in her lap or on her arm. And I remember the Anti-Swan Ball that Paul Sloan, with whom I practiced law, held in the woods of his family's farm on the night of the high-society Swan Ball at the Belle Meade Country Club. I remember feeling out of place at the victory celebration at the Opryland Hotel when Lamar Alexander, from John's law firm, was elected the Republican governor. And I recall buying furniture at the fairgrounds flea market and at an auction in Lebanon, and refinishing it in the backyard with John, as his mother had taught us.

And I remember the sad day we were driving to watch the U.S. Open on television at George's house. We were trying to turn left in a residential neighborhood, but there was a car stopped, blocking the lane ahead. I could see a man in the car holding a woman around the neck with his right arm and slugging her in the face with his left fist. I jumped out of the car and pulled open her door. As I pulled her out of the car, he swung open his door and headed for us both. It occurred to me then that I had always inserted myself into these situations on the premise that a man wouldn't hit a woman, and that premise clearly didn't apply here. But as he stepped toward us, John was standing there. Calm down, man, John said. He walked the man back along the road, talking to him, almost whispering to him, as I took the woman across the street, into someone's yard under a tree and went to the house to get help. Her face was covered in blood. The police came, but the woman wouldn't press charges. The police would not arrest him based on what I saw without her complaint, and so we all got back in our cars and drove away.

I saw them both about a year later at the grocery store, an old yellow bruise on her cheek. I suppose I had always thought that even strangers could intervene and make things right, if only they would, and this was a hard lesson that it wasn't always going to be that easy. You couldn't always fix everything.

CHAPTER 6
RALEIGH

I've now come to a chapter that I knew I would have to write. By an unspeakably vast margin there is no part of my life, or any life, that speaks more to what this book is about. I found a community that stood by me in the worst of times and allowed me to emerge, eventually, from a place of profound pain. I will try to write from a repose that should come with the passage of the years, but I cannot honestly say that it does. I do not want to endure the writing of this chapter, but I will. I will write it because it is a story of tribute to those who stood with me, not simply a story of our loss.

I awoke early. It was a crisp New Hampshire morning, like the mornings before it during which my daughter and I had visited private schools to which she had been accepted. Cate was still asleep in the other bed at the

Exeter Inn. I dialed home. John was taking depositions in Charlotte, so Wade was home alone. He finally answered. We had talked the night before, too, about his junior paper, due that morning. He had been sitting at the computer, typing his last corrections, when we talked. What did I think of this change in wording? Did I think he needed to make this section two paragraphs rather than one? He knew it was better; he just needed me to say so, and of course I did. And I let him talk to his sister — sweet words from her, I knew the same from him. Then goodnight. The morning call was shorter.

"Are you ready for school?"

"I'm up."

"Really up? Are you standing up?"

"I'm up, Mom. I love you."

"I'll see you tonight. I love you." That was it. No more talking, no more teasing. No more hugs. Click. That was it. It was over. It was April 4, 1996, and those were the last words I ever said to my boy.

The plan for all of us to meet at the beach for spring break was toppled by a wind that blew his car from the road. And Wade, just sixteen, could not stop the car from flipping and crushing some part of him that made him stop breathing. When he had tried to get his car back on the highway, maybe he overcorrected, maybe he moved too quickly, all the maybes for which I have no answers, except the final answer. The car fishtailed, then flipped on the road to the beach, and by the time an EMT who was traveling alongside him got there, Wade was dead.

I didn't have some second sense that he was in trouble. Cate and I were flying home from New Hampshire. John met us at the airport, and we talked about the high schools she had visited, the choice she now had to make, and the long-awaited week at the beach. Wade had gone on ahead with three classmates — two cars with two boys each — leaving after school with hopes of getting down early to catch the last of the sun on that first day. So the driveway was empty when we pulled in, and empty as we began packing for the week, and empty when I walked through the living room to call upstairs to Cate that we would leave in half an hour. That's when I saw it, the state trooper's car, pulling into the driveway and up our hill. I opened the front door as the driver stepped out of the cruiser.

I spoke before he did. Pleaded, really. It could only be one thing.

"Tell me he's alive."

"Is this the home of Lucius Edwards?"

No one but his friends making fun used Wade's first name.

"Tell me he's alive."

"Is this the home of Lucius Edwards?"

"You have to tell me he's alive." My voice breaking.

There was no gentle way to say it.

"He is dead."

I suppose every death has its own story. Our story began before we came into it. John had been working and Cate and I had been away, so there was only an empty house when the patrolmen came the first time. As the troopers circled, our neighbors began to find out the terrible news. By the time John and Cate and I first heard the trooper's words, people had gathered, waiting. The doctor from down the street with sleeping pills he thought we would need; our friend and John's partner, David Kirby, who would drive us to the hospital where he lay; Wade's friends; our neighbors. All in waiting, waiting for us to learn, waiting to reach to hold us up and to hold each other.

If I make myself think back on that night and on the next days, I can see everyone, I can bring everyone back. But it is so hard to do it without also bringing back that pain. The heat of it. The chill of it. What's important and what's not? People came, that's what's important. They were there. For Wade, first. And for us. A woman who had worked for us years before was at the sink, washing dishes the next day, not talking to anyone much, probably because she didn't know them. Becky, who helped us with the chores now, wanted to make sure Wade's room was clean; she busied herself elsewhere when she saw the sign my sister, Nancy, put up not to vacuum or change the sheets. I wanted the room to smell like Wade as long as it would, so Becky just helped in the kitchen. Chris, who cut all our hair, stood by the kitchen door. My brother, who is a filmmaker, sat with a camera in the living room and interviewed the children about Wade. He left the tapes for me, but I cannot yet watch them — even ten years later. Kim, whom I knew only slightly from having worked on a PTA project together, sat with the house while we buried Wade. Whole families came, because we had known most of these people as a family — through school events, soccer teams, the Jaycee Center and the YMCA, sitting on blankets at Pops in the Park, walking the downtown mall on First Night — and they were all there, helping and holding us and one another.

And the letters. I still have them, though they, like the memories, are hard to revisit. I didn't revisit them to write the notes I should have written. I didn't thank every teacher he had ever had, all of whom came to the funeral. I didn't thank my UNC basketball e-mail group or the gardener; both sent flowers. The food, the flowers, the notes, people stricken and desperate, and I was apart from it all and held up by it all at the same time. They allowed me to do what I needed; I just immersed myself as much as I could in Wade and held on. And I loved them, for what I will always believe was their love for him.

David drove us to the Duplin County Hospital that night. John sat silently in the front seat for the hour drive. Cate and I were literally huddled in the backseat. Everything outside was black. Everything inside was black.

The little hospital waiting room was full. The parents of the other boy in Wade's car, who escaped with a turned ankle, and the parents of the two boys in the second car were there. A local husband and wife with whom John had worked had come and with them an elderly woman from their church, who brought cookies and lemonade. I'll never forget her kindness, but I only wanted one thing, and she couldn't give it to me. We walked back outside and, with the help of Dick Henderson, a tall and gentle man whose son was in the car following Wade's, went up the stairs to the small morgue. He left at the door. John and I went in. There, on a cot, lay Wade, as beautiful and peaceful as I ever remember him. Sleeping, really. Couldn't he be? There was a bruise on his forehead, and as I stroked his face, I saw that the lobes of his ears had darkened as the blood pooled there beneath the skin.

I do not know what killed Wade. It doesn't really matter. It wasn't alcohol or speed. Knowing what killed him wouldn't tell me why, and it couldn't change the one thing I did know: he was dead. We called our parents. John told his parents; I told mine. Or I told my mother, since my father didn't speak on the phone much after a massive stroke in 1990 narrowed his once wide life and quieted his once gregarious voice. I heard Mother cry out, and I heard her tell my father. Then I heard the real sound of grief. Dad couldn't form words easily, so the sounds he made were not the no, no, no, no, no, no, that I screamed when the trooper broke my heart. His voice was the sound of pre-language pain, guttural and uncivilized, and the most powerful and mournful sound man can utter. He opened his mouth and the sound bled through the phone line and wouldn't stop. I hear it today.

That first night Cate slept with us. Our bedroom was downstairs. She and Wade shared the second floor, and it seemed too much to ask this child, who had just turned fourteen, to return up there alone. We pushed two club chairs together, with an ottoman between them, next to our bed, and she slept there that first night, and the second and the third. She slept beside us for two years, finally sleeping upstairs again when she was sixteen years old.

Wade died on Maundy Thursday. With Easter weekend, we could not have the funeral until Monday. The days in between were impossible and, if I can use an odd word, wonderful. Every day our house was full of food and flowers and friends. The washing machine was running. The kitchen was swept. And when we finally slept at night, they went away. But they were back in the morning, with more food, more support. I had never thought about how our lives had managed to intertwine with all these people, but they had, with some by just living, with most by doing — reaching out, helping out, coaching, carpooling, just being there. And now they were all here for us.

Hargrave had volunteered to come early that first morning. When she came at 8 A.M., John was already sitting on the front porch with his father, consumed by grief. Cate was up, and she and Hargrave hugged and cried. I was sitting at my computer printing out the phone numbers of the private schools that had admitted Cate for the next year. "I know it seems irrational," I told Hargrave, "but I have to contact all those schools this morning first thing to let them know that Cate will not be coming. She can't go anywhere."

By midmorning the house was full. Diane Payne, the principal from the high school, and a clutch of teachers arrived asking what they could do. Martha from next door, or Ihrie answering the door, Sally or Bonnie answering the phone, Tricia or Ellan or Lisa — it could have been a dozen people — making hotel reservations for family coming from afar, and everyone intercepting reporters. Soccer teams from the twelve years that John had coached, and book clubs and PTA. People from the church we attended. People from the Y. From basketball and Urban Ministries. Lawyers and maids and secretaries and bankers. All there. The house was crowded with them, and yet in the most important way, the house was empty for us. There were people, just not the one person we craved.

There were things we had to do, impossible things that all parents who lose children have to do. We had to pick out a casket and flowers for our boy — cherry and a blanket of pure white roses — and ride around in the back of a sedan while Chuck Gooch from Oakwood Cemetery showed us the available burial plots. Sitting in that car, Chuck's tender voice could not change the fact that he was driving a knife into us with each word. *Here's where you can bury your son. Here's where you can put him in a box and let us cover him with dirt.* I leaned into John. *Make it end.*

The visitation was on a cold rainy night, and I am told it lasted for hours, but time had no meaning for me. We stood in a long room with Wade's casket at the one end. We had decided to bury him with letters from each of us. His father and his sister wrote long letters to him. I had sat with my paper and stared. "My dearest Wade," I wrote. "You know." That's all I could write. We each placed our letters in the casket and had the top closed, so it was just a lovely box at the other end of the room. But it was Wade, just as surely as if he had been lying on that morgue cot, only a vinyl bag around him. The line of friends and neighbors, teammates and classmates, teachers and coaches went out the building and down the block. I had a moment, or should I say hours, of clarity, and I knew the name of every person who came through the line, even names I did not know I knew. Except for one. An older woman came up. She had to have waited in the cold rain for at least an hour, maybe two. I reached for her hands, searching her face. No, I did not know her. Then she spoke.

"Is this the line for Joy?" She was there for another visitation entirely.

"I am so sorry. This line is for our son, Wade. I don't know where she is," I said, then added as her tiny hands squeezed mine, "But if you find joy, please let us know."

The funeral was the same. Our church was full. Even though it was spring break, people had come back — every one of Wade's teachers, from preschool through his junior year, the boys with whom he played soccer and basketball for a decade and all their parents, the girls from cotillion, our friends, his friends, Cate's friends, and family — including my niece Laura from Indiana, who was to be married the following Saturday, and my Uncle Troy from Florida, who had buried his dear son David after a car accident almost twenty years before to the day. They stood with us, and they cried with us, and they prayed for us and, more importantly, for Wade.

We had always sat in a pew about two-thirds of the way back, far enough back that it wasn't a distraction that Cate, with a purseful of crayons, and Wade, with a nub of a pencil, were drawing during the sermon. That was our pew for fourteen years, but not today. On Easter Monday our pew was the first row, and at the end of the pew was the casket we had chosen. I suppose it was the one we had chosen, but honestly I do not know because I could not look at it. And I had to not look at it for an awfully long time, as the service went on and on. The three of us who remained were to speak, and Wade's friends and some of the adults with whom Wade had been close. I could have listened forever to the voices of those who loved him. But first the associate minister spoke. He was a dear man, but he did not know Wade, and in what would turn out to be a terrible decision he chose to speak from *Lament for a Son,* Nicholas Wolterstorff's book about the death of his son Eric. It must have seemed a right choice, a love song to Jesus, really, occasioned by Eric's death. And as the minister read, as Eric emerged, a selfish boy took form. "When I got angry at him," his father wrote, "it was usually over his self-centeredness." Who was this boy intruding on Wade's funeral? He was not Wade. Wade was imperfect — we all are — but he was never once selfish, never once self-centered. Did anyone here think this was Wade? I wanted to scream out, *That's not him.* The sermon about this stranger and his tormented father went on and on. I leaned into John. *Just make it stop.* On it went. *Please make it stop. Please.* And finally it did. It was finally time for the rest of us to speak.

Unimaginatively, we had always called Wade's friends — who nearly lived at our house — "the boys." It was now the boys' turn to speak. They had met at the house of one of our neighbors and planned what each would say. They stood together in front of the altar, and each one in turn stepped to the pulpit to say one special thing about Wade.

One boy stepped up but couldn't speak.

His face was dissolving in grief in front of fifteen hundred people. It was all I could do not to leave my pew and go to him, for these weren't just "the boys"; they were my boys. They had been a part of my every day for years. Another boy, the boy I always thought of as the closest to Wade in spirit, went to him. After they finished, Cate spoke, reading something she had written and speaking with the beautiful grace that has always accompanied that child. She was fourteen, and she transcended age.

John read from Wade's Outward Bound journal. Wade had climbed Mt. Kilimanjaro with John the previous summer, and, in order to get himself acclimated to the heights, he had gone to Outward Bound Colorado to spend time at high altitudes. He had told me about the journal he wrote at Outward Bound, but we hadn't read it until he died. The hardest to hear was the last he wrote. And John read it aloud. "The course director said that the solo is where you become a man. I disagree with that. I think that you become a man by slowly maturing. I think that it takes different experiences to help you mature and I think that you never really stop maturing and growing as a person. . . . I know that when this course is over I will be very proud of myself and very self confident. Whenever I have an obstacle to overcome in the future, I will think back to this course and know that I can conquer it. More than any other goal that I have set for myself I want to show my love and appreciation to my family for all that they have done for me. . . . I really want to do something great with my life. I want to start a family when I grow up. I am going to be as good a parent to my kids as my parents are to me. But more than anything, when I die, I want to be able to say that I had a great life. So far I have had a wonderful life (and I hope it keeps up.)" Across the church, people who had squirmed through the sermon were crying into Kleenex or the shoulder of a neighbor. And before this room full of sobbing teenagers, I got up and read a short poem by William Butler Yeats, changing the last word. *I sigh that kiss you, for I must own, that I shall miss you when you have gone.* My voice could hardly be heard.

For a time, the house was noisy with visitors, and then it was mostly still. The damp funeral flowers, as Edna St. Vincent Millay said in "Interim," "strangled that habitual breath of home," so we sent the lilies to the retirement communities around us, places

Wade had gone with his Latin class to carol and to dance. The hours passed, then days, then weeks. Each evening two friends came to our house. David Kirby and Gwynn Winstead, who was a friend of mine who had lost her son eighteen years before. From dinnertime to bedtime, we sat in our family room, the television off, the music off, the only sounds our voices. We relived sixteen years with them, night after night, week after week. For months. Sally, the mother of Cate's closest friend, came nearly every day. Hargrave and Ellan and Martha, who lived near me, kept watch. Did I need anything? Could they do anything? Jim, who had written a column in the paper about Wade a few weeks before he died, was a welcome sight at our kitchen table. Letters daily, wonderful letters about the difference Wade had made in his sixteen years. "He was the good one," one boy said. Most of these gestures were small, but a walking stick is small compared to a man, but when a man needs one, that small stick is all that will do. And we leaned into it.

Still the quiet house was hard for all of us. The Weather Channel with no sound. The Weather Channel with sound. Then C-SPAN. Then news. Finally sports. But even that was background. In the foreground was silence.

In order to tell the real story of the extraordinary people who gathered around us then, I have to tell the story first of a noisy house. And I don't mean it figuratively. Our house had been so full, so loud, before Wade died. Cate's friends, who had sometimes gathered at our house, were now asking her to come to their houses, their parents undoubtedly thinking they were helping. Maybe they were, but they left behind the silence.

Before Wade died, Cate's friends had gathered in lots of places, our house included, often locked away in her bedroom teaching each other to dance, talking about middle-school romances and middle-school humiliations. Wade's friends, on the other hand, filled every part of our house every day — and every weekend night — for years. Our house was the hangout for his class. My kitchen would fill up after school until I chased them back to the basketball court or upstairs to the playroom. I had a sign on the drawer where I kept the snacks for lunch that reminded them they could not eat from that drawer and another on the cabinet where we kept basketball tickets and travelers' checks that said, "If this isn't your house, stay out of this cabinet." But they ignored the notes, because it really was their house. They would tell me their grades, talk to me about politics, ask for my help with homework and projects. One Sunday night before Mr. Baker's famous leaf project was due in biology, my kitchen was filled with children, and I mean actually filled, most of whom — but not all of whom — I knew. Until late into the night, I helped freshman boys, friends and strangers, mount and label pressed leaves, many the extra leaves Wade had collected just in case any of his broke while being mounted. Report cards, PSAT scores, driving test results, breakups with girlfriends — it was all reported in my kitchen.

Just as they were learning to drive, one or more among them decided to take a truck from our driveway. The housekeeper listened to their plan and was there when they left, but she didn't intervene and went home soon after, without calling me. So when I did get home, the house, which was never empty, was completely empty. And the truck was gone. I called John at work. *Do you have the truck?* No. In every puzzle there is a most likely solution, and the most likely solution here, where there was a house with no boys and a driveway with no truck, was that there was a connection between these two facts. I moved my car to the neighbor's driveway, which couldn't be seen from our house, and walked back home. Watching from a window about a half hour later, I saw the boys — Ryan and Ellis in front, Wade and Tyler in the back — pull the truck into the driveway and carefully, very carefully, back it up and forward until it was precisely where it had been. They got out and walked up to the back door laughing and high-fiving one another. Until they opened the door and saw me. Then there was complete silence.

"Ryan, up to Wade's room. Ellis, to the living room. Tyler, to the kitchen. And Wade, come with me." Alone with him, I asked Wade what happened. Nothing. He told me absolutely nothing. He wouldn't say who was driving. He didn't tell me what the housekeeper later told me about his resisting the idea. He said nothing at all. I tried the others, one at a time. Each one caved, telling stories that differed only slightly, as the teller of each version and Wade were portrayed most sympathetically. Lots of "Wade and I tried to talk them out of it." Lots of "It was not my idea." Lots of "Ryan/Ellis was driving." After I had grilled all of them, I put them back in the same room. And I talked about the fact that they were fifteen and sixteen years old, that in five or six years they would be entering the same world I was in, doing business with me, trying to sell me a house or a car or insurance. And I told them they had to start acting like responsible people, because I wasn't going to forget what they had done. They were getting too old for do-overs. Did they understand? They said yes, apologized, and started to get up.

"Not so fast," I told them. "I have something else." They sat back down. "You all are lousy friends. Really lousy friends. You have a lot to learn about loyalty. Every one of you — except Wade — told on your friends, not reluctantly, not eventually, but immediately. What kind of friend does that make you? If you want to have friends you can count on, you cannot wait until the day you need them. You have to be true and loyal friends every day before that day." I had exactly the same conversation with those boys that I would have had with my son; it never occurred to me to do less. The relationship we had — and have today — wasn't won simply by buying enough soda and string cheese. It was won in hard times, by treating them as if I cared about what happened to them. Which was easy, because I always have. I talked to them about everything, and Wade, bless his heart, would sit there — maybe embarrassed, but always patient with his mother. When a boy showed up proud with a hickey on his neck, I tried to explain that it was not a mark of passion but a mark of ownership. When there was a conflict at the high school over the Confederate flag, we talked about that. When they would twitter and laugh about a slang word that meant breast, we would sit at that kitchen table and, as coldly and dispassionately as I could, we would say every slang word for breast over and over until it was no longer funny, no longer cool. Girlfriends, teachers, politics, sports — nothing was off-limits. If they wanted to get away from Wade's mother for a while, they would bound up the back steps to the playroom or run to the backyard and the half-court's worth of cement that we called a basketball court. Wade would linger to the end, give me a hug, and then join them.

When Wade died, these friends lost a friend on whom each one had relied at one time or another, on whom they knew they could depend for a lifetime, whom they loved. They also lost their way of doing things, or thought they had; they lost their place for doing things, or thought they had, until we reassured them that this was always home to them. At first they were there all the time, not so much for us, I think, as for each other. As time went on, one or two would come by every day or so. They would stay awhile and talk softly to us, as if they were in a library. Honestly, it couldn't have been much relief to come to that quiet kitchen and talk to those sad parents. John and I knew we had to break this pattern, for them and for ourselves. So we asked the boys and the girls if they would come by every week for dinner. They could come more often — and they did — but every week, every Tuesday, all of them could come at once. (Since I used to feed some of them five nights a week, this was actually less often than before.) And they came. It did me such good to come home to the sound of them. Together, like it had always been. We cooked steaks or spaghetti, or if it had been a tough day we ordered pizza. A dozen children one week. Twenty the next time. They took a picture for the senior yearbook at that basketball court in the back. When Mother's Day came, the boys brought me a dogwood tree. The girls brought a framed poem surrounded by pictures of Wade. Still it was grades and sports, and politics and

168

teachers. And soon it was colleges. They kept coming, until they graduated from high school the next year. And while they did the house was loud again, filled with stories of Wade and with stories of life that had happened after Wade.

Seeing Wade's friends happy was the best thing and, honestly, the worst thing for me, but there was never a question about what I wanted. I wanted them to be happy. I want them to have the joys he did not live to have, the success he cannot win, the family he cannot raise. And they are the carriers of his memory. So once a week we would eat and talk, and they would tease one another until it was finally late. Sometimes a child would slip out of the kitchen and go upstairs to sit in Wade's room. We would find them, with tear-streaked cheeks and red eyes, sitting on the edge of Wade's bed. Why did this happen, they would wonder, but we had no answers, then or now. We would hug them, and we would leave them, letting them sit as long as they needed. I surely love those children.

I want to make clear that Wade was not perfect. Only the youngest of children who die are perfect. He loved us, knowing our shortcomings — I don't think I was an easy mother — and we loved him with his shortcomings, though he was really a very easy child. Only once in the last five years that he lived did we quarrel. Of course, I had to tell him to leave his sister alone, and he wouldn't; or to bring in the soda from the car now, not later, and he would dawdle; or to turn off the television and study, but I would still hear the music to *Saved by the Bell* coming from the playroom. But these were little things, truly. He found such pleasure in whatever was around him, stumped only by vanity or betrayal. John says something about our younger son, Jack, that was also true of Wade: he says, "I wish I had the same joy about anything in life that he has about everything in life." The raw material for a fine man was there in Wade. And it gave us pleasure, and now it gave pain. But we were finding our footing. Wade was helping; he wouldn't be, as we had feared, easily erased.

It was easier, too, because so many had hold of our waists, holding us up as Dick Henderson had held us up that first night when we walked to the morgue. Hayes Permar, a classmate of Wade's, came by and played a song he had written for Wade, about wishing they had had more time. *I want to rock you in the water in the river of my mind. I want to thank you for your laughter; I only wish we had more time.* Wade's English teacher told us a story of how special he was. In her AP English class, they had been studying *The Snows of Kilimanjaro* the week before Wade died. They discussed it for four days, and Wade participated. But until she read his obituary, she did not know, because he had not mentioned, that he had climbed Kilimanjaro the year before with his father. What child, or adult, could have refrained from such a boast, she wondered aloud. He had done the same thing when he was one of the winners in a national speech contest a few weeks earlier; he told his friends he was going to Washington "to look around with Mom." Nothing about his award. There was another song by a friend of John's, one that would be included in his band's CD. Wade's essay on voting with his father, for which he went to Washington, would be in a North Carolina textbook the next year. The yearbook, on which he worked, had just enough time to get in pages honoring his memory. An editorial in the newspaper entitled "A Great Kid" was one of the best gifts of all.

Gene Hafer, an attorney and the father of

one of Wade's preschool classmates, came by and asked if he could set up a foundation for the contributions that were coming into the high school in Wade's name. What's more, he had some ideas about how to spend that money. John and I had written out the things Wade cared about — writing and soccer and computers, Broughton High School and the University of North Carolina — and we used that list as our guide to what we might do in his name. When Gene suggested a computer lab adjacent to the high school, it seemed right. Wade had complained one day that an assignment was marked with the words "Ten extra points if your paper is typed." Not everyone could type their papers, he'd said. Not everyone has a computer. It wasn't fair to them. Well, now Wade could level that playing field. In his name, we built the Wade Edwards Learning Lab. I asked Matt Leonard, who with his father had climbed Mt. Kilimanjaro with John and Wade the previous year, if he would be the first director. He had just left Yale and was looking for something into which he could throw himself. He said yes. From the reconstruction of the office building to the wiring for the computers to selecting the Internet service provider, Matt cajoled and badgered and worked harder than anyone around him, until in October, six months after Wade died, the Wade Edwards Learning Lab — the WELL — was open and students who had no computers at home were at the long desks, checking their e-mail and writing their papers.

I had known Gwynn for eight years, since our daughters were in kindergarten together. And yet, after she took me to my first Compassionate Friends meeting, a meeting of bereaved parents that she moderated, I realized I owed her an apology. I hadn't been such a good friend to her, I said. I hadn't read the scars that the death of her precious son Drew had left nearly twenty years before. I hadn't had eyes that allowed me to see, or maybe there was a part of me that did not want to acknowledge the possibility of burying a child. Whatever my excuses, I hadn't been a good friend. I learned two things. From Gwynn, I learned that I needed to be more like her, to be someone who stepped forward when others stepped back at the death of a child. And she didn't step up because it gave her an opportunity to talk about Drew — and you cannot know, unless you have been here, what a temptation that is. She stepped up and let a mother grieve her own loss. That's what she did with me and with John. For years, really. So when I was campaigning in 2003 and 2004, I knew not just to hug someone who whispered in my ear that they too had lost a son. I held them but pulled back enough to look them in the face, my arms still around them, and I asked his name and when he had died and how they were doing and whatever else my time would allow, because it is not just a box to check for deceased children. Their boy deserved to leave more marks, and he could leave one with me. As I learned from Gwynn.

I also learned for myself that I had to give the people who cared about me instruction. I had to let them know what I needed, what would help. I got pretty good at that, although I was considerably less good at saying what didn't help. It certainly didn't help when a man I know, complaining that his son wasn't getting into college where he wanted, told me that at least Wade was spared that unhappiness. It certainly didn't help when a trainer at the Y said she had visited her aging grandfather and, boy, I sure wouldn't want Wade in that condition. I didn't want to teach them. I just wanted to run away from them, and I did. They weren't trying to be hurtful, few are; they just had no clue. For the others, I tried to help them help me. It wasn't always pretty. And frankly they didn't always volunteer.

I carried a picture of Wade in my pocket, in one of the stiff sports card sleeves into which he put his best baseball cards, so it wouldn't get bent as I fingered it — and I did finger it. If, in a restaurant, I felt Wade about to overtake me, I would go to the restroom and take out the picture. If someone, anyone, was there, I showed them the picture and told them about my boy. I know it made some people feel awkward — I could see it in their faces — so I was always sure to say how much it meant that they had listened, so that at least they would feel good to go along with the feeling awkward. In a while, I felt more composed and could go back to my table. Maybe it was the time I needed; maybe it was the sharing. But what made it work was the willingness to reach out, the willingness to take a chance on the decency of strangers. And, frankly, no one ever ran out of those restrooms; they always stayed and listened.

Nothing was easy. Sometimes what I needed was to be left alone. The grocery store was a hard necessity. How many times could I pass his favorite food, his choice in soda? Not as many as I needed, it turned out. Once he came crashing in on me, and I was literally thrown to the floor. I sat sprawled in the soda aisle at the grocery store and cried uncontrollably. No one bought sodas for about five minutes. Although the store was crowded, no one walked down the aisle in which I sat, flattened by Cherry Coke.

Because of moments like the grocery store — I finally asked friends to go for me for a while — or restaurants, I tried to keep on a pretty narrow track. The house, the middle school Cate attended, the cemetery, Compassionate Friends meetings, more and more the Learning Lab, and Cate's softball and soccer games. I started substitute-teaching at the high school Wade attended. Where people knew me, where people knew Wade. I didn't need to go farther. I didn't want to go farther.

John still coached Cate's soccer team, and although the season was mostly over by the time we lifted our heads, there were still games to be coached, a tournament or two to attend. One dreadful tournament in Wilmington, near the beach house, was down that same highway where Wade had died. Cate's team stayed across the street from the motel in which Wade and I had stayed — in a front corner room I could not miss — when his team attended the same tournament the year before. I would stare at the door to our room and wonder if I was ever going to be able to go anywhere again.

Despite having a mother who seemed to be made of ashes, Cate was trying to push through her year as cheerfully as possible. I went to all her softball games, where she pitched, and to her school programs, where she collected honors. She was doing her part; I tried to do mine. I took my camera so that people would see I was busy and wouldn't feel they had to be solicitous. I was Cate's mom then, not the mother of the boy who had died. It was good for her, and it was good for me. It was, I have to believe, good for them, too. They could give me a hug, and they did, without fear that I would collapse in their arms and they would have more than they could handle. So there was this unwritten boundary: I could be sad, but I just couldn't be too sad. If I played my part, I got enormous support, support that continues even now, ten years later. But I couldn't ask too much, or the deal we had implicitly forged might be broken.

It might have been an impossible deal for me to keep — remember, I did sit and cry in soda aisles — except that I had other places to put the grief, other things I was doing that let me parent the memory of Wade, and, as I will tell you, other places to be the desperate grieving mother.

First, I had John. In every activity, in every project, in every moment of grief, I had John. For years, I had been writing a letter to my children, a letter that they would read, I thought, when I died — my "dying letter." I read it to myself when Wade died. Afraid I might not be there to interfere with whomever they were choosing to marry, I expressed my opinion in advance, on paper. What they had to understand, I wrote, was that passion is not a constant river from which they could drink for a lifetime. What kept the passion there, what filled the gaps when the passion hit a drier spot, were respect and friendship and love and communication. And I was now living such a time. Though we were both filled up with emotion, overloaded with emotion, there was no room amid the grieving for passion. And yet our relationship was deeper as that river dropped. For the first six months after Wade died, John and I were only a few feet apart nearly every single minute. Some couples grow apart; I saw it happen in couples in Compassionate Friends. It had happened to Gwynn. But we had what I had hoped Wade would have, and what I still hope Cate will have: a relationship in which there was passion, respect, friendship, love, and communication. And there was something else, something that is just dumb luck: we needed basically the same things in our grieving — not entirely, admittedly, but basically the same things. So we walked together, and still do.

So first and last, there was John. And Cate, whose two-chairs-and-an-ottoman bed in our bedroom also had a little bit to do with the lull in passion, but who brought much more than she took away. Cate, who worried that the good child to whom she could never measure up had died, although it was Cate who got most of the awards, Cate who was the better athlete, Cate who got the best grades, and — this like her brother — Cate who had devoted friends. She was there for me; I only worried that she wouldn't let me be there for her. When she was seven, she couldn't blow a bubble-gum bubble, so she went to her room, practiced for as long as it took, and came out only when she had mastered it. The year before Wade died, she said she wanted to be a softball pitcher. None of us could help her with the exaggerated slow-pitch windup. But she got a pail of softballs and stood in the backyard each afternoon, until she was the starting pitcher on her team. And when the league changed to fast-pitch, she did the same thing all over again. No one could have asked more of herself and less of her mother. I always had the feeling that the support I gave her was the support she thought was good for me to give, rather than what she needed. But it was something, and, after a decade, it still is something.

And I also had Matt Leonard, whom I had loved for almost his whole life, and whom I could fuss over like a mother while he fussed over the Learning Lab. He'd have to tell you if it was good for him — and time might give me a break on his answer — but I know it was good for me. I fussed too over the WELL, like a lioness protecting her den. John, and Cate, the WELL and Matt, the cemetery and the staff there — they were my companions.

And Wade, too. Every day I would sit beside him, on a blanket with a thermos of water, and I would read the Bible aloud to the place on the ground under which he was buried. I read from the Bible my mother's parents had given me in 1957, a zippered New Revised Standard edition that was worn before I started. It got so much use in those next months that it is now too fragile to be taken from my house. After I finished that, Wade's godfather, Glenn, sent me *Sages and Dreamers* by Elie Wiesel, and I read that aloud. When Wade's senior year started, I read aloud all the books on the twelfth-grade reading list. The whole thing. As I did, I remembered our years of reading together, his head on my lap, his fingers linked in mine, as first he read and then I read and then it was his turn again and then mine until he would sleep and I could feel the deepness of his sleep in the long and even passage of each breath, and at last I could close the book and read the face of my child instead. And at the grave, I would do the same — read until I closed my own eyes, seeing then what I could not see with open eyes, the edges of his eyelids, the lashes soft against his cheek, the freckles climbing across his nose and around to the edge of his eyes and then fading into the soft short hairs at the tops of his ears. Where I once ran my fingers through his clean straight hair over and over, I could only finger my own, twisting it in dissatisfaction around my finger. And as I once watched his chest rise and fall beneath my arm, I could now — if I watched closely, and I did

— watch tiny greenbugs work their way among the blades of grass above his coffin.

Chuck Gooch, the foreman, Wink, and the Montenard workers at the cemetery became part of our family. We would see them as we read and as we carried water for the flowers we planted. They would know we had been to the cemetery before them when they would find the fallen twigs in our section of Oakwood neatly stacked along the curb. They would stand back or spin their lawn-mowers off in another direction while we prayed or when we needed time alone. But they would join us at the grave while we worked or planted, asking if we needed water. Or Wink would come, shovel in hand, and dig where I pointed. We gave them presents on Wade's birthday and at Christmas, and they replaced a small statue of an angel when someone stole a similar one from Wade's grave. Just like family.

Mother's Day, when Wade's friends brought a pink dogwood for me, was a hard day. Six weeks. They had planned to plant it that afternoon, but in the early hours of Mother's Day, a fraternity fire in Chapel Hill claimed the lives of five young people, including Ben Woodruff, who had been a senior at Broughton High School when Wade was a freshman. "The boys" — and some of their older brothers — were part of a wide, happy circle from which large shavings had now been cut, and the circle would never roll again straight and carefree. So the boys delivered the tree and went to be together, again, as they had when Wade died. Although Wade and Ben were not friends, Ben had been good to Wade in soccer and in Latin activities. It was startling to read his obituary. Born in Nashville, as Wade had been. Latin, soccer, Woodberry Forest Sports Camp, all like Wade. And now, like Wade, buried in Oakwood Cemetery. We went to Ben's parents. The day before we went, we knew everyone who had gathered in their house better than we knew the Woodruffs themselves, and now, on the day Ben died, we knew Bonnie and Leon better; we recognized ourselves in their vacant eyes. I don't have to see them often to know that we are forever linked.

When John and I came from seeing Ben's parents, we planted the tree in the backyard. The girls brought a collage of photographs and a poem they framed. And they answered my request to dig through their pictures and find any with him in it. Wade worked on the yearbook staff — as I had done decades before and as Cate did in the years after him — and his friends there found pictures of crowds of students in which, they assured me, that was Wade sitting behind the fellow in the cap or leaning against the bleachers near the wall, as they pointed to a dot I could hardly see.

There were things that came up that spring and the next year that Wade would certainly have done. Honors breakfasts, literary magazine readings, assemblies. The only question for us was whether there would be a hole where he would have been or whether we would fill it. So there was no question at all. We went. And sometimes there was a moment of grace. At the spring honors assembly, Wade was to get several awards. We went to receive them for him. Watching the children who marched in together and sat in the honorees' chairs was one of the hardest moments I'd had. I could only bury my face in my hands. *It was stupid to come,* I thought, *stupid, stupid, stupid. What did I expect?* When we stood to accept his first award, however, the entire student body rose in a spontaneous standing ovation — the other honorees, then his classmates, the whole school applauding him softly, then strongly as they stood. We were overwhelmed. Their love for him that day convinced me always to be where he should be, whenever we could, no matter how hesitant we might be to face his absence.

I went every day to Wade's grave until our second daughter, Emma Claire, was born, because that was what felt right to me. Whatever we do — going or not going to our children's graves, sleeping with a toy, or closing the door to their rooms — has only to be what we each need, what we require to make it through each day without them. There is no other yardstick. It served me best to visit Wade's place daily. On my way through the cemetery, I passed the graves of other children I knew to be well loved and did not often see their parents. In some ways, I suppose, I envied that they had a way of facing the death of their children that was not so vulnerable to weather, that did not require checking the papers to schedule around large funerals, that did not have a locked gate at sunset. It meant nothing to me that they came less often; I didn't think then or now that they loved their children less than I loved Wade. We were, undoubtedly, different people before our children died, and we are different yet, with different ways of reaching for some measure of acceptance of this.

I went to Oakwood then, and I go now — though less often — because the rest of the living world ends at that cemetery gate. There his body lies, surrounded by the bodies of families, by stories of lives long and short, and there the inevitability of death seems like but another chapter. And there I could not help but speak to him. I read him letters that people had written to us about him as if they had been written to him. I took his SAT score out to him when it came in the mail. He would have been able to go to Carolina, where he so wanted to go. I told him, too, that Matt had gotten a good score. Before Wade died, I had kept trying to chase his great friend Matt home when he and Wade would sit at Wade's computer, Wade helping Matt prepare. "Wade has to prepare himself, Matt," I would say. But Wade wanted to help, and Matt stayed. And when Matt happily shared his score with me, I shared it with Wade's grave. But it wasn't just Wade I talked to. I also spoke to Oliver and Gerald, young brothers who died, each at two years, half a century ago, before I was born, and their brother Robert, who died in World War I, and to Ben and Emily and Betsy, who died within months of Wade's death. I would speak to Wade and pray and read aloud. And I planted and tended and cared for the space that now surrounded his body. I cleaned around

Wade, like cleaning his room, and I cleaned around the graves of the children like Oliver and Gerald, since next to each child were his or her parents, who died after them and were unable to tend the graves themselves. I placed flowers on the grave of Barbie, who fell from the Bay Bridge in Maryland; her parents lived too far away to place them there themselves. I never knew her, or them, but when I read her obituary, read that she would be buried at Oakwood, I thought how Wade, who was her age, surely would have liked her. I cared for the grave of Ida's baby daughter, and I cleaned the cross of John, who died at twelve, carefully washing the dirt that had gathered in the words inscribed on his cross: *In his mouth was found no guile.*

It doesn't matter to me whether all this sounds odd. I did it because it made it easier for me, easier for me to think that there were mothers who would come after me and tend to Wade's grave when I no longer could. Easier to think that we were all in this together, that we formed a bond, a community — these long-dead mothers and I, and the mothers who would come later — and the creed to which we all subscribed was the sanctity of the graves of our children.

CHAPTER 7
RALEIGH, AND NOT
RALEIGH

I found a special place to share what I couldn't share with every stranger and what I couldn't inflict on every friend. Wade had introduced me to the Internet back when Prodigy and CompuServe were the only commercially available providers. He and I bid on sports cards on the sports card group on AOL with people like Stratfan and Bocephus69; I argued about grammar on the English-usage newsgroups with Bob Leiblich; I shared song lyrics on the music lyrics newsgroup with Ron Hontz. And when I needed it, I found the grief newsgroup. A newsgroup was — and is — like a bulletin board where someone posts a message and other people post responses. Sometimes a message gets no responses, and other times there is a long line of responses, called a thread.

One night, when I could not sleep, I found alt.support.grief, the newsgroup for the bereaved. I later discovered GriefNet and, there, grief-parents, an e-mail group for bereaved parents, and I found Tom Golden's wonderful website on grief and healing. All of these became homes for me, but at first, it was only alt.support.grief, ASG. For several nights I read the stories of those who had died posted by those who buried them. The pattern was the same. A new poster would tell his or her story, and the family of ASG would comfort him. And soon the new poster would be the one comforting another new griever. When Astrid, who lost her son Christian, introduced herself and him in wonderful stories about his too-short four and a half years, I responded in much the way all first responses were framed. *I am so sorry about the death of your son, Christian. His death is part of the incomprehensible workings of a world we once naively thought fair. I hope that you find in this group what you need. Some of us will be angry on days you need resilience. Some will be cheerful on days you need to wail. Some will feel exactly as you feel on a given day. But all of us will be in pain on every day on which you feel pain. And in that, oddly, is the gift, the bond that allows us to be gentle with each other. You know that the person across a continent of irrationality understands the immense weight that emptiness and absence can have inside you. Do not misunderstand: no one else has lost Christian; no one else knows just what an incredible boy he is. But all of us are willing to learn that from you. There is no time, not months or years from now, that we will tire of him. With great regret, I welcome you to alt.support.grief.* It was what I truly felt, and it was my part of the great web we were weaving — each strand weak and vulnerable, but all together strong, or at least stronger. And I was stronger for having curled myself around Astrid's tender thread. And so it was.

I flip through the printouts of my e-mails now. *"Fred, I am so sorry about the deaths of Maritta, Regan, and Jeff." "Stefan — That your father hid from himself in a bottle does not mean he loved you less than he should; it means only that he loved himself less than he should." "Joanna, I remember vividly the accident that took Ginger." "Irene, I am so very sorry about the death of Gabe."* And on and on. It is a chain today and tomorrow that will not be broken.

There were threads on how to decorate a gravesite at Christmas and what to do for birthdays. People shared poems and lyrics. There were threads of pain and threads of hope. And those people and that place were home for me for the year — and more — that I needed it. I wrote at ASG words I could not say aloud, words too raw for the stranger in the restroom, words too hard for the friend who dropped by to check on me. In that safest of places, I described the importance of it, and places like grief-parents, when I wrote: *In our families, we nurture and protect; our pains hurt those who love us, so without thought, we temper the manifestations of pain. Can I really let my mother, who hurts so for my son and for me and for herself and his grandfather, can I really let her see the depths to which I go? I cannot. But there is here. Thank God, there is here.*

And, honestly, those people are as real to me today as if they were standing beside me. Bill Chadwick was almost always the first to respond to any post. I have never met him, so I don't know what Bill looks like in real life, but in my mind he is a bear-like man with huge hands he uses to grab your shoulders and an open face that he brings close to you when he speaks, telling you that God will help you as He helped

Bill when his promising son Michael died. Lana must be small and strong, with a face perfected by weather, and she might offer to plant your child's favorite flower in Brooke's Garden, her form of parenting her daughter's memory after Brooke was hit by a train. Sue and her son Wally. Pretty Shelby and her precious toddler Chase. Eloquent Carl and Wilem. Gigi and her seven-year-old Kelsey. And Christian, sorely missed by Astrid. We paid attention to each other, trying to anticipate the shards that would hurt our friends. Lana was from Massachusetts, and when I read of another train accident in North Andover, another child killed the way Brooke had been killed, I wrote. It's what we did. There are more than a hundred names I kept in a book by my computer, their birthdays and death days marked so I would remember to send my prayers and wishes. It was simple: none of us wanted our children to be forgotten.

By the time I got to ASG, I had already found some relief at the keyboard. Wade and I had been bidding on sports cards when he died, and the auctions were still ongoing. We had a good reputation for paying promptly, and I didn't want that to be tarnished. I felt, and still feel, a responsibility to his reputation. So I asked a friend to post on the board what had happened, promising that I would pay for whatever Wade had won and asking that the sellers be patient. They were much more than that. Understand first that this is a community in which sports cards were auctioned. Souls were not bared, confidences not shared. This was sports cards. Or so I thought. Within days of Wade's death, the e-mails started coming in. Stratfan, from whom we had bought many cards, wrote that we had "after such a long time, become friends through this forum, and that trust and friendship will never be forgotten." He told me, too, the story of his son, Ronnie, with whom he had collected, describing the same intimate enjoyment Wade and I had shared. And then he told me that two years before, on Father's Day, Ronnie had drowned. He warned me that the pain would not go away, and he promised to stay in touch and did. But it wasn't just the bereaved who reached out. SptInvstr, whose real name was Brad Drown, wrote, *All of us who are here on-line are to some degree a family, and the fact that we've never met doesn't matter at this point. We share your sorrow.* And so it was from DeputyCarl and Blankster, KidFlash 95 and Bottom9th, from RiSpec and Pogman, and

Jim Harpp, known as Bocephus69. They may have had silly names — okay, they did have silly names — but they didn't just coast through. Even in this online venue, which allowed the least personal of interactions, they made it personal. And they made it better.

I had an even closer group online. For a couple of years I had been corresponding in e-mails with some UNC basketball fans. We had first posted on the America Online bulletin boards made for UNC fans, but it became increasingly peopled by "anybody-but-UNC" fans, and we found refuge in private group e-mails. We were spread out across the country, e-mailing our comments about the program, the recruits, and the games to one another. We'd cheer when someone's child would be admitted to Carolina. We told each other our triumphs and our defeats. Though we had never seen each other, we were friends. In a lull in the season — Thanksgiving or Christmas of 1995 — I had noticed that one of the participants, John Schoo, had an interest in adventure travel. Over several weeks, I talked to him about Wade's trip to Kilimanjaro and his desire to go on another adventure with his father the following summer. I asked him what he suggested, and he told me of a trip he had taken with his son. He sent me a picture of a handsome blonde young man and himself perched in an open-topped Jeep in the Nagar Valley out from Hunza in the north of Pakistan, six of the seven tallest mountains in the world at their back. "The most important trip of my life," he said. John Schoo and I lived more than a thousand miles apart, but we had close friends in common — his brother-in-law and I were godparents to the same twin boys. And through that connection, I heard why it was his most important trip. Months before he joined our group, his son, Nielsen, had died, falling over in his living room, maybe as the result of an aneurysm. Whatever it was, it killed him. When Wade died, John told me about Nielsen. And the telling and my outpourings to him opened the gates of grief again for him. I know the price he paid for every letter of support he sent me over the next months, and I love him for it, always will. It was John Schoo who wrote the day after the funeral and reminded me that Wade had a life away from me and John among his many friends, a life and stories and photographs they would be happy to share, but I would have to ask. So I did. And he was right. Before we were about to meet for the first time at a basketball game in the fall, he warned me, *If you think I am immune from the tears . . . think again.* Other members of my e-mail group — people I had met only once or not at all — wrote immediately, wrote constantly, wrote gently, checking on me, reminding me of things I had told them about Wade, which meant they remembered, and cried with me, too, when we were finally together. Catherine. Tony. Eddie. Now more than just names on an e-mail header. Now family, too.

But just like family, they couldn't spend every minute with me grieving Wade, and the conversation had to turn back to basketball — it was healthy for it to do so. But not for me. I wasn't ready. And I had found friends with a need that mirrored mine at ASG and grief-parents, and my e-mail box, once full of news about recruits, was now full of misery and grief, as — it is odd to say straight out — I needed it to be. All grievers in these online communities are not the same. Among the grieving, there were a couple of dozen I wanted to meet and hold, whose children's pictures were taped on the wall behind my computer monitor. There were two to whom I was particularly drawn.

I started a conversation with Gordon Livingston, who, impossibly, had buried two sons. The Emily Dickinson poem "My life closed twice before its close" might have been written of his life. And the end of it befit him: *So huge, so hopeless to conceive, as these that twice befell. Parting is all we know of heaven, and all we need of hell.* I have now known Gordon for a decade, but I have met him only once. We had dinner in Durham when his daughter Emily started at Duke. Gordon, who lets life in and lets it have its way against his great powerful soul, is forever a part of my life story. To Gordon I could even write about the limitations in support others offered and not worry that he would think me an ingrate. To Gordon I could write, *Someone else writes me to ask why I am not getting professional help in my "recovery." He views mourning as a goal-directed task: rally the troops, make a list, get it done! That has so little to do with the way I feel, and I cannot find words to make him understand. How can I tell him there is no cure for me? I cannot express how deeply this boy had grown into my being, and how I will suffer his loss every day that I breathe. I cannot be* cured of it, any more than I can be cured of breathing itself. I suppose there will come the day when I will need to clean the dining room, when I must box the pictures, when I will decide what is to become of the things in his closet, when I will not be able to visit his grave each day. But we simply eat in the kitchen, and I do not walk into his room, and I make time for the cemetery and Wade, because it is important to me that he have some time in each day that belongs just to him. And if I started putting him away and blocking him out of my day, would I be recovering from his death? Well, the problem is that it also seems awfully like ignoring his life. The image I have for our family is grapevines, twisting around each other, interweaving, leaves pushing through until it is impossible to separate the vines without destroying much of their beauty. And this vine was, without warning, ripped from us and from among us. We heal only by growing around the wound, in constant recognition of its absence. It reminds me of a story my brother told of a woman who, having lost a son, was seeking some way to reconcile this loss with what she thought she knew of life. She went on a retreat where she was asked to walk into the woods and find a tree, *her tree, to contemplate, to look for answers. She balked, it sounded useless, but she walked anyway and picked out a tall old tree for no apparent reason. She sat there for some time, staring at it without seeing it. Finally, bored, she approached it and studied it. There was an odd place in the bark, and as she fingered it, she realized that a stake had — some time before — been driven into the tree. The tree, obviously, could do nothing about the stake, so it had grown around it, acknowledging the injury but living nonetheless. I have had, in a sense, to reinvent myself, a mother of a boy who was, for I can never have an existence that does not acknowledge him. I could not excise that spike even if I wanted to.* Our conversation paralleled and then exceeded the conversation on ASG, as his voice, time and again, pulled me back from the abyss into which I could write myself. It still does.

And then I found Phil Lister. He came to ASG before the then-inevitable death of his younger daughter, Liza, claimed by leukemia, which also took Gordon's youngest son, Lucas. Phil had come to the newsgroup asking for advice on what books to read. He'd been met by a chorus of the best

199

books on grieving, but it seemed to me that was not what he was after. I thought he meant something else, and I recommended Eudora Welty, and that is, in fact, what he wanted. We didn't unlink. Phil's voice was — and is — what the word *dulcet* was invented to describe. Dulcet and mournful. He would send his extraordinary poems, and I would read them aloud to John, and neither of us tried to stop the tears that formed silently as I read of the tree they planted at Liza's school or the sofa on which she had lain and died. One of my favorite things of Wade's was a box in which he kept his most treasured belongings. When Phil and his wife had a son, I sent a box for a boy.

It wasn't just bereaved parents who gathered at ASG. It was sisters and sons and girlfriends. We would be supportive, but we would also be firm. I wrote to Robin. Her boyfriend's son had died, and her boyfriend was spending time grieving with the boy's mother. Robin was sad, and she was angry. After I expressed my condolences, I added, *I do not mean to be harsh, but now you need to focus on him, on his needs, on his pain, on his loss. The more you focus on your own, the further you will be from him.*

One girl who lost her fiancé wrote about her mother wanting her to move on, and though I knew nothing about a loss such as hers, I wrote. Because that's what we did. We tried to help. *Grief is a long process of untangling ourselves from the physical reality of the person and from our expectations of our future with them. You will not, I imagine, decide one day that it is time, that you are ready, and then go out and find someone. You certainly won't do so because someone else, even someone with the best intentions like your mother, has decided it is time. It happens the other way, I suspect: you will instead discover — some day in the future — that you have made a new emotional connection. Then you will know that you have been ready for someone else in your life. I am the mother of a dead son and a living daughter. As the mother of a dead boy, I want to tell you to keep Bill's memory a part of your life, but recognize, as much as it hurts, that it is but memory, that he is dead. As the mother of a living daughter, I want to tell you that you do not have to serve the memory to honor it; you honor him more by valuing the fullness of life.* It was a lesson I was having trouble practicing, I have to admit.

For now, almost everything I did was centered on Wade. The Learning Lab certainly, and we met with the North Carolina English Teachers Association — including a professor named Collett Dilworth, with whom I had gone to English graduate school a quarter century before — and set up the Wade Edwards Short Fiction Contest for North Carolina high school juniors, which awards college scholarships for stories that inspire. We went to the Wake County awards ceremony for literary arts and accepted an award for a short story Wade had written — given, fortuitously, by Jim Jenkins, the sweet man who had written the column in the paper about Wade before Wade died. And John read aloud from Wade's short story at a reading of the literary arts winners at our local bookstore. So many children asked for pictures of Wade that I wrote to Lifetouch, the yearbook photography studio, and asked them — though it was past the time for ordering — if they could send more of his junior pictures. I enclosed a check, which they sent back when they sent the pictures. I wrote to the boys with whom he had gone to Outward Bound Colorado and sent them a story Wade had written that was loosely based on that experience. Letters from those children and the ones with whom he had gone to Washington three weeks before he died comforted us. We went to a reading by the splendid author Kaye Gibbons, and before she read from her new work, she read from Wade's journals. "Like Hemingway's Nick Adams stories," she said. I could have lived for a month fed only by those words. We traveled to Myrtle Beach, where the trial lawyers' association was announcing that the high school mock trial competition it sponsored would be named for Wade. A tree at his elementary school. There were so many gifts. And on ASG, I talked about the gifts, the ideas on which we followed through, the ideas left for another day. I gave advice on foundations and encouragement where I could. I hadn't thought, though, how it all might be received.

A speaker came to my meeting of bereaved parents, a respite from our usual commiserating, I suppose. After he spoke, he turned to me and said, "What are you doing to honor the memory of your son?" Out of the blue. It hadn't been the topic at all. But, coincidentally, that morning we had gotten the brochures from the foundation we were starting. It had pictures of him and descriptions of several projects in his name. I had brought one to share with Gwynn.

Without thinking, I pulled it out, and it was passed around the table. And then he asked the other parents the same question. One woman, who had just moved to Raleigh and had little in the way of support, said, "I pick up money I see on the street; I always think it comes from my son. And I decided I would do something for him, so I counted the money, and it was $2.73. I didn't want to add to it because the 'found' money was from him. Then in church they said they needed crayons for the Sunday school, so I used the $2.73 to buy crayons." As she spoke, I slowly put the brochure back into my purse. What she had said was so sweet and lovely, and I told her so, but I could not erase my own blessing. Although she had been at every meeting before that, she did not come to the next meeting or the next, and it broke my heart. After that, before I posted a blessing on ASG, I thought of her out there, listening and alone. Of course, I am glad I am able to parent Wade's memory so vigorously, but the height of the gestures measures nothing at all. They were all just expressions of our continued love, whether in the form of a computer lab or a box of crayons.

We went to Wade's spring Latin program — another blessing. It had been renamed

Attic Night, for his name in Latin class, Atticus. The Latin class was small and had been together since freshman year. Each year the energetic teacher, Jennifer Holt, gave them new Latin names, and each year the names got closer to their personalities as she got to know them better. Atticus had been Cicero's best friend, and he was emblematic of friendship and loyalty. He was also known as a mediator who used his persuasiveness and gentleness to forge compromises. It was the perfect name for Wade. But for the next year, for fourth-year Latin, Jennifer would give them all the names of gods in a ceremony that took place on Attic Night. We watched his classmates move up and on without him — that was the first time we had to do that — and as I sat there, I could see him, I could see him standing beside his good friend Todd, his head thrown back in laughter at the foolishness of comparing themselves to gods. The tears came silently, and we left quickly, John to our room and his books, me to the computer and my friends there. The writing on ASG was raw. We were all so unprotected, skinless really. I felt I could tell them everything, and I did. Four weeks after Wade died, I wrote, *Today is four weeks. This is the hour he died. The phone message light is blinking. Please be Wade, I whisper. "Hey, Mom." If I could only hear that. "Hey, Mom." Instead the words, "Hello, Mrs. Edwards." My chest aches.*

At three months, I joined a discussion about whether to change the room of a child who has died. *I know it has only been three months, but I do not know if I ever will be able to take it apart, since he put it together. Since he was only sixteen, he put so little together, I cannot take anything apart. There is already too little of him here on earth. I need the places to grieve, but I do not need them to feel close to Wade. I go to his room only in my worst moments. I pull his comforter back and smell him in the sheets. I take his things from his backpack and put them back again. I run my hands over his books on the shelves. But I feel close to him when I am sitting here, or when I sit at his grave, where he never was while he was alive. Or when I pass his parking place at school or when his friends come by. And when I look across a long yard or read a novel with a perfect image. Wade is with me everywhere. The beach house, his room, these are places I have to deal with. But I cannot confuse them with keeping Wade close to me.* Did it help Bob, who was trying to decide what to do with his daughter's room? I don't know. I do know it helped me. It helped me think about all the parts of this terrible uprooting, sort them out, and give them places. That was such an important part of what was happening: our helping, or trying to help, was helping us. It provoked me to think about how I had responded in the past when other children had died, and I thought of Kellam Hooper.

I dated Kellam a little when I was at Mary Washington College. He died in an automobile accident in 1969, our sophomore year, returning to the University of Virginia from a date with another girl in Fredericksburg. Ten years later, the year Wade was born, I went back to Charlottesville to interview Virginia Law School students for summer jobs at my Nashville law firm. I drove by the house Kellam had lived in, a house where he and I had once sat up all night talking, and I stopped outside, looking up at what had been his windows, and I thought a lot about him — as I had for years. When I went home, I wrote a story about him, a story I then put in a drawer. After Wade died, I realized I should have sent the story to Kellam's parents. So I set out on a mission to find them. It was good for me. The search swallowed me up. Since Kellam had died before graduating, the UVA Alumni Association had no record of him. But they did have the address of Joey Tennant. It was Joey, wasn't it, who had been in the car with Kellam and survived? I remembered his hair and his open face; I doubted he would remember me. When I finally reached him in Texas — he had been camping with his son's Scout troop, I liked the adult Joey immediately — he said I was right, he had been with Kellam, and he added, "I think about Kellam all the time and wonder if other people do." Joey gave me some hints about where to find Kellam's family, and using them, I finally found Mrs. Hooper. Improbably, she had moved to Charlottesville. I called and spoke to her, and twenty-six years after Kellam died, I told her how I had so often thought of that remarkable boy over the years. She told me her husband had died a few years before, and I was filled with regret. I told her what Joey had said, and I told her I had written a story about Kellam and apologized for not sending it years before. She told me about getting her hair done that morning and about playing bridge, and she asked if I would send the story now. And I did. Seventeen years late.

Kellam's mother, the bereaved parents at the Compassionate Friends meetings, my new family at ASG — we were linked. It is why I felt linked with mothers whose children had died — and those who feared for their children at war, mothers I hugged and held as I campaigned across the country in 2004. We were alike in the most essential of ways. We wanted — needed, I suppose — to hug someone who truly knew. Like the men and women who sat alone in front of monitors and typed out their fears and tears and nightmares hoping for a listener who understood.

Write as we all did, there was no elixir that could return us to the world where unbridled happiness was possible. We were all searching. Keep his things? Pack them away? Change his room? Move altogether? Not moving, moving; being surrounded by their things, being isolated from them — these were but rearrangements of the physical and could not reach the part of us that needed redesign. What we all had to face was not something present but something absent. And although anyone could escape something's presence, there was, we each discovered, no way to escape its absence.

The picture I need to draw, to be accurate, is not an engaging one. We weren't really trying to escape. We were trying to immerse ourselves. We all sat reading and writing about dead children. I wrote about my dead child and, for hours on end, I would read about theirs. I did this for them, for their child, and they would do it for my child. It is selfless and selfish all at once. What you're afraid of, as a mother of a child who died young, is that he will be erased, and there is nothing you can do about that. Acknowledging these children is an affirmation that we won't allow them to be forgotten. In that society, you were not alone. When I was with the parents of my son's friends or my daughter's friends, their sons were alive, their daughters were alive; I was the different one, I was the oddball. In ASG, I wasn't the oddball. We were all the same, wounded. In Annie Proulx's magnificent book *Shipping News,* Quoyle is a misfit who moves to a community in Newfoundland, a land that's unforgiving and hard and bitter, and all the people who are there are one form of misfit or another. And there miserable Quoyle becomes happy with this life — the odd man out who finds comfort and happiness in the community of like people. I too was out of place anywhere else. I couldn't express myself fully anywhere else. Here everything that I felt could be wide open. And so I'd walk in there and open my coat, and nothing could have been better for me.

It functioned in the very best ways communities can function. Everybody comes in need, and everybody wants to get their needs filled, at the same time they understand that they have a role in filling everybody else's needs, too. The one thing I hated to happen was when somebody would start a thread and nobody would respond. I felt obligated to post something in that thread so that that person wouldn't feel like they were just shouting into the void. Because that's exactly the opposite of what we were supposed to be. It was the very best functioning community — and it was made of people who were probably not functioning at all in their real lives. People who didn't know me well would offer me antidepressants. I had my antidepressant, this wonderful community of support. I didn't need a drug, didn't want one. A drug would just make me feel numb. These people made me feel like I was home.

It was nearly Wade's birthday. What had been such a day for celebration was now what? When Wade was born, John had said to me, "Thank you for giving me what I always wanted." Could we still celebrate the gift of his life? We could try. We went to Pullen Park, where we had taken Wade and Cate so often, and gave the concession stand the money we would have spent on his party. Then I made a card, with Wade's picture, that read, "July 18 would be the 17th birthday of Wade Edwards of Raleigh. Please use the attached coupon to celebrate his birthday." As we had arranged, the coupon could be turned in at the concession stand for an ice cream treat. I went to Kinko's to have them print the cards on nice card stock. They printed them, but they read them, too, and they wouldn't let me pay. John and I took the cards to the public pool at the park and handed them out. The children were dubious when we started, the littlest ones asking the older children to read what it said and asking about the boy pictured on the card, but the first child who returned from the concession stand with a Nutty Buddy convinced them to join in the party. We stood, satisfied if joyless, in a sea of children with circles of ice cream around their mouths. Wade's seventeenth-birthday party. And then we drove to Durham to see Cate at "Math Camp."

Cate was at the Talent Identification Program at Duke University. She had been the year before, and — whether or not she liked the six weeks of classes — she loved the program and the young people from across the South who attended. We thought it would be best for her to go again, to get out of our gloomy house for a while, and — bells, whistles, and fireworks — attend what I called "Math Camp." Of course it also meant that for that time we were not in control of her life, that we couldn't protect her. Three weeks after Wade died, a substitute teacher in one of her eighth-grade classes had asked how many in the class were only children. And it was about to happen again. Her precalculus teacher at Duke had called one day to let us know that he had decided to take a break in class and have the students write an essay. His topic: "What I like most about having a brother or sister, or being an only child." He hadn't known about Wade until he read Cate's essay. Apparently she handled it. It was clear, however, that despite all the efforts to prepare those around our child, we could not count on that. We would need to prepare the child herself.

It was hard to prepare Cate because even at fourteen she was strong and independent. The next school year, her biology teacher interjected in class that the lovely old trees at Oakwood Cemetery, where Wade was buried, were large and full because they were fertilized by the decaying bodies around them. When I was told, I put my head in my hands. When she heard it, she just looked down at her book and willed herself steady. She had always done it. And it was hard to prepare Cate because she busied herself with making our lives easier, caring for John and me. Could she bring us dinner? Did we want to play a game? Want to walk down to the creek? How many times, then and now, I have thought of the line from Isaiah, "And the little child shall lead them." For we were led by Cate, reminded of joy by Cate, and blessed with Cate.

So seeing Cate on Wade's birthday helped. But the day was still hard. I wrote on ASG that night, *We need sometimes to place our feelings about someone in a box. We place the boxes on shelves in our hearts, some high, placed where we almost forget them, until some picture or invitation — maybe a song — reminds us to pull it down and open it. I had to place Wade in a box of his own. A dark cherry box long enough for a six-foot boy. It is difficult to write, for words and tears are poor company for one another. The tears must go to make room for the words, so I focus hard on a picture of Wade at ten, his head leaning against the arm of an old sofa at Holden Beach, his pale blue eyes wide and filled with as much love as any photograph could possibly capture. The tender edges of a smile cross his face. We had come in from the porch crowded with cousins and second cousins, come into the dark wood room away from the heat and the talk of family in South Carolina. Wade had come, too, and rested with us a bit. He was the oldest young boy, and as we sat and talked about how sweetly he had cared for the other children, how tirelessly and patiently he had played with the youngest of them, he let that smile in the picture come over him: happy to have been the one whose company was cherished, and proud that we thought his gifts to his distant cousins so thoughtful. And we told him, as we often did, how sweet he was, how much we loved him, and how proud we were. The camera captured the cherished boy smiling tenderly back at us. A moment it was, before someone came in and offered iced tea, and in that moment a perfect portrait that slid away, a captured moment that was Wade.*

Sometimes the exchanges seemed odd when viewed from any distance, but we were all right there, naked and needing each other's warmth. I remember a teacher of mine in graduate school. Dr. Eliasson taught Old English. (Didn't know I knew Old English? Well, I don't anymore.) One day he talked about the varieties of the English language and about the language of intimacy — the pet names, the peculiar phrasing, the shorthand we use with our families. That's how I think of these exchanges, as the kind of family talk for which we give ourselves additional latitude, as when I wrote to Steve, who was so disconsolate over the death of his mother that he could not even summon anticipation for the upcoming birth of his first child. *Thank you for talking of your mother. My son died in April. I ask God daily to take me instead of taking my boy. I often think of what he would feel if God granted my wish and Wade lived and I died. He would, I think, be much like you, disoriented and lonely. I speak to you now as I would speak to Wade if he stood in your place.*

You are my precious son. In the months I had you inside me and the years I had you beside me, I imagined for you every happiness. As you were my firstborn child, I had to learn to be a mother. I learned the names of trees so I could teach them to you. I would finish the books I read to you even after you fell asleep, with the same cadence and inflection, listening in the pauses to your deep breath. I would hunt for old lullabies to sing to you, picking out the tune on the piano until I had made the song my own, your own. And later I stayed up all night typing your papers as you dictated. I searched the stores for a special box for your first corsage. And I bored you with parables so that you would know instinctively the way to be a good man. You never failed me.

There was never a point in my parenting you when I would have chosen to hurt you the way you hurt now. And I grieve to think that in death I have caused you this pain, that I have made you feel even that the birth of your child will be insufficient joy. I meant to give you life, to give you joy for life. And when I died, knowing I had done all I knew to do to give you that joy, I died satisfied. My most important work was done. And now my death undoes that, unwraps my work, and leaves you without the tethers to character and strength and compassion that I worked so hard, so lovingly, to tie.

But, son, the best of me did not die. I gave

the best of me to you. All I valued and all I cherished, all I knew and all I dreamed, I gave to you. It can die, of course, if you let it. Or it can live the full and magnificent life I hoped for you. And you can teach that baby all I taught you about living well, and I will live on again. My legacy — my life's work — is in your hands. Take hold of life, son. It is all I really hoped for in life or in death. Almost nothing else I wrote was as therapeutic for me, because I know Wade would, if he could, admonish me as I had admonished Steve.

My turn then for the doldrums. Another day without Wade. That's how I started a post three weeks after his seventeenth birthday. It wasn't getting any better. *Today two letters drifted in, two late voices wishing us comfort. A few days over four months since I heard my son's own voice. How sweet to hear these, and yet I read them once and put them down. I have no strength to face his death. Even comfort about his death brings me to the floor.*

I cannot look it in the eye. I cannot sit there with his picture before me and look at the edges of his smile, at the fold of his eyelids, or his thick soft clean hair across his forehead. I cannot sit too long with his handwriting before me, the uneven line of letters, so painstakingly drawn or so haphazardly scrawled; there is no way to tell the difference now, I cannot ask him. I cannot sit on his bed and pull out the drawer, knowing I will find the things most precious thrown beside the things that meant nothing at all. A small notecard from his sister on which she had written "Good Night, Wade. I ♡ you. Your sister," and left it on his pillow. And he had saved it, as he had saved each thing he treasured. All the little pieces of his life up there in that room. Papers from every year tucked in folders, neatly labeled in his desk. Lists of things to do, including the last list of all, which we took from his pocket.

And what am I supposed to do without him? If I cannot face his memory, have I nothing left of him at all? This boy is the dearest thing I ever knew, and now must I ache even to say his name?

Last night I dreamed of him, which I do not often do. A shallow sleep, and a remembered dream. He got out of his car and spoke. He had heard the most awful thing about himself, but he would not tell me then, for we needed to be together first without my knowing. I searched his eyes. On his cheek there was a spot of blood, though his face had not been cut at all when he died. We drove in silence to no place at all, and I did not speak because I knew the awful thing was that he had died. And we both were silent, loving and protecting the other, holding on as long as it might last. For while we did not speak of it, he was beside me. There was no sleep afterward.

Today I opened the laptop I had not used since he and I had traveled to Washington three weeks before he died. We had gone for him to accept an award. Between events, we sat on the hotel beds, and he would tell me what to type for his junior term paper. The Development of Labor Unions During the Depression. Now the battery has run down in the laptop. So today I plugged it in. The day and date had to be reset. So I set it for April 1st, three days before he died. I pressed Enter, and I hoped that God would finally take me up on my offer to move back in time, to let me take his place. Enter. Nothing. It is still August. The rain has stopped, and the steam rises from the slate outside the study.

I don't know how many days without him I have left inside me. When I was little I used to make-believe that I only got so many total steps in life, but I had convinced myself that *steps that I took while eating a Saltine cracker would not count in my total. So I walked around with a long bag of Saltines in order to save my allotted steps for later in life. That is what I am doing now. I only have so many days in me that I can dream of him or really look at him. It uses up my life. So I live the other days by looking at the edges, the high part of his cheek near his ear lobe where the soft nearly invisible hair is short; there I can look. But I do so miss looking my boy in the eyes.*

Does this make any sense? Looking at the edges because I cannot stand it if I do not look at all. Save the eyes, the freckles with a glimpse of God, for a day when I can crawl up against that shoulder. You're so pretty, Mom. You're such a sweet liar, son.

Where are you, merciful Lord?

Bill Chadwick, the "father" of ASG, always warned about putting on the clothes of grief. And there was, admittedly, plenty of that, as we felt sorry for ourselves. But it was our children's loss, not ours that was the real loss. I wrote to Sharon, whose son John had died, *I have seen, in the months we have shared this sad place, you carry your love for John higher than you carry your grief.*

It is not as common as it ought to be. But it was not unnatural, either. Our children became not children but the cause of grief, as solicitous friends would tell us, "You have been in my thoughts." What I wanted was that Wade, or Lana or Nielsen or Liza, be in their thoughts. No matter how I managed to work with my own grief — work through, I suppose, the stages of my grief — I could never work around Wade's losses: his loss of love, of his own children, of his successes and failures and pleasures. Nothing in the books I read could tell me what to do about that. But there was plenty on grief.

There are five stages of grief, according to Dr. Elisabeth Kübler-Ross, the pioneer in the field. Denial and isolation come first; I suppose I went through denial. I drove past people mowing their lawns or planting a tree and I wanted to yell, *Stop, don't do that, don't change anything, God is just about to grant our wish to turn back time and you are only making it harder.* I would open a drawer, and as I closed it I would see something unfamiliar that caught my eye. I would open the drawer again, and I knew I was looking for Wade. I did it from the first: I had only to find him and bring him back. I looked in his towel closet and under the clothes in his bureau. Certainly this was denial. I thought so often of the book Wade and I had read together for his freshman English class, Ray Bradbury's *Something Wicked This Way Comes*. In it, there is a carousel of death run by a satanic figure. Goodness, in the form of two boys, finds a way to move it backward, to move back in time. So round and round we continued, hoping against reason to move fast enough forward or fast enough backward to feel his face and hear his voice above the screams inside my head.

The second stage, anger, I never felt. With whom should I be angry? There wasn't anyone. It was the wind. Physics and engineering and meteorology took him. Science took him. There is somewhere some blasted equation that can be written to explain why he was dead. It was something that could be explained fully, and something that could never be explained satisfactorily. So there was no one with whom to be angry, not even ourselves, except that we failed in some larger sense to keep him safe. Many parents blame themselves, play a tortured game of "What If?" I wrote to one such parent once: *His is not a life you might have saved by some different action. We who have lost children to accidents all think "if only" we had done one thing, a phone call, a chore, even an argument, we could have changed the course of time. But which "if only" is it? My husband called my son before he left the house, I did not. If we each think we are responsible, I would have called and he would not, and Wade would have been where he was nonetheless. It is not us. It is not you. It just is.*

Now, the bargaining stage — maybe I am still there, since part of my daily prayer is that God takes me and lets my son live. My head knows they are just words, but I feel it so desperately, when could I ever stop offering?

And there must have been depression, the fourth stage, but honestly, we so quickly threw ourselves into our post-death parenting — the WELL, the Short Fiction Contest, a bench at his high school — that we had to plow through whatever roadblocks depression might have put up. John was and is a great life force, a bright piece of energy. It was why I fell in love with him. I had seen that energy dimmed by Wade's death, but he had relit himself, redirected himself, a sadder self for sure, and now he was pressing that life force against all we needed to do to parent Wade's memory, pushing it forward. Depression was a poor match indeed for John and for me.

The last stage is acceptance. It is not an adequate word, and neither is resignation. Edna St. Vincent Millay, whose poetry I have loved since I was thirteen, wrote, "I am not resigned to shutting away of loving hearts in cold ground. . . . Down, down, down to the darkness of the grave, gently they go, the beautiful, the tender, the kind; quietly they go, the intelligent, the witty, the brave. I know. But I do not approve. And I am not resigned." What is the word for the battle-weary, who at some place deep within him continues to rail but whose voice is now quiet, beaten finally into silent submission by reality? The levels of our being are like stories upon stories of a building through which a fire has run, weakening everything, making life on any of these other levels precarious, causing us not to walk to the edges but stay in the middle of the rooms with the false sense that we are there protected. (At least, we imagine, we might see another fire coming at us and might not be caught so unaware.) But on the floors that remain, we carry on with a life that seems, in its sad serenity, both to acknowledge the wreckage below us and to embrace the life about us. Maybe Yeats described it best, and certainly most simply: "I am accustomed to their lack of breath." Not resigned, or accepting, just accustomed. I know I have a relationship with my son, a relationship that had been fuller and changing and promising when he lived, but now it is different, flatter, without promise, not so unlike the relationship you might have with a family member who has moved far away, about whose new surroundings you know nothing. So when you speak, it is easier to talk about what you do share, although it means your relationship is time-stamped on the last day you lived together. That's what I have, and that's what I make the most of.

The Learning Lab was getting built, so there were building plans to approve, wall colors to choose, study tables to buy and . . . the list kept us busy, doing in our lives what he might have done in his. I read a wonderful book, *After the Death of a Child* by Ann Finkbeiner, whose son TC died in a railroad accident. It discussed parents who had lost their children five, ten, twenty years before. My favorite parent was Lyght — not just for his name but for his gentle spirit. He worked for Hospice, in an unspoken way for his son. When Ann posted on ASG once, I wrote her, telling her how much her book had helped me, how I had followed her advice to let friends know that I would still hurt in the next decade and the next, and if they wanted to really help, they could remember Wade then. I told her how much I admired Lyght. And then I got an e-mail from Lyght. She had told him, and he had reached out. You see, we really are a big — much too big — family.

When we had asked his friends what they wanted us to do to remember Wade, I have to admit that they didn't say a computer lab. They wanted a bench in the outdoor lunch area at Broughton High School. We went to Shaw University one day and I saw a lovely stone bench with a plaque on the back that said "In Memory of Anne Hollins." That's what I first had in mind when we went to Thomas Sayre, a sculptor and artist in Raleigh. Thomas was our age and a close friend of friends of ours, but we hadn't known him. His vision for the bench exceeded our pedestrian expectations. He started with an idea of a series of poles in a spiral shape throughout the picnic area. Poor Thomas, the idea made me cry. Wade was already too scattered, I said, his image like the rings of a skimmed stone spreading outward but fading. I needed as much of him as possible gathered together. And Thomas, sweet Thomas, needed to find another idea, one that didn't make me cry. And he did.

A Place in Time is one hundred feet long, most of it a long weaving tiered bench that forms the tail of a comet shape. The head of the comet is a small courtyard, with an inscription, written by Wade at the end of his sophomore year in an essay in Latin class. "The modern hero is a person who does something everyone thinks they could do if they were a little stronger, a little faster, a little smarter, or a little more generous. Heroes in ancient times were the link between man and perfect beings, gods. Heroes in modern times are the link between man as he is and man as he could be." He was fourteen when he wrote it. At the front edge of the little plaza is an irregular wall made up of eighty blocks, large pillows of concrete on which the handprints of the people with whom Wade had grown up were placed — children with whom he had gone to child care, classmates, teammates, and friends. Each child went to Thomas's studio and placed their right hand slowly, evenly into a wooden box of warm wax. Thomas poured cool water over their hand, and they could feel the wax harden. From those molds came the seventy handprints that formed the face of the wall, seventy hands coming forward, pressing themselves against the plaza's space. Thomas described the hands by saying, "The head of a comet is made up of a lot of parts. And one of the continuities of life is that there iscommunity that lives on, that gets replenished." The bright light that was Wade was passed on. The bench is public art, and sonow and again someone will skateboard across it, leaving black scars on the edges of the benches. I fought it at first. And then I cleaned it. And Thomas cleaned it. But now I don't really mind. It means that it is a living piece, with young people, not so unlike Wade, enjoying it.

Cate had started high school in the school Wade attended, in math classes with his classmates, since she had gotten ahead of her own classmates in that subject, passing his friends in the hallways, and I grieved for her. At her first open house, John and I walked through her schedule, just as we had done for Wade three years before. How many laughing faces of parents turned to see ours and a look of great sadness swept over them? We couldn't say, *Don't be sad for us.* They wouldn't listen even if we could say it. I honestly didn't know what to do. In being a mother, I relied on instinct and intellect. In parenting a child who has died, I had no resources. And despite our wide circle of support, sometimes I needed even more. I signed up to substitute-teach.

My first substitute teaching assignment at Broughton was hard. It was supposed to be honors chemistry, but there was a mix-up, and it was AP physics. Wade had signed up to take this course, and the class was filled with his friends. As the children worked in groups on worksheets that the teacher had left, I could not help myself — where would he be in these exchanges? I finally asked Maggie Whitmeyer, one of his friends. Right here beside me, she answered sweetly. While the children worked, I tried to push out the images, tried to read a book of essays I had brought with me, *The Devil Problem* by David Remnick. But the title essay was about Elaine Pagels, the religion professor at Princeton who lost her husband and five-and-a-half-year-old son within fifteen months. Quite a remarkable and thoughtful woman, but I needed to close the book on her. So I picked up the papers from the classroom floor and watched the children eating lunch outside. One of the papers was the ballot for Homecoming Court, much different from my high school days — all seniors still, but boys and girls. Of the twenty-five young people who served as pallbearers and honorary pallbearers at Wade's funeral, three of them went to boarding schools away from Raleigh, while the other twenty-two went to Broughton — and all twenty-two were nominated for the court. Wade's life passing on without him, Wade's class talking and exploring and learning without him, Maggie with an empty desk beside her. I let my mind wander.

The fall was very hard, on me, on all of us, as Broughton High School was in perpetual mourning. A drunk driver severely injured a student getting out of a car at 7:30 in the morning. Another boy was in a coma after a car accident. The assistant minister at the Presbyterian church — a favorite of many of the children and the father of one — succumbed to a cancer that had been attacking him for years. Jackson Griffith, from Wade's class, the captain of the wrestling team, was playing in the swollen creek across the street from our house after Hurricane Fran came crashing through, and he was grabbed by a whirlpool near an old dam and — though he was strong — held under the muddy water for days. Endless painful days. He had been studying Japanese, and his classmates marked his death with the Obon ceremony I had loved as a child in Iwakuni. But it was all impossible. And about to get worse.

On October 29th, we called back to Raleigh on our way home from a soccer trip with our daughter and a car of girls. "I have bad news." Another child from our school. Our school of just under two thousand, children who mostly grew up together in the part of town where people do not move, where the children have gone to the same schools, played ball in the same Y gym winter after winter and soccer on the same teams, gone to the same camps, belonged to the same youth groups.

Wade, then Ben in a fire, then Jackson drowning, and Edward in a coma. And now Betsy Draper, a sophomore, a promising soccer star, fell to the floor while dancing with a friend in her bedroom. That night, we were told, she was unable to breathe on her own and was in a coma with a cerebral hemorrhage. It was grim. And the children who remained were reeling. What were we to say? The world makes no sense? Your life is held by the thinnest of threads? And with their innocence gone, they did not want to leave each other's side. The girls in the backseat huddled, holding hands. So like what Cate and I had done six months before.

The next day I wrote to my family at ASG, *I have four images in my mind. One is a picture of Wade I carry with me, three weeks before he died, handsome, happy, at peace. The second is Wade's still face as he lay in a permanent and cherubic sleep. The third is the flat empty faces of the children I saw today at the hospital, uncomfortable where they were, unable to be anywhere else. The last, juxtaposed oddly, is an image from this weekend's soccer tournament: the girls, having won the semifinals in a shootout, linked arms and skipped across three fields to where the championship game would be played. The perfect picture of blissful childhood. Eighteen hours later, there was no joy whatever in those faces.*

As I type, Cate has pulled out Wade's yearbook from last year, looking for pictures of Betsy, I know. She will not find what she really seeks: some reason, some explanation for the injustice of these tragedies. I want to hold her and tell her I will keep her safe, but now, such words would be wasted: she knows better.

The deaths of our children confound us. The foundation blocks of living have been upset. As time passes, we start putting together the crumbled wall, trying to find in life enough rationality that action, even the action of living, makes sense. But the assault is too fast: do not rely on fairness or right, we are reminded over and over. When Solomon speaks to his son in Proverbs, he promises that a righteous life will be a long life; it turns out that is not true. The story of Cain and Abel is the truth: no one will step in and protect the pure from death. And if that was not enough, we learn we cannot rebuild the wall even with mercy and grace, for too many of the blocks are now missing. I am so very tired.

I used to think that the greatest gift you could give a child was the sense that anything was possible. Now that gift has a horrid twist: anything is possible. You tempt death as you sleep, as you drive on a clear day, as you walk, as you dance. Maybe this is all naive. Maybe the cocoon never was there. Instead it is like the public service announcements on breast cancer, I wrote eight years before finding out I had breast cancer. *One, two, three, four, five, six, seven, you get breast cancer. One, two. . . .*

Tomorrow I substitute-teach at our high school. I will try not to look at them as targets of irrational tragedy; they will try not to look at me as the symbol of a dead child.

In the midst of this, the Learning Lab was about to open, the bench about to be dedicated, and we wanted to find a grand way to do that. I wasn't much in the business of making things joyful these days, so my friends — my dear friends — took over. Tricia, who had experience organizing such events, took control of a day of celebration, and everyone pitched in, including women I didn't know well. The dedication of Wade's memorial wall and bench went as well as I could have possibly hoped. The day was cloudless, with only an occasional breeze. Wade's high school is an old stone building with a clock tower in front. There was a large white tent in place before the front doors, seventy yellow-clothed tables topped with pink geraniums. There was nothing reminiscent of sadness. It was to be, and looked to be, a celebration. There were eight hundred people there, eating lunches made by a local caterer, the mother of one of

Wade's closest friends. Thomas was beyond eloquent, describing his sculpture as the image of a comet like the short life of a child, brightening our skies and then extinguishing. John spoke of the Learning Lab and how it would level the playing field for students of different means, as Wade had wanted, and of the generosity of everyone who had come. Governor Jim Hunt spoke and was quite good, as education is his chief interest and gentleness came naturally to him. And I spoke of Wade, and of Ben, and Jackson, and Betsy.

"When we sat after Wade's death and wondered what he would have us do, we first wrote the things for which he stood. And then the things for which he cared. We recognized, as we wrote, how well Wade had followed the Apostle Paul's last instructions to his young companion Timothy: to be an example in love and honor and charity.

"The notion of these projects is to do what Wade might have done had he been given a full lifetime. To inspire those people he might have inspired, to help those people to whom he might have given his hand, and to encourage those people who needed encouragement. Those here who knew Wade know that he would have inspired, and supported, and encouraged in his adult life, for he did those things in his young life. He knew that it was not always easy to do the right thing — but that in the end, the right thing served you best.

"We are blessed, John and I. It does not seem in our circumstances that we should be able to say that, but we do. We have been blessed by the presence among us of wonderful children. Some of them sit with us now, and we dearly love them, and some of them — wonderful children all — do not. Wade. Ben. Jackson. Betsy. This is not a moment to mourn their absence — although we each mourn, of course — it is a moment to celebrate their collective presence among us. They have not gone as long as we feel their presence in our lives, as long as we each listen for their voices within us, as long as we touch the things they touched, love the friends they loved, and, as we do here, do what they might have done."

When I was through, Cate spoke, a single simple sentence, dedicating, on behalf of her brother, the bench and the Learning Lab. Sarah Bolton, a stunning friend of Wade's with a voice even more lovely, came to the microphone for the closing. Without accompaniment, Sarah sang "Hymn of Promise" from the Methodist Hymnal, her clear young voice filling the tent and the front lawn. And while she did, Cate took her place behind her. Then other children rose from their seats and slowly worked their way to the stage, joining Cate, noiselessly forming a semicircle behind Sarah. Brad, who had been Wade's friend so long he had his own toothbrush at our house. Cate's best friend, Settle, who had been raised with Wade as the big brother in her life. The boys, Todd and Matt and Michael and John, Chas and Will, Tyler, Ryan, all of them. And the girls, Addie and Erin and Katherine, Maggie and Julia, all the others. Solemn friends, the young people whose handprints were in the wall of the comet. As the last verse rang across the long lawn —

In our end is our beginning; in our time, infinity;
In our doubt there is believing; in our life, eternity,
In our death, a resurrection; at the last, a victory,
Unrevealed until its season, something God alone can see

all seventy children — healthy and strong — stood together. And my father wept inconsolably. I had tried to prepare him for what would happen, but as he did not see these children often, their promising faces were too much for him.

After the grown-ups dispersed to the Lab and the wall and back to work, the students from the high school were let out early. We had soda and ice cream treats for them and a popular local band playing, Sarah singing again. We gave out fifteen hundred treats, and they had to go for more. It was hard, and it was splendid.

When we came home, Cate had left a note about her whereabouts and her journal, which she allowed us to read. Her journal was more pained this time than I remembered it being. Her brother's comfort with himself, which was so hard-won, seemed to her to be a part of his being, and she longed for it: the wide respect and popularity, the easy way he seemed to take it all in stride. I had to remind her of weekends he sat with us, when his friends, all older, all drivers, had forgotten to pick him up or assumed someone else would for a party or a concert, remind her of his disappointments and frustrations. I hadn't any doubt of the end of Cate's story, but it was natural that she should.

At church that Sunday, I missed him terribly. As soon as I sat down in our pew I knew I could not do it. I left and walked the blocks around the church until midway through the service, when John came and found me and we went on to the cemetery. Another family, whose pretty daughter Emily had died on the same stretch of road as Wade the previous spring break, were fixing a tire that had split when it caught a brick on the narrow roads in Oakwood. They had been up to visit Wade's grave. My parents were at the grave, which was good, except that I did not want them to see my despair. We stayed on after they left. A woman came to put flowers at the grave of her mother and her brother, but she could not find them; she had forgotten where they were buried. It broke my heart for them, and it reminded me of our blessings. I could go home.

More happens in a cemetery than you might imagine. A man, maybe my age, but worn — as I was becoming — came one day wearing his work clothes and carrying his small dog in his arms. He came to visit his father's grave in a section of the cemetery near Wade. He came more often than anyone else around us. Since I had already been to the cemetery earlier that day, I had left John alone at Wade's grave to pray, and I walked, picking up some of the sticks that remained from a storm. The only tree in the man's section of the cemetery had fallen in that storm, and it had fallen across the grave of his father. His pain and helplessness were overwhelming. I made a small bouquet from the flowers at Wade's grave and took them to him. He usually brought something for the grave, but that day he was empty in every way. Sometimes we pressed on as if we were not weakened, and then we saw ourselves in someone else.

CHAPTER 8
RALEIGH, BREATHING AGAIN

After the WELL opened, John spent more time at his office. He agreed to represent a young girl who had been critically injured as the result of a defective pool drain. It was good for him, I knew, and the girl and her family surely needed him. We had been used to giving him up to the families he represented for however long he was needed. It helped that Cate and I had the WELL to absorb us. Cate would come over after school — the WELL is across the street from Broughton — to tutor older students in math, which, I have to say, they took pretty well considering she was a tiny freshman. These students who came to the WELL were strong; they just wanted a chance, and they grabbed the opportunity there. We set up hundreds of e-mail accounts in those first weeks. They started in right away making their own web pages. Seventy-five to a hundred students would come each day to use twenty-two computers, and Matt and I learned their names and what classes they were taking. We would meet their parents, and sometimes we stood in as their parents. *No, you can't pull up websites with crude lyrics.* Or *Try this search engine for that assignment on rare diseases.* Crystal wrote well but got no encouragement, so I agreed to read her work and help her improve. I bothered her all fall until she applied to college. No one else was going to do it. And it wasn't just Crystal. It was the Jeremiahs and Michaels and Pearls and Lakias. Just as the boys on the soccer teams John had coached had become mine, and just as the boys and the girls who gathered at our house had become mine, these children became mine, too. And since I'd started substitute-teaching, the circle of children grew larger and larger.

But they weren't really our children, I had to remind myself. John and I sat one rainy day and wondered if this was what life would be now. A house once full of life was still quiet. A child who should be comforted was comforting us. And a child who should be applying to college was in the ground. Other people's children were coming and going from our lives. We were investing ourselves in them, and that gave us pleasure. But where, we wondered, were we going to find real joy? We couldn't pin the responsibility for creating joy entirely on Cate, although she'd certainly have tried to meet the challenge.

We asked ourselves, what gives us joy? Well, that was easy. Children gave us joy. Should we have more children? That would be wonderful, but I was forty-six. Could we? We went to my doctor, Shep, who sent us to a specialist, who after a round of tests said it would be tough, but we could try. We only needed the tiniest hope, and we had untapped hope to spare. So we decided, after we got Cate's blessing, to do just that. Cate couldn't have been more supportive, and we set out with an optimism we thought we might never feel again.

But the process was slow. Tests, appointments, procedures, failures. It was not until the week of Wade's eighteenth birthday that the shots and medications and good fortune were translated into a pregnancy. I speak less of this not because it was unimportant. This pregnancy and the one to follow were two of the most important events of my life. I speak less of it because I did what others who wanted children did: I spent hours on-line looking at the faces of children who might be adopted. I read the online postings, almost as full of pain as anything on ASG, of women who had tried fertility treatments and failed to get pregnant. I heard the grief of women who had gotten pregnant and were unable to carry the pregnancy to term. It was heartbreaking. When John was in the Senate, a London newspaper contacted me. Did I want to do a piece for them showing them how older women can get pregnant? No, I said. The chances are so slim, and false hope is a bitter poison. People will have unreasonable hope, as I did, without me. But I could not encourage it, for I knew the cost of it when there was not a baby at the end of this difficult path. The paper should tell its readers to get pregnant younger, I said.

About this time, there was an interesting post on ASG by a sixteen-year-old girl who was born after the death of her brother. Her parents told her very little about Stevie; they did not want to talk about him. Did she even really lose a brother? she wondered. *Dee,* I wrote, *You did in fact lose a brother, and for that I am very sorry. And, from your description, you lost a chance to know him and also a chance to know of him. That is no one's fault, for the treatment of grief has changed. None of us can speak for your parents; none of us can say whether talking of Stevie with them now will bring them disproportionate pain or will bring them solace that you are interested in knowing your brother as well as you can. I can tell you that one of the things that naturally occurs to a parent who has lost a child is the desire to rebuild their family and reintroduce joy into their lives. No one who has lost a child really believes they can replace the child they buried. A child can bring joy, but the grief is always there. You said that you felt unhappy with yourself, but that is not fair. You are responsible for the joy and you are not responsible for the grief. The fact that you felt this burden, however, is edifying to those here. You have probably helped some parents who intend to have additional children think about issues that they might have neglected, and for that, I thank you.* Those thanks were personal. Dee provoked me to read about something called replacement child syndrome, when an after-born child feels responsible for replacing the dead child. John and I decided that one way to let a child know that he or she was not replacing a lost child — and no one could — was to have more than one child.

If we could.

While we were adjusting to our lives without Wade and praying for more children, we clung, too, to the things we had always done together. Cate and I went to Quail Ridge, our bookstore. I was looking at the new Southern fiction, and she was looking for books from her freshman list to read. She came back to me holding Mark Helprin's *A Winter's Tale.* Mark Helprin was no older than thirty-three when he wrote "The Schreuderspitze," a short story of grief and redemption that only an old man should have been able to write. "It's long," she said, "but my teacher said it was good. Can I get it?" I asked if she was sure she wasn't supposed to get Shakespeare's *A Winter's Tale.* She said she had read a little of this while standing there, and this is what she wanted. When we got home, she did start instead with *Death of a Salesman,* considerably more manageable in size and bearing the endorsement of Wade. I got the Helprin first. Mark Helprin had also written the foreword to my friend Gordon Livingston's book, *Only Spring,* a book and a foreword to which I turned often. "The cruelties of the world are often associated with sin, but this cruelty was visited solely by nature, which, by nature, is itself without sin," Helprin wrote of Lucas' death. "What kind of God would allow the world He created to act so coldly upon the most innocent and vulnerable . . . ? The answer is a God who, in ravishing you, eviscerates your faith and trust in him while at the same time leaving you with nothing but the hope that He exists and will in another world extend to you the missing pieces in His puzzle of mercy." Yes, I would read the Helprin first.

The words of Mark Helprin touched precisely the weakness in my online family — our differing views of a God who did not prevent the deaths of our children. Those differences, our religious differences, tore at ASG and at grief-parents, at the wretched souls seeking solace from one another, and for a time there was no solace there.

Most of the groups' active participants were Christian, as I am, but among our number there were differences of belief and hope concerning whether God would or could protect our children, concerning so many things about their eternal condition. And there were also plenty of active participants, and presumably some silent ones too, who weren't Christian, some who were surely hurt by well-meaning mourners who celebrated — who needed desperately to celebrate — that their family's particular religious practices were their children's passport to heaven. From any distance — and understand we had none — it is easy to understand how difficult this issue would be. Christians, non-Christians, doubters, all hurting just as much, all wanting just as much, all hoping just as much for a reunion somehow, did not want to hear that their child might not have followed the right set of rules. Some people, people of sensitivity and integrity, spoke their hearts and unwittingly stabbed other parents at the same time. Others fought back, and what had been a place of solace was now a place of war. People about whom I cared were in palpable pain. It was too cruel, for absolutely everyone.

My God was a benevolent and humble God, I knew that, and I couldn't accept, still cannot accept, that He would deny glory to those children who lived by his creed but had not learned His name. I had grown up watching the grace and forgiveness of the dance teacher Toshiko, and I knew my God would smile on her. It was fine to share Biblical passages and spiritual experiences. We all wished we had even more of those to share. We just had to be careful not to hurt others by suggesting that the children outside this experience were also outside God's grace.

As the debate went on, the community we desperately needed was becoming a battle-field, and in spite of ourselves it was falling apart, with no sense of the promise of support, tomorrow or the next day or next year, from a precious family that we knew understood something of our grief and our love. When Debbi turned out to be a paid Catholic bereavement counselor and was asked to quit posting sectarian requirements for the eternal life of our children, it was the small rock that started an ugly avalanche. There were many defections of people who could not endure the pain of this kind of debate. Not wishing to add our frustration to the messy public forum, Gordon and I wrote privately to each other every night about the plain constant shape of our grief: *The day was bad enough,* I wrote him after following a particularly contentious exchange, *and the weather good enough to justify two trips to the cemetery today. That will be my measure for a crummy day now: a two-cemetery-visit day.*

I was desperate. I needed this place. I wrote to everyone involved in the discussion privately, and I spent whole days and nights typing letter after letter to each of the participants. To Cheryl, a Jehovah's Witness, I wrote, *You do not need to defend your faith to me. I respect your faith. Am I remembering right that your son Keith loved Isaiah? I have been thinking about the God of Isaiah today, thinking that God demanded loyalty and promised blessings in return. And thinking also what that God promised for those who did not follow him. It is harsh, Cheryl, you know it is. How cruel it would be to quote some portions of Isaiah to those of different faiths, to those who pray daily for the eternal protection of the souls of their children, but do not pray to the God in Isaiah?* I thanked Debbie, who wrote privately but never posted, for her support, and I stated the problem bluntly, *I was simply asking that someone think about the Jewish man before they order pork for everyone's plate.* To Lois, *The tremendous strength of your own faith is not a measure; I wish it were. The vulnerability of our community is the measure. Yet here, of all places, you say we are on our own.*

I hope you will not unsubscribe, I wrote to Maribeth. *Even in our worst moments, we are strong because we are connected. Next week and next month we will need each other. Not just you needing us, we will need you. When someone leaves, I do not think of just the adult leaving, I think also of the memory of the child leaving our midst. I would miss Gregory.* To Donna I wrote, *I think you and I have some special gifts. Our boys, who both died in automobile accidents in which the passenger walked away, left wonderful writings defining their views of life, their hopes and expectations. You have shared Charlie's wonderful poem "The Future," I remember. I remember thinking how like Wade's prose writings they were. Having these gifts does not make us better, but it makes us stronger, more able to weather the worst of times. And then there are people like Marge, whose son killed himself at sixteen. Her frailty is written in the few posts she makes. It is almost as if she cannot get the words to the page. It is easier for us. It is impossible, I know, but it is easier. And those gifts, like the gift of faith, place on us a special burden, to be gentle with those without the gifts, without the tributes, without the strength of unbridled faith.*

This story would not be accurate if it seemed I had been roundly persuasive and that all was well when I spoke. It was not.

But in the end, the differences were bridged, the community salvaged. Publicly, with great relief, I wrote, *Our children lived for minutes, or for decades, or not at all on this earth. We stand here, a group of parents who dearly loved their children, loved them so much that we need support from places like this just to move through the days that we must now live without them. A thousand foolish things separate us, yet we somehow manage to ignore those things that might have, in the halcyon days before, have kept us from one another. And now we stand together. We are like the web of a spider, each strand fragile and vulnerable, yet somehow strengthened by our connections to one another. The whole is still unwieldy, and it must still be treated gently. I asked only for tenderness. I ask for it still.*

This is not about whether we should use a grave blanket or how often we visit the cemetery: this is about the eternal condition, about the souls of our children. It is cruel to assume that we can state our views on this of all issues and if it strikes at the core of another parent, if it hurts them in their consideration of their chances for heavenly reunion, well, they always have the delete key.

Among us are the weak. Weak and weary, hoping and desperate. Trodden by death and despair, they need acceptance on the most important spiritual issues from you who have offered your hands and your ears when they worried over less consequential things. For me, this discussion is not about religion. It is about grace. It is about looking at my son's face, at the blush in his cheek and the few freckles that remained. It is reading his words and finding, I hope, the charity, humility, loyalty, and love that might be the requisites of any heaven. I close no doors that might lead him to eternal protection, that might lead me one day to his side. And I honestly believe that if we are not enlightened by the death of our children to the frailty of man, we will never be enlightened. And if we do not respond with compassion to that frailty, we have failed a very easy test.

The dialogue was full of pain, even among the believers. There were those who had had faith that God could have intervened and saved their child, but that for some unknown reason God did not. Their faith was given the most pitiless test, and some felt immense anger. It is not surprising that Job — whose children were taken from him in a test by God provoked by Satan — found his way into many of our online discussions. *We are not Job,* I wrote, *though the wind took away our child. These deaths cannot be tests of our faith. The level of malevolence or ambivalence from a god that this conclusion requires is unthinkable. We may each, like Job, face questions of faith, including facing questions of our own pride. The lucky among us come to a complete and comforting faith. It is hard not to wish for us all the peace that comes with that acceptance.*

I never accepted a God who might have chosen to intervene in the death of my boy but did not, who could have decided to stop the invisible wind that killed my son, but decided to do nothing. I listened to the Bill Moyers PBS series *Genesis* in which someone stated that what was not admirable could not be God's motivation. The response was that we don't have a God we want, we have the God we have. Both were right, maybe. God did not cause our children to die and did not wish them pain or suffering, and it was not that — this time and not another — he allowed such a terrible thing to happen. I came to understand and accept a God willing to stand back and not intervene in accident, disease, violence.

It may not be the God we want — certainly it is not the God we now want — but it is the God we have, a God who lets man's actions and the balances of nature take their course whatever the earthly consequences.

It was so in the Bible when God did not stop his beloved David from murdering Uriah because of David's lust for Uriah's wife, Bathsheba. Where greed or jealousy results in murder, where the lack of moderation results in accidents, when nature is cruel and God does not intervene, we must not be surprised. The causes of grief have always been part of life. The love of God is very different from a promise of protection from tragedy or pain, as perhaps all love, which is so tender, must be. Whether or not our God weeps at man's calamities, I do not know, but I believe in the promise of neither intervention nor protection but only of salvation and enlightenment.

I would speak to Wade of all that happened. Although I knew him well enough to know what he would say in response, he did not speak to me. As the weather got cold and the ground colder, we decided to place a bench at the graveside. It was meant to mark his grave until the headstone was completed, to replace the license-plate-shaped metal marker the funeral home had placed there. Our dear friend Thomas helped us lay it out. When we went to his studio, he had made a mock-up. Wade's name along the side of the cardboard bench seared through me, the heat turning my insides to ashes. Thomas was getting used to seeing me cry. But I had to see it one day; I am just glad my first day was with John and Cate and Thomas. Within weeks, it gave me comfort to see his name there. And Thomas introduced us to Robert Mihaly, a young sculptor who had come to meet him before starting as an artist in residence at the National Cathedral. Thomas' father had been dean at the Cathedral, perhaps its most influential dean, and Robert wanted to meet Thomas before going. Thomas told us about Robert and his work, and he arranged for us to meet this weird and wonderful young man. At our first meeting, Robert sat with a drawing pad on his lap, and he would lean down and peek into it, lifting the corners of the pages so no one else could see. We were enchanted and confused by him, and — happily — we agreed that he should carve Wade's headstone. It was a great relief to know that it was under way, although it would be a year before the sculpture was in place.

The late days of autumn were gray. The cold and dampness never left. Even in the worst of summer, I could take my water jug and a book and sit with Wade for hours. As autumn closed, the cold settled in my joints and I was not with him long before I was thinking of myself, of my own comfort, and not of Wade, so I would leave. Robert, the sculptor, brought the plaster model for the headstone, and it was extraordinary, an angel caressing him. I told him I could live with it forever, which was the only test I knew. Our only hesitation was the scale, as Robert wanted magnificence and we wanted intimacy. An oak that was felled by the hurricane that had claimed Jackson Griffith came out, and we planted in its place a magnolia, as the magnolias had fared better in the winds. Things were coming together at the grave. We wondered, though, what would busy us when it was done.

The Learning Lab busied me. I worked on developing a web page for it, but, with no experience and no tutor, I was lost. I finally put something up using the free Geocities pages that had easy instructions for even the most simple-minded, in which group I was apparently included. It kept me busy. And children came to use the Lab when I was there, whether it was technically open or not, so I had company. All of which made John, who was deep into his trial, feel better, allowing him to concentrate his energy where he should, on the precious child, Valerie, whose future was in his hands. Cate was bringing home the same worksheets Wade had brought home three years before, asking me the same questions he had asked. I was busy, but it didn't always help. I so often felt like a used decanter, a circle of wine in the bottom, the smell of wine at the top, and completely empty in between.

So now we were back to just the usual pain. And there was plenty of it, as Christmas was approaching. I got an e-mail from a friend. His son, Elliot, was in a class taught, coincidentally, by a woman who had lived in my Atsugi neighborhood when we were in high school in Japan. So I heard about Elliot's essay through his father and then again through his teacher. Misty had asked her students to write about the one gift each would most like to give that holiday season. Elliot wrote, "If I could give a gift to anyone in the world, it would be to Wade Edwards. . . . He died in a crash while going to the beach for spring break. . . . If I could give him a gift it would have been to let him reach the beach house. He deserved to live a full life. Also to be able to become the lawyer he wanted to be. I think he would write a book because of how good of a writer he was. I never met him but when I asked my mom about him there were tears in her eyes." I wrote back. "You did give a gift today. Your paper gave a gift to us, Wade's family. I, too, wish Wade were waiting at the beach house, wondering what in the world was taking us so long to get there to join him. It cannot be, however. Wade, as a human being, is now only a memory. And memories are very fragile things; they can break apart and the pieces can be so small that no one can even imagine what the remembered boy was. So it is really important to parents who have lost a child that people take good care of the memory of their children. You, Elliot, are taking very good care of Wade's memory, and that is a wonderful gift, maybe the best Christmas gift we will get."

I love Christmas. I love the decorations and the music and the smell of the kitchen. I love the caroling and the Hallelujah Chorus and the live nativity, the little girls draped in sheets with tinsel and coat-hanger halos and little boys in their fathers' shirts and mothers' scarves around their heads, broom handles for staffs. I love the wrapping paper and the elegant lights and the gaudy ones, too. Every Christmas for the previous twelve years we had had an open house. It was one of the best-known parties in Raleigh because we invited children as well as adults. How often we heard from parents that their children wanted to know if the family Christmas party invitation had come yet. The children liked to think they were coming to an adult party, but in truth the children were upstairs with cookies and punch and the adults were downstairs with slightly better food. We started it when Wade and Cate were small and we had to hire sitters for upstairs, who were given the instruction not to let any of the older children throw any of the younger children out the windows, and if possible no blood. The year before, Wade had been the primary sitter — and he had spent a good deal of the night, his last Christmas party, trying to find a lost Barbie doll. We would send four hundred or five hundred invitations, maybe more — I would handwrite each one — and usually about eight hundred people came. I would make all the food myself and never pretended to be a hostess. If you wanted to talk to me, come to the kitchen. It was loud and happy, and it was a hard tradition to give up, but it was an impossible tradition to repeat this year. Cate relented and agreed

261

that we could forgo the party. But the truth was that I didn't want Christmas at all this year.

Sally and Gwynn, then Tricia and Ellan, came by to help decorate the tree. The usual three trees — one for the children that they decorated themselves, one for Hallmarks and other ornaments, like the children's old mittens and handmade ornaments, and the last for my glass ornaments — would be reduced to one tree for Christmas 1996. The glass tree had fallen three times in recent years and the sight of smashed Radko ornaments that I had collected and cherished had been hard in easier times, so I left the remaining Radkos in a box, and we hung the more unbreakable ornaments on a single tree. If it is possible to decorate a joyless Christmas tree, we were doing it.

We used a check we got from Wade's small life insurance policy to buy Cate a pearl necklace. It was her present from Wade. As far as I was concerned, there was no other gift in the room. Christmas began and ended with opening that box, fixing that clasp, and imagining a brother's pride in his beautiful sister. The rest of the days were minutes to get through. There were nice things: Jim, the columnist who wrote about Wade, had his articles framed for us. I do not wear jewelry, but I asked for and received the obligatory bereaved mother's locket. And more books. I even bought us new bookshelves, for the floor in the bedroom was nearly covered. We ate a late Christmas dinner with Gwynn and her daughters.

Driving home Cate asked if my Christmas was merry.

"I loved being with you."

"It is not what I asked."

Caught. "Merry is too much to ask. I don't know when I will be able to describe myself as merry again. You made it the best it could have been made. I hope that is enough for you, for it is enough for me."

The last, of course, a lie.

Nothing could raise my spirits, although, bless her heart, Cate tried. She gave me a book entitled *One Thousand Things To Be Happy About* — but the only thing that was making me smile was the child handing me the book. The week before Christmas I posted on ASG. *And his stocking is hung. No little boy in new red sleepers will sit on the steps until it is time to come downstairs. No young man in a flannel nightshirt will complain that his father is not yet awake. I will not* spend my afternoons running my hands over sweaters he might like or my evenings wrapping them. Instead I went today to the nursery; the gardenia at his grave the latest casualty of nature, pansies and lavender for remembrance now in its place. And as I stood there at the counter of the nursery, my arms full, my heart broke, again, as I bought for his grave instead of for his closet. A magnolia now stands where the oak that shaded his grave once stood, the one I liked to think was a part of a thread that started with the oak at Allonbacuth, the oak of weeping at Deborah's grave. Nature again, furious, had felled it. Winds more powerful, but less terrible, than the wind that took him. All of this, the oak, the gardenia, the season, the stockings, the tears, it all comes and goes, the wind a fitting metaphor. A young man carves a piece of marble for his headstone; it, too, will pass in time. The only thing that will not change in my life, in generations, is that he is dead. Where is solace, where can you find it, when all there is is mutability and death? Death. The counterpoint of a gay stocking in needlepoint, made years ago in that naive belief that I could make the world gay and perfect for him. I see him sitting on the sofa, that stocking in the curl of *his leg, awaiting his turn to discover its contents, laughing at whatever foolishness was in his sister's stocking, anticipating someone finding his contribution to their stocking. That image, too, is impermanent. If I can carry it with me until at last I too die, as I hope I can, it will die with me, and one more piece of him will be extinguished. The only thing we cannot touch will be the last to stand: he is dead. How I wish that he had children and they had had children and something of him would pass through the years, mocking death's attempt to cut him short. How I wish . . . but what use is it? The girl he never kissed, the baby he never held, the stocking he never filled. Death has won. All that is left will fade, will erode, will die. He is beaten, and so am I. The house is still again. I will never become accustomed to the permanence of this silence.*

The most faithful stepped up, as I knew they would. But Christmas was having its way with all of us. Sue, whose son Wally — about Wade's age — had died, resisted her husband's efforts to celebrate. *We do what we do now for others,* I wrote. *My husband played Santa this year, as he did last year and the year before, for a child care center in the housing projects here. He and his partner provide Christmas for sixty-five children there. The office staff are "Santa's Helpers" and last year, when Wade worked in his office as a runner, Wade was a Helper. A couple of the kids had clung to him throughout last year's party, sitting on his lap, playing with his Santa hat. He dearly loved children. This year, without saying so to anyone, I know John was Santa in memory of Wade, giving whatever joy he could. It was a sad day for us, highlighting as it did Wade's absence, but our sadness is permanent. The joy of Christmas for these children is so fleeting, a bright moment in a life filled with less light than a child's life should have. For John, maybe for your husband, it was not a celebration in the way you use the word.*

And New Year's Eve was no better. As it approached, I started worrying. *This morning's paper brought the year-end stories. It was a hard year here. Good riddance, they say, to 1996. And I try to find my own feelings in this. Do I want the last year he spoke and ran, the last year he touched me to be gone, to be history? The march begins; it will be one year ago, then two, a decade, then two, and more, since I last saw my boy. It does not mat-*

ter, of course, what I want. This year will end, and the next.

1997. I had once thought this year would make me sad for he would leave and go to college, and I would write him letters he would not care to read. In anticipation, I had been buying him silly cards whenever I saw them. They sit in a slot above the telephone. Several dozen cards — wordplay and foolishness — all to remind him his mother loved him. I should have buried them with him, for now I cannot throw them out or send them to someone else or look at them. No one warns the grieving that New Year's will be hard. You expect Christmas. You expect birthdays and the anniversary of their death, but, as I wrote on New Year's Eve, *I did not expect this. I did not expect the evening's celebration to press against me so. But it has. Why do I keep being surprised? I ought to learn but somehow I do not. There is this constant tugging. I want to get up, walk away from here, leave this life and all the sorrow it has brought, find somewhere else where maybe I can be someone who has not lost her son. I know it is useless, that the loss is not here around me. It is in me, in my every thought, in my empty arms, in my weary, beaten heart. And there is part of me that does not want to leave, does not want to go a place he has not been, see faces he did not see, wear clothes I had not owned when he died. He is, I sometimes think, only in those things that he touched, upon which he gazed, or that he simply knew. I do not want to see Montana; he is not there. I will not travel to Stockholm; he cannot see it, too. And I do not want this new year to come. It has, I know, but I do not want it. I do not want it. Everything was the same as last year. We did not go downtown together to First Night as we had in some years. We stayed home. Last year was home and football and finally Dick Clark. Wade came and went throughout the night, as was his way; between parties or for no reason whatever, he would come home for a bit. The headlights in the drive. His door slamming, maybe he would finish listening to a song before coming in. And then up the steps, two at a time. And he would come in the family room and try to sit just where his Dad was sitting. They'd pretend to fight, and I would make room next to me. Come sit with me, son, I have room here. And he would sit with me, press himself against me. And then as soon be off, returning in an hour or two to repeat the whole routine. That was last year. The year that is gone, is history, like he is. By midnight last year his father and I were in bed, watching the festivities unfold on television. Wade came in a few minutes after, crawled over me, and lay between us. Happy new year, son. That little kiss, the most one could hope for from a young man. Are you in for the night? Yeah, I'm home. Love you guys. And he crawled over me again. I could hear him bound up the back stairs. If I had known it was the last new year's eve, would I have done anything differently? The edges of the night are a blur, where had he been? I would get that back. I would write that down, write everything, what he wore, what he ate. (Well, that was likely a cola and string cheese. But I would write it down nonetheless.) Write so many details that I could walk into it whenever I wanted, be there again. Once since he died, I have felt that same presence beside me, not the weight of him, but the warmth. In the stillness of night, have you felt something there? I think it was my memory on which he is sufficiently impressed that I can feel his warmth but I cannot quite get my mind around the rest. I want my mind to stop protecting my heart. I want to feel him all. If only I could feel his arms.*

Maybe if it were last year, I could feel him, feel the weight of him, his breath close against me, and his own smell. Maybe if the year would not change this time. But it changes. And he seems, by the simple changing of a single digit, so very far away from me. And I feel so very alone. I typed and pressed send and went back to bed. The hard edge of it would not turn away from me. *The time, the celebration of birth, the comfort of families, the changing of the year, are like measurements. What has changed, what has stayed the same? And there will, each year, be changes, new years to be crossed, births and marriages, graduations, graying hair. One thing will not change: Wade is dead.*

Anna Virginia Johnson is buried not far from Wade. An English boxwood planted by her grave decades ago when she died, as Wade did, at sixteen. I think about Anna Virginia, though I only know her name. There is no sign she is otherwise remembered. If there is no life eternal, then Anna Virginia is gone, faded, only a name on a stone, a stone being slowly covered by that boxwood. We can cry out, I do cry out — but I cannot change it.

On Talk of the Nation, Science Friday on NPR they talked of the origins of man. How recent, a caller asked, are the differences in man we attribute now to race? Very recent was the answer. Race has emerged in the last 100,000 years. There was so much in this: if 100,000 years is recent, what then is sixteen years? A blink, less than that. And even something as seemingly basic as race is mutable. It exists briefly, maybe to be washed away again as gradually we intermarry and live in common climates. It confounded me, but the words that cut me were the truths I confronted every day: *Parts of death — at least parts — are cruelly permanent. I will not brush his hair from his eyes, I will not feel his arms wrap around me as I work, I will not watch him as he shoots a basketball in the backyard, I will not sit beside him at the table now or in ten years or twenty. This is the life I must now live and in this life he is forever dead.*

New Year's Day was followed by the nine-month anniversary of his death, on January 4th. In the nine months since he died, I had been to the movies only once. It was *Emma.* I could do that. I went once to a light opera, *Amahl and the Night Visitors.* I could not do that. As Amahl's mother held him and loved and watched him, I could not stop the tears, grateful for the curtain calls to come and the darkness that allowed me to cry. And finally for the first time we watched something besides sports or a convention or the news on television. I walked into the family room and sat down with John. He was watching *The American President.* Michael Douglas walked down the portico from the Oval Office, the boxwood gardens to his right. Three weeks before Wade died, I had walked that portico with him, the gardens to our left, when he had gone to Washington for the speech contest. And I knew, as I watched the movie that night, that all my strength and all my smiles were doomed. It would always come down to this. That sweet boy, my precious son, lay in the ground, his hands, his long squared fingers, crossed on his chest, wearing that same jacket he wore on the portico. Everything was hard.

I thought endlessly of odd moments, not necessarily happy times but intense times, times when having Wade as my son took everything from me. When he was in Colorado for the eighteen-day journey with Outward Bound, it was unlike other camps he had attended: I could not speak to him or write him, and he could not write to me. On the day he was to fly home, I had calculated when he would be at the Denver airport, and I arranged to be home if he might call, as I hoped he would. He did, but he called earlier than I had thought, and when I came home, there was only the tail end of his collect call recorded on the answering machine minutes before. It sounds foolish now, but I was inconsolable. I had saved up all my expectations, for days I had been anticipating his voice, and now I had been frustrated. Hours passed while he walked the Denver airport and talked to other boys who were leaving on earlier flights, shopped for shampoo and washed his hair. Hours that I sat there, staring at the phone. John tried to distract me, but it was no use. I wanted my boy.

He did finally call, exhausted and less than interested in telling me right then everything that had happened to him in the preceding eighteen days. So I waited the interminable hours until he would be home, got to the airport early, and watched each plane land, searching the windows of those that taxied by for his face. Finally he was in my arms. I would only have him for hours before he left with John for Africa, to climb Mt. Kilimanjaro. He bathed and ate and slept, and I watched him sleep, sitting beside his bed, my elbows on my knees and my chin in my hands. I rose to move his laundry or, when he woke, to get the newspaper articles I had saved for him. But I needed that contact, his smell, the soft brush of his hair. I ran my hands over his fingertips and across his newly shaved face. I drew my finger softly against his eyelids and brows, and I traced his lips. I could not leave his side. I could not get enough of him, particularly since I knew he would go away again. I just never knew there would come a time when he would go away forever. I wished for one more touch. But it would not be enough, I knew. I would only ask for another, or for the warmth of his breath. Things I could not have and for which I should not have even dreamed.

The Learning Lab kept me from dreaming, because it kept my mind in the present. Most of my time was spent working on the web page, which I had finally improved on since my first Geocities effort, keeping the students reasonably quiet, making sure the e-mail was running and that the printers had paper, that the candy wrappers were in the trash cans and the students' questions answered. It was rewarding, demeaning, and exhausting all at once. And there was no place I would rather be. I was there one night when I got perhaps the best gift of all.

The director of the Lab was Steven Killion, a gentle man of quiet strength, enormous intelligence, and astounding patience. When John and I finally left for Washington, we confidently left the physical care of our son's memory to Steven and to Sarah Lowder, who matched Steven in gentle goodness, and our ability to do so says all I ever need to say about these two.

One night, Steven was at the Learning Lab late, again, and I sent him home. John was working, so I could stay on with the two students left at the computers. They were a sturdy girl and a younger boy, her brother undoubtedly, and she was helping him. After a while, the telephone rang, and the woman at the other end asked if Alyse was there. I turned and looked at the girl. Could that be Alyse? Alyse Tharpe? It was. I called her to the phone and asked her to see me when she had finished. A few minutes later she came over, and I told her who I was. Alyse had been in elementary school with Wade. They'd been in the same classes, and they had, memorably, been in the same fifth-grade production of *Julius Caesar,* which looked from the audience like an indistinguishable clutch of twenty-five ten-year-olds, who — because there were three fifth-grade classes — would periodically walk offstage and be replaced by another indistinguishable clutch. I cannot remember anyone else's part, not even Wade's, but I do remember Alyse's role. Alyse was the seer, and the line she delivered is now my favorite: "Beware de Ides of de March." Alyse and Wade had gone on to different middle schools and then to different high schools. They had lost track of each other. And now she was here at the Learning Lab.

"Alyse, I'm Wade's mother." Pause. "Wade Edwards." Pause. She looked blankly back at me. "Wade, from Root Elementary."

Her face lit up. "Wade!" She hugged me, and then she pulled back in horror and in grief. "Wade?" She looked at his picture on the wall. "I know that face. I just couldn't remember why. Oh, Wade." She hadn't known he had died. She hadn't linked the boy she knew on the playground at Root with the name on the Learning Lab she was using. Now, for the first time, she began to grieve the loss of her friend. We hugged each other in the middle of the Lab, and then we sat and I told her about Wade.

When I got to the Learning Lab the next day, Steven handed me a letter. Alyse had given it to him, and he had read it — which

I loved because he only knew Wade through a mother's description, and who could trust that? But now he had Alyse's eloquence, Alyse's eyes to inspire him each day. And I had it, too.

Dear Wade,

I just found out it was you that the Lab was dedicated to. I'd like to say that I'm impressed and you wouldn't believe how much the students are grateful for it. There are some kids who do come in and cut up but I guess that's just you given them the sillies. I hear you climb a mountain! I'm so proud that you climb it but that could never be me, I'm not that brave.

Listen, I just wanted to say something that I didn't get to say when we attended school together. You were my only real friend and the only one since then. I want to thank you for being there and taking up for me when everyone else didn't. For sitting with me at lunch when I thought I had to eat by myself and making sure everyday was a good one. Even though I acted up all the time I'm glad I had someone to make me be serious when I needed to. I might not have gotten out of there without you, I have so much to thank you for because you make me the person I am. In being there for others, not judging, doing my own thing, being able to establish trust for and from other people. Thank you will never be enough neither will this letter or this poem but I hope that my heart is sufficient and my soul a light.

I don't feel sorry for you or sad other than the fact that elementary was the last time I saw you. I am hurt because of that. But your in a very special place right now so enjoy it. Don't send down no teardrops of rain because you're lonely (joking, cry all you want). You know what you did that was really special? You understood me most of the time and when you didn't you tried. When other people didn't understand me or what I was saying, they call me name, but not you! You were that light I tried and continually try to follow, but your too bright. I wont give up though. I come to terms that it was you that pulled me to that picture in the lab everyday. I'm sorry it didn't click. When your mom hugged me, I so badly wanted to cry, but I held it in. I didn't want to make her upset. I still make paper hats, footballs, and boats you taught me how to make and I still remember the last score in the last football game we played. 37–17!! I never beat you, you were just too good! God bless your soul, I love You.

White Sand
My friend, the white sand on the beaches,
that gives us heaven on earth
And the sun that shines brightly over,
tripping on the clouds and winds,
of obstacles, but never hurt.
A martyr in my mind and others,
forever my brother.
Sunny days are when you smiled,
and life awakens in your pretty blue eyes.
My brother, white sand on the beaches
    and the sun,
pure as diamonds and precious as gold,
the bestest friend I've ever known,
When I'm sad, I hope your there to hold
    my hand.
When I'm happy, I hope your there to hug
    my neck.
Because if it wasn't for you my life would
    be a total wreck.
And for you my companion, I love you for
    that.
Your in my heart, forever!

The spring came. We restarted a conversation we had had before Wade died about whether John should run for the U.S. Senate seat held by Lauch Faircloth. David and Jim and John sat at our kitchen table, readying for the fight. John went by the state Democratic party headquarters and was greeted quizzically when he said he thought he would challenge Faircloth. He went to Washington to talk to Bob Kerrey, who was the head of the Democratic Senatorial Campaign Committee and who didn't greet him quizzically at all. Bob knew as well as anyone that some fights are brewing inside and you are ready before anyone else knows. While John was away, I thought I would straighten the study. It sounded simple enough, I know, but it was covered in papers. What it meant, of course, was going through a lot of paper that had to do with Wade: cards on which he had written his bibliography for a paper, the notebook of his papers that his English teacher gave me, his list of companions for his Outward Bound trek, a hundred little things he'd left behind. The night before he'd died, he worked late in the study on his junior term paper. When I got home, the computer screen still had his scanned photograph of striking workers during the 1930s. His books from that paper were on the coffee table still open beneath newspapers with stories of his death.

Putting his things in folders, taking the steps to put them away, was much harder than I had anticipated. Well, in truth, I had not thought at all. Stupid me. It was no consolation that he would have had it all filed by now, in his desk or his closet. He would have thrown out most of the mail, although I could not. I finally stopped, unable to do anything. But John was due back the next day, and he would be tired, so I had to steel myself to finish it. There was no easy way around any of this. After I finished, I drove to the cemetery. The rains were headed toward us, but it was bright and breezy when I first got there. At Wade's grave, the stone basket of flowers, a large metal angel, four smaller angels, and one of the potted plants were missing. Someone had tried to move the large angel that replaced the one my sister had brought (which had been stolen earlier), but it was too heavy. The mud from their hands had left marks on the angel's face.

I cannot express the way this violation made me feel. I had failed to protect this boy when he lived. I loved him, yes, and he had known that, yes. But my first responsibility had been to keep him free from harm, and I did not do that. I do not feel guilty. I did all I knew to do. It simply was not enough. And now I could not even protect his place. I stood and cried and screamed. A couple walking came to console me, and Chuck, the cemetery director, came and sat with me. At first I was glad that at least they had left a mark — that large angel would have their fingerprints.

I called the police and then told Chuck to go home. The rain started to move in. It would wash away the fingerprints, I thought. So I took two umbrellas from the trunk and arranged them to cover the statue. To hold them down, I covered the umbrellas with a sheet and then a quilt. (Fortunately I clean my trunk about as often as I straighten my study.) Then I sat on the bench and finished my prayers. The police did not come. I called again. It was nearing five, and the gate would be locked soon. The rain was steady now; there had been accidents; no one was available. I persisted, and they sent someone.

It turns out you cannot get fingerprints from that surface. The wait had been fruitless. I put the umbrellas and linens back in my car. More had been taken from us, of course, than simply the trinkets that comfort us at the grave. I was so tired of being impotent, of being reminded I was impotent. And I was just plain tired.

For John's next trip to Washington, I went with him. But this time it wasn't for the Senate. This time it was to give out a college scholarship to the national winner of the contest in which Wade had been a winner the previous year. We sat in the Old Post Office while bright high school students ate their lunches, and we talked with the two women who had managed the children the year before. Carolyn Naifeh, who had been Geoff Cowan's assistant at Voice of America, and Ann Orr, who worked with Sheldon Hackney at the National Endowment for the Humanities, did not know then what great friends of ours they would become. All they knew was these were the sad parents of that sweet boy from North Carolina they had met a year before. So their faces were something to remember when John told them that he was running for the United States Senate. John had told me about the faces at the state Democratic Party headquarters when he had made a similar statement, but now I saw what he meant. The little side glances to one another might as well have been accompanied by shrugs. We laugh about it now.

Soon there would be the graduation of Wade's high school class. It wasn't just me, of course; bereaved mothers across the country were facing spring concerts and banquets and graduations. Graduation was hard. We didn't want to sit too close — there were so many families who had living children graduating who should be close, but from where we sat at Wade's graduation, I could hardly see the candles that were lit for Wade and for Jackson. I felt, as I often had, outside myself: the grieving mother, the solicitous friend, the dutiful parent of my surviving daughter, but all as if I were a puppeteer, stripped of the ability to evoke anything other than rudimentary motion in my puppet body. Real life was something other people had, something I'd once had and could not imagine having again. The people we once were are like characters in stories from a book; we were drawn to them, to their fullness and hope and happy naiveté, and yet we could not get to them. It was nearly impossible to believe that once we were them.

It was more than a year since Wade died, and still it seemed there would be no light. On ASG someone wrote of the perils of holding on to grief as a means of holding on to our dead children. *His death knocked* me down once, and it knocks me over each day, again and again, and I see no end to that, I responded. *I can sit and let the pain grow within me. I can feel the tears wall up against the backs of my eyelids, and my face flush, my cheekbones fill with the pressure of the coming torrent. I can rest my mind on his car, rising up in the air, of his terror, of the weight of that car pressing the life from him. I can feel just the way the air felt on the porch as the patrolmen pulled into our driveway. I rub my skirt between my fingers and beg them to tell me he is alive. I hear my No, a wail that they finally stopped outside me but which has continued inside me every day. And the intensity of that pain is greater than any emotion I ever had. Not love, not fear, not wonder. The greatest of all is pain. And I am inclined, on rainy days, or on days we might have celebrated had he lived, or on days when I cannot account for my unsteadiness, on those days I am inclined to wrap myself in my mourning, a comforter, a hairshirt, my son. There is no question that as I pull it closer about me, I feel his presence run through me. It is pain and memory, and I cannot release its hold on me. And he cannot, I remember, release my hold on him, him as a dead boy, when I do this. For when I do this, the fullness of him is gone; all he is the object of my grief. I deny him when holding on to him in pain. He becomes but a dead boy. Gone is the tender boy, the selfless boy, the tired runner, the easy laughter, all that was important to him, all that he loved, it is withered and replaced by that mesmerizing pain. I know I must let the dead boy go.*

I could, sometimes, and John and Cate helped. Life was Cate's softball and Cate and John's soccer — he was still coaching — and the WELL. I might have had to make some Latin flashcards, but Wade had saved his in a labeled folder — so typical — and Cate didn't need many new ones. And we turned our faces northward, to Washington. It was politics now. In our kitchen or in John's office, looking at videotapes of commercials sent by political consultants who wanted John to hire them. Meeting with these strangers who were checking him out like he was a thoroughbred they were thinking of buying. I was sometimes surprised they didn't open his mouth and check his bite. And I was still trying to get pregnant again. It felt like endless appointments and hundreds of shots. Cycles and failures, but I didn't have the same anxiety I saw in the doctor's waiting room and read about on-line. I had had children; I knew I could handle a pregnancy. I was just old. I say, "just old" like it was nothing, but it wasn't nothing. It was a real hurdle. But it wasn't hopeless, either. I knew what hopelessness felt like, and this was not it.

Part of the process of using pharmaceutical help to get pregnant is getting the drugs in you. The clinic nurse handed John an orange and a syringe so he could practice giving me shots, and he promptly handed them to me.

"It is not someplace I can reach, hon," trying to hand them back to him.

To which he responded, "Then we will have to figure something else out, because I do not want to give you shots." Cate, always helpful, was very clear: if Dad wasn't doing it, neither was she. But John solved the problem. A warm nurse who reviewed files in his office stopped by the house every day — it was only about two blocks from work — and gave me my shot. When John started campaigning across the state more often for the Democratic nomination for the U.S. Senate, I was particularly glad Gail Campbell and not John was my shot giver. John would arrange his schedule around weekly appointments, but it would have been much too limiting to arrange it around daily shots. When I finally got pregnant — around Wade's eighteenth birthday — John was there to celebrate our real but muted joy. And Gail was there to teach me how to give the next round of shots I would need, which were fortunately in a place I could reach. And when Emma Claire was born, Gail was there, as proud as if she were the mother, snapping pictures and giving hugs. It went smoothly — well, pretty smoothly; as a result of the medication I did get a uterine cyst, which had to come out, and I did get gestational diabetes, which I controlled with diet. But I kept going to softball games and the cemetery and the Learning Lab, and John kept campaigning until, ten days before the Democratic primary, Emma Claire was delivered by Watty Bowes, who treated me as if I were his granddaughter — which, given my age at the time, forty-eight, I particularly appreciated.

Emma Claire developed jaundice because her blood and mine, like Wade's and Cate's blood and mine, were incompatible. She required transfusions and special lights, and John stayed with me, with us, when he ought to have been campaigning. Finally Cate and I made him go, and Cate took care of me and her new sister, with the help of

Nancy Speroni. And by the day of the primary, ten days later, Emma Claire was strong, and John's three girls — Emma Claire in a tiny onesie embroidered with John's campaign logo, made by the campaign staff — stood with him onstage as he accepted his party's nomination and prepared for the fight to come. After the klieg lights were turned off and the television cameras were packed away, Cate and I went back to the room in the Velvet Cloak hotel where we had waited for the evening's results. She spread out across one of the beds. Harrison Hickman, our friend and pollster, came in and asked her, "Isn't this a great night?" Her response: "I just want to go home." It was hard on her, I could see that. And there was more to come. When John won the Senate seat, I told him the truth: in our house, if you were not a baby or a candidate, you didn't get much attention. Take her on a trip, I said. And that Thanksgiving he did. He and Cate went to London.

Although I had a busload of teenage girls and nearly as many empty-nest mothers who would have been glad to care for Emma Claire, allowing me to go out on the trail, I stayed out of the campaign for Senate and remained with Emma Claire. I did listen to the television and, on the way to the cemetery, to the radio, and I would call the campaign office when new commercials against John broke or with something I had heard, but I barely campaigned.

I liked the campaign — from a safe distance from the cameras — and I particularly liked the young people in the campaign. They were smart and committed and poorly dressed. They were happy and energetic, and did I mention poorly dressed? The older folks — most younger than I — were fine, but it was a job for them, yet another job in a long line of political campaign jobs. They dressed like they had taken time doing it, not like the young people, who dressed like it was a blasted necessity every morning that slowed them on the way to what they really wanted to be doing. For these young people, for David Ginsberg and Christina Reynolds, for Brad Anderson, John Dervin, Hunter Pruette, for Julianna Smoot and Jennifer Skalka and Jessica Wintringham and Laura Godwin, it was a passion. Cate worked with Jessica in the press office. Laura was Emma Claire's first babysitter. I could almost feel the mesh winding around these young people, binding them to us, and us to them. My role was purely supportive, and with a new baby, I liked it that way. John, who had lost his first, second, and third wedding rings running, needed a replacement ring. I could do that. I went to a jewelry store. "I'd like to see what you have in size nine gold wedding bands," I said. She brought out five bands and placed them on a little square of velvet. I looked at them for only a second, and then, to her great surprise, I said, "I'll take all five." He only needed three in the campaign, but Emma Claire lost the fourth, so perhaps five was a good number.

The next months were hard. We had a taste of what to expect when Lauch Faircloth, who was the incumbent Republican senator, ran a commercial against John the week before the seven-person Democratic primary, before John was even the nominee. It wasn't that the commercial was so bad; it was silly, really, attacking John for the legal work he had done, of which I was very proud. And we were prepared for the possibility of attack and had a response on the air right away. But it was a shot across the bow, a warning of what we could expect in the weeks and months to come. Wade's nineteenth birthday came, reminding us what real hurt was, providing us that shield against the foolish barbs headed our way and reminding us of what a wonderful community we had. Ellan and Sally and Hargrave came by. Glenn Bergenfield, Wade's godfather, would call. Erin Maness, one of Wade's favorite friends, a beautiful girl, talked with me for the longest time, sitting in Wade's room, both of us fragile, both of us lonely. Jim Jenkins, his gravelly low voice warming his words until they were melted butter: "Knew it was his birthday. Went to the cemetery today." He says it every year, same thing, and it is always music.

In the summer, John had a decision to make. President Clinton, whose wife had been the subject of relentless attacks by Senator Faircloth, wanted to come down to North Carolina to campaign. The Monica Lewinsky scandal was in the news, but there were still denials from the White House. John's staff was against a Clinton visit, but John said he wanted him to come, to talk about the accomplishments of a successful Democratic administration. He planned to come July 30th. It was, it turned out, the week before Lewinsky's blue dress turned up. Cate and I were planning to be in Rhode Island that day, looking at colleges. We had flown up to Pennsylvania and rented a car, and we were driving from one college campus in which she had an interest to the next, with a little sightseeing in between. I figured it was better to go before her junior year, when her excitement about colleges could be translated into a good performance in her important junior-year grades. We were in Maine when Clinton's visit to Raleigh was confirmed. Cate and I parked the rented car, left our suitcases in the trunk, and flew home. It was exciting. Air Force One taxied up to the UPS terminal where we were all waiting on the tarmac; we met the President, and then we were shuttled to the fairgrounds in black SUVs, traffic stopped along the way for the motorcade, John with the President in one car, Cate and Emma Claire — then only three months old — and I in another.

It was wickedly hot, and the fans in the tent where people had gathered to meet the President might as well have been props, they did so little good. Inside the arena where Clinton and John would speak, it was certainly warmer, but you didn't feel it because there was such a sense of excitement. We all entered the arena together, and after John and the President spoke, we left together. But there was an overflow crowd of thousands in nearby Dorton Arena, so the men headed over there to speak again. We sent Emma Claire, who was hungry and tired, home in another car headed directly to our house, and Cate and I went to our assigned motorcade vehicle and waited. Our driver didn't really know where he was supposed to be or where my husband was. That should have been our first hint. We waited as the crowd dispersed, and then he drove around to the arena. No one was there. He apologized and drove out to the UPS terminal, where John had left the car, where Air Force One was sitting. Only by the time we got there, Air Force One was no longer there, and neither was our car. Only the UPS workers were there. The driver dropped us at the terminal nonetheless, and Cate and I stood by the gate to the UPS parking lot, waiting — for John, for another SUV, just waiting to go home. We tired of standing, so we sat on the curb by the gate. And then there was a shift change, so we moved away from the gate and sat farther away on the curb, still dressed in the outfits we had worn to meet the President, as fifty cars and trucks of UPS employees left and fifty more came into the parking lot. And then it started to rain. We had no coats, we had no umbrellas, we had no place to get out of the rain. Cate turned to me and said, "In the President's motorcade one minute, in the rain on the curb outside UPS the next. Not much of a chance to get big-headed." Whenever we are given a dose of humbling reality, we always say, "Just like UPS." We were still laughing when a UPS worker came out to tell us that John, who thought he was meeting us at home, was on the phone. He came to get us, we went home and changed, and then we went out for our usual anniversary dinner — this was our anniversary, too — at Wendy's.

My sister, Nancy, came to help with the campaign. She lived in Florida, and she did the books for a dental practice over her computer. So her office moved when her computer moved, and she moved it all to Raleigh to help with the campaign. It was not a little thing. She stayed in a hotel for months. She knew no one other than us and a few of our closest friends. And she had no experience in campaigns. She had never done anything like this before, and she was given no model from which to work, but she created a volunteer campaign in our biggest counties. Of the three children in our family, she is my father's daughter. Once when we were all in Washington, she arranged a trip to Annapolis, her family and mine and Jay's and my parents. It was after my father's stroke, and Dad didn't walk well, so we insisted he use his wheelchair, as we were going to be covering long distances. He was in the wheelchair when we visited the Hall of Fame. We found Dad's picture as an All-American lacrosse player, and we showed Ty and Louis, Jay's boys. There was a guided tour nearby of Japanese tourists. Nancy brought them over and pointed to the picture and then to my father. "That is this man," she said. And they applauded him. We all pushed back tears, including my father, and I was so grateful for my sister, for the gift of her ability to reach out to strangers. It was a gift she put to great use in the campaign. If you didn't want to work and work hard, you had better hope Nancy didn't have your home number.

As the campaign moved into the fall, the Faircloth campaign used that Clinton visit. There were relentless attacks on John and his character, played over the radio and on television, including the televisions in the lunchroom at the high school Cate attended. When one commercial called John and Bill Clinton lying lawyers, with caricatures of both of them growing Pinocchio noses, all the students sitting around Cate turned to look for her reaction. Her reaction was that she had had enough.

"Can they just make anything up," she asked us that night. "Yes," we told her, "it doesn't seem right, but they actually can make just about anything up. We just have to trust that people will see it for what it is." We hoped we were right, but right or wrong, it didn't make it any easier for a sixteen-year-old girl who had already lived through an assault on her family. But this was Cate, and she just dug in and started putting in even more hours at the campaign headquarters.

I'd like to think that the negative advertising failed. I'd like to think that John's refusal to take the bait, that his running a positive campaign, worked. But the truth is, I don't know why John won. I only know he should have won and did. The excitement of that evening, sitting in the hotel room of the Hilton where the post-election festivities were planned, was unlike anything I had ever experienced. We sat on the two beds, baby Emma Claire propped in the middle of one, surrounded by our dearest friends, and watched as John's picture flashed up on the networks. Winner. And then it was a flurry. We were taken on the kind of circuitous route to the ballroom victory party that you see in the movies, and which seemed hardly necessary. Down service hallways, through the hotel kitchen, along the corridor to the laundry. Finally we emerged into a room that sounded like it was full of people, but the lights were so bright in our faces that I couldn't see a single one. John spoke, and we finally got to hug all those young people who had worked so hard.

The next day John was headed to television interviews, and Kym Spell, the press secretary, knew that some of the younger staff were eating at IHOP. So John stopped there on his way to the interviews to thank them. The real thank-yous came that night when we gathered at the P.R., the Players Retreat, a Raleigh institution, if a pool hall and bar can be an institution, and John sat with a group — David Ginsberg, Christina Reynolds, Brad Anderson, John Dervin, Jessica Wintringham, and Josh Stein, who had probably been the youngest statewide campaign manager in the country that year — none of whom was over thirty. Toward the end of the night, a customer from across the room offered to buy John a beer, and John said, "Thanks, but we should probably go." "We've got a sitter," I told him, "and you only win your first election to the Senate once; I think we can stay a little longer." We talked on, and one of the young people at the table — who had talked to John for months as they traveled the state — said,

"It is so weird to be sitting here talking like this to a United States senator."

"No weirder than being one," John replied.

CHAPTER 9
WASHINGTON
THE SENATE

When Cate graduated from high school, she gave her six closest friends blankets embroidered with all of their names and the years they graduated together from Root Elementary School, from Daniels Middle School, and finally from Broughton High School. The blankets marked a span of their history together that easily could have been broken when John was elected to the United States Senate and — during Cate's junior year in high school — his job moved from Raleigh to Washington, D.C.

Except for one thing. I myself had moved to Washington, or more precisely to Alexandria, Virginia, for my senior year of high school. All the activities that had made up the tapestry of my high school experience, all the friends I had known, who had known me as I was becoming me, were gone, and — with the exception of my brother and sister and one friend, Barbara Bradford —

I'd had to make a start from scratch. Of course I couldn't run for class office, though I had been class president at Zama. I couldn't be a cheerleader again; the Hammond cheerleaders had been chosen the year before. I wasn't going to be editor of the yearbook as I had planned, either, for that position had also been long decided. I managed, of course. I joined the debate team — that was still open — but my senior year of high school should have been more than that. And I wasn't going to let it happen to Cate. She had lived in the same house since she was born and had the same neighbors and the same friends for her whole life.

We had talked about Cate leaving Raleigh for high school, going to a school where she wouldn't place out of all the math classes sophomore year, where she would be challenged in a way that our public schools — as good as they were — were not equipped to do. But that proposed move, which didn't happen after Wade died, would have been a move for her and for all four years of high school, not a move for John that stripped her of her last year and a half. We promised her that when Dad won — the optimistic way we always phrased it — she and I, and now Emma Claire, too, would stay in Raleigh until she graduated with her class.

So we stayed put. We went up in January when he was sworn in, a swirl of festive activities and deferential treatment to which we were not accustomed. We had a lovely dinner at the Naval Observatory grounds with Vice President and Mrs. Gore, and after dinner we — along with the other new Democratic senators and their spouses — walked through the warm January night from the house to the observatory and looked through its great telescope at the rings of Saturn. Except for seeing Saturn, it was more like the evenings to which we were accustomed: a pleasant dinner with pleasant people.

The Senate spouses were very organized about welcoming new families to the Senate. There were sessions to explain the location and furnishing of offices, the role of the Capitol Police, where to get your ID card. And they gave each new spouse a "big sister" to show you around. Mine was Linda Bird Johnson Robb — no one could have a better big sister. The wife of the senator from Virginia, and of course the daughter of Lyndon Johnson, she had been in this Capitol since she was a child, and she knew every nook and cranny. With a constant flow of stories about what happened here or there, or when this or that painting had been hung, she marched me from one place to another.

Now, there are places in the Capitol that only senators can go — unless you are with someone like Linda Bird, who has been there longer than almost anyone. I saw much I would never have seen without her, such as the corridor behind the Senate president's desk, but I also got shooed out of more places than any other new Senate spouse. I was constantly apologizing — "Sorry, I'm sorry, I'm leaving" — but that wasn't Linda. "Yes, yes," she would say, "but first I want to show her this desk." I wouldn't have traded her for the world.

Washington life didn't feel like real life, not like we knew it. Certainly walking around with Linda Bird did not resemble any part of life as I had known it. And it wasn't just seeing the flesh-and-blood faces that I had watched in the news; it was also the news itself. Reporters were everywhere, many trying to figure out who we were. I was talking to a reporter I did know when another new Senate wife, whose husband had been in politics for a while, intervened. "Don't talk to them," she warned, standing between us. I was shuttled back into an extraordinarily decorated Senate office and away from a perfectly nice conversation. Was life going to be like this? I wondered. Guarded conversations, perfect clothes? "People," she told me, "will befriend you in order to use you, and the press are the very worst." I decided that when we did move to Washington, I wasn't going to live that way; I wasn't going to assume that everyone was out to get me, out to use me. I couldn't be looking at what everyone's motives were. If I enjoyed them and they appeared to enjoy me, I was determined simply to accept that. I sure didn't want to spend my time looking under everybody's skirts, as my grandmother used to say. Being hustled away from a single conversation proved to me that it was a lousy way to live.

The flip side of being used, of course, is using — using every person or event as a political opportunity. Who is the most important or influential or visible or rich person in the room? Where is the camera? I don't want to mislead here. Sometimes in political life you — the politician and the spouse — are looking for political opportunity, for press coverage, for financial support. But not every minute. We had dinner with Howard Fineman, the reporter, and our friend Harrison Hickman, who was John's pollster in the Senate campaign.

Above left: My father, Vince Anania, at Kiski Prep in Pennsylvania.
Above right: My beautiful mother, Elizabeth Thweatt, Punahou High School, Honolulu.

Below: My father, the commanding officer of VU-5, a squadron in Atsugi, Japan, in the cockpit.

My brother Jay in a traditional Japanese boys' school uniform, surrounded as usual by Nancy and me, wearing kimonos in our family quarters in the Army housing area at Sagamahara, Japan, in 1954.

In June 1959, Dad received the Distinguished Flying Cross, the highest aviation medal that can be awarded outside of wartime, for saving the Mercator he was flying and its crew after they were attacked by MiG fighters.

John and I in front of the altar at which we had just been married on July 30, 1977. It's hard to tell from our smiles that Bethel Baptist Church in Chapel Hill, North Carolina, was not air-conditioned and the room temperature was about 85 degrees.

Grungy from spending the day packing a moving truck, John and I ate dinner at Wendy's with my mother and father, who is taking the picture. It was July 30, 1978, our first anniversary and the beginning of an anniversary tradition.

Above: John and I were as happy as we look in this picture with Wade, not quite a year old, in front of our first home, in Nashville, Tennessee, in the spring of 1980.

Below: Wade, who loved to hug and cuddle, and me at the beach in 1992. It is my favorite photograph of the two of us.

Of the many pictures we have of Wade hugging Cate, this one at Rehobeth Beach, Delaware, in 1986 is my favorite.

Christmas 1993 in Raleigh with Wade and Cate.

CELEBRATE WADE'S BIRTHDAY

July 18 would be the 17th birthday of Wade Edwards of Raleigh. Please use the attached coupon to celebrate his birthday with an ice cream or treat from the Pullen Park concession stand.

The gift you can give in Wade's name is to do something nice for someone else.

Above: John and I handed out 100 of these coupons to children at the public pool at Pullen Park in Raleigh on July 18, 1996. It occurred to us later that this would have been a happy way to celebrate Wade's birthday if he had lived. Instead, the delight on the faces of the children as they returned from the concession stand with ice cream treats was a sad reminder of what the day might have been had Wade lived.

Left: The headstone for Wade's grave at Oakwood Cemetery was sculpted by Robert Mihaly, who started it when he was artist-in-residence at the National Cathedral. The bench was designed by Thomas Sayre and the small garden was planted by John and me.

Mother's Day, May 12, 1996. The boys—Wade's friends—brought me a dogwood tree. *Left to right:* Matt Nowell, Todd Misenheimer, Will Henderson, Tyler Highsmith, Chas Scarantino, John Brewer, and Ryan Bock.

The girls—Wade's friends—brought us a collage. *Left to right:* Julia Marslender, Meredith Moore, Addie Soldin, Erin Maness, Maggie Whitmeyer, Emily Younger, Alice Walton, Katherine Honeycutt, Sarah Bolton.

Even a crowded campaign bus can allow for tender moments. Jack and I share one in September 2004.

Above: Christmas 2002. Emma Claire, John, and Jack in front of Dad, Louis and Ty—Jay's boys—and Mother. In back, me, Nancy, Lee and wife Laura and Jordan (Nancy's daughters), Cate, Jay and his wife Jackie.

Left: Our traveling campaign family. Ryan Montoya is in the plane with pilot Jim Bruning. Hargrave McElroy, Brett Karpy—our other pilot—and Karen Finney stand with me.

Left: The Military Moms with a Mission became friends during the campaign. Maura Satchell, Pat Heinemann, Lara Bertsch, me, Lisa Lietz, Ann Runyon, Nita Martin.

Center: Our dear friends Hargrave and Rick McElroy in July 2004 in Boston on Hargrave's first day with the campaign.

Below: Cate and I laugh at ourselves at Radio City Music Hall after singing "This Land Is Your Land" on stage in July 2004. *Photograph by Diana Walker.*

During the meal, Howard told me that a certain wife was the best political spouse he'd ever seen. Why? Because she took his business card and entered it into her Palm Pilot right at a dinner just like this one. For me, this was a conversation stopper. It sounded rude, not splendid; I thought, perhaps naively, that we were getting to know each other. I had nowhere to go in this line, so I just asked Howard about Pittsburgh, his — and my dad's — hometown. Sometimes, it seems to me, you have to turn that "political wife" thing off and enjoy the moment without thinking about any gain from this person or that place. Sometimes you have to let out that part of you that gets excited walking around with Linda Bird Johnson Robb and not worry whether or not you are impressing her. John and I saw plenty of symptoms of political opportunism all around us, and we soon promised each other that if we stopped enjoying each minute for what it was, we were going back to North Carolina.

And then Cate and Emma Claire and I went back to North Carolina so Cate could finish her junior year of high school.

While we were in Raleigh, John lived in a little apartment in Alexandria and came home every weekend. When he was home we'd sometimes lose him to meetings with constituents, a trip to Fort Bragg, a rally, or an opening now and again, but the truth was I had grown up this way, and Cate and I, and Wade in those days, had lived this way before, when John would try cases for weeks on end and come home Friday in time to coach a soccer practice. In those days, he would come home for the weekend, but he would work on Saturday, except for coaching the games, and on Sunday he would prepare for trial the next week and then he'd be gone again, for another week. We accepted it then, because we knew how important the work he was doing was to the people he was representing, usually parents who cared for a brain-injured child. Who could complain? Who would? And this wasn't that much different. He was off doing what needed to be done, and we would see him when he wasn't needed there.

The truth was that with a "family-friendly" Senate schedule — that's what they actually called it — we saw him more often than we had when he'd been practicing law. I had been warned by Bubby Smith, who went to high school with me in Japan and was then a lobbyist in Washington, that a senator's schedule was very hard on wives and on marriages. This is going to be very different, he said. I told him, and it turned out to be true, that I didn't think it would be any harder than the life we were leaving. In fact, I think military wives and trial lawyers' wives might be the best-prepared wives in the Senate. And when John was gone to the Senate, it was in some ways better than it had been before. During trials, on our nightly phone call, I'd get the five-minute version of what had happened during his eight-hour day. He wanted to talk about the family and what we'd done, not the trial. But now we had C-SPAN2.

I had watched C-SPAN and C-SPAN2 for years, watched the empty Senate floor while a single senator gave an impassioned speech to just the clerks and the presiding officer, watched the well fill up with loitering senators as votes took place. I used to watch the way they moved in relation to one another, who turned his head away as he passed a colleague, who spoke intimately and wrapped an arm around a confederate. To a family of huggers and touchers, it said a lot. But now we weren't watching for that, we were just watching for Daddy. And now there were no empty seats, no impassioned speeches, no votes. There were no committee meetings, no time for constituent visits. John stepped into the Senate and was immediately sworn in as a juror in the impeachment trial of the President of the United States.

In the wide shots from the gallery, we could pick John out, leaning over his desk, his chin in his hands, watching the proceedings below him, and watching, frankly, in some horror. The founding fathers had not anticipated that Congress, once filled with orators and writers and thinkers, would be filled with politicians with no skill whatever in making a clear point or in eliciting a pertinent piece of evidence in a proceeding that resembled a trial. John and I did not talk, and frankly we should not have talked, about the substance of the case he was hearing, so our nightly conversations usually involved Cate's activities, Emma Claire's achievements of the day, and the House managers' procedural incompetence. It wasn't partisan. We had the same conversations later as we watched Democratic lawyers argue in Florida state courts in *Gore v. Bush*. It was professional, or at least it was the profession he was leaving, the profession I had left the day Wade died.

If you think about the impeachment process in a way that would make sense, the House of Representatives was like a grand jury. The articles of impeachment were like a criminal indictment. The indictment is sent to the Senate for trial, but now the grand jurors — or their representatives, the House managers — are the prosecutors and the senators are the jury. The House managers were apparently not chosen because of their skill in presenting a case; they were partisans, making political speeches, inside and outside the chamber. The President, on the other hand, had real defense lawyers, and the Clinton defense team was good at what they did. The evidence would be the sworn statements the President had given special prosecutor Kenneth Starr, and the evidence of three key witnesses — Vernon Jordan, Monica Lewinsky, and Sidney Blumenthal. The House managers and the Senate wanted — rightly, I think — to avoid the spectacle of Monica Lewinsky in the well of the United States Senate, so it was agreed that the three witnesses' testimony would be taken by videotaped depositions. The House managers and the Clinton defense team would do the questioning, and representatives of the jurors — six senators — would preside over the depositions.

In his first weeks as a senator, John was chosen to be one of the six presiding officers. It made sense; he had more trial experience, and more recent trial experience, than anyone else in the Senate. In a place where seniority means everything, it was an extraordinary opportunity to participate in this moment of history. Extraordinary, too, was the fact that John's first speech on the floor of the Senate would be given from the well of the Senate to ninety-nine other senators and to the Chief Justice of the United States. Most senators speak for the first time on the floor of the Senate from their desks to a nearly-empty chamber, and they wait months to do even that. This was very different.

John called me from the Democratic cloakroom, which is just off the floor of the Senate. His Senate staff had written a speech that tried to bridge his displeasure with the President's conduct — horror really — and his conclusion that the House managers had not proven an impeachable offense. So couched was every phrase that the draft, which tried to disparage the President's conduct while exonerating it, managed to say nothing at all. John called me to say he didn't like it. "Write your own speech," I told him. "It's what you should have done in the first place." John always had this management style: he would let younger lawyers make the opening argument in a trial; he would let them question key witnesses. It was training, and it was opportunity. I always complained about it, because I thought the client always deserved him. He was doing it again, and I said what I had always said — no one can say it like you can say it.

The speech wasn't hard for him. John wanted to do the right thing and be responsible. He had said to me many times that if he thought Clinton was guilty, politics would not have kept him from voting to impeach. But it was never an issue. The House had miscalculated on the charges in order to get the most political effect, but in doing so had charged him with offenses on which no jury would have convicted him if they were following the law. The best proof of this was in a question that John and Herb Kohl, senator from Wisconsin, asked the House managers, the prosecutors: "Would you agree that whether President Clinton is guilty or not is an issue about which reasonable people could disagree?" If the answer is yes, that means it is reasonable to have doubt and he's not guilty as a matter of law. There was always a rush among the House managers to see who would get to answer a question, who would have the nation's attention for the next thirty seconds. On

John's question, Lindsey Graham, now a senator from South Carolina, won. Or maybe he lost, for he answered, "Well, of course I would agree that's true." That's the equivalent of saying there was reasonable doubt and as a matter of law the President was not guilty.

The entire experience was an object lesson in so many ways. The obvious ones are the ones wives liked to cite about fidelity and basic respect for your spouse. But the other lessons, about hubris and hatred as motivators, were there for anyone to see.

During the impeachment trial — which lasted for months — it honestly did not feel like John was away. We talked several times a day, as we had our entire marriage, except when he and Wade were on Mt. Kilimanjaro. We watched him every day at his Senate chamber desk. I'd watch after the proceedings to see if he would talk to reporters at the Ohio Clock, a place the media sets up cameras after sessions to interview senators. He would never stop; the best I could hope for was to see him walk behind the senators who were being interviewed. I guessed that after years of trying cases, he just couldn't imagine the jurors talking, midtrial, to the media.

But eventually the trial was over, and John

went from being a juror to being a senator. It took a little time for John to get his office just right, but he did. Josh Stein, who had run the campaign, came to Washington for a while, until we unfortunately lost him to the attorney general's office in North Carolina. Finally, Miles Lackey, a North Carolina native who had worked in Washington for a number of years, took over the Senate office, and he is still part of our extended family. Another North Carolinian, Will Austin, managed John's schedule, saying no to some requests in just the same nice Southern way John would have. Before the real bonds were formed, everyone reached for easy connections. And the easiest connection was our Southernness. Victoria Bassetti, who was John's first legislative director, and whose family was from Louisiana, would charmingly explain at length her Southern roots. Laura Godwin, Emma Claire's first babysitter during the campaign, finally had her first paid job with John, and she stayed in the Senate office until the end, becoming more invaluable every day. Lisa Zeidner and Jessica Wintringham from the campaign came too. Cory Menees, whom John had coached in soccer on Wade's team, worked in the office. David Sherlin, the older brother of one of Wade's good friends, stayed until he went to law school. Ann Berry, Elizabeth Nicholas, Justin Fairfax, Mike Briggs, Lesley Pittman. And then, as John's reputation and responsibilities grew, so did his staff. Stephanie Jones, Robert Gordon, Derek Chollet, Carlos Monje, James Kvaal.

There are a hundred names, maybe more, and it is hard to skip even one, because they were — and are — so close to John, and even to me. They would humor me when I would call with whatever I had heard on the radio or on C-SPAN or the news. Miles still teases me about an early-morning phone call. He always says I called at 5:30 A.M., but my mother taught me the wait-until-after-9-A.M. rule, and I (almost) always follow it. He picked up the phone and heard me say, with no hello first: "Plywood. We have to do something about plywood." I had just heard about shortages in hurricane-devastated areas because the military had bought so much plywood for Iraq that there wasn't enough for what was needed at home, and the price had skyrocketed. Couldn't they do something about it? Could he call me back later on this, he asked — like when he was awake? I know I will never get the real truth from any of them about whether they liked my calling with my ideas or peeves of the day or whether it was its own joke. I do know that with me or without me the office had a warm feeling like they were all on the same big boat, each with their own jobs to keep it afloat, but watching each other's backs, too. A giant green plush rabbit got passed around from office to office — if you were gone for a day, you could be sure that the rabbit would show up on your desk. It was clear these people were genuinely fond of one another, happy being where they were, and happy doing what they were doing. The affection was authentic then, and it is authentic today. And the last time I saw that green rabbit, someone had deposited it in our garage.

Back in Raleigh, as Cate's senior year started, she was beginning to grow anxious about losing her friends when everyone moved on to college. I had convinced her to apply for early decision somewhere, and she had narrowed the choice to between Princeton and Duke — in my view, the school she really wanted and the school where she would be closer to her friends. She finally applied to Princeton, and then she complained to me for months that I had made her apply there, away from her friends. It was endless, and as the end of school approached, it was constant. When, just before graduation, Cate's eighth-grade English teacher returned letters to the students that they had written to themselves four years before concerning their ambitions for high school, I was vindicated. Cate had written that she wanted to finish calculus by her sophomore year, which she did, that she wanted to play varsity softball all four years, which she did, and that she wanted to go to Princeton. Princeton! Right there in her eighth-grade handwriting, before I had mentioned colleges to her! Rarely does a mother get a break like that.

But I understood what was behind Cate's complaints. She had only known one place, one group of friends, and although she was not afraid to face a new place — she had gone to lots of camps and the TIP program at Duke, places where she knew no one — she was afraid to lose the place, and the friends she knew best. I told her she wouldn't lose them, she'd add to them, that it's like when you have a child and think you couldn't love any more than you do, and then you have a second child, and it turns out you can love twice as much. No sale. It is like Jesus and the fishes and loaves, I tried again — there is always enough for the people you know and for the people farther up the beach whom you haven't come to yet. Again, no sale. Time, of course, has proved to her what her mother could not convince her of: that her lifetime friends would always be her lifetime friends. They have part of you, part of your life, in them, so you don't want to lose them. But you don't lose them because you also have part of them in you. It changes. But it doesn't evaporate. I knew this to be true, even for relationships that hadn't incubated over eighteen years, for my life was scattered across an entire country of people with whom I had shared it and about whom I still cared. When I moved to Washington, I went to the Jacob Lawrence exhibit at the Phillips Collection with Martha Hartmann, and it was like the thirty-four years (thirty-four years!) since we had been friends in Atsugi, Japan, had slid silently away. I had lunch with Maggie Ketchum this winter, thirty-two years after we were in graduate school together; I still love her.

I was trying to coax one child to decide on colleges while changing diapers for a second and trying to bring yet another child into our lives. I was still trying to get pregnant again. It was looking more and more like the end of the mothering road — then in August we learned I was pregnant again. We were overjoyed. The Senate was on August break, so John shared in the excitement of the news face-to-face, and he went with me to my appointments, even just to get my blood tested. One of the blood tests sounded an alarm. My estriol levels were supposed to keep going up, at least doubling each day that I was pregnant, only one day they didn't, and the doctors feared that meant that I had lost the pregnancy. We went in for another pregnancy test. John and I sat in the doctor's office, hand in hand, waiting for the results. The doctor came in, holding a little plastic square with a negative sign across it, and said he was sorry. He left us alone, and although we were unhappy, we knew how lucky we were to have Emma Claire. We resigned ourselves to the great gifts we had in our daughters, and we'd started to get up to leave when the doctor ran back in. In his hand was the little plastic square, but perpendicular to the negative sign another line was forming. It was impossible to say who was most excited. And when we left happily, the doctor chased us out to our car; we'd forgotten the little plastic square with the perpendicular lines; he was sure we'd want that for the baby book. Those perpendicular lines would soon be our son Jack. There were, however, a few intervening events.

Cate's life was in overdrive — she had the senior year she deserved. And we finally did some things we needed to do at our house. The family room had always been the center of our activities, or at least our activities outside the kitchen. We had so many memories of Wade coming home to that room, bounding through the front door, spotting us, sitting next to John, on top of him, really, pressing himself into whatever space John was in, and John would push him and tease him. When Wade was seven, it was there we watched Wade's favorite team, the Denver Broncos, lose the Super Bowl. Wade had taken an orange football helmet and taped on the side a drawing he had made of the Broncos' trademark horse. He sat in that family room, his chin in his hands, that enormous helmet atop his head, and tears streamed down his face as the Broncos were unable to stop the New York Giants. We had thirteen Christmases in that room. It is where we watched Tar Heel basketball games, political conventions, and approaching hurricanes. It is where we read whatever was assigned in English class, cuddled under a blanket my mother bought during my father's last tour of duty in Italy. And it was now a room we did not want to enter, a place so filled with happy memories that it made us too sad to be there. Finally in 1999 we decided to make a change, and so the rooms changed places — the dining room, the living room, and the family room played a kind of musical chairs that disrupted the house through Cate's entire senior year and through my last pregnancy. And through even more.

After Al Gore secured the Democratic nomination for president in the spring of 2000, Warren Christopher, perhaps as a courtesy, visited all the Democratic senators in an attempt to help Gore find a running mate. The famous Christopher reserve we had seen on television was, according to John, exactly what you got in person. He asked John about other senators, and John spoke highly of each one. All in all, an interesting experience. And Christopher certainly hadn't tipped his hand to John, so with the rest of the country we waited for the names on Gore's list. I admit that we weren't on pins and needles. We had a growing two-year-old, and all of Cate's end-of-senior-year events, assemblies, and parties were crowding the schedule. We were glad to be looking forward to them rather than dreading them, as we had three years earlier when Wade's class graduated.

And I was very pregnant. If Trent Lott,

then the majority leader in the Senate, agreed that there would be no votes that day, Jack would be delivered on May 19th. Honestly, we waited to schedule Jack's birth until after Senator Lott agreed that there would be no votes. The doctors had been adamant that at my age, and after three previous cesarean section deliveries, Jack would be delivered by cesarean section a few days earlier than the due date. On John's request, with Senator Tom Daschle's help, Lott agreed, and May 19th it was. Cate and John and I went over to Chapel Hill in the early morning. Jack — John Atticus Edwards — was delivered before 9 A.M. He looked just like his father, in every wonderful way but in an odd way, too. His hair looked almost combed, and in his father's hair style, when they first showed him to me in the delivery room. I thought it was a joke Valerie Parisi, my obstetrician, was playing on me, but it wasn't, that's just the way he came out — coiffed. His hair hasn't been as neat since. Like Emma Claire, and Cate and Wade, he had complications from ABO blood incompatibility with me, but in a day or two we were all home, trying to find places for Jack to sleep out of earshot of the ill-timed remodeling.

And that was the scene — Cate's graduation paraphernalia spread across the kitchen, invitations, awards, robe; Sam and Charlie putting in a new ceiling in the once-dining-room-now-family-room; Emma Claire under constant watch so that she didn't get harmed by the construction and so that she didn't, at two, overreach with her new brother; Jack, mostly trying to sleep; company coming by to meet him and to say goodbye because we were moving to Washington a week after graduation; boxes and suitcases open in the hallways so that whenever we had a minute to spare we could pack something; me at the computer scanning my favorite photographs so we could take copies with us to Washington.

It was the Friday afternoon a week before Cate's graduation, two weeks before the move, and John was due home from Washington anytime. The phone rang, and a very proper elderly man with a whisper of a voice asked for John. Could John call him back when he got home? Andrew Young was picking John up at the airport, so I called Andrew, who relayed the message that Warren Christopher had called, but John, seeing no urgency — he assumed Christopher had another question about another senator — waited to call when he got home.

Over a hungry baby, a toddler trying to

get her returning father's attention, banging hammers, and adult chatter in the next room, John could not quite make out what Christopher was whispering; he could understand about every other word. John was apparently in a final group of potential running mates, and Christopher wanted to know if John would submit to a vetting. When John got off the phone, I asked what he had said. "Well," said John, "I can tell you what I think he said. I couldn't hear him." Had he said John was in a final group? That he was pretty sure of. How many others were in that group? No idea. What did vetting entail? No idea. The one thing he had heard clearly was that this was a secret and we could tell no one. So we told no one.

Well, vetting, which started right away but for me was just background noise — or among the background noises — involves turning your life inside out for someone to see. Professional, financial, social, academic, everything. All of our income tax returns, all of John's medical records, every legal case he'd ever done. A campaign finance expert went through John's contributions. Everything was scrutinized. John met with the whole team once, in a small office used by Senator Ted Kennedy and once used by

John Kennedy. The vetting by an entire team of investigators was secret, since John's place on the list was secret, and the small office tucked into the Capitol was away from all possible press scrutiny. Eventually I was quizzed for an afternoon by Bill Taylor, an affable Washington, D.C., lawyer. All this time, we told no one.

Of course, a select group of people in the office knew, people who had to pull together John's votes and speeches. And a select group from the Senate campaign was particularly useful. In political campaigns, you investigate the other candidate's records, of course, but you also investigate your own, put yourselves in your opponent's shoes and see what would turn up in an investigation of you. Although it was not as intensive as the vice presidential vetting process, the campaign research staff, David Ginsberg, Christina Reynolds, and John Dervin, were invaluable. John and I could talk to them about it, but to no one else. The talk everywhere in Washington was all about who the vice presidential nominees would be, on both sides. Everyone assumed that the reason I never said anything in these conversations was that, since I had just moved up there, I knew nothing. No one suspected that the real reason I was quiet was because

I knew something. This went on for weeks.

I said nothing when Bill Taylor came to the house. I said nothing as we turned over our financial records to a stranger. And I said nothing when a car with tinted windows picked John up at our house — within walking distance of the Gore residence — and drove him to his interview with the Vice President. We weren't tense. It was, we knew, an extremely long shot. Our first clue to that, of course, was that no pundit, no gossip hound, no insider ever even whispered John's name. And the second clue was that the names that were mentioned in the press — John Kerry, who had been in the Senate for twenty years, Evan Bayh, who had been a two-term governor, Joe Lieberman, the longtime senator, George Mitchell, former majority leader of the Senate, Bob Graham, the Florida senator, Jeanne Shaheen, the personable governor of New Hampshire — were, well, all more likely choices. John thought he was there as a fallback. In the post-Lewinsky world, Al Gore was understandably intent on finding a running mate who was not vulnerable. So John was the untarnished choice, we figured, in case other candidates collapsed under the vetting. Apparently we were wrong.

John jogged with Evan Bayh regularly.

They are about the same age, both easygoing, and both were new to the Senate in 1999. And now both were on Al Gore's short list. When John left the Senate gym to run with Evan one Monday, he and Evan — in private — could talk about what they hadn't mentioned in public. They talked about Gore's selection process. Evan had had his interview with Gore the preceding Friday, and John's was scheduled for the next day. Evan, who could have resisted giving John any advantage and so could have stayed quiet, instead told him about his interview as they ran. It had been very low-key, he said, very friendly. They'd just talked about family and history they shared. He'd thought Gore would be tougher, but the Vice President hadn't asked him anything hard. So that's what John expected when he went for his interview.

When John arrived at the Vice President's residence on Tuesday morning, he was taken to a pleasant sitting room. John waited there for Gore, looking at the paintings and the photographs. Sarah Gore, one of Al and Tipper's daughters, came in, and then the Vice President, and John engaged in the same idle chatter Evan had described. But then Sarah left, and the room went quiet. John broke the silence, pointing to one of the photographs: "Is that your dad?" Gore glanced at the photograph and in one breath said, "Yeah-now-can-you-answer-a-question-for-me?" "Sure," John said, a little taken aback by the shift in tone. And it was about to get worse. The Vice President asked him how he would explain to the world that he had picked somebody who'd been in office for a year and a half to be a heartbeat from the presidency. The first question out of the box. John talked about the attributes of leadership as he saw them — honesty, steadfastness, strength in times of adversity. He'd survived that question, but the whole interview was like that — hostile, difficult. Gore asked about everything, policy, family, politics, how to distance himself from Clinton's conduct. On his lap there was a notebook — of the vetting material, John assumed — and he flipped through the pages and peppered John with questions. The tone never changed, and John only knew it was over when the Vice President stood up. They walked to the car, Gore thanked him for coming, and then he surprised John by adding, "You should feel very good about this interview." Did he mean that, or was he trying to cheer up the new kid? We didn't know.

That afternoon John ran with Evan again,

and Evan asked how the interview had gone. They were very close, and John told him the truth: It was really tough. Evan listened thoughtfully as John related the questions, and then he said, "That's bad news for me. He's serious about you, and he wasn't serious about me. That's what that means." Until Evan perceptively said this, neither John nor I knew how to read the interview. But Evan knew how to read Al Gore. John was still thinking that he was probably last out of those in the running, unless Evan was right and Evan was last. We were still not arranging our lives around this. A few weeks later, on a Friday, everything changed. The *New York Times* reported that Gore had his list down to three people — John, Lieberman, and Kerry. It was the first time John's name had been mentioned at all, and now it was mentioned as one of three.

The press, in a swarm, started staking out our house. Cameras lined the sidewalk across the street, and if we walked to the car, they would come up alongside us, snapping away, and we would have to close the door on a camera lens. But it wasn't going to last long, we knew, because Gore announced that he would make his choice on

Monday. On Friday, John went to North Carolina for Senate business for the day, and while he was being mobbed there, the children and I were stalked at the D.C. house. Mary Louise Oates and Ellen Bennett, two veterans of these kinds of things — and good company besides — came over to see about me and to see if I was ready. I had been out of maternity clothes for less than two months. I was not ready.

They took my closet apart. I had just had a baby, and at my age, I was not bouncing back into shape, yet here I was, standing in my underwear in front of women I had known for only a month, while they had me try on what they thought might be suitable, which, frankly, was not that much of my wardrobe. So distressed were they with my clothes that Ellen took off her designer jacket and gave it to me. "Try this," she said. I declined. "I really can't take your clothes." She changed her tack. "Wear this," she ordered. When they left, they had a small — very small — pile of what they thought might be acceptable, and they promised to be back. When John came back from North Carolina to my clothes thrown all over our bedroom, I didn't even try to explain. Despite the cameras and the Attack of the Clothes Police, we still thought that John was the last choice, third now of three, but still last. After the day we had had, sleep came easily.

Saturday mornings were like Saturday mornings in every house with a new baby and a two-year-old. Jack was crying, Emma Claire wanted breakfast, and — our new twist — there were seventy-five members of the press corps camped out in front of our house. About 9:30 A.M., the phone rang, John was changing Jack, and Emma Claire and I were eating breakfast. It was Bill Daly, Al Gore's campaign manager. He told John that he had just had breakfast with the Vice President. And then he said it was between John and one other person. Oh, my gosh. He may have said more, but who heard anything for a minute? Then he said to John, "Now, I don't know you, and I feel like I should know you because I'm going to have to help advise the Vice President, so I need to meet with you." John asked where, and Daly suggested his apartment. John said, "That's fine, but there are TV cameras out here, and they're following me everywhere I go." So they arranged a cloak-and-dagger drive-into-the-underground-Senate-parking-garage-and-change-cars-and-drive-to-Daly's-apartment plan. Which worked. John met with him for about an hour. Daly was very friendly and open. Everyone liked John, he said. Everyone was impressed. But he was still worried about the fact that John had not been in office long. They talked about it, and at the end, Daly told him that his family needed to be in place on Monday, all of us, because if John was chosen, the campaign would be sending a plane to take us all to Nashville, where Gore's campaign headquarters were.

I don't know whether Mary Louise was being careful, whether she was perceptive, or whether she had inside information from her husband, Bob Shrum, who was a top consultant in the Gore campaign. Whatever it was, she was back at the house that morning to dress me. Mary Louise didn't hand me any of her clothes — she is a good six inches taller than I am. Instead she made plans for us to go shopping. When she picked me up, I was dressed in comfortable North Carolina clothes, and four hours later she dropped me — now dressed in smart slacks and a leather jacket — back at the house. With all the press camped out at the front door, we decided — actually, Mary Louise decided — to leave all the shopping bags in the car trunk, and I retrieved them after dark, after the last of the press had gone home for the night. The attempt to avoid press coverage of my shopping trip was apparently unsuccessful, though, as the shopping trip showed up in David Broder's column in the *Washington Post* — and syndicated around the country. Not exactly the national introduction I would have hoped for, had I ever hoped for a national introduction.

I got home from shopping just before Cate and her friends arrived in the airport shuttle van from Baltimore. The girls — and there were about six of them, all of whom John had coached in soccer or basketball — were coming for four days. They had graduated from high school together and within weeks they would be headed off to different colleges, so this was a farewell fling for them, one they had been planning for weeks. When the van stopped in our driveway, the press leaped up and ran across the street, leaving spraying soda cans and pizza boxes in their wake. The girls sat paralyzed in the van for a minute, and then, unable to contain girlish giggles, they fell all over each other and finally out of the van. The press figured that one of these was our daughter, but which one? Did anyone know what she looked like? I don't know who looked more confused, the press or the girls. The press was snapping and filming them all, asking which one of these girls was Cate Edwards. For a few minutes, all the girls had cameras in their faces. They were all Cate Edwards. From that point on, the girls never left the house without looking terrific.

The next morning we watched the hosts of the Sunday talk shows eviscerate John. It was, "These are hard times. We need a president with experience, and this guy's been in office for a year and a half. How can you even be seriously considering him?" Representatives of the Gore campaign were countering with things like, well, Abraham Lincoln had been in office for two years when he was elected president of the United States, and George Bush had been governor for four years in a state where the governor didn't have much authority. The best defense of John was, oddly enough, given by John McCain, who was on *Meet the Press;* he said he'd worked with John and John Edwards was really talented and smart.

We lived in a residential area, so I went out in the early afternoon on Sunday and asked the press if anyone needed to use a bathroom. We had a first-floor bathroom they were welcome to use. Of course they did. They all poured in. And while they were waiting, they pored over the mail that had collected on the front hall bureau. Bad boys, I said, retrieving the mail. They were not asked back.

We spent the rest of the day talking to the girls when they were home, playing with the children, and talking about the news shows and my new clothes. Sunday night we went to dinner with Julianna Smoot, who had been working for John since the Senate campaign. In every campaign, you get to do exciting things and you have to do boring, menial things. I got such a kick out of Julianna because when she was tired of doing the menial jobs, she would complain in frustration, "But I went to Smith College!" Even when she was complaining, she was good company.

We went to bed Sunday night believing that in the morning Al Gore would pick John Kerry as his running mate. Joe Lieberman went to bed believing that Al Gore would choose John Edwards. In the morning, the television news and the ringing phone simultaneously announced that we were all wrong. He had chosen Joe Lieberman. John talked to whomever it was on the phone, and I got up and walked downstairs to Cate and all her friends. They were still sleeping and spread all over her room. I stepped over legs and luggage until I could lean over Cate and whisper, "He picked Lieberman." She didn't open her eyes, just "Uh-huh." "You can sleep in." As I walked back upstairs, I looked across the street and nothing remained of the seventy-five people who had clicked their cameras every time we opened the door. Nothing but a line of trash.

It was as if Cate and I were once again sitting on the curb at UPS in the rain long after Air Force One had left Raleigh. But I didn't despair then, and I didn't despair now. I had Cate and all those precious girls sleeping in her room, I had a little girl covered in a mop of yellow curls, I had a new baby boy with a freckle in his palm, and I had John. Instead of getting on that plane to Nashville, we made reservations at the children's favorite restaurant for dinner. And John took a trash bag and picked up the remains of this adventure from the sidewalk across the street. Having these girls there — although they were just eighteen at the time — made it so much better. We had known them so long, coached them and watched them grow, and now, without knowing it, they were there, a soft, embracing pillow that — with our own children — broke what might have been a fall. We went out to dinner with the girls and the younger children, everyone laughing, the children misbehaving, everything back to normal.

It's hard to explain, but we did not have a great sense of loss when we heard Lieberman's name. We never really thought John would be picked. Our period of expectation was only the forty-eight hours or so after Bill Daly called, and I got a new wardrobe out of it. We heard the back story later — it drifts out, it always does — and it seemed that John was closer to being chosen than we had imagined. Once, months and months later, after the recount and the last concession speech, I saw Hadassah Lieberman at a Senate spouses' event. She was nice, saying she had thought about me a lot and wished me well. I told her I had thought about her, too, only — after the recount and the election that would not end — I had thought, *There but for the grace of God go I.* I need to be a little more careful about what I say, I think.

All of this took place in a house we bought in Washington. We didn't want to dismantle our home in Raleigh, couldn't really, since we would be home for holidays. So we bought new furniture, or more accurately, I bought new furniture, for the D.C. house.

To do that, I stepped into a world I had not known, of decorators and upholsterers, refinishers and showroom representatives. And they were fantastic. B.A. Farrell is an architect and designer who grew up in Troy, a town near where John is from. I accuse B.A. of designing a space and then having such allegiance to the space that he doesn't want someone to ruin it, so he helps decorate it, too. He will take his collection of clients, mostly women, to High Point to buy furniture and fabric so the integrity of the space is retained. As odd as it sounds, this traveling group is its own community — "B.A.'s girls," perhaps — women whose only connection is B.A. You travel with whomever B.A. collects for a day, women you don't know, and you always have a great time. I went with a woman whose husband is an active Republican in the state. John came home and said, "Why is there a George Bush sticker on the car in our driveway?" "Well," I told him, "she left her car here and we rode with B.A." And I spent a day pulling out fabrics for this Republican woman's bedroom, saying, "Would this look nice?" It was great fun.

We all know B.A. never feeds us, so we've learned to bring our own food. It was always good to go when Jane Henderson went, because she would bring her fabulous chocolate chip cookies. One time five of us went to Farmville, Virginia, to Green Front Furniture. It's a good drive to Farmville, but worth it. They have furniture, but we were going for the carpeting and the rugs. We were each looking for carpet for ourselves, but as we moved through the huge rolls, we would call out to the others — "Is someone looking for a light blue?" We'd have to get Ricky, who worked there, to get carpet down for us, but even finding the rolls was hard work. After several hours, we stopped and ate the lunch we had brought. We just sat on one of the big carpet rolls and opened our thermos and bags. And we got Ricky to take a picture of us.

The women eating lunch on the carpet roll, the woman with the Bush sticker on her car — these are not women I knew before, but now, having traveled with them, having worked on something together with them, I knew I could trust them. And it was not just the women. It was also the people with whom we traded, with whom I still trade. Ricky at Green Front, Ginger at Market Square, Red at Latimer Alexander, Anthony and Pete and Doris — a whole world of friends disguised as business contacts. Like everything else I have ever done that would have been fun no matter what, it was miles more fun because I got to know the people from whom I was buying fabric or whatever it was.

B.A. and I were shopping with Ginger recently, asking about her daughter's new house and the changes at her workplace, when another couple joined us, looking at furniture in the same showroom. They could not understand our relationship — who was the salesperson, who was I, why was a customer pulling out catalogs for them — because our relationship didn't bear any resemblance to the model they expected. Somehow we have gotten to a place where we aren't supposed to know the name of cashiers — although almost every one of them wears a name on their shirt. We don't call by name the bag boy whose name is on his shirt or the waitress who told you her name when she handed you the menus. And I think we are worse for it.

Bobby used to serve the iced tea at the Belk's cafeteria — "Sweetened or unsweetened?" — and his face would light up when he would see us, his friends, in line. And our faces would light up when we saw him. The last person to check me out in Target was Amy. The fellow framing our new house is Mac, and Steve is laying tile. So for our house in Washington I didn't just buy furniture in High Point, I made a whole town of friends. And for the life of me, I cannot see why everyone doesn't do the same thing. When I get on the phone to say the cable service is on the fritz, I listen for the name on the other end, and then I use it. I know that it may be a false name; when I call and reach someone named Harley in what is obviously India (which has happened), I am pretty sure it is a false name. But I use it nonetheless, because it is the way to treat people. Coincidentally, there is another benefit: unless I am mistaken, you actually get better service from people you have treated well. I spoke to a health care providers' convention recently, and I told them to personalize their service. None of us wants to be "the patient in room 206." Yet that is how so many otherwise good people think about the mailman and the maintenance man and the bag boy, as if they were all nameless. But the mailman is Edward, and the maintenance man at the children's school is Drew, and the bag boy at Harris Teeter is Sam, and my life is better because my children and I can expect to be greeted with a smile by Edward and Drew and Sam.

So Washington, where people are treated as various levels of royalty, where a magazine publishes the A-List of the most desirable dinner guests for the upcoming year, was probably not a perfect match for me. But as long as I didn't fall into that trap, I would be fine. I admit that I was pleased to sit at lunch with the wife of the ambassador from India — she is a genuinely lovely woman. And it was a great pleasure, an honor really, to go to the British embassy. The people were interesting and friendly, and I enjoyed every minute. But I also enjoyed Evelyn and Mr. Clare in the book room of the Goodwill retail store and Jimmy and Shakira, elevator operators in the Capitol. I still start up conversations with the person behind me in line at Home Depot.

My less-than-perfect fit with Washington was nowhere more evident than at an event the Senate spouses had for the First Lady. Every year, we had a luncheon for the First Lady, and every year she would return the favor. This particular year was Laura Bush's first year, and the theme of our luncheon for her was, predictably, libraries. We had oversize bookshelf displays for photographs, and we had lots of table decorations, including piles of books that would later be donated to needy libraries for children. I was working with Liz Jeffords, the terrific wife of the Vermont senator, on a portion of the planning, but everyone on the committee, regardless of their assignment, was asked to come for a "workday" to set the room up the day before the luncheon. I had done this dozens of times — not First Lady luncheons, of course, but PTA book exchanges and middle-school silent auctions. Since everyone had been asked to come, it must be a lot of work, I figured, so I came dressed for work — in overalls. Apparently that is not what was meant by "workdays" for, except for Fran DeWine from Ohio, who was at least wearing slacks, every other spouse was wearing a suit, a very nice suit. There was even one suit with sequined lapels. And there were heels and stockings. And then there was me, in overalls and sneakers. Even the Senate building staff — who were, it turned out, the real workers doing the setup — were dressed better than I. At least I was a hit with the Capitol Police at the entrance nearest John's office; I don't believe they had seen a spouse in overalls before.

CHAPTER 10
AMERICA, THE
PRIMARIES
THE WINDUP

The evening of December 29, 2002, when John called the people closest to him and told them that he was going to run for the Democratic nomination for president in 2004, was, in one sense, the end of a process that had been going on for more than a year. Of course, in another sense, it was the beginning of an even more excruciating process, and in the ensuing whirlwind, it was impossible to sort out just the moment when he had first stepped onto this path. I remember talking in 2000 to a reporter for the *Washington Post,* Rich Leiby, who asked a question John had been asked a dozen times before: when did John decide to run for the Senate? The answer I gave applies here. "Are you married?" I asked. Yes, he was. "Then you courted your wife and loved her and maybe marriage was on your mind and maybe it was not, and then one day you realized that perhaps that day or the day before or the day before that you had fixed in your mind that you wanted her to be your bride. It didn't happen in an instant; it was a collection that finally, invisibly, reached the tipping point."

It is easier to date John's definite decision to run, although even that is in important parts a collection of little pieces from which the decision finally came when, at the end of 2002, he put the puzzle pieces together. After the 2000 election a number of people who had worked in the Gore campaign and had supported John as the vice presidential choice were looking ahead to 2004. It was what they did. And this time they came to John. Now, frankly, these same people might have gone to others as well, urging them to run, but I do not know that. I only know they came to John, and came, and came. They said the right things: he was authentic, he came from a working-class background, he spoke plainly and passionately. He brushed off the first compliments and the first few suggestions, but he finally agreed to talk about the notion of running. The people promoting the idea — some of them members of his staff — set up a two-day meeting to talk about the possibility and what to do if John said yes. I mention members of his own staff because there is a joke in Washington that every senator gets up in the morning, looks in the mirror, and sees a potential president. It may be true, but it is also true that every staff member looks at their boss and sees a potential president . . . and, I suspect, imagines their own West Wing office. We are always positive that our staff is different, that our staff is suggesting he run because of their belief in him and loyalty to him, but the truth is probably somewhere in between.

For two days, a Sunday and Monday, we met in a large room on the first floor of our Washington house. As with every meeting John ever had at the house or elsewhere, there were no assigned seats. To normal people, this will not sound strange, but in the political world, with pecking orders and limited chairs at the table, it was, we were assured, unusual. And there was no assumption that John would get the best seat; it was first-come-first-served seating, and as John usually came in last, he usually got the worst seat. Tom Donilon, who had worked with Warren Christopher and who had a diplomat's acumen as well as a diplomat's caution, came to every meeting pressed and fresh; he had a particularly comfortable seat on the couch for his one day. He could not be there on Monday, and his seat was snagged the next day by David Ginsberg, who had worked for John in the Senate campaign and had, in the course of those months, become family to us. David came equipped with the latest laptop computer, a BlackBerry on one hip, a cell phone on the other, and he became, by virtue of his appliances, the scribe. Erskine Bowles from North Carolina, more recently Bill Clinton's chief of staff, didn't need a chair. He stood for the whole meeting — his back was bothering him — and from his position, leaning against a post, he said he believed in John and wanted to devote himself to making him president, which was of course heartening to hear.

The media consultants Bob Shrum and his partners at the time, Tad Devine and Mike Donilon, were there. They were the veterans. Bob and John had become close when Bob did the commercials for John's Senate campaign, and I hope their warm personal relationship will survive the stories I will tell about him here. Bob, who came to no meetings pressed, spoke a great deal, as he had the most experience, and when he wasn't speaking he was popping gum into his mouth so he wouldn't smoke. Mike, who is Tom's brother, sat, as he always did, on the edge of the chair, leaning into the conversation, and although his might have been the most reliable voice there, he just leaned in, didn't talk much, but he did stop John afterward and said he wanted to be a part of this if it happened. I will skip ahead to say that Bob and Tad and Mike wound up working for John Kerry. The decision, known in the press as the Shrum Primary, was one that made us sad and relieved at the same time. These are experienced, brilliant men, but one of their skills — appearing as surrogates for the candidate on television — was a skill that could undo some of what John brought to the campaign as a new face, as an outsider. They were the consummate insiders, and therefore their skills could not be exercised if they worked for John, which would mean that neither John nor they would get the full benefit of the relationship. John and I had that difficult conversation with Bob before the decision was made. But before that decision — and after it, I believe — Bob was a friend and a champion, albeit a quieted champion during the primaries.

Harrison Hickman, John's brilliant, funny, committed, and — he wants to rid himself of this adjective — sometimes prickly pollster was there. He and John are the same

347

age, although Harrison has the distinguished gray hair that the press and I always complain John doesn't have. Miles Lackey, John's legislative director at the time and a former White House staffer himself, and Jeff Lane, John's chief of staff, were there. Soon Jeff would move to a law practice and Miles would move into his job. Rebecca Walldorf came, energetic and more connected than her pretty, ageless face would suggest, as did Ed Turlington, who was a member of our church in North Carolina but, more importantly, was one of Bill Bradley's most trusted advisors, so he brought even more experience into the room. Julianna Smoot, who had managed the fund-raising in the Senate campaign, and Tom Girardi from California, who would be important in fund-raising if John ran, came, Tom with his distractingly beautiful wife, Erika — who brought flowers.

The room was full, and full of purpose. The one difference in this meeting over the less formal ones that preceded it is that there was a firm agenda. Now, political consultants and pollsters cannot help themselves, and there will always be the anecdotes about the last campaign or the one before — Bob, who worked for Gore, would tease Ed, who had worked for Bradley —

but there was a lot to cover and people held, or mostly held, to the outline in the binders each had been given. For two days we all sat there — going through all the issues, setting the table, though we didn't know it, for a conversation that would last another fifteen months. One thing we did conclude: if John was even thinking about saying yes, it was not too early to start laying the groundwork. Everyone left with their assignments for the next months.

The meeting took place on September 9th and September 10th, 2001.

And then there was September 11th. In some respects, it was not unlike Wade's death. September 11th wiped everything else off the calendar, off the map, out of the conversation. For us, for everyone. Erskine decided he needed to do more than help with a race, and he decided that day to run for the Senate himself. We thought more of him for that decision. For now we were all, like the country, focused on that terrible morning, focused on our families and our larger national family, and it is not too much to say that John was focused on the new challenges the Senate would face.

Although our family was scattered when the planes hit the Trade Center and the Pentagon and crashed in a Pennsylvania field — I was shopping, John was on his way to the Senate, Jack, almost sixteen months, and Emma Claire, three, were taking a walk with Jennifer Madison, who helped us care for them — we quickly gathered in our house in Washington. Phone lines were jammed, so neither Jennifer nor I could reach our North Carolina and Florida families or Cate in Princeton. The Senate was evacuated, and John came home. The sounds of planes and helicopters, which were usually constant at our home near the vice presidential residence, were gone. There wasn't much traffic. The world went quiet except for the sound of the television set. Within a few hours, the Capitol Police came to the door to pick up John to take him to a secure location. Was the Senate meeting there? No. Was he required to go? They would like him to go. No, he said, he would stay here with his family. We did what America did that day: we watched in disbelief and sadness, together, and we reached for one another.

The next morning we all drove to Princeton. We needed to see Cate, to touch her and hold her. The local paper, the *Princeton Packet,* started in those first days publishing the names of local residents who had been lost. I suppose everyone read those stories in the *Princeton Packet,* or the *New York Times,* or their own newspaper. But many of us read the names and the stories differently, envisioning the life that was lost, and by our careful reading doing the little we could to pay homage to those who had died. I knew that my alt.support.grief family was doing this, each in our way, silent and separate, honoring lives that should not have had to be reduced to a paragraph. Those who remained couldn't know we had done it, but doing it was right and fine, and so many of those people who died that day and those that remained to mourn them, people we never knew — mothers and sisters, sons and fathers — have stayed with me. One who has stayed with me is not one who died but one who survived: a woman with a son whose husband died on September 11th. She could not talk to the *Princeton Packet* reporter who called. She could not give her name or his. She could not talk at all. Not wouldn't. Couldn't. Her paralyzing grief, which I well understood, was heartbreaking.

In those days and for many weeks afterward, as John devoted himself to his duties and I devoted myself to the children, there was no mention of the two-day meeting. But our lives, like the lives of so many others, finally started to regain a rhythm. By January 2002 the discussion of a possible presidential run started up again, and John's scheduler, Will Austin, whom we adore, called to set up a trip to New Hampshire. A senator's schedule is not his own. He is controlled by votes and committee meetings, by constituent responsibilities and party caucus obligations. These — and any possible campaigning — are juggled and contorted by a magician called a scheduler. Everyone in John's life with an interest in his schedule gets on a weekly conference call and argues for John's time, and it is in these calls that I play the nasty witch of the west. Since no one else on the call had children, and even if they had, they didn't have our children, my job on the calls was to make certain his children knew John's face. Other than on television.

The children did see a lot of John on television. During the day, C-SPAN2, which covers the Senate, was always on in the hope we might catch him speaking or at least voting. My children looked at men (and a few women) in suits all day. At night, I would turn on the arts channel, and they would be lulled to sleep by an elegantly dressed woman singing an aria or a man in a tuxedo playing a piano concerto. We hadn't realized what a skewed view of the world they were getting until John, leaving one night for a black-tie dinner, reached down to kiss Emma Claire good night, and she, looking at him quizzically, asked, "You play the piano?"

It was my job to make sure they knew a little more about their father, and I had a two-nights-away rule. He had to sleep in our house every third night, no matter what. We kept that rule — until we didn't keep it. But in these early days, certainly on this first campaign trip, we were keeping the rule. In February 2002, with an icy rain blanketing southern New England, John and I visited New Hampshire.

There is something comforting about the election rituals in New Hampshire and Iowa, even for a neophyte. I hadn't campaigned in the Senate race to any significant degree, and I wasn't actually campaigning now. I was along for the ride, and the ride was taking me to Manchester. We stayed at the Holiday Inn, where politicians thinking about the New Hampshire primary have always stayed. A friendly journalist warned me that the cleaning staff could be bribed for a tidbit about the secrets of the rooms of politicians, so even though I couldn't imagine we had anything to hide, I carried our trash, in the ice bag, to the lobby trash can each day. I wasn't very good at being secretive, however. On this visit or the next, one of the reporters for a North Carolina paper forgot his shaving cream. I saw him forlorn in the small hotel store being told they didn't have any. So I took him up to our room and, while John was getting in a morning run, he shaved using John's bargain shaving cream over our sink surrounded by our toiletries. No secrets.

When John was back from running, we made our obligatory trek to the Merrimack Restaurant. It is a typical old-style diner with a dense darkness that bespeaks years of conversations, important and frivolous, with deep booths, a waitstaff that has been employed there for decades, and truly great diner food. And it is the place where every potential presidential candidate, at one time or another, makes a stop, or two, or three. John made his early, and it was recorded by CNN and *USA Today.* He and I sat in the back corner booth while two reporters peppered him with questions. Susan Page from *USA Today* said, "We've got the most recent poll from New Hampshire and you're at one percent. Why in the world should anyone take you seriously as a possible presidential candidate?"

John wasn't the least defensive. "What's the margin of error in that poll?" he asked.

"Three percent," she said. You could tell from her tone that she was anticipating his excuse that he could be as much as four or five percent in the poll.

Instead, he said, "So if I'm one percent, and the margin of error is three percent, I could actually have negative support?"

"Yeah," she said, laughing, "I guess that's true."

Instead of moaning or making excuses, he had taken a swipe at himself even bigger than the one she had taken. And that was the attitude we had. You give this your best effort, but the fact that it is important doesn't mean that you are important. You have fun at the same time, and you cannot let yourself think it has anything to do with who you will be when it is over, one way or the other.

We began that weekend by meeting the local faces connected to the names we had read over the years. There was a Lou D'Allesandro, whom we would court for months to come — the warm Italian American, with hands like my father's, always

355

outstretched, and his incredibly patient wife, Pat. We came to know of their children and their grandchildren, his daughter's wedding and his brother's illness, and we stopped thinking about them as political contacts urged by the staff and started thinking of them as friends. And here's how I know: as I type Lou's name, or Sharon Nordgren's or Lucy Hodder's, it is hard not to look in my Rolodex and find their numbers and give them a call. Yet if I did this throughout this book — and I have weakened more times than I want to admit to my editor — I would never finish it. John didn't win them all. Peter Burling, whom I greatly admire, finally came with John, but only after his friend Dick Gephardt left the race. Dan O'Neill, who belonged to John's brother's union, the IBEW, would never make the commitment, but, honestly, John still enjoyed seeing him, because though it was politics, it was also the only life we were going to get, and we were determined to enjoy it. And John enjoyed Dan.

John had his first house party that weekend in Manchester. Ed Turlington had convinced Chris and Kristin Sullivan to open their Concord house to us and, what's more, to invite their closest friends so that

John could introduce himself. It was like riding a bicycle for the first time: John could do it, he was nimble and athletic, but it wasn't always rewarding. Was he moving forward at all? As a senator, John had weekly town hall meetings — in North Carolina if he was there, in the Capitol for visiting constituents if he was not — so the give-and-take of the house party questions did not bother him. But these people were not just looking for answers to their questions. They were looking for a horse to ride in the 2004 primary, almost two years away, and many of them — most of them — would not decide anything on their first or second or third chance to check out each horse. They had seen it happen before, potential candidates testing the waters — some ran, some didn't. No need for them to get wet yet. All of this was new for us. Honestly, we didn't know anything about the process, and the withholding of support by people who clearly liked John left us less than sure-footed.

My role in this was to smile, shake hands, and make small talk. I could handle that. As John spoke in the living room, I stayed in the kitchen playing with the assembled babies — Jake Sullivan was not yet born, but there were plenty of babies — and I looked carefully at this precious house. Kristin had made café curtains and painted and stenciled the walls. Pictures were framed with handmade mats. They hadn't just let us into their house, they had invited us into their home, and when you let yourself feel that offer, it made all the reservations in the next room meaningless. Chris and Kristin probably had a lot of conversation after that day about whether to support John; I had already made up my mind about them.

It was a series of houses that weekend, repeating over and over what we had experienced at the Sullivans'. The last, in Nashua, at the Foster house, which was surrounded in every direction by ice, left us with lots of questions. Not about Joe and Marisa — they were terrific — but about this process and about what John needed to do, if he was to convince a constitutionally skeptical audience. One thing he would need, he said, was more concrete answers about where he wanted to go. The criticisms were easy, the solutions were not. So when we returned to Washington, John set about developing a real platform.

This was a year of politics and policies in our house. The meetings we had in our home were just like the meetings we had always had with the people on John's staff. I was on the inside, of course, because I was married to John, but in truth everyone was on the inside. In David Ginsberg's story of joining our campaign family, there is a clearer picture than I might draw. On New Year's Day 1998, David drove down to North Carolina to join the Senate campaign. It was his first time in the South other than traveling I-95 on the way to Florida, and everything was foreign to him. It was sixty degrees out, and he was wearing shorts; less than twenty-four hours earlier, he had been freezing at a New Year's party in New York City. His dad had helped him drive down, and he helped him bring his things into the hotel room, as David hadn't found an apartment yet. When his dad pulled away David had the oddest sense of complete dislocation. Not only was he in a city where he didn't know a single person yet, he was in an entire region of the country where he didn't know anybody. He had never been here before, and he had just committed to live here for eleven months based on a ten-minute phone call with some trial lawyer down in Raleigh. He was twenty-two and pretty scared. Within weeks of meeting us, meeting the campaign family we had assembled around us, all that seemed far in the past. David said it was as if he had gained two new families — the family of the campaign, with the team-like spirit of singular focus, then the additional layer of John and me on top of that. It was an amazing transformation, going from totally disoriented and lost to feeling right at home. And that wouldn't have happened if it weren't for the way we all treated one another, the sense of community in the campaign, and the personal care we all took with one another. Opening our home was just a symbol of opening ourselves to these people who had committed themselves to John. It was easy.

The rules at our Washington house were the same as the rules in Raleigh. If you are expected for a meeting, just walk in and announce yourself; don't make someone get up from the meeting to answer your knock. If you want something to drink or to eat, the kitchen is in there; you can have anything you want — as long as you fix it yourself. When we moved to the house on P Street in Georgetown, it was the same. The feeling in all these houses was a good one, with many threads of our lives crossing one another, from our personal lives, from the children's lives, from neighbors, from these young people — and older people — who were helping, and from friends. There was noise and life all around us in the meetings — the meeting might be in the library, but there was always another conversation in the kitchen, and the children coming in with book bags into the front hall. I participated, but I also listened and learned. All the little pieces I picked up fleshed out answers I would later give when I was on the road. All the anecdotes gave life to the policies, and I would tell them and retell them. After a televised town hall in Harrisburg, Pennsylvania, one man called in to say that it was probably easy to tell all those facts and stories since I had cue cards. My mother was furious, but I was just amused; I couldn't have cue cards at a town hall with a dozen questions. My cue cards were the hours and hours — days or weeks, even — I spent listening to these bright young men and women share what they knew with John and, by osmosis, with me.

And so it went for the next months. Between trips to Iowa and return trips to New Hampshire, there were meetings on health care and the environment, on domestic security and education, on the military and on the military family. This will sound strange, but the tone of the meetings wasn't actually partisan. I doubt many meetings like them are. The complexity of the problems that faced America was daunting and the solutions difficult. There was no room to find anything except the right answers. Again, I don't want to mislead; Emma Claire and I were sitting on the floor talking as Robert, James, and Derek were coming in and claiming chairs for yet another meeting. C-SPAN was on, as usual, in the background. There had been a Senate Judiciary Committee hearing. Emma Claire looked at the television and, at five, astonished me by asking, "Which one is Orrin Hatch?" I pointed him out, and she said he had a nice smile. "Politicians have nice smiles, Emma Claire," I said, "but you can't pay attention to that; you have to listen to find out if they have nice words, and the words have to . . ." I probably talked on for three or four minutes until, completely bored, she got up and went outside. It was the typical reaction I got from my children over the years. When Cate asked me a question, she had learned to complete it with, "One word, if you can, Mom. I don't need a dissertation." I may have left English graduate school, but I never stopped wanting to teach, and here was my — somewhat — captive classroom.

My main job for years to come will be — until I am nearly too old for it — raising children, but the raising of these youngest children took place with James Kvaal laying out the intricacies of health care policy and Orrin Hatch smiling from the television screen, with Adrian Talbott bringing by homemade olive oil for the children and the first bulky Internet telephones sounding their alarming rings, with John Auchard and me spread out across the library editing John's book *Four Trials,* piles of papers around us, Elizabeth Nicholas bringing lunch and dinner so we could meet a deadline, editing sometimes with the Disney Channel in the background and two small figures sitting cross-legged on the floor between us, watching Mulan or Hercules or Mickey himself. I can say all this without embarrassment at my parenting, as I spent the day in which I am typing this at two soccer games and a baseball practice. But the truth is that in the chaos and the openness of our house was a lesson for these children, the lesson we had taught the children before them, a lesson that would serve them well: let it all in. The boy with the hickey, the speechwriter with the tender little voice, the academic with the analysis of health care costs — let them all in. There's always room.

Of course, it was about to all come in,

into our lives and our house. John spent the fall talking one-on-one to his advisors, consultants, and staff. He would open the discussion about whether he should run for the Democratic nomination for president, and then he would let them talk. Miles, Nick Baldick, Jonathan Prince, David, John Dervin (who knew more about John than he did about himself), and Bruce Reed (who knew more about running a political campaign than the rest of us). Although it was not unanimous — Mike Donilon, for example, said he should run but should wait until 2008 — most of the opinions were that he should run now. John was so professorial in his questioning that even I did not really know what he would ultimately decide. And while he was deciding, he was laying out an agenda in a series of speeches on education, the economy, homeland security, even reform of the criminal parole system. The speeches moved the campaign forward, but they also did something else, something more permanent: they solidified the bonds we had been building. Jonathan was now firmly a member of this family; Stephanie Jones, who worked with John on the Judiciary Committee, brought her brilliance into the circle. Derek Chollet, who handled John's foreign policy in the Senate office, found a permanent seat at the table. Wendy Button joined us, bringing not just her skill with words but a gentle sensibility as well. There were the more experienced voices, too, people like Bruce Reed and Gene Sperling, and though they were welcome, would always be welcome, we knew that they had seats at lots of tables. I think of them as you might the children of an amicable divorce: they'd do Christmas at your house but Thanksgiving somewhere else. Others were somewhere in between. Peter Harbage, Tom Donilon, and Michael Dannenberg come to mind. We tried, not always successfully, not to ask more of any of them than they were ready to give. It was selfish, really; we liked them and respected them and didn't want them to have to make a choice that could leave us without their company and counsel.

The result was long Saturdays when Bruce might bring a six-pack of beer and Gene and Tom would find comfortable chairs. I would sit at my desk, Robert would be at the table with his laptop open in front of him, Jonathan would come in late but get the last chair, and John and Miles, as the last ones into the room, would be left with the ottomans, and John's speech on the economy would take shape. Nearly the same group reassembled on each subject, with

Derek taking the lead when the discussion was foreign policy, and Robert again in charge on education. The emphasis in the domestic policy discussions was always the same: close the gaps in the country.

There were counterparts in John's Senate office. John was on the Health, Education, Labor and Pensions Committee, and he was working on developing public service programs in high schools. Wade and Cate's high school had a public service requirement: students had to complete one hundred hours of public service — twenty-five hours a year — or they would not graduate. I was really interested in the policy, and I kept asking Robert, John's brilliant legislative director, about it. Robert would talk to people who were providing volunteer programs in different places, in order to figure out the parameters of the programs and how much it would cost. One day, when I was in the office, I went by to see Robert and ask how it was going. Robert answered that it turned out to cost about $2,000 a child to have a public service program. Whoa. I told him how the public service program works in our high school. One woman, a neighbor, Jane VanGraafeiland, runs the volunteer office. The PTA helps her out; I think she has even had paid assistance now and again. But the office really is Jane. Students who find it hard to schedule community service can do their volunteer work in Jane's office, taking telephone calls from people who have public service opportunities, making cards about the opportunities and posting them on the boards for other students, and making the confirmation calls when students turn in the hours they have volunteered. Jane found opportunities around the school for kids who had a job after school and couldn't manage volunteering except during study periods. The WELL offered lots of opportunities, from tutoring to planting to painting at the Learning Lab. The Senior Center across the street. The child care center in the nearby projects. There was plenty of need. And managing it all, one full-time employee for a school of two thousand students. I am reasonably certain Jane doesn't make $4 million a year, which is what she would be making if the federal government were paying $2,000 for each child. We needed to go back to the drawing board. This was Robert's baby and John's, not mine, so I left him with that. As positive an idea as it is — instilling in young people the habit of community service — I am pretty sure it never became legislation, probably for more than

367

one reason. One is politics. The well-meaning interest groups that have a vested interest in the $2,000-a-student programs are powerful. The second is politics. No potential Democratic presidential candidate would be allowed by a Republican-controlled Senate to have a significant legislative accomplishment while running. And, honestly, the opposite would have been true if Democrats controlled the Senate.

This was my role in the Senate office and in the campaign. We hadn't been in Washington for long, so we knew what public schools were like, we knew how crowded the emergency room is in a small city, we knew about bridges that needed repair and response to hurricanes and the elimination of coastal wetlands. And we brought those experiences to the table when policies were being discussed. When Michael suggested a College for Everyone program, John insisted on a work requirement, not because of something he'd read, but because of what he himself had learned. "I unloaded UPS trucks. It was the hardest work I ever did. I swept the mill, cleaning around men who stood at looms for six, seven, eight hours straight. The easier jobs in the cushioned chairs in the offices? Those, I learned, were for college graduates. Work is good, it made me do my homework." And the decision was made. It was all collaborative: policy and real life and all these voices, young and earnest, older, wiser. No one was ever ridiculed — I think I would have been first on the chopping block if that had been the practice. No one was ever out of order. So we got the best people had to offer, unfiltered.

As 2003 approached, there was a deadline of sorts: money raised in 2003 could be matched by federal funds, and if he wanted to run, an early 2003 announcement made the most economic sense. Andrew Young in Raleigh arranged for office space, should it be needed, and phone service, should it be needed, and a website, should it be needed, all to be available at the first of the year. Prospective staff, John Robinson for example, did not take other jobs, waiting to see what John would decide. Over Christmas, the staff called our house at least hourly. No, no decision yet. After Christmas, John and I talked. He had what he needed from other people. He needed now to consult himself, away from them, away from me, away from the children. He went to the beach for three days. Still the staff called hourly. Still my answer was the same. I wanted to end their misery, but I honestly didn't know. This was the presidency; I wanted him to ask himself every question he needed to about whether he was doing this for the right reasons, about whether he knew he could do this, because in the end it would be a solitary job. And I had told him I was with him whatever he decided.

CHAPTER 11
AMERICA, THE
PRIMARIES

THE PITCH

There can't be that much suspense in this: John decided to run. The announcement was January 2nd, so that January 1st we could first tell our friends, who gathered that day in our backyard. The press assembled on the street surely knew what John had decided when the cheer went up, but the public announcement was the next morning on the *Today* show. Our dining room became a television studio so that John could announce his decision and I could sit by him in support. After the show, John spoke to the press. I looked around the kitchen, and the staff had done what Wade's friends had always done: they had eaten everything remotely edible. My car was parked next door, so I slipped out and drove to Panera to get more breakfast food. As I walked out with two large bags, a woman nicely helped me with the door. When I turned around to thank her, she had this look on her face: *Didn't I just see you on . . . ?* Yes, I smiled back.

I made rules for the campaign. I didn't want the staff to ask John to do what he wouldn't normally do. Yes, he could walk to the creek with the children — he did that all the time. He could make pancakes, his Saturday-morning specialty, but he couldn't flip them on a stage. He doesn't wear hats much, so no hats. And — there was never any argument about this one — no costumes. Win as John or lose as John. That was sometimes easier said than done. Preparation for candidate debates was the worst, as some smart someone would come up with a line they particularly liked — and usually John liked it, too. Bruce Reed and Harrison Hickman were particularly clever. But then the whole debate preparation would be about how to get that line in. The experienced voices said that the after-debate analysis would turn on a sound bite, so John tried to use the chosen line. It wasn't until he stopped trying and was just John that he finally saw his support grow. It was a lesson he would not forget. Politics is not so different from other interaction; we sense the genuine and reject the manufactured, even when the manufactured is cleverly packaged.

The calendar was simple. In 2003, John would raise money and campaign in Iowa, where the first caucuses would be held, New Hampshire, where the first primaries would be held, and a collection of states — South Carolina, Oklahoma, New Mexico, Arizona — that would follow. At first he did most of it on his own; I stayed home with the children. Soon enough it would be my turn.

From the pieces I picked up listening to John and sitting in the policy meetings in our library, I wrote my first stump speech. My baptism would be at the Concord, New Hampshire, home of Tenley and Peter Callahan and their precious, athletic children, who would come in and out as I spoke — children were the only things for which I was prepared. It was an inauspicious start — David Ginsberg spilled coffee all over my fortunately dark-colored pants suit on the plane. C-SPAN, unable to get permission from the campaigns to cover the candidates' fund-raising events, covered the Callahan house party. My very first campaign event, and I had a camera on me as I spoke, and a huge microphone on a long boom followed me as I moved around the room meeting Tenley's friends. My conversation about the Teletubbies? Caught on tape. And I am caught on tape again wishing that I had a Noo-noo, a vacuum-cleaner-shaped robot that would clean Teletubby spills and make Teletubby beds. When I gave my speech, I stood with my back literally against the wall of the Callahan kitchen and rattled through it at breakneck speed, all the while twisting the notecard on which I had written an outline around my index finger until, forming a perfect tube, it was useless as a speech aid. There was a woman there with whom I had gone to high school, and I could not convince even her to support John. It was two years away, she said. She would think about it.

The thing about terrible is that there is only one direction to go from there. And lovely Tenley did not jettison me or, more importantly, John. Each time I did a house party, or later a town hall, I learned something about myself — and I learned something about the people with whom I was speaking. There are a lot of ways to have this experience, but I only knew one, the one I had learned growing up — open up, let them in, and find out what we share. You didn't have to be perfect, but you had to be open. But that made something political into something personal. I wanted Chris Black or Rob Nordgren or Deb Nelson to support John because I liked them and I knew they shared something important with John and with me. As with Paul Robitaille in Gorham, who grew up like John did, in a mill town in which the mills were closing, I fought for the connections and then I fought for the support, and I was disappointed when one did not lead to the other.

I made friends in New Hampshire: Kristin, Tenley, Lucy Hodder — at whose house I had my very worst house party — and Pam Yorkin, women who were simply fun to be with. And it wasn't just voters, it was staff, too. Meghan Scott, young enough to be my daughter, became a friend, as did our state director, Caroline McCarley — you have to like anyone who, as a child, would name her dog Hugo Black. And it was at a luncheon honoring Caroline that I met Colin Van Ostern. We would eventually convince Colin to be John's press secretary in New Hampshire. I knew immediately on meeting him that this was a young man to whom I could feel close. I was right. After all the primaries were nearly over, as Colin and I walked different directions to get to our respective gates at the Buffalo airport, knowing that this was likely the last time we would do this, I was simply sad. Not sad for the coming end of the campaign, but sad that there was no excuse now for Colin to be a part of our lives. I was wrong, though: Colin is still a part of our lives. I still see him at reunion parties — yes, we have them — and talk to him on the phone. And Meghan and Jay Heidbrink. And Pete Cavanaugh, who returned to Georgetown University after the election. Pete would stop by our house or, if we weren't home, leave notes on our car. I was used to a house full of young people, and in a sense that's what I still had.

As much as I liked the people, New Hampshire was always a struggle politically. It made sense that it would be. Howard Dean was from Vermont, John Kerry was from Massachusetts. There wasn't much oxygen left for other candidates. John was Sisyphus — everything we did was uphill. And sometimes it was a struggle because the campaign hadn't done what we needed, which led to some frustrating visits. There was one ill-planned trip when more thought had been given to the press than to the event. I was to meet voters at Dusty's, a diner in Claremont. We got there, and I met one supporter who wanted to say hello before he ran to an appointment. That was fine, I thought, until I moved into the room where I would "meet voters." My schedule should have said "meet voter." One elderly man, not always clear in what he said, was sitting at the table we'd reserved. And there were one television and two print reporters to capture this campaign low — or what I thought was a low until we left there and drove to a senior center to meet people during lunch, only to learn that we had mistimed it — it certainly wasn't because I had dawdled at Dusty's — and gotten there after lunch. With a print reporter still in tow, I spoke to the lone man there, who was sweeping the lunchroom.

The primary season was punctuated by candidate debates, and the first one was May 3rd in South Carolina. George Stephanopoulos, who moderated, immediately got John Kerry and Howard Dean to do what we knew their staffs had spent all week telling them not to do: they got in a spat. Dick Gephardt got in a plug for his health care plan. John got in his line in response — something about Enron. And in what seemed like minutes, it was over.

John and I left immediately after the debate. John was to speak the next day at the Kennedy Library in Boston, so the two of us took a chartered plane from Columbia to Logan Airport. As the pilots flew around a storm off the coast, we could see the skies light up. And in that vastness where the sky seemed alive and the heavens seemed open for a glimpse, we fell apart. It was Wade. It was how much he would have enjoyed all of this. It was how much we missed him. And it was the pressure of the moment, even with a decent performance behind him, that all came crashing in at once — and the illuminated sky was the perfect backdrop. We recovered, we always did. But the difficulty of talking to George Stephanopoulos or Tim Russert or Bob Schieffer will never compare with the difficulty of not talking to Wade.

In May 2003, I made my first solo trip to Iowa. We would always say that the people of Iowa were, at their core, so much like the people of North Carolina, and everyone assumed it was political rhetoric. It wasn't. We felt at home in Iowa. Brad Anderson, Aaron Pickrell, and Kim Rubey, John's Iowa press secretary, were with me when in Jim Larew's packed office in Iowa City, I just talked, like talking to friends from home, except that I gave Kim a start when I said, in the intimate way you would say such a thing, "Can we go off the record for just a minute?" In politics there is no such thing as off the record. When you say it in front of press, you might as well be shining klieg lights on yourself and announcing, *Listen up, this could be good.* I don't remember what I wanted to be off the record — maybe my comparison of John and George Bush's athletic history. All I remember is that it wasn't worthy of the newspaper, which made Kim very happy.

The summer of 2003, after countless Democratic dinners, forums, and debates, after dozens of polls in which John did not make the top one or two or three, our family took a two-week bus tour of Iowa and New Hampshire. In preparation, I bought the children a new round of play clothes to replace the ones with holes and stains, and myself something that was casual but — there is no other way to say this — First Lady–like. Needless to say, I had nothing like that in my closet. And I made copies of The Song Book.

Since I was in college I have been writing down the lyrics to songs. Before computers, I would take the lyrics down in shorthand, transcribe and type them onto notebook paper, and alphabetize them. Word processors made corrections easier, and then the Internet made the process almost effortless. The only qualification to get into the songbook is that I have to be able to sing it. "In-A-Gadda-Da-Vida" by Iron Butterfly is not, for example, included. Children's songs, old rock-and-roll, folk songs, country, bluegrass, and swing-era songs — my favorites — are all included. The songbook now includes the lyrics to well over five thousand songs. It takes more than one large notebook to hold them, so the day before the trip, I sat in my study and, with the help of Marc Adelman and Elizabeth Nicholas — who were young enough to keep me from including every song Jo Stafford ever sang — I made an abridged version for the bus tour. Marc made a cover — which included a mock bus with all our photographs in the windows, the last window filled with his cat, Bootsy — and we made enough copies to pass it out on the bus. I was ready.

I would like to say that I made everyone sing. But you can't actually make people sing, just like you can't actually make children sleep. You can put the children in bed, and you can hand the staff member, supporter, reporter, or whomever a copy of the songbook and hope you will get cooperation. So that's what I did. And we sang our way across Iowa, and then across New Hampshire. When Cate joined the bus trip a few days late, she looked at the stack of songbooks and said, "Oh my goodness, she's doing it to you, too." On family trips I was always the last one in the car. I would step in and then reach down and pull the songbook to my lap. "Not the songbook," Wade and Cate would wail, and I would always say, "It'll be fun. Where shall we start?" It was alphabetized. "How about J for John?"

And that's what I did on the bus. I handed staffer Josh Brumberger the songbook, and good-naturedly — he is monumentally good-natured — he sang "How'd You Like To Spoon with Me?" though the boy was born in 1979 and the song was written in 1905. Hunter Pruette, who traveled with John, recording his speeches and getting his sodas, used his cell phone's camera to secretly record Josh crooning, "Sit beneath an oak tree large and shady, call me little tootsy-wootsy baby." Miles Lackey, who plays concert piano and reads three biographies of historical figures rather than one so his opinion will not be skewed by a single biographer's point of view, could usually be convinced to sing only if we sang "Lemon Tree," the old folk song. He had held the songbook in his lap through dozens of songs, but after we sang "Lemon Tree," which has a limited range, he decided that would be the one we would sing. I couldn't complain; I couldn't get David Ginsberg to relent for even a single song. David, who had been with us longer than anyone, would simply sit there, his laptop propped on his knees, studying whatever it is that campaign staff study. John would constantly pick at him, teasing him, saying David's strategies were the reason that John hadn't surged in Iowa, and John gave him the nickname "Surge Protector," which we use still whenever David is taking things too seriously.

John Wagner and Robert Willett, from our hometown paper, were the most agreeable members of the press when handed a songbook — although I think John mouthed more than he sang. Even mouthing, I gave him credit. Adam Nagourney of the *New York Times* wouldn't even take the book. His interview with John was over; was "Good Night, Sweetheart, Well, It's Time To Go" going to ruin his journalistic impartiality? A little aside here about the press. I liked the journalists. I admired what they did. They seemed to be a lot like me, so I did what I always do when I like someone — I would seek them out. Once in Des Moines, Jennifer Palmieri, our press secretary, organized a casual get-together. I sat at a table lined with reporters from television and newspapers and wire services. When the conversation died for a minute or two, I asked everyone what they would do if they had to do something other than what they were presently doing. It sounds like a Miss America question, right? Well, no one balked. Ron Fournier would be a policeman like his father. Dan Balz would be an architect. So, by the way, would I. I remember that late afternoon as one of the most pleasant — and normal — in the entire campaign. The next day, one of them asked John what he would be. A sports reporter, he said.

After the Baltimore debate, I went up to Chuck Todd and Craig Crawford in the spin room, a large hall where journalists could talk to the candidates or their surrogates about how the debate had gone. But Chuck and Craig were off to one side, alone. "Don't you all need to be talking to someone other than each other?" I asked. Craig smiled. "How are we going to know what Conventional Wisdom is unless we talk to one another?" I doubt I could have gotten them to sing.

Aaron Pickrell, who ran the Iowa staff, and the entire Iowa staff, whenever they were on the bus, would sing. They were great sports about everything. Aaron would sing while bouncing Jack on his foot. Only

Brad and Patrick, also from the Iowa staff, could also manage that feat. Rob, who'll bounce his own baby when he returns from Iraq, was the most reticient. Johnny, who drove — and owned — the bus, was the music man, whether he sang or not. As we approached the site of a speech or a town hall, Johnny would turn on the music on the bus's exterior loudspeakers, which drew in everyone age seven through thirteen in the surrounding blocks — none of them, of course, voters. When he moved from bus driver to disc jockey, he would take off his driving hat and put on a cap with a long ponytail attached.

Brenda, his wife, was just as polite as he was mischievous. It says something when the best-dressed woman on the bus is the driver's wife. I could sometimes get Brenda to join in the singing. She had a prettier voice than she would allow, but whenever she would catch me pulling out the song-books, she would start preparing something in the bus's tiny kitchen to get out of singing. Brenda would feed us and feed us. She reminded me of the Cher character Rachel Flax in the movie *Mermaids* who, for breakfast, lunch, and dinner, served her daughters hors d'oeuvres. We ate sausages wrapped in just about everything. We had pizza shaped in every way except like pizza. We had stacks of cheeses and meats and crackers cut into quarter-size circles, so we could make the smallest Dagwood sandwiches imaginable. And I don't want to suggest we put our noses up. We ate it all. There were times when Randy Galvin, who watched the children, or Jennifer or Cate would beg Brenda to get some apples or something green, and she always would, but left to her own devices, it was pigs in a blanket. The only times her food was snubbed were when Sam Myers brought fresh corn aboard from a spot called Camp David in Iowa Falls and when we stopped at the Iowa State Fair. As John was giving a speech in the Iowa Falls restaurant, I was talking to the waitresses — since the customers were listening to John and no one at their tables was ordering anything. "That corn looks great," I said. "Came in about noon," one said. "Picked this morning," said another. She saw the look on my face, a look born of two straight days of appetizers-as-meals, and she said, "We can cook you up some." Without hesitation, I motioned to Sam. We still talk about that Camp David corn. And Brenda — and her tiny bus kitchen, it wasn't a fair fight — was also outdone by the Iowa State Fair pork-on-a-stick. It's called pork-on-a-stick, even though the stick is really the bone, but no one was quibbling. It was the best meat of any kind we'd ever had.

After Cate — who knew not to bother complaining, just join in the singing — Jennifer Palmieri was my most reliable singing companion. She would sing anything. She would sing anytime. Jennifer is also a child of a military family, but she is more like my father than me, jumping with both feet into every experience. She had moved enough to know the part of *The Great Santini* that is absolutely accurate for nearly every family: traveling in the wee hours and singing all the way. There are people who are so full of life that being around them either makes every moment delicious or exhausts you. Sometimes, admittedly, Jennifer would exhaust John. Sometimes, frankly, I would exhaust John. But she and I never exhausted each other, and I could pull out that songbook first thing in the morning or last thing at night, and she would start flipping through. "Ooh. Ooh. Ooh," I can hear her say, " 'Don't Sit Under the Apple Tree'! Let's sing that." Cate and I would reach for our songbooks.

Sam Myers, a Missourian who had been making trips like this longer than anyone, had the best voice on the bus — no surprise, as his parents were music teachers. Most of the time he didn't need the songbook; he already knew the words. Although Sam had made lots of bus trips, he might not have been on one like this before. When Jack got on the bus for the first time, he gave Sam the once-over — checking out his hunting vest, the pockets filled with all the items Sam had needed in emergencies on previous trips, asking what the hair was that was growing under his nose — until he noticed Sam's woven sandals and asked, "Why are you wearing girls' shoes?" From that point on, Sam and Jack were a reliable comedy routine on the bus. Sam would be pointing out the route to Johnny, the driver, and Jack would be in his lap and in his way the whole time.

When James Galvin, Randy's husband, brought his guitar out, he controlled the song list, which meant that the songs were keyed to a younger generation. Cate and Josh and Hunter and Aaron knew all the words, and by and large, I knew none. But that didn't matter. I liked the great sense of fun that music brings, creating a community chorus that crisscrossed Iowa between oceans of cornfields and then navigated the narrow roads and sharp turns in the mountains of New Hampshire.

Colin Van Ostern, the New Hampshire press secretary, calculated that, during the one-week New Hampshire bus tour, we drove 1,757 miles, went to twenty-six towns for house parties and other events, had ten town hall meetings, had forty stops, 168 cans of Diet Coke, and 245 bottles of water. And through it we sang. Colin took Kim Rubey's place. Meghan replaced Brad — and was a more agreeable singer. Some of the people who came on the bus for a day, such as Sharon Nordgren and Lou D'Allesandro, never got handed a songbook, because we were trying to get their support and someone thought when we had the songbooks in our hands we looked less like a campaign than a family on vacation. Exactly, I thought. It was that feeling of being a real part of something, something the candidate himself was a part of, not remote from, not smiling down from the mezzanine boxes, that constituted part of the campaign's magic.

The bus was a moving G-rated pleasure palace. Emma Claire and Jack each had someone to watch them at events — Randy and Elizabeth Nicholas most of the time —

so that John and I could talk and meet caucus-goers. They claimed the back of the bus, with the long benches on which to take naps and watch DVDs. Many a time John would have three or four reporters on a leg of the trip with us, but he would give separate interviews. The reporters-in-waiting would be banished to the back of the bus, where they would watch Kipper, the most civilized dog in the cartoon world, with the children. When John gave his first speeches, the children watched from that rear perch, opening the back windows. Having the children with us — which we did on weekends and when school was out — was good for all of us. And it was best for John. The family feeling was not one we lost because, well, we were a family. So sometimes the children would invite other children onto the bus during an event, as they did in Tama, Iowa, and sometimes when the children would tire of events, we would give them time away from the bus. Meghan, Randy, and I took the children to the Lost River Gorge caves in New Hampshire. With the steep drop-offs and bridges over gorges, I spent an entire day nervous. We thought there would be a lot of hiking, but we were wrong. There was a lot of crawling. Emma Claire and Jack gleefully climbed through caves and around rocks on their hands and knees — followed, I have to admit, by Randy and Meghan, whose combined ages didn't add up to mine. I got good at saying, *Meet you on the other side.* The children went skiing on another trip with Chris Black. And swimming at Bev Hollingsworth's daughter's house. A campaign for John, a vacation for them.

As John campaigned, it was not unusual to meet up with people who were not going to be with you in the election. John was doing a town hall in Durham, New Hampshire, when I spotted a man with a video camera — not unusual — who had been at the last two events — unusual. One of the staff asked him if we could help him with anything, and he said no, he was just the Republican tracker. His name was Steve, and he had been hired to follow John and tape his public events. Oddly enough, even Steve became part of the family. We'd walk in somewhere, and there he would be, sitting right in the front so he could get a clear shot. Hey, Steve. Hey, Mrs. Edwards. After months of hearing John talk, he even allowed that he thought John made sense and he might even vote for him.

We kept plugging on, despite events with

only a few people, despite low poll numbers. In late summer there was a labor rally in Iowa attended by all the candidates. John Kerry spoke before John, and the head of the union, who introduced the candidates, handed Kerry his personal $1,000 contribution when he introduced him. Geez. This was a group — working people — to whom John could appeal, and their president sent a clear message to go another way. With all of the polls putting Howard Dean on top and Dick Gephardt next, Kerry and John were fighting for the third spot, and it was certain that only three of them would come out of Iowa with their campaigns alive. When John started speaking, the crowd sat back in their chairs, arms folded. It didn't look good. But as he spoke, they leaned forward, and then they started applauding what he was saying and finally they were on their feet. It was good, but the numbers didn't change.

We continually worked on our speeches. John was starting to frame his stump speech in new language, using a phrase he had heard Christina Reynolds, who had been with us since the Senate campaign, use after she heard John talk about two school systems, two health care systems, two tax codes, one that benefited the rich, the other for the rest of America: It was Two Americas. And it was the beginning of a speech that would electrify audiences, but was it too late?

Campaign momentum would constantly be broken by debates. It wasn't all bad. It meant television coverage, more people seeing the man, hearing the message, but it was also completely out of control. A one-hour debate would consume half a day and might result in John speaking for four minutes. And the questions were not the questions that we heard at town halls; no one there asked about polls or about money raised, and yet part of nearly every debate — and sometimes nearly all of them — would be these process questions, all inside-baseball, all irrelevant to most voters.

We drove in a van to Baltimore for a debate, and fifteen people had to stay quiet for the trip because John was on an hour-long telephone call from Bill Clinton, who was giving his advice on the debate. Sam Myers may have been used to being still for long periods, but it was painful for Jennifer, Jonathan Prince, and honestly me. In the New York Pace University debate, Cate and I sat in front of the Sharpton family. At each debate there was a different lineup of candidate families — Jane Gephardt and I were the most reliable, then Teresa and Gert Clark, but this was the only time I had seen the Sharptons. Al would be holding forth onstage and Al's two daughters would be saying, *Just answer the question, Daddy. That's no answer. Oh, Daddy.* It was pretty clear that Al got the same amount of grief from his daughters as John got from his.

John had a brutal schedule. Once when he was in Washington, we walked down to M Street to eat dinner. In the narrow, heavily traveled streets of Georgetown, we each had hold of one child, until John Kerry's car pulled up alongside us. Kerry jumped out on the corner of Prospect and 34th. While I held both children, he and John talked about how hard it was to get heard in Iowa over the clamor for Dean. People say I should drop out, Kerry said. Will he? I asked after the Kerry car drove on and the traffic juggernaut it had caused dispersed. No, John didn't think so. But, he added convincingly, it's hard to keep going when nothing's going your way.

Not much was going John's way. We had a core of supporters in Iowa and a core in New Hampshire, but as Dean's rocket was taking off, the pool of people from whom we could try to garner support was dwindling. By November, it looked like the big unions were going to go with Dean, unions that might have — with a different tableau — gone to Dick Gephardt or to John, based on their policies and histories. The whole ship was tilting. We kept plugging in the same way we always had, but the holiday break was welcome. We called the campaign office in Washington to find out who was staying in D.C. for Thanksgiving, and then we called the "Thanksgiving orphans." *Dinner will be at 1* P.M., we said, *don't be late.* Cate and I put together a menu, and whenever one of the staff arrived — Miles or Marc Adelman, Jennifer Swanson or James Kvaal — we would hand out assignments: stir the mashed potatoes, fill the water glasses. Then John and I sat down with the staffers and our children — in other words, our family.

It was that Thanksgiving weekend, though, that John and I sat one quiet afternoon in our house in Washington and talked about whether he would stay in the race. There is a tired you get when you are working hard but you are seeing the product of your work, which buoys you. We were not that kind of tired. We were just plain tired. There was no payday in this. Should he get out? I didn't think so, for all the same reasons I had believed in him before.

"But we're not gaining anywhere; how do we get any momentum?"

"Remember Gephardt?" Even Gephardt told John to remember Gephardt. On November 15th, as we had stood backstage at the Iowa Jefferson-Jackson Day dinner, a huge Democratic dinner that — once every four years — is a cheerleading contest between the various campaigns, John and Dick talked. "Don't worry about the numbers now," Dick said, "things move quickly in Iowa." He should know. Dick had come from nowhere before Christmas to winning the Iowa caucuses in 1988. We wanted Dick to be right, of course. After singing "Happy Birthday" to Jennifer Palmieri at a staff dinner after the Iowa Jefferson-Jackson festivities were over, Dick's encouragement was the topic of conversation.

We'd just keep working. It would happen, or it wouldn't.

We didn't become panicked. In fact, the polls released a lot of pressure. To give you an idea of the relaxed mood, the morning after Jennifer's birthday, Emma Claire kept interrupting John's preparation for an interview. It might have been fine, except that C-SPAN was filming the preparation. Emma Claire wanted to know what Jennifer's husband had gotten her for her birthday. "I don't have a husband," Jennifer said. "What did your boyfriend get you?" "I don't have a boyfriend." "Why," Emma Claire wanted to know, "doesn't anyone like you?" It was all caught by the C-SPAN camera, and Jennifer's love life, or absence thereof, was shown nationwide on *Road to the White House,* like a very targeted personal ad: WFS — Democrat.

And it turned out that Dick Gephardt was right: things can change in Iowa quickly. After Christmas, the crowds at John's events started to increase. We didn't have any money for polling, but we would hear from other campaigns that John's numbers were creeping up. John had tried to set a positive tone in his dialogue with other Democrats — no reason for them to stand in a circle and shoot at one another, he figured. And his decision had kept the other campaigns fairly positive. But as the caucus date — Monday, January 19th — approached, negative campaigning started. Dean was losing ground, and he struck out. Gephardt hit back. We would come into the hotel room, turn on the television in those last days, and shake our heads. If this works, John loses. But it didn't seem like John was losing. The crowds were bigger and bigger for each event.

On January 6th, the *Des Moines Register* held a candidate debate. It was enormously important. Caucus-goers would be polled a little more than two weeks later, and more than three-quarters of them watched more than half the debate. It was a very good debate for John. Anyone could see his strength, his personality, his warmth. Everything came through. He had shut down his advisors thirty seconds after they began proposing sound bites for the *Register* debate. *I don't want lines,* he said, *I just want to know facts. Give me the facts and I'll go out there and be myself.* And he was great.

The following weekend I was back with the children in Washington when very late on Saturday night John called. "You are talking," he said, the excitement in his voice unrestrained, "to the endorsee of the *Des Moines Register!*" The editorial in the most important newspaper in the state was titled "John Edwards — His Time Is Now." We'd been telling ourselves for so long that John was the voice we needed, and finally — I'll be honest with you — here it was, the first really objective positive thing that had happened. I am surprised I didn't wake the children, I was so excited. And in New Hampshire the staff celebrated, too, Colin buying wine for the staffers of other campaigns who were at Cotton with them getting the news on their BlackBerrys as he and Meghan were cheering.

We weren't doing polling but Kerry was, and he knew the race was no longer between Dean and Gephardt; it was between Kerry and Edwards. Dean didn't do well in the debate, but it didn't matter, really, as the tide had shifted. And though we had no polling that confirmed the shift, we could tell because of the crowds. The crowds that had been coming to John's events on word of mouth about his message increased geometrically after the *Register* endorsement. The places Sam had selected weeks before for events were now too small. The crowds that in December had been thirty, forty, maybe fifty people, went to two and then three hundred. I was campaigning separately with a two-man staff, driver Tommy Vietor and navigator Brad Anderson. We would be in a library with thirty people and hear that John had five hundred. We were stuck outside the town hall in the snow in Centreville — Tommy having misplaced the car keys — hearing that there were seven hundred people at the next rally. No one had seen anything like it — three hundred to seven hundred, then one thousand, then fifteen hundred.

There would be overflow crowds, and John would give two speeches instead of one at each stop. I still had a separate schedule, and I was in Clinton, Iowa, a river city, at a Democratic hall, talking to about forty people, when Brad got a call about a new poll — John had passed Dean. We stood there in the muddy parking lot and the freezing cold, remembering all the events that had disappointed us for months and how incredible the moment was. We headed then to join John at the National Czech and Slovak Museum in Cedar Rapids, where he was to have a rally. I sat in the backseat, eating a tangerine, happy that people were finally seeing in John what I saw, when I noticed that the tangerine juice had made a huge stain on the front of my shirt. There was no way to cover it up. Can we find a place with Shout Wipes? Tommy pulled into a discount grocery store where items are sold in case lots. No Shout Wipes. Iowa is a beautiful state, but it is not the shopping capital of the country. We drove on, looking for a clothing store, a regular grocery, anything — no luck. We were getting close to the museum. Then I spotted a Goodwill retail store. Stop here, I said. Brad and Tommy looked at each other. Here? Yes, stop here. I went in the Goodwill and bought a sweater set for three dollars. I put it on in the dressing room and wore it to that event.

I am so glad I didn't miss that event. It was in a square room with a platform for John. The room had very high ceilings, and Edwards signs covered the walls. The line outside the double doors at the hallway was backed up for twenty feet as people tried to get into an already full room. The press was crowded against the walls as more people poured in. At the far corner of the room open double doors led outdoors. There, people were standing in the snow, jumping up in the air periodically to see. I had been traveling in my own little polite and orderly world — I'd go to a library and people were nice to me and then I would go on to the next event. This was my first taste of what John was living through. After John spoke, people were tearing the signs off of the walls. They were handing up anything that could be signed — napkins, envelopes. Here's the back of my deposit slip, sign that.

They couldn't get enough, and John couldn't get out. As Dick Gephardt had predicted, lots had changed in Iowa.

The following Sunday when the *Des Moines Register* headline was "Kerry, Edwards Surge," the world, which was already fireworks all the time, erupted further. John had a staff meeting to thank these incredible Iowa staff — young people who had stuck in there through months of single digits in the polls. The campaign office was a converted auto parts store with one working bathroom — on good days — right on a major thoroughfare. We could hardly get in because there were so many TV cameras. Every press person you've ever heard of was there. Tom Brokaw knocking over George Stephanopoulos, Kelly O'Donnell screaming for her cameraperson, Tim Russert waving at the children. I stepped back to look at the chaos, and a polite Japanese reporter came with his cameraman. "Why," he said, "do you support Senator Edwards?" "Well, I have lots of reasons, but one of them is that I am married to him." Surprised, he asked a question or two more, then ended by saying, *"Domo–arigato."* To which I responded, *"Do–itashimashite."* One word in

401

Japanese generated another five minutes of questions.

The Iowa caucuses take place on a Monday evening. It makes the Monday important and useless at the same time. Basically, you have done all that you can do, and the day is often spent making certain your supporters will turn out that night. We had a morning of television scheduled in which we would do that reminding. John got up first, showered, and left for a series of interviews. My first appearance would be on the *Today* show, an interview with Campbell Brown. I showered and dressed. I had lost my hairbrush the previous day, but we had stopped at a drugstore and, from a meager selection, I hurriedly picked the best replacement. And now I was standing in front of the mirror at the Hotel Fort Des Moines, drying my hair and trying to style it with this new brush. I reached around to the back of my head, wrapped the damp hair around the brush, and held it there while I aimed the dryer at the brush. And then, as I have done thousands of times, I tried to pull the brush away. It wouldn't come. I put the dryer down and tried to work the hair loose from the brush with my fingers, but the brush was in the back of my head and I couldn't see which way to work. Five minutes, then ten, and the brush was still there. I was alone and due downstairs soon. I called Jennifer, sure she could fix it, but she didn't answer — she had gone with John and, during his interviews, had turned her phone off. I called Miles Lackey, John's chief of staff, in his room. Hearing the alarm in my voice, he hurried down. Now, Miles grew up with only brothers, he was balding, and he hadn't any notion how to help. He pulled and wrestled with the brush, but it did no good. Then I had another try, and he would BlackBerry Jennifer in panic. I couldn't go on television with a hairbrush sticking out from the back of my head. Finally he spotted a fork, left over from a meal someone had eaten in our room the night before. He washed it and used the tines to pry the hair loose from the hairbrush. Every yank hurt, and every yank was bliss. Finally it was out. I combed my still-damp hair with John's comb and hurried downstairs. With only a minute to spare, I fell into the seat opposite Campbell. I have no idea what I said or how I looked; I only know that I was no longer wearing a hairbrush.

Cate had exams at Princeton, so we spent most of caucus evening on the phone with her, reporting what Miles, Rob, David, Aaron, and Jennifer were hearing from the people in the field. And it looked good. John, who had been a distant fourth a few weeks earlier, was a close second in Iowa. We had heard, through one of Kerry's field generals, that if the caucuses had been three days later, the places would have been reversed, so pronounced were the trends. But we were not unhappy. Dennis Kucinich called first, then Dick Gephardt, and then Howard Dean, all congratulating him. John called John Kerry to say, "Good race." And then each of the candidates went out to speak. The great showing was John's, but it also belonged to the Iowa staff. Rob Berntsen was the oldest person on the Iowa team, and he was thirty-two; most of them were in their early twenties, some were paid, some volunteered, and they worked every bit as hard when John's numbers were at 5 percent as they did at the end. John's speech was a tribute to them. But there was no rest. We left the stage and the state, and at 1:30 A.M., in a hangar in Concord, New Hampshire, we had a rally.

By seven the next morning John was in front of a television camera again, about to be on the *Today* show. As he waited to be interviewed, through his earpiece he could hear Katie Couric and Matt Lauer talking about Howard Dean. John had no idea what they were talking about. John spoke in Des Moines and we went straight to the airport. We were probably the last people in America to hear about what came to be known as The Scream. I want to be clear: The Scream did us no good. We had always heard that two stories come out of Iowa, and what we wanted was for John to be one of them. If The Scream hadn't happened, Kerry and John would have been the stories coming out of Iowa, since they had garnered 70 percent of the caucus-goers between them. Since it did happen, Kerry and The Scream were the stories. And there was no New Hampshire bump. All the might-have-beens.

We thought there might be a bump anyway. The crowds in New Hampshire that week rivaled the Iowa crowds. The locations again were too small, but I was traveling with John more, and I would take John's overflow crowds and answer their questions in a warm-up town hall. One of his first post-Iowa town halls was in a high school gym. Glenn Close was traveling with us, entertaining the children with her Cruella

De Vil persona from *101 Dalmations* and taking her not inconsiderable knowledge about health care to forums as John's surrogate. She and I were crouched on the stage as John began, but Miles came and tapped us on the shoulder. *Could we go to the overflow room?*

The overflow room was a whole other gym, and the bleachers there were filled with four or five hundred people. I saw Jonathan Alter, whom I admire greatly, come in. I memorized where he was sitting and then never looked there again. It was possible to look at Sandy Mucci like she was someone from my hometown and just talk to her. It was impossible to look at Jonathan Alter and use that same conceit. The first question I got asked was from a Lyndon LaRouche supporter about why we wouldn't let LaRouche on the Democratic ballot. The crowd, tired of LaRouche supporters disrupting town halls, started booing the questioner. I asked them to stop. People can ask anything. And then I turned to her and said, Candidates don't decide who is on the ballot, but if it had been up to me to decide, he wouldn't be on the Democratic primary ballot — he's not a Democrat. It set the tone for everything after that: there was no restriction on the questioning. Miles hadn't actually seen me do a town hall, and when he came back in to see how I was doing, I was answering a question on North Korea. He listened and left. I'd be okay.

Exams at Princeton were now over and Cate was campaigning with her father and on her own. Her roommates and a dozen more of her friends from Princeton — Sun Jung, Adrienne, Courtney, Hayden, Erica, Jenna, Catesby, George, Steve, and others — had come up to New Hampshire to canvass in the record low temperatures, joining their friend Pauly, who had been there for six months. John had a rally in a church in Portsmouth, and Cate's friends, who were volunteering all over the state, all came. And listened, most for the first time, to what their friend's father was saying. They heard him talk of Two Americas and say it didn't have to be this way, and many were moved to tears. I'd seen it happen over and over — the effect of hope, but it was different to see these young people — clearly on the soft side of the Two Americas — take hold of John's message.

Months before Laurie McCray had told me that she had narrowed it down to three candidates and John was in those three. She was smiling, as if that was good news. Not good enough, I told her. She would come to town halls and ask about nursing, the profession she loved but had left. And maybe then it was down to two. And finally Laurie came on board. She and her son Michael, who is now a happy, handsome teenager, had a pleasant, organized, busy life, and she was managing a lot — including Michael's extra chromosome — to make that so. But when Michael, seeing John again at another town hall, would reach to hug him and John would grab him and give him a bear hug back, I could see the beginnings of tears in Laurie's eyes. Life was harder than it should be, and it didn't have to be this way.

We still weren't polling, but we knew we hadn't cracked the Kerry-Dean juggernaut in New Hampshire. The night before the primary, the entire traveling entourage — Sam and Jennifer, Miles and Colin, Hunter, Jay Heidbrink, Meghan and John and I — worked until there was no one left to talk to, and then we started looking for dinner. John wanted to go to Outback Steakhouse and a bookstore. It is nearly eleven, Hunter said. Okay, just an Outback. They were closing the restaurant when we arrived, but they kept it open and cooked for John — and, since we were there, the rest of us. In the nearly empty restaurant we sang and laughed as if we had reason to celebrate early. Which we didn't.

Though room after room would be closed by the fire marshal because the crowds at John's rallies had gotten so large, though at event after event crowds of people had to be turned away, there was no bump from Iowa. Kerry finished first again, then Dean. Clark, who had skipped Iowa and concentrated on New Hampshire, beat John by less than eight hundred votes. It was January 27, 2004, and we were headed South and West with no momentum. A week later there were primaries in five states and caucuses in two. People and organizations that had endorsed Dean when he was on top were bailing out, but it wasn't helping us, as they were signing on with Kerry, who was now on top.

So it was on to South Carolina, and John Moylan or Robert Ford or Bill Clyburn taking one or the other of us to beauty shops and university campuses, farmer's markets and diners. And then I was on a plane to Oklahoma and then, nearly as soon, to Missouri and then New Mexico. There was less than a week before the primaries, and there was too much ground to cover. I knew it almost didn't matter how well I did. I watched the Super Bowl between the Patriots and the Panthers in New Mexico, and first thing in the morning, I flew to South Carolina. I arrived in time to watch the clock wind down in Columbia. John won in South Carolina and gave one of the best campaign speeches of the year that night. But, except for Oklahoma, Kerry won elsewhere. It was going to be hard to derail that train.

There were primaries in Tennessee and Virginia the next week. Again, I campaigned on my own, in Norfolk and Virginia Beach. My cousin Robert and his wife, Rachelle, helped with a women's luncheon attended by one of Cate's first-grade teachers. I left energized; we might be down, but we could still do this. The volunteer driver, a handsome college boy, dropped me at the airport so I could fly to Richmond for a Democratic event that night at which all the candidates would speak. I was still feeling great, until my flight was canceled. I called the office. *Any other flights?* No, but just wait, they'd said; they would figure it out. *That's fine, but I'm not waiting. It's not far, I'll rent a car.* And I hung up. By the time the office reached me I was on I-64 headed west. Before the event in Richmond, the Governor, Mark Warner, endorsed John Kerry. And again in Virginia and Tennessee we finished second. Now we were headed to Wisconsin.

We headed to Wisconsin a little earlier than John Kerry expected. When the first numbers from Tennessee and Virginia started coming in, we flew to Milwaukee. We were at a rally at the Slavic Center when John called to congratulate Kerry. Kerry was floored. "You're in Wisconsin? The primary was today. What are you, the Energizer bunny?"

Wisconsin wasn't a last stand, though it came close. The primary was two weeks away, and unlike the previous weeks, we could concentrate on one state. Home base would be the Pfister, a refurbished hotel with a large lobby that served as the meeting place for press and children and staff. And best of all, our niece Jordan, my sister's youngest, was the staff person in charge at the hotel.

I spent two weeks driving around Wisconsin, talking to as many people as I could. Donsia Strong Hill helped set up meetings, and Brian Brooks drove me — using

Mapquest directions faxed to him from Raleigh, which often left us on the wrong side of lakes. *Um, Oshkosh is right over there,* he said, pointing west over Lake Winnebago. When Meghan and Jennifer joined us, it became the girlmobile. We sang — without the benefit of the songbooks — and Brian was a good enough sport to join in.

When we were near Milwaukee, I would try to stay at the Pfister so I could see the children. But the children were being well cared for without me. I came in and dropped my suitcases one time, and Jordan pointed to the nearby couches. I walked over and there they were, Emma Claire and Jack, one on either side of Nick Anderson, a *Los Angeles Times* reporter. He was reading them a book. He looked up and said, "Miss my own kids. You don't mind?" Of course not, and sat with them.

"So," he asked, "what would be a victory in Wisconsin? A thirty-point loss?"

"I'm an optimist."

"A twenty-point loss?"

"I'm an optimist."

"You surely don't think he'll win."

"I'm an optimist."

John was getting good crowds, and he had positive interviews with several newspaper editorial boards. I felt good. The *Milwaukee Journal Sentinel* debate went well. After the debate John was still standing onstage, cameras still running, when Howard Dean came over and said, "We've got to get together." John asked when, and Howard said, "Whenever you want." "How about tonight, then?" Howard agreed. He said he wanted me to be there. I think Howard might have been skeptical the first time I told him I had known his brother, who had been killed in Laos, when we were both at UNC, but Gerry Cohen, whom we had both known, had made a scrapbook of Charlie's time at UNC and sent it to Howard, who was no longer skeptical — I'd been friends with his brother, and that was good enough for him. I understood completely.

That night we went out to dinner with the children and Chris Downey, a good friend from Washington. Our table was on a platform with curtains around it that the children were enjoying closing and opening. We knew Howard would come shortly. But before he did, four journalists, E. J. Dionne, Dotty Lynch, Walter Shapiro, and Meryl Gordon, came in and were seated at the table next to ours. I got up and told Sam that Howard couldn't come into the dining room unless he didn't mind this being public. Sam found another space, and when Howard arrived, we drew the curtains on the table, and John and I slipped out. We went up a darkened staircase to a private party room. It was empty except for chairs stacked on tops of tables, a bar, and Howard. We took chairs from the tables and sat. It's hard to explain the rawness unless you have been in the center of the storm, but there is nothing subtle at this point. We all knew why we were there.

John said, "Thank you for coming. When are you going to do something?"

"Well, you know, I don't know."

"It looks like you're going to finish third here, Howard. You know you'll have to get out of the race." Silence. Howard was grappling with all that was inside him, all that had been inside him since the extraordinary tower he had built started collapsing.

Howard did not think John Kerry should be the nominee. I don't know whether that was political calculation talking or the residual effect of the nasty campaign between them. But he believed that John, not Kerry, could beat Bush. Everyone was focused on Ohio being the big swing state. "The shop foreman in Ohio, those people will vote for you. They will not vote for Kerry," he said, "because they feel a connection to you and they don't feel any connection to him."

"But the way things are going, he will be the nominee, Howard. You have to do something. You can't just stand by and watch."

Howard paused. "When," he asked, "are you going to get traction? You beat me, but you lose here by about twenty-five or thirty points, it's over." Why should he go out on a limb for somebody who was not going anywhere? It was a perfectly reasonable question. What we didn't know — and he didn't know — is that it wouldn't be twenty-five or thirty points. It would be six. And Howard took eighteen percent of the Wisconsin vote.

We didn't push him. This was a deeply personal decision. Howard and I hugged, and the men shook hands warmly. Howard left, and John and I waited upstairs so that no one would see us leave with him. Howard was trying to talk himself into doing something. That's why he was there. But, John said, he's not going to do anything, and I agreed. He's grieving, I said. It was natural. Everyone assumed he had a completely clear path to the nomination. When we'd go back to Washington, *The Washingtonian* would have big articles about what a Dean administration would look like and who would be doing what. He'd been on the covers of *Time* and *Newsweek.* And then, in what seemed like an instant to all of us, it was over. And Howard knew that, but it was just too hard to let go.

What we didn't know was that around the corner, on Monday morning, the *Milwaukee Journal Sentinel* would endorse John. Unlike the *Des Moines Register,* which endorsed eight days before the caucuses, this endorsement was the day before the primaries, too late for us to add that endorsement to television commercials and signs. The public polling at that point — and we had no money for private polls — said that John was anywhere from twenty-five to thirty-five points behind.

By the afternoon of the Wisconsin primary, John had already started doing satellite television into the Super Tuesday states. He was in his chair in front of the camera when he saw the staff buzzing around whispering to one another.

"What are you all talking about?" he asked.

"We've gotten the first exit polls," Miles said.

"Don't tell me. We'll go to the room. You can tell Elizabeth and me both."

I was getting ready to go down to the coffee shop to have lunch with Meryl Gordon when they came in. The early exit polls were showing a virtual tie. John had won the expectations game. The press was stunned by this comeback, but again in the end, it was second. It was Kerry's face, not John's on television screens above the words Wisconsin Winner.

That night we didn't fly out at midnight.

Wisconsin, we knew, had been our best chance to turn the tide in the race for the nomination. It wasn't just Howard, we all played what-if games. What if the endorsement had come earlier? What if Howard had pulled out before Wisconsin, or Clark before Oklahoma or Tennessee? But those are parlor games. The real contest is out there, in America, and there, we knew, it was nearly hopeless. There were two more weeks until Super Tuesday on March 2nd, when California, New York, Ohio, Georgia, and six other states would go to the polls. I talked to Amy, the pretty, bright, and endlessly energetic woman who had been a leader in the Dean campaign in Minnesota, and John talked to their group; John might get their endorsement when Dean withdrew. I went to Maryland to campaign — like so many other states, I was able to say I'd lived here, my brother and sister were born here — but Maryland would go to Kerry. The point was to stay alive, and staying alive meant winning somewhere. The next week would be Louisiana, Mississippi, and Texas, and the public polling there still showed John with a significant lead. It was two weeks of insanity, really — stay afloat, stay afloat.

Larry King conducted a debate in Los Angeles with John Kerry, Dennis Kucinich, Al Sharpton, and John. Before the debate, I went to a forum of students, professors, and consultants and press run by Geoff Cowan of the USC Annenberg School of Communications. Geoff had been head of Voice of America when, three weeks before he died, Wade was one of the national winners of the contest VOA had sponsored with the National Endowment for the Humanities. Holding those little pieces together, as if my life made sense, as if Wade was still a living, changing part of it — *see, here he is in California* — filled me up and emptied me out at once. I'd always choose to have those moments, as when Wade's friends would drop by to tell me about a job or show me a picture of the girl they were planning to marry, but each time they took away a little of the conceit that Wade was just away somewhere, at school maybe.

We did these things in the last two weeks before Super Tuesday with the knowledge that this was Everest and we hadn't the right gear. The last debate, hosted by CBS in New York, was on Sunday morning. Again it was Kerry, Dennis, Al, and John. There was no audience; each candidate could have one person in the studio. I sent Cate. John was splendid. The last question was asked by Elizabeth Bumiller of the *New York Times:* "Is God on America's side?" Kerry answered, "Well, God will — look, I think — I believe in God, but I don't believe, the way President Bush does, in invoking it all the time in that way. I think it is — we pray that God is on our side, and we pray hard. And God has been on our side through most of our existence." Elizabeth turned to John, "Senator?" And John answered: "Well, there's a wonderful story about Abraham Lincoln during the middle of the Civil War bringing in a group of leaders, and at the end of the meeting one of the leaders said, 'Mr. President, can we pray, can we please join in prayer that God is on our side?' And Abraham Lincoln's response was, 'I won't join you in that prayer, but I'll join you in a prayer that we're on God's side.' "

That night Cate, Colin, now heading our press operation in New York, and I went out to dinner. We asked at the hotel where we should go, and they directed us through a garage door, down two blocks to an Italian place. Good, we thought — comfort food. So we sloshed through the cold rain and landed at a diner with a drag queen pianist dressed — honestly — like a clown, singing the songs from *The Sound of Music*. The food was dreadful, and the place was smoky, and Cate and I just looked at one another. Back at UPS!

It wasn't the only misstep that week. I had campaigned in Ohio with Chris Redfern, the state legislative leader who, like John, will not age, and Matthew Nelson and I were scheduled to take a flight back to Washington from Cincinnati. I had promised the children that I would take them to school in the morning. We boarded the plane, but the doors wouldn't close properly, so the flight was canceled. There were no other flights. I could go straight to New York, the office told me, but I had promised the children. Passengers from the flight were still standing around the counter, so I walked around saying, "We are renting a car; we'd love to have additional drivers if you want to drive to Washington." We only had one taker, a fellow named Dean who worked for the Republican National Committee, so Matthew, Dean, and I drove and talked and sang for the next ten hours. Ask me anything you want about Matthew's very large family; I now know all there is to know. When Nick Baldick found out I had ridden and spoken for ten hours with someone from the RNC, he grilled me for nearly as long. No, we hadn't said anything at all about the campaign, the candidates. Nothing. It was the forbidden subject. Most importantly, I got there to keep my promise: I took the children to school. And I paid for it the next day when I tried to do four or five events in New York, the last starting at 11 P.M.

The last days of the primary campaign were spent in Georgia. On primary day there was, as usual, little to do to influence the voting. Midday, Cate and I were looking out the hotel window when Jenni Engebretsen and Jennifer Palmieri came in to get us for lunch. *Look,* we said, *there's an Eatzi's.* Instead of getting bad food in Styrofoam containers, we could get good food in Sty-rofoam containers. How far is it? *Well, it looks like a couple of blocks,* I said. And it did look like a couple of blocks when viewed from the fortieth floor. Cate said, *You can come if you want, but we are definitely going. That's what we'd do if Dad wasn't running; that's what we're doing now.* The walk there wasn't too bad. But then we bought lunch, or over-bought, and four overdressed women had to haul bags of food along a broad thoroughfare back to the hotel.

The distance to Eatzi's was like the campaign: everything seemed closer; everything seemed within grasp when it really wasn't. On Super Tuesday, when the exit poll numbers from the various states started coming in, John and I were standing in a room at Georgia State University. John turned to me and said, *It's over.* I didn't say anything. He said again, *It's over,* making sure that I was getting the message. *This is over.* I didn't say no, but I couldn't say yes. It was his decision to run, it was his decision to stop running. I just wasn't very good at giving up hope. Having said the words aloud to me, he came close to saying them when he took the stage that night. And his near-concession went out to Minnesota shortly before the Minnesota caucuses began. John finished second there, too, and we got on a plane and flew back to Raleigh.

The plane ride back to Raleigh — David, Jennifer, Hunter, Miles, Jim Andrews, John, Cate, and I — was, oddly, magic. The campaign was over, we all knew, but it didn't matter. We were together, we were laughing; it was as if a weight had been lifted. We had had fun, we'd given it our best, we had made a difference, really. It didn't seem like we had just lost a presidential primary. That came two days later, that came in the quiet of the aftermath.

The next morning we spoke to the staff, first me, then John, and when his voice cracked, so did the room. And then we all went to Broughton High School, Wade and Cate's school, for the last rally. Here we were in front of all our friends, people who had stood with us through so very much for so very long. We tried to make it a celebration, and I think for some it was, but it was hard to look across that room, peppered with young people, their heads down, their cheeks streaked, and not wonder what if. All the near misses, Iowa, Oklahoma, Tennessee, Wisconsin . . . what if?

After we left Raleigh, the campaign office was cleared. Nick went home to Liz and his children. JRob to a new job. Rebecca, Sharon, Skye, Georgie, off to the next war. Boxes of memories were packed and posters came down, and the young people who had powered that engine went home or went on vacation. All of the people who had gotten strength from one another, working beside one another when it looked bad — and it looked bad much longer than it looked good — were scattered, and they couldn't lean on one another now. And those, I think, were the worst times. Because we weren't together.

But it wasn't long until we were together again. John started calling supporters right away, thanking them for coming with him and for staying with him. The magic returned when once again we had meetings at the house on P Street. If you can imagine family meetings at the dinner table, that is what they were. Sometimes contentious, always lively, but most importantly there was — and is — a circle of trust and comfort. We may have been talking about big issues and big things, but we were just people — friends — sitting around talking about how to move forward together. After a little talking about what if.

CHAPTER 12
AMERICA, THE
GENERAL ELECTION
IN THE STARTING BLOCKS

When John Kerry called my husband in Washington to ask him to be on the Democratic ticket with him, I was in Raleigh, in my doctor's office, lying on an examination table, dressed in a lovely blue cotton backless robe. It was 8:20 A.M. My doctor had agreed to see me earlier than the office usually opened, and my friend Ellan had gone with me to the appointment — we were planning to go out to breakfast afterward. I expected to take a late-morning flight back to Washington. As I was lying there, looking at the fluorescent lights on the ceiling, I heard my cell phone ring in my purse across the room. At the same moment I heard Ellan scream from the waiting room, where she had been watching television.

The nurse handed me the phone. It was Emma Claire. Fifteen words: "Kerry picked Daddy, he just called Daddy. Here's Jack. He wants to tell you, too." Now it was Jack's improbably deep voice. Mom. Yes, Jack. I swam all the way across the pool with my head out of the water. That's what he wanted to tell me. To him, these two pieces of news were roughly equivalent.

There is prelude, of course. Aside from the eighteen months of prelude that were the primaries. The previous week we had been to Disney World with Cate, Emma Claire, and Jack. It had been like hundreds of thousands of Disney World trips taken by families before us. Although John was recognized every once in a while — once as we were celebrating my birthday early at Cinderella's Royal Table — vacationers were mostly, and rightly, concerned with their children. It was relaxing. And then Mary Beth Cahill, John Kerry's campaign manager, called. Could John meet Kerry in Washington the next day? I'm with my family in Orlando, John said, I'll be back on the next day, on the second; how about that? No, it had to be July 1st. They would send a plane to get him; he could leave Orlando after lunch, meet with Kerry in the early evening, and return late that night. Of course John said yes. He'd said yes to an earlier Kerry request to meet with John's top financial supporters — a meeting where John Kerry was peppered with questions about whether he would choose John as his running mate. He'd said yes to a Kerry invitation to dinner at his lovely Georgetown home — fortunately before the press started staking out the house — where he and Kerry had excused themselves from Teresa and me at the table to talk privately about the vice presidential slot. He'd said yes to the vetting process, in which we had opened our tax returns, our records, our histories — again — to a team of lawyers and investigators. And so he said yes, he would go to Washington on July 1st. Cate and I would take the children to Toontown and Frontierland without him.

Thursday night when John came back from D.C., he was tired, but I was too curious to let him go to sleep before telling me what had happened. He related a positive but guarded meeting at Madeleine Albright's house. There was no ask, there was no commitment, but John felt good about the meeting. We woke the next morning to our last day in Disney World — with our four- and six-year-olds, with Cate, and also with Andrew and Cheri Young from Raleigh, who had come with us to Orlando with their own two young children. Four children under six will take your mind off almost everything. But not everything.

The evening of July 2nd we were back in Washington, and Cate began packing to move to New York and a new job. The children were slowly coming down from a week of character breakfasts and amusement rides. And John and I were reading in the paper that Kerry had met with "his choice" at Madeleine Albright's house Thursday night — and that the choice was Dick Gephardt, the only name in the perceived pool in town that night. Now, I could pretend that I was agnostic about this, that I did not care whether John was chosen, but I was not. I am like most wives: I believe in my husband. And this election was a fight for which we didn't want to be on the sidelines, as we had been in 2000, when there was very little role for the almost-chosen. As interested as I was, there was still life to manage. So Sunday night, Cate flew to New York to meet a moving van at her new apartment. And Monday morning John flew to Boston to give a long-planned speech, and, when he returned Monday night, we did our usual tag team with the children. I left them in his care, and that night I flew to Raleigh for a doctor's appointment Tuesday morning.

As I said, I was not agnostic. Monday night wore on as I restlessly padded around the Raleigh house. The Kerry campaign said that the selection would be announced by e-mail to supporters on Tuesday morning. The next eight hours could change the course of my life; I figured I could sleep tomorrow. So I walked into the family room to watch cable news, then back to the computer to press Search on Google News. Would the choice be leaked anywhere? Well, it was leaked, but in an unlikely place, an airplane mechanic's blog. Didn't know there were such things? The Internet is the most democratic medium we've ever known. A mechanic posted he had been in the secret hangar where the plane with the new Kerry-Edwards logo was hidden. But I didn't see the blog.

What I did see was a *New York Post* on-line article that came up about 2:30 A.M. It said Kerry had chosen Gephardt. I might have just gone to sleep then, assuming that once again John had been the nearly chosen, except . . . the *New York Post* article was oddly worded. There was no reference to a source for the information, and the byline said that it was from *Post* wire reports. The *New York Post* has a wire service? I didn't think so. So I stayed online for an hour or two longer, still re-pressing Search. No other news media picked up the article.

Nothing on the Internet. Nothing on CNN. Nothing on MSNBC. Finally, I went to bed as the sky was beginning to get light, figuring that whichever way this played out, a little rest would be good.

After learning from Jack that he could cross the pool with his head above water and from Emma Claire that Kerry had picked Daddy, I begged off breakfast, and Ellan took me to the airport instead. I was back in my D.C. house before lunch. Or at least it might have been my house. It was now filled with people I knew — our family and John's staff from the Senate office and from the primary campaign, all family, too — as well as with people I did not know, the people the Kerry campaign sent as John's first skeletal staff. Peter Scher, the new chief of staff, had gathered Mark Kornblau, who would be John's press secretary, and — happily — Sam Myers, who would be John's trip director again. They'd arrived at the house on P Street within a half hour of the Kerry phone call. There were six hundred cameras on the street, Peter said, though certainly there were fewer. Peter rang the buzzer. Nothing. He rang again. Nothing. John was upstairs showering; the children had left for summer camp for the morning. So with six hundred — or fewer

— cameras clicking away, they'd finally had to step into the house shouting *Anyone here?*

There were Secret Service agents already gathering outside, neighbors slowing their walk to wish John well. A woman from whom I had bought some suits during the primaries was on the doorstep with garment bags of clothes in case I needed anything else . . . and in case I wanted to buy them from her. Kevin, who cut our hair — and colored mine — came in case any of us needed him before heading out on the road for — well, we didn't know how long. Cate, who had spent the previous day unpacking her suitcase in New York, packed it again and headed back to Washington. Televisions were on in every room, with constant replays of Kerry's announcement of his choice at a rally. Dahling, who took care of the house, was laying out every snack food we had, and Matthew went out to get more. Lexi Bar and Miles were glued to John's side. Jonathan Prince and Ed Turlington, who weren't in Washington, were on the phone. Elizabeth Nicholas was answering the door and attempting to slow, if that was possible, the flow of people into our bedroom. It was loud and chaotic, and there wasn't anytime in the foreseeable future when it would be any different. By midafternoon, we had met John's new staff, gotten instructions from the Secret Service, talked to our parents, packed — without any real notion where we were going or for how long — and dressed the children.

John's chief of staff for the general election would be Peter Scher, a handsome, open-faced man with an easy smile. When his cell phone had rung the previous week, Peter had been driving to a Baltimore Orioles game with his wife, Kim, and two boys. He didn't recognize the number, but he answered anyway, and the first thing he heard was "This is John Kerry." A robo-call! Peter figured he had just gotten one of the automated calls with taped messages from candidates that campaigns everywhere use. "Oh, cripes!" Peter said to Kim. Then, from the other end of the line, "Is that the way you answer your phone?" Oops. It wasn't a robo-call. It was actually John Kerry, asking Peter if he would be chief of staff to the vice presidential nominee. Kim busied herself bribing the boys to silence, while Peter pulled over and talked about the offer. Would Kerry tell him who it was? No, he wouldn't. Peter thought about it, and, it is our good fortune, agreed to do it, blind.

The next days were so terrifically public that it hardly seems I could tell anyone anything that they didn't watch on television. We left our house about 3:30 in the afternoon. As we moved the children toward the door, I heard the television still on in the study. I went in to turn it off, but before I did I called to John to come look at the image on the screen. It was our front door, live on CNN. Just as we were to walk out that door, however, Jack, who is a congenitally cheerful child, tripped. He started crying and saying he wasn't going. John picked him up and told him he was going. More tears. We're going, son. And then John opened the front door. Jack, the natural politician in the family, took one look at the assembled cameras and the gathered crowd and instantly became again an engaging four-year-old. We came out of our house to a street full of black SUVs, television cameras from one end of the block to the other, and the spaces in between filled by our neighbors — neighbors who knew that they would be inconvenienced by the Secret Service in the months to follow — applauding and wishing us well.

The Pittsburgh to which we flew was not the Pittsburgh I remembered as a girl. I remembered working-class neighborhoods and soot from the factories that clung to your hair and the folds in your knuckles when you played outside. We were headed to the incredibly lovely Heinz farm, pristine and gracious. There was not a single thing not to like about this home. We stayed in a cottage next to the main house, and the children were in a perfect bunk room downstairs. Teresa played effortlessly with the younger children as they swam, and John Kerry and John had their first few minutes to talk alone as a team. Except for Teresa's eldest son, all the children were there. A few of Teresa's friends were there, including the lovely photographer Diana Walker. A person's friends can say very nice things about them, and having Diana Walker as a friend said a lot of nice things about Teresa.

The next morning — a truly glorious day — was the formal announcement. Both families, rows of children of all ages, gathered with the Pennsylvania hills as backdrop. If you judge a photograph in a campaign by how much pain it gives the other side, and many do, this was a painful tableau. Myself aside — I don't think I looked particularly good in a new suit that didn't quite fit me (could I possibly have gained weight since I tried it on the day before?) — this was an extraordinarily good-looking group. That didn't stop the criticism, of course. Later, when I got on the Internet, I read complaints that John and I were somehow using the younger children by bringing them to the formal announcement. This is one of the problems, of course, with the devolution of political campaigns into waves of assaults. Who, I had to wonder, would not bring their children to the announcement that their father was the vice presidential candidate? I imagined the conversation as years later the children looked at pictures of the event. "Where am I, Mom? Was I alive then?" "Yes, you were alive, but it was a little too important an event for you, so you were home with a babysitter." A lot of people I met in the following months would reassure me about the children, but they needn't have. The complaints rolled right off my back. Just like they did when there was a flap because Teresa tried to get Jack to take his thumb out of his mouth. He'd never done it before, but we were all doing things we had never done before. I didn't notice the thumb go in, and I didn't notice Teresa pull on his hand to get it out, but for goodness' sake, if someone I know wants to wipe one of my children's noses or tuck in a shirt or pull out a thumb, I am completely fine with that.

There were less happy times, of course, when we didn't bring the children. They did not, for example, come with us to Faneuil Hall for the concession speech four months later. I did not think they would one day look back and say, "So why didn't you bring us?"

I promise not to use the word whirlwind about shopping in twenty stores or spending two weeks touring Italy, but the next days campaigning were a whirlwind. Imagine that we had the national press corps and the international press corps traveling with us. The local press corps joined in wherever we landed. There were two families of children, young and not as young, and one of them, Alex Kerry, had her own film crew with her all the time. There were staff — John Kerry's and Teresa's established staffs plus John's nascent staff and not really enough seats in the staff section of the Kerry plane for all of them. And then there were Secret Service details, and details, and details. Getting us anywhere was like tying a bow around Jell-O. And so it was to Cleveland, and Dayton, and St. Petersburg, Florida.

And then it was New York. There was a fund-raiser scheduled for Radio City Music Hall. We had been told that at the end of the event the families would come on stage to sing Woody Guthrie's "This Land Is Your Land" with the entertainers John Mellencamp, Dave Matthews, and Jon Bon Jovi. Everyone knows the first verse, but we were going to sing four verses. So that afternoon, as we sat in the hotel room, Cate and I pulled out the songbook and started to memorize the verses. After we had learned them, we dressed for the evening. We got in the elevator with John and the Kerrys, and Cate and I remarked how hard it was to learn all the verses quickly. Everyone looked at us blankly. You didn't learn them? No, they hadn't. Cate and I gave sidelong glances to each other. They were going to sing at Radio City Music Hall? And they hadn't learned the words? Boy, were they going to be embarrassed. What dopes. I was going to have only one chance in my lifetime to do this, and I did not want to be stumbling over the words.

At the end of the entertainment, John Kerry got up and spoke. He asked Teresa to speak, and then John. By this time, I was pretty sure what was coming, and I was racking my brain about what to say. Usually I just introduced Teresa, but this was out of order. And, though I knew the words to "This Land Is My Land," I had no speech prepared. So when John handed me the microphone, I didn't give a speech. I just said thank you to the people who had given money to attend, and I said, maybe impolitely, that the election wasn't about them. It was about the young boys from Harlem who had sung for us earlier. It was about the people who would come in after we were gone and clean up the hall. It was about the mothers who that night could not find sleep because of a son or daughter in Iraq. Less than a minute, I figured. When you are unprepared, I recommend sincerity and brevity. Within minutes after that, the stage had filled up — Meryl Streep and Chevy Chase, Sarah Jessica Parker and Jessica Lange, Whoopi Goldberg and Paul Newman. The music for "This Land Is Your Land" started, and Cate and I smiled at each other. For this, we were prepared. But just as it started, a light came on above the audience, a big square of light, and the lyrics we had so diligently learned scrolled across, big enough for everyone on the stage to read. Diana Walker took a photograph that night of Cate and me. We are standing face-to-face, our arms on each other's shoulders, and though the photograph cannot capture it, we are telling each other that we were the dopes, and we are laughing at

our too-serious, overprepared selves. Once
a square, always a square.

We continued to travel with the Kerrys
for four days, ending with the largest and
maybe warmest rally in North Carolina history in our home town of Raleigh. As we
had stayed with the Kerrys at the Heinz
farm at the beginning of this trip, we asked
them to stay with us in our considerably
more modest Raleigh home. My friends, if
you haven't figured it out already, are
spectacular. Bonnie, Ellan, and Gwynn, Tricia and Sally, with muscle from Andrew
Young and Ellan's son, Joel, cleaned and
rearranged, changed lightbulbs, and swept
sidewalks. This was a house in which we
lived only a few weeks a year now, and there
were cobwebs in the corners, linens that
could stand freshening, and more than a
plant or two that needed replacing. They
did it all. Our guest room, on the third floor
with two single beds angled in the small
room, would not be satisfactory for the Kerrys. Cate had a nice room with a large bed,
so the Kerrys, my friends decided, could
stay there. But it was a college girl's room,
with homemade posters and funny adver-
tisements pasted to the walls. So they took
down and threw out, they bought and
moved things around. Bonnie bought new

linens for Cate's bed, and Sally made her take them back. No, that's too expensive, she said, Elizabeth would never buy those. Go to Tuesday Morning; she shops there. Bonnie found something less expensive. And they absolutely transformed our house. It was like coming home and finding that Martha Stewart had been there: it looked great. It turned out the Kerrys used Cate's room to change clothes and rest, but they didn't spend the night. But now Cate has nice new bed linens. And we had an evening free to take those fantastic friends to dinner.

One night off and then John started campaigning again, nearly full time, and I went to Washington to start thinking about the next months, for me and for the children. The Kerry campaign assigned a sweet young woman, Laura Efurd, as my temporary chief of staff to put together a full staff for me; what they may not have told her was that there was no budget for the vice presidential candidate's spouse. I was, rightfully, low man on the totem pole, although I had been campaigning on my own, doing town halls and televisions and even a little fund-raising for the past year. I sure didn't want to start being window-dressing. Laura had some friends volunteer to help in the beginning, women as young as my daughter, who treated me as window-dressing, talking about me in the third person when I was standing in front of them. We should have Mrs. Edwards call . . . *Wait! I'm standing right here. Speak to me.* It didn't stop. After a few frustrating days, I chased them away to other parts of the campaign. Despite that, a staff was built. Petite and blonde, a gentle powerhouse, Lori Denham became my permanent chief of staff. Pretty Kathleen McGlynn, who was working on the Democratic convention, promised to join after it was over, but — having heard that I had chased two volunteers away — told no one about the job. If she was only going to have the job for a few days, why talk about it? She stayed for the whole campaign; I couldn't have done it without her, she is unmatched in thoroughness, innate good sense, and good humor, and when John needed a scheduler for his poverty and political work after the Senate, Kathleen signed on with us again. Now, I needed a crew who would travel with me: a trip director, a press secretary, and an assistant.

I have known Hargrave McElroy since the summer of 1981, when we both moved into

441

the same apartment building in Raleigh. In her self-effacing way, I suspect she would describe herself as medium. Medium height, medium brown hair, a medium to slight build. That would only describe her when she is still, and she is never still. She has life and joy about her; she's the kind of friend who, when you are in your fifties, will still get tickled at the prospect of the two of you buying matching pajamas in Target, which we did late one night when I had left my pajamas in the previous night's hotel. Only she looked prettier in them than I ever could.

Twenty-five years ago, when John and I came from Nashville to John's new job at Tharrington, Smith & Hargrove, we lived across the hall from one another in the same apartment building. Hargrave and her husband, Rick, had come from Buies Creek, North Carolina. She was a lawyer for the Army Corps of Engineers. The complex in which we lived was in the process of turning leased units into residential hotel apartments, and not only were our apartments not yet renovated, they were in terrible condition. The air-conditioning was unreliable, the pipes would back up, bugs were a constant problem. I had been there alone with Wade, who turned two that summer, while John worked. When the McElroys pulled up and started unloading little boys' toys into the apartment across the hall from ours, I was — it is not overstating it — euphoric. And a little pathetic. As they unpacked, I quizzed them.

Where are you from? Originally South Carolina. Oh, my husband was born there.

What do you do? We are both lawyers. So are we!

You must have children with all these toys. Twin boys.

How old? Almost a year and a half. We have a two-year-old!

I don't think I actually said *Please be our friends,* but I honestly might have. We had a lot of friends in Raleigh, but they had jobs that kept them busy the same hours that John was busy.

Whether I asked or not, we did become friends. Our boys carved pumpkins together, shopped for Christmas trees together, bathed together while we made popcorn and watched a movie in the next room. Hargrave's husband and I, now pregnant with Cate, were looking for jobs, and both families were trying to save money for a house. It was like living in a dorm, no money and hand-me-down furniture, except in our version, there were children. We became so close that when, after my water broke at the Ringling Brothers circus and I went to the hospital to deliver Cate, Wade spent the night with the McElroys. Naturally we asked Hargrave to be Cate's godmother. And naturally I wanted Hargrave's sensible, wise, and patient presence with me for the campaign.

We picked up the second member of our troop when I was in New York looking for something to wear to the convention. In between shopping, Laura Efurd scheduled an interview for me with an extraordinarily beautiful and extraordinarily tall young woman. She had spectacular credentials, but that's not what I was looking at. It was someone else's job to make sure she had the skills to be my press secretary. I needed to find out if I could spend four months in close quarters with her. The interview lasted as long as a cup of coffee, but if she would take the job, I knew immediately I wanted Karen Finney with me. Even if she seemed a full foot taller than I.

The final slot was not filled until the campaign train trip in August. I was introduced to Ryan Montoya, who had coordinated the train stop in Las Vegas, New Mexico — he even had a building repainted that would be the backdrop for the stop. Nick Baldick called me from Washington. Ryan's the best, he said; the only question was whether I would like him. It was a five-minute interview. I said, *Tell me a little bit about yourself.* He did. Thinking of the campaign songbooks, I asked, *Can you sing?* He was hesitant, but he said *Yes.* So I said, *Great! See you next week.*

Ryan had a lot of experience. He knew that the A-teams on these staffs are with the presidential and vice presidential candidates and that he would be forced to make do with less staff and less money, and he'd heard, despite the puffball interview, that I expected a lot. But he took the job anyway, thinking wrongly that the job couldn't possibly entail that much. As my schedule became more and more complicated, so did Ryan's life; he was driven to mailing his dirty laundry to Washington so that it could be cleaned and sent to him at a later stop. Although I didn't know it until much later, he, like Kathleen, didn't tell anyone that he had taken the job. When he was asked what he was doing for me, he would say he was just filling in temporarily.

The rest of the staff was collected by Lori Denham while I was on the road. Rebecca

Werbel signed on to help Kathleen with scheduling. Courtney O'Donnell would help Karen Finney. Puja Pathak and Susan Ochs put the briefing books together that I got every night. Briefing books are notebooks with the positions of the campaign and the information about the places we went. If I was going to Buffalo, essentially this notebook would say, *Here's the deal on Buffalo. Here are your talking points.* I remember when Cate looked at her first briefing book during John's primary campaign. *Where are the facts?* she asked. *I don't need to be briefed on rhetoric.* Well, I had the same problem with the Kerry campaign briefing books. They were written like arguments for a position. I could do the arguing in my own words better than I could do it in someone else's, but in order to make the argument, I needed the facts, good or bad. I didn't want to be surprised. I didn't want fluff, and I sure didn't want spin. Except when I was keeping the breast cancer a secret, I never pretended to be anything other than what I was, and I didn't hide that I was upset that the campaign was spinning me instead of informing me. At first, I filled in the facts myself, going online after nearly everyone else had gone to sleep. When we finally got the briefing books right, I also got a little more sleep. And then Ryan devised a system of cards so that I had information about every state, every place we went, every issue I talked about. The average income in West Virginia, the percentage tuition increase in Pennsylvania colleges, jobs, wages, health care costs, Medicare premium increases. I would have all the pieces, so I could give people the right information. I wanted to convince audiences, and to do so, I had to be candid and honest. The facts gave me the ability to do that. Poor Puja and Susan, and Michelle Jolin and Lisa Ellman, who handled policy on my team; I don't think any team worked as hard. And every day, I went to two or three or four more places, and they had to do it all over again for each one. Each night I would update the cards with the briefing book they sent for the next day, and before each town hall or interview, I would look over the cards, *Do I know this well enough to talk about it?*

I will admit here that I was tough on these people. I didn't think of it as being tough, at the time, and I don't think of it as unfair now. I don't think I asked any more of anyone else than I asked of myself. But

447

looking back, I know I asked a lot of all of us. The election was important, and I didn't want to make or hear excuses. I called from Cincinnati once. I was about to have an event at the new Freedom Center. What, I needed to know, had John Kerry done on African American issues while he was in the Senate? It wasn't in the briefing book. Well, he's going to . . . No, no, I stopped them. Not what he's "going" to do, I want to know what he "has" done. There'd been a lot of civil rights legislation in the past twenty years; had he cosponsored any of it? How had he voted on it? Silence on the other end. Let me know when you find out, and then I will go to this event. It wasn't their fault, they had gotten the "He's going to . . ." answer from the Kerry policy desk. But wherever the problem, my team was taking the heat.

As long as I am being candid, I admit I had a lot of eccentricities that were not likely to make my traveling team more comfortable. I didn't want to stay in grand hotels, and the first hotels in which we stayed were nicer than I would have chosen. Some people who had contributed to the campaign would never miss the $2,000 they sent in, but some supporters who gave $25 or $50 could have used that money for something they really needed, and for them, I didn't feel right staying in a nicer hotel room than I really needed. As a consequence we stayed in some pretty lousy places. Ryan remembers coming into a room in Iron Mountain, Michigan, so late that he didn't even turn on the light, he just fell into bed. When he got up in the morning, he was horrified that his room was covered with cat hair. Remembering that I am allergic to cat hair, he rushed to my room to find out that my only problem was no hot water. After Iron Mountain, Ryan intervened to make certain that frugality was not being taken too far.

We ate pretty much only on planes or in our hotel rooms. At first, the meals we were brought were from the nicest restaurants in town, beautifully served and exquisite. It was lovely at first, but it soon became too much, at least for me. Can I just get salads, I asked. So salads it was, for all of us, and always the same, always chicken Caesar salad, lunch and dinner, day after day, until I finally cried uncle and banned chicken Caesar salads from the menu. How about meatloaf? From then on, it was meatloaf or chicken, occasionally steak — sensible food I might have made at home.

And then I didn't want to rest. There

were, at the beginning of my schedule, lots of rest days. But when I had those rest days at home, I was restless not resting. So, at the end of September I said, *I'm not going home again until this is over.* The children would join John or me or both of us on the road on weekends and for rallies, too, if they wanted, and they were the only reason to go home. And when I stayed out, so did our little team.

Where we stayed, the Secret Service stayed, and what we ate, the Secret Service ate. So when I wanted meatloaf instead of something more highfalutin, they ate it, too. But they were trained not to complain. They were trained to be nearly invisible. One of the agents told me that the way to find out if you are Secret Service material is to put on your best suit and stand completely still in your backyard for eight hours. I knew I was going to like the agents. They may have been less sure about me. Soon after the announcement I met the lead agents who were assigned to protect me. We met in our D.C. living room. I sat on one love seat; Kevin Pain, who did the talking, sat opposite me on the other.

"We're going to be around all the time," he said. "I know."

"We are here to protect you, so we can't carry your luggage or your purse; we're not being rude." "I know."

"Our offices will open all your mail; do you know all the people who send you letters and packages?" "No, I get a lot from eBay sellers, packages from all over." "We heard that," he said. I thought, *Geez, they heard that?*

"The other agents on the detail are not being rude when they don't talk to you. The lead agent will initiate all conversations with you." "Fine."

"And everything we see and hear is confidential." Okay.

The conversation was formal and fast. To me, Kevin Pain is just a stitch, even then at his most regimented, clicking through a checklist. He is such a straight arrow. He talks as if he's reading a movie script for a Secret Service agent. He talks about "the roommate," that's his wife. On intense questioning, I could get him to talk about the house he and the roommate were building in Texas or about hunting with his son, but he was pretty much a look-straight-ahead guy, and he ran a very tight ship. Having grown up in the military, I knew him before I knew him. And I honestly liked him. I suspect I got more smiles from Kevin

Pain than any protectee — that's what we are called — ever had.

I had grown up around formal and disciplined. I had grown up with men standing straight-backed for hours watching everything around them. For some protectees it was hard to get used to having someone always there. One kept insisting, wrongly, that the Secret Service had set up cameras in his bedroom. Others balked, got irritable under the constant watch, even yelled at the agents. Shoot, I was going to spend just as much time with them as with Hargrave and Ryan and Karen — although the Secret Service agents did rotate, so maybe not quite as much time — and I figured that the better we got along, the better the experience. The rotation allowed the agents, who had been pulled from all over the country, to go back to their home bases, get home for a while and have dinner with the roommate, for during their two- or three-week shifts they only went where I went. Sometimes we would skirt their hometowns. It's how I met Bob Rolin's family and Bill Cousin's son. Bob was as easy a smile as Kevin was difficult. He was a cheerful, happy man, and it honestly made me feel good just to be around him. Bill was a sweetheart, and he had a sweetheart. We teased him about Mary, the pretty woman who would show up at Michigan events now and again, and then, after he asked her to marry him when his shift was off right before the election, we got him a card and teased him some more. Don Cox, the fourth lead agent, was a student of history and culture. His being in the Secret Service made him a witness to the history he loved, a part of events that mattered. And the man knew everything. Lani Breda, though blonde, was more like me than the others — a sensible-shoes sort of woman. The other women could all play Secret Service agents in the movies: gorgeous Sonyia Rouel with her Ralph Lauren ponytail; Joanne Moses, who would have played the intellectual but surprisingly athletic agent; Lindsey Taylor — whom we eventually lost to Jack and Emma Claire's detail — was the homecoming queen turned Secret Service agent; and Laura Hughes, well — Laura actually was in a television documentary about the Secret Service that was shown while we were on the road. I can only imagine the ribbing she took. Each of them, Michael, Bart, Patrick, and the list goes on, three dozen, I'd guess, names and faces and stories. It's hard to leave any of them out.

We didn't leave them out of any of the

fun. I didn't get them to play Boggle on the plane, but when it was time to sing, I would hand out the songbooks I had refurbished for the general election and ask them to pick a song. I would do it only when we were in the private plane we eventually squeezed out of the campaign, because that was a controlled environment where they could have something in their hands and on their mind other than watching out for me. Kevin would never sing, of course, but nearly everyone else did, and even I caught Kevin flipping through the songbook once or twice.

As the end of the campaign approached, the shifts were having their last days as part of our little team. A few days before each shift left for the last time, we had a goodbye party. The first was in Reno. Hargrave and Karen's room was on one side of a common room, and mine was on the other, and in between we laid out a feast. Cake, piles of fruit, nachos, and things to drink. Actually, when I write it, it sounds terrible, but it wasn't. And even if it had been, it would have been terrific, because the agents there — and later for the next crew at the party in Kenosha — were so unbelievably appreciative. One said that in twenty years with the Secret Service, covering all kinds of people, never had anybody done this, ever. He turned to the younger agents. "So don't expect this again. People," he said, "don't even say thank you." Honestly, that broke my heart. They were supposed to act like furniture, but that didn't mean we should treat them like furniture.

In mid-October we piled into the Secret Service SUV as we always did, heading out from the airport to a town hall in Grand Junction, Colorado. On a bench outside the airport gates sat a man, perhaps in his sixties, his hair thinning, the color of his faded jacket and the color of his weathered skin nearly the same, and on his lap he held a handmade sign, maybe twelve by eighteen inches, and on the sign a single word, plainly printed: FATSO. I watched him, there was nothing else to watch, only a parking lot behind him and the road ahead. And as we drove, he watched us too, watched the tinted windows of the line of SUVs. When we passed, I looked back and saw the man get up. He was walking to his car. The sign, I realized, was meant for me. It was a thrust of ugliness and meanness, meant to throw me off. This man had made the sign, driven to the airport, parked and sat on that bench for who knows how long, waiting for me to come by so I would read his sign, so I would see that someone, a plain old man, called me Fatso. When I saw him get up, I turned to the others in the car — there were three Secret Service agents and my little team, more than the usual load. "Did you see that guy?" I could tell two things from the way the Secret Service responded: they had hoped that I hadn't seen it, and they were mad. Well, the Secret Service is not there to protect me from meanness, but if you could have seen their faces and particularly the faces of the younger agents, who had seen him from the cars in front of us and behind us. When they rejoined us at the town hall site, it was as if each of them wanted to find a reason to give this fellow the once-over. It was their job to protect me, and I now knew that they actually wanted to protect me. I wish I could have told that nasty man that although he was trying to hurt me, he had given me a very-nice gift.

John and I had been to the 2000 Democratic convention. John, like most of the junior senators, had a five-minute speaking slot in the early evening. When he spoke, the audience was mostly the loyal North Carolina delegation. I sat with the North Carolina delegation and the Overseas

Democrats delegation — each group had equally terrible seats — when Hadassah introduced Joe Lieberman. In 2000, John was a footnote to a footnote to a footnote, the dismissive slotting of the almost chosen. The experience of the 2004 convention was entirely different. In the first place, I didn't see much of Boston. I spoke at breakfasts at hotels to which I was delivered by the Secret Service SUV. At the convention hall, I was shuttled from one network booth to another. Thank goodness for Peter Jennings, who told the ABC makeup girl, my third makeup girl in an hour, that I looked just fine, quit fooling with me. I would go up to our family box to see my family, Jay and Jackie and their boys Ty and Louis, my sister, Nancy, and her daughter Laura, and to see my friends — they were all there. And John's family, his parents and his sister, Kathy, and friends who had become supporters and supporters who had become friends after two-plus years of working together. Then back to the hotel room to work on our speeches.

When Cate and I came back into the room, John pulled out a T-shirt someone had given him, boasting that he'd been told it was the highest-grossing T-shirt in Boston. The shirt, made by a group of Harvard women, had a line drawing of John and the words "John Edwards is hot."

Cate took one look and said, "Dad, that's disgusting. Do you want to burn that or do you want me to?" "Oh, yeah," he answered, "I think it's weird." Then he showed it to the next three people who walked into the room. Cate said, "Dad, you are so proud of that." "No, I do think it's weird." "Okay then," she answered, "stop showing it to people." John never had to worry about getting too full of himself with Cate around. Bless her.

The night we were to speak, John and Cate and I were each in our own worlds, going over our speeches one last time, pulling at our clothes, watching the convention coverage from any one of the seven flat-screen televisions in the absurdly plush suite the campaign had chosen. In another room, Heather North was dressing the children, and they traveled separately from us to the convention center. Although I had bought their outfits, I had never seen them in them. So when they walked into the hold room under the convention stage that night, I had my first glimpse. Emma Claire, who usually wears her hair in a ponytail, had her long blonde curls down, and she looked like the lovely, serene child that she is. And Jack, I took one look at him and said, "With him in that seersucker suit, the rest of us could go out there naked and no one would notice."

We had gone out to the stage the night before, just so we would know what to expect. There would be TelePrompTers to our left and right on which the words we had written would scroll out as we spoke, and best of all, there was a big-screen Tele-PrompTer straight ahead of us, just behind the seated delegates, which, they neglected to mention, would be entirely blocked when the delegates stood or hoisted signs, which was all the time. Cate spoke before me, eloquent, poised, and lovely — how had she learned that, speaking only to college groups of forty and fifty? But I remembered her composure at Wade's funeral, and I wasn't surprised. Whatever fears I had had about walking out there were mostly banished: if Cate could do it, so could I. Any remaining fears left when I stepped out and, instead of seeing a sea of strangers, I saw the faces I had seen over the past two years. The Iowa delegation was immediately in front, and Mike Fitzgerald, Ro Foege, and Susan Salter were smiling at me like they had dozens of times before. The North Carolina delegation was to my right — I knew every face. In each state, in each delegation, hands I had shaken, people I had hugged. I spotted Kathy Sullivan and Carole Appel, and there was Patsy Madrid, Virgie Rollins, Donsia Strong Hill. Everywhere, faces of friends, Joe Maxwell, Mari Culver, and their faces opened memories. I remembered the day Paul Shomshor had signed on to the campaign and my first event with Chris Redfern. I look back at the pictures from that night, pictures in which I am smiling or pointing or waving. There is no doubt that they put me at ease. I wasn't talking to millions of people who didn't know me. I was talking to them, and they did know me.

I left the stage to John, to the speech I had heard him give twenty times in our room at the house, and yet it wasn't the same, because now it was punctuated by explosions of applause, and now when he promised that *Hope is on the way,* those words echoed throughout the Fleet Center. At the end, our family, less Wade, was on stage together. When John took Emma Claire in his arms and walked to the far side of the stage, the cameras followed him, and I blew Wade a kiss.

John Kerry spoke the next night. We watched the beginnings of John Kerry's speech from the family box, but then we moved to the hold room, where we re-combed hair, retied shoes, checked lipstick. We listened to the end of the acceptance speech huddled in a four-by-four space behind the backdrop, the adults in front and a collection of children of all ages on the stairs behind us. And when it ended and the convention center erupted, first John, then Teresa, then I went out, followed soon by the children and the balloons, then friends and politicians and party leaders until the stage was full, and all the while, I was watching to make sure the children — intent on keeping the falling balloons afloat — didn't fall off the stage. Nothing should take away from this night for John Kerry.

The evening was capped off by a concert by the Boston Pops with James Taylor. Once when my dad was head of the NROTC unit at Chapel Hill, he decided that we should take a space-available free military flight to Puerto Rico for Christmas. My mother packed a miniature tree in one suitcase and we went. We went to San Juan, of course, and across through the rain forest and down to Ponce. It was an extraordinary trip, but Jay was angry the whole time. He hadn't wanted to come. He didn't want a miniature tree. And then, as the final blow, when we returned to Chapel Hill we were told by our neighbors that we'd missed joining in the caroling . . . with Chapel Hill native James Taylor. That was the early 1970s, and my brother is still angry about it. When you meet someone, famous or unknown, you reach for what you have in common, and being in Chapel Hill — or in this case not being in Chapel Hill — is what I reached for, but I don't believe James Taylor heard a word over the fireworks and the aahs of the crowd. After another late-night stop, we finally crawled into bed about 3 A.M. We were up at 5, packing and dressing for a rally that would be carried live at 7:15 A.M. and a bus trip that would last nearly a week. It was July 30th. Our twenty-seventh wedding anniversary.

Chapter 13
America,
The General
THE RACE

John and I have always celebrated our wedding anniversary at Wendy's. It started, as so many rituals do, without any thought. We were moving out of the townhouse in Virginia Beach that day, packing to move to Nashville. We were wearing cut-off jeans and we didn't want to stop and shower, so we went to the nearest fast-food restaurant, Wendy's. The next year, we found ourselves at Wendy's again. The trip the third year sealed it, and it has been Wendy's ever since. So the campaign allowed that we could stop the caravan of full-size buses, filled with families and press and Secret Service, and eat at a Pennsylvania Wendy's.

The patrons at Wendy's were not alerted. Not only were cameramen suddenly leaning over them, not only were Secret Service agents filling every available square inch of floor space, but even if they had been able to get up, there was no way to leave, unless they had walked to the restaurant. The parking lots were all blocked. We all ate. Teresa had chili, John Kerry a hamburger. John and I ordered our usual: number one combos. Also celebrating were Cate, the Kerry girls, the Heinz boys, and Ben Affleck, who was traveling with us for those first days. We ate and got back on our respective buses. At the next stop we were asked about the gourmet meal we had eaten. It was great. Wendy's always is. Not Wendy's, the reporter said. The five-star gourmet meal delivered to the bus after the Wendy's stop, how was that meal? We had no idea what he was talking about. It sorted itself out in a day or two. It turned out that the Kerrys had never eaten at a Wendy's, and although they were willing to go with us, they made sure they had a backup — a quite nice backup, willing to deliver to a bus — if they hated it. One side note of the Wendy's trip: everywhere I went, in rope lines or in town halls, people would hand me Wendy's gift certificates. We used some for our anniversary dinner the next year, in 2005. Even if the Kerrys don't go, it is clear Wendy's is getting plenty of business.

Early in the campaign, our family had a bus tour separate from the Kerrys, a bus tour of the South. We worked our way through Louisiana, where we tried alligator meat and Louisiana barbecue — and where the campaign decided later not to fight. We had a great rally in Arkansas on the banks of the Arkansas River, where Jack and Emma Claire stole the show by sweeping the stage during everyone's speeches — and where, again, the campaign decided later not to fight. We had a beautiful day in Missouri, where once more the campaign withdrew, deciding not to fight. The entire experience was delightful and unbelievably frustrating.

The bus tour ended in St. Louis, where we joined the Kerrys for a train tour. And you should have seen this train. The Kerry car was the back car and more luxurious than ours, but ours was terrific. Truman, we'd heard, had ridden in the car in which we traveled, perhaps slept in the bed in which we slept, maybe written a note at the mahogany desk in the small lounge. It was like the first time stepping into the Senate chamber, rubbing your fingers over the names of senators carved there over the years. It was wonderful and inspiring and important. We left the grand Union Station and headed west.

Not every moment was a perfect moment. And there were times on this trip that were not perfect. It is a sad fact that Teresa was not permitted to be nostalgic about her first husband, Jack Heinz, the Republican senator from Pennsylvania who died in an airplane crash. No one begrudged me missing Wade. And yet Teresa was not allowed to miss Jack. She and I had an awkward interview on the train with the St. Louis paper; while Teresa reminisced to the reporter about Jack, her press secretary paced, and the staff squirmed. I was supposed to be there to right a ship that wasn't really a kilter. Then the first night out, the Kerry staff, which was supposed to share the available bunks with the Edwards staff, put Keep Out signs on all the private room doors and locked John's staff out; John's staff slept in the seating cars. They thought we didn't know. A reminder, I suppose, of still-unreleased animosities that had grown during the primaries.

And then there was a worse moment. It was late one night. We'd gotten behind schedule, as the stops had lasted too long during the day. Now it was 12:30 at night, and we were making up time barreling through Kansas. John was lying on the bed, and I was sitting beside him talking to him. The door to our room was open, and I could see out the window across the narrow hall. Of course, it was night and there was nothing to see. And then, all of a sudden, there was something to see. There were hundreds of people on a train platform — where were we? — and there were signs and lights, and, saddest of all, flashbulbs going off as the train raced through what turned out to be Lawrence, Kansas. Those people came out, and we didn't even slow down, I said. The train can't go back tonight, John said, sensibly enough as the train barreled on. And then we looked at each other. But *we* can go back. I wrote an entry for the Kerry blog about how much John and I loved Lawrence. We'd traveled through when we were in law school, and a generous soul had fixed our ailing brakes for a more than fair price, which was pretty important to two students working their way through school. We would come back, we promised Lawrence. We went to bed unaware that later that night we would pass the Imus Ranch, where there were more people waiting, including children. We hadn't even known it was scheduled. I only found out weeks later, listening to Don Imus one morning complain that the train had raced through there too without stopping.

All the little snags aside, Mort Engelberg, who put the train trip together, was responsible for one of the most splendid experiences a campaigner could ever have. I could have sat on the back of that train, talking to the folks who gathered along the tracks, at rallies and at train crossings, watching the country roll by for months if I had had the chance. Families gathered at the places where they knew the train would slow and waited, sitting on lawn chairs, the children playing beside them, a homemade sign ready to be hoisted when we came by. Men and women working in plants and shipping yards alongside the tracks would stop their work and wave their caps. How could you not love this? I liked walking through the press car, with papers and jackets and empty cardboard coffee cups strewn everywhere, then walking through the immaculate Secret Service car, grown men who weren't on duty, sleeping upright in their seats in coats and ties. Although John and Cate and I each thanked Mort as we left him in Albuquerque and returned with the younger children to Lawrence, those thanks could not convey our appreciation for the gift of that incredible trip.

And then there was Lawrence. You should know we have a love affair with Lawrence.

On a day's notice, a rally was put together in a park, and then it rained and it had to be moved, and still thousands of people found us. John spoke inside and then went outside to talk to the thousands more who could not get inside after the fire marshal closed the doors, and he spoke again. When John was speaking to the crowd indoors, Jack, who was standing with me, whispered that he wanted to talk, too. Daddy's talking. Another tug on my slacks. I want to talk. During the next round of applause in John's speech, I went up to him and whispered that Jack wanted to talk. What's he want to say? he asked. I shrugged. John was sure he was going to say "poopy-head" or some other phrase four-year-olds find amusing, but he gave him the microphone anyway. Jack held it close to his face and, after a long pause, he repeated a line he'd heard his father deliver dozens of time. In his unlikely deep voice came the nearly whispered words, words John had used in his convention speech and in every speech since then: *Hope is on the way.* The room erupted. That night, Jack did a reprise of sorts. As he was stepping into the bathtub, he smiled and said *Soap is on the way.*

Summer was ending. In mid-August the

469

children's school would start. We needed to get them back into a routine, so the children and I went back to Washington. It was from there that I was to leave for my first solo venture as the wife of the vice presidential nominee. I was going to Ohio in early August. Jennifer Palmieri was the press secretary for the Kerry-Edwards campaign there. She had called me before taking the job. Should I go? Of course, I said and then added, with no premonition whatsoever, that's the election, right there. Go. Well, she had, and now she had put together an event in Columbus to thank a woman restaurateur who had registered hundreds of single mothers in her restaurant. I would use the opportunity to talk about why this election was so important for women. John Kerry and my husband had campaign planes. Teresa had her own plane. I was flying commercial — which would not last long — and now I wasn't flying at all because the flight had been canceled and there was no other way to get there. Ryan's first job as my trip director was to tell me that there was no trip. I started that day asking for a private plane.

Our new team was still feeling its way. My schedule was, at first, made up of panel discussions with women on different topics.

The campaign would locate women in various towns to talk about health care or education or domestic security. The stories I heard were incredible; the women I met were strong or crumbling or fighting. But it wasn't a format I liked much, because I was too much an emcee making sure the shy panelist spoke up and that the vociferous panelist — and there were one or two or more of those — gave others a chance. It seemed to me, too, that the women on the panels and in the crowd had already decided how to vote. I was preaching to the converted. Maybe those were the only people they could get to see the spouse of a vice presidential candidate. I could understand that. But when I read in the nightly press clips that my events were open only to Democrats, I was livid. So even if an undecided voter had wanted to hear me, I asked the staff, they couldn't? No, the press had it wrong, they told me, but I think the press had it right and my staff, who didn't yet know me, was trying to protect me. Maybe they were worried that if I was able to get so exercised over a briefing book, how would I respond to a heckler? It would not have been an unreasonable concern, except that, as I said, they didn't know me yet.

I had met hecklers. When John announced

his candidacy at the University of South Carolina, a half dozen boys with Bush signs had been disrupting the speakers before me with chants and shouts, so when I took the microphone, I spoke first to them. "We have press here from all over the country," I said in my most motherly voice. "I just know you boys are going to show them some good Southern manners." That's all it took, and they never said another word. It's all in the tone of voice. When protesters gathered outside a community health clinic where I was doing a town hall, I was disappointed that I hadn't seen them until our SUVs were pulling away. I told Ryan I wanted to thank them, for no one before had ever found me important enough to bother protesting my visits. He said nope, not a good idea.

But I wanted to talk to them, to anyone who might be persuaded, even those others had written off. I had been trying in those early weeks to make a point about the closed and ticketed Bush and Cheney campaign events, and apparently — because of an excess of caution or a misunderstanding — I was having them, too. I was adamant: I wanted to speak to Republicans, I wanted to speak to independents, I wanted to speak to undecided voters. When the staff insisted the press was still getting it wrong,

I was all over Karen Finney to make the openness of the events a talking point with every reporter and in every press release for my appearances. To make it clear they were complying, my staff had T-shirts made. On the front they read Elizabeth's Staff, and on the back they read Open to the Public. It cracked me up.

Everything has a name, whether or not the name makes sense, and the handshaking that takes place after panel discussions, town halls, and speeches is called "working the rope line," although there was rarely a rope between my stages and the audience and although the "line" was three and four deep and, like a basket of puppies, constantly in motion. And it was dear to me, for that was the place where I could really touch those who had come. Women would reach to hug me and, as they did, they would pull me close and whisper in my ear: I lost my son, too. Every day. Debbie, the waitress in Sioux City, who cried as she asked for my autograph; things were so bad for her, and it was so emotional to be with someone trying to change things. Or they would come to me, as a pretty young woman had once, crying, saying I don't even know why I am crying. Or they would know. Her son's National Guard unit was headed to

Iraq. The county couldn't pay for her eight-year-old's glasses anymore and she couldn't afford to pay for them. Her husband's employer was closing his factory. *My parents . . . my daughter . . . my brother.* It was almost never about themselves, which just added to their sense of impotence and hopelessness. There was anger, too, and optimism often, but there was always sadness. They had been stripped of health care, jobs, eyeglasses, and hope, and most importantly of the dignity of feeling that they were self-sufficient and could weather whatever was handed to them. Now they couldn't. *It didn't used to be like this,* they'd say. And all I could say was I know. And then work as hard as I could.

Just as in some respects each rope line was the same, each was unique. In late August at the University of Nevada in Reno, we had a great town hall on education issues with the Wolfpack students and the public. I had practiced saying the state name all morning so I wouldn't embarrass myself as I had during my previous visit. Apparently the rest of the country mispronounces *Nevada.* We all say "Ne-vah-dah," when we should be saying — as I now say — "Nev-add-ah." After the town hall, a woman in the rope line reached to hug me, and I reached back as I always did, but she grabbed my neck. You look tired, she said, and I am a massage therapist. Right there, she started to give me a massage. The Secret Service stood behind me in each rope line, one hand on my back in case they needed to pull me away. They hadn't ever needed to before, but this time an enormous agent from Miami, pulled her fingers, one by one, from my neck.

Ryan Montoya, who managed the entire trip — from making sure my luggage was with us to queuing the music for my entrances — was almost always unflappable. He must have been thrown off balance once, though, when, at a Sioux City senior center, a woman tapped his shoulder and said, "José? José?" "Why," asked Ryan, "do you think my name is José?" Completely unintimidated she just repeated it, "José, do you teach Spanish lessons?" He came back to the hold room and complained to Karen, Hargrave, and me, so, sympathetically, we called him José for the rest of the week. It was Ryan who pointed out the road signs for an upcoming Dairy Queen on a long drive to Tucson. In forty miles. In thirty. In ten. Bob Rolin, the unbelievably agreeable

Secret Service agent from South Carolina, allowed that we could stop if I wanted. So we did, and we bought Blizzards for the agents who had never been in a Dairy Queen, and we generally upset the entire place for the twenty minutes it took to feed all of us.

I talked to the families in Dairy Queen, and I would speak to young people wherever I went. The politically astute nine-year-old on the flight back to Washington who recognized me and talked politics the whole way. The Florida boy outside the fruit market wearing a Bush T-shirt. (Tell me why you support George Bush. *I like war.* Now that's a conversation stopper.) The round-faced boy with a Mohawk haircut at the Dickinson County Fair on the Michigan Upper Peninsula showing me the goldfish he had won. I refrained from reminding him, as I would have reminded my own children, that all balloons pop and all goldfish die. In September I read one of my favorite children's books, *Cloudy with a Chance of Meatballs,* to Connie Chouinard's second-grade class at Lincoln Center Elementary in St. Paul, and that afternoon, after being introduced by the student body president, Marcus Mason, I spoke to incredibly well-informed high school students at John Marshall High School in Rochester, Minnesota. Mostly they were worried about the rising cost of college, although I did get an interesting existential question, which I couldn't have repeated immediately after she asked and I cannot repeat now, from a beautiful girl dressed entirely in Gothic gear. The daily schedule for that visit warned, "There is no air-conditioning in John Marshall High School." They were warning me, from North Carolina, that there was no air-conditioning in a Minnesota school in mid-September? Hargrave and I had a good laugh.

In August and September, I visited people's houses to hear the stories of their neighbors and friends and answer a few questions from the press. The campaign hoped that the event would get enough press coverage to justify the expense of putting the whole thing together. Long before in the primaries, I had abandoned attempts to manipulate press coverage, and that left me to what I enjoyed most, having conversations, with the homeowners, their neighbors, the participants, and yes, with the reporters. Whatever happened happened. Some of what happened was funny. At the Gonzalez home in Burbank, I sat next to a man who was in all the press photographs of me and bore an uncanny resemblance to Dick Cheney. It must have confused more than one newspaper reader.

In a hilly Little Rock neighborhood I sat in the home of George Word, who had been in the military but was having trouble getting the military to continue health care coverage for his wife, who was in a coma. I remember his neat home. I waited before the event in the bedroom shared by his two daughters — decorated sweetly, carefully, by a man with much too much on his plate. In Green Bay, I sat next to Donna for a midday house party she hosted. It was midday because the Packers game was at 4:15, and she was not going to miss it. Donna, her husband, her children and her house were all dressed and decorated for the game. The picture over the sofa was of Lambeau Field. When she opened her home to me, she told me the story of buying it. She and her husband and two boys had been living in a mobile home, but they worked two and three jobs each to save for a house. Finally they were able to buy this immaculate, well-loved house, and she told the story of when she told their sons they were moving to a house. A house, she said, with a sidewalk. A sidewalk. And they didn't believe her. No, she told them, choking away the tears, we really do have a sidewalk. I fell in love with these people.

When I think about campaigning, I don't think about the anxiety of speaking to strangers, of the hesitation in eating unfamiliar food, or of the fear of being trapped in some obligatory and excruciating event. I am certain that because I grew up in so many places, surrounded by the faces of so many ever-changing people, I long ago quit worrying about that and started enjoying the ride. And let me tell you what letting go of all that anxiety, hesitation, and fear gets you: you get to enjoy, completely enjoy, an experience like I had on Michigan's Upper Peninsula. I had spent the morning in Lansing with the incredible Michigan Governor Jennifer Granholm, and I had left a health care discussion in Traverse City. Now on a bright September day we were flying across Lake Michigan, low enough to see the shadow of the plane on the water, to inspect the tiny forested islands near the coastlines. My guides were Bart Stupak, the congressman from the district and his wife, Laurie. It was a Route 2 visit: first one way on Route 2, then the other. First was the

Dickinson County Fair, where during a bingo game, I was introduced to the unique accent of the Upper Peninsula. Bee-ee fou-our-de-en. I was intrigued. Karen was just delighted I didn't win — she did not want a bingo prize to be the press story of our visit.

After an afternoon at the fair we went to Iron Mountain High School. It was Friday night, and on Friday nights on the Upper Peninsula, just like on Friday nights in Raleigh, North Carolina, your whole world is playing, or watching, high school football. The Mountaineers were playing Gwinn High School, also from the U.P. Gwinn was built as a model city for returning World War II veterans, and the team is burdened, or blessed, depending on your point of view, with the team name The Modeltowners. Fewer than five hundred students attended each school, and yet in the stands and rimming the field there were two thousand people, in black and gold for Gwinn or, confusingly, yellow and black for Iron Mountain. And there must have been more at home or at work listening to the game on the radio, because both teams broadcast the game on different radio stations.

After I posed with a group of four-year-old cheerleaders, dressed in perfect minia-ture replicas of the Mountaineer cheerleading uniforms, I sat down to watch some football. It wasn't pretty. As the first half neared the end, the Mountaineers had scored at least three times, and I don't recall a single Modeltowner first down. My press secretary Karen came down to get me out of the stands. "They'll let you join them on the radio," she said. As we climbed to the press booths high above the field I said, "That's great." And I thought, *And what do you want me to talk about?* I talked football — John playing high school and a little college ball, my Dad being a stand-out college player. The two Mountaineer announcers, who did terrific fast-paced color and play-by-play, asked a mild political question or two, and I gave a mild answer. I knew the people who were listening to this, and even if they liked politics, they were listening to hear football. So all I was really saying was who we were — Friday-night-football kind of people. And then I moved to the Gwinn booth. There was only one announcer, one exhausted fellow trying to find ways to convey any excitement over the airwaves when his team was getting so badly beaten. I sat through a play or two, as Gwinn failed to get a first down, listening to this overwhelmed but still game fellow try to do the play-by-play. It was painful. Had the regular play-by-play announcer abandoned him, gotten up in disgust at some point in this game and left him to carry the whole load? Whatever the problem, it was highlighted when Gwinn punted. "All right, there goes the punt," he said. "It's a high one. Number twenty-eight for the Mountaineers has picked it up in the end zone. He's running it out. Now he's down, and — oh, there's a flag." And then he stopped talking. The referees were conversing, but there was no sound going out over Gwinn radio. Nothing. It's radio. Finally, I couldn't stand it and I said, "Pretty much has to be a clip." Karen was standing behind me, her lovely brown skin turning white, thinking, *What is she saying? Does she know what she's talking about?* It was a tremendous relief to her when the voice came over the stadium loudspeaker. "Penalty on the Modeltowners. Clip."

For me, it was a perfect night. Not for the Modeltowners, obviously, but it was crisp and clear, the setting was verdant and alive and, well, American. I used to sit in the YMCA in Raleigh and watch Wade, and then Cate, play basketball on Saturday mornings. Parents in sweatpants and glasses — no one having put in their contact lenses yet — sat in folding chairs with their hands around warm cups of coffee watching seven-year-olds dance down the court or shoot at the wrong basket, and no one would criticize. And if, by chance, one of the seven-year-olds scored, the coffee cups would be set between knees all the way down the row and the parents of both teams would clap. And I used to love to see it. This is what we are about, isn't it? This is the America I missed as a child, the America I embraced as a parent. And I was embracing it that night in Iron Mountain.

None of this had anything to do with being a Republican or a Democrat. Maybe the best politicking doesn't, and shouldn't. It shouldn't in Canton, North Carolina, or Asheville, where John and I toured after Hurricane Ivan devastated those mountain communities. It shouldn't in Millvale, a working-class town in Pennsylvania where Ivan left some of his last markers, and where I visited in late September. The people in these places were cleaning up and helping each other out, no questions asked. I filled plates at a makeshift cafeteria in Millvale and then ate a little lunch with those who were taking a break from cleaning. The room was filled with people, with strollers and walkers. And young people, high school boys, I'd bet, wearing baggy skate-boarder pants covered in mud, were sweeping the floors, taking out the trash cans as they filled with paper plates, just doing what they could. And when their crew had finished eating, they put down the brooms and went back outside to work again, picking up their shovels at the door. I left Millvale, this devastated place, with a sense of real hope for us all, because people, even young people who were supposed to be too self-absorbed for such things, cared about their communities.

The day's lessons weren't over, either. That night when I got to Ohio, a group of Ananias, who had told my staff we might be related, was waiting for me at the Holiday Inn. The staff set up a little room with sodas and snacks, and I went down to meet these Ohio Ananias who might be related to my dad, a Pennsylvania Anania. Here's what I discovered: it doesn't matter if they are family or not — they are "family." Pete Anania, his arms crossed as he stood against the wall, clearly the one who'd had to be convinced to come, and his wife, Betty; Vicki Anania with a collection of handsome children and grandchildren, Angela and

484

Eric and Dominique and — how did he get in here? — Tyler; Tony Anania, more like my father than any of the others, always a smile and another story. And more cousins, pretty girls who looked like my own cousins. We spent an evening being family, and I am still on their e-mail list and suspect I always will be.

At first we traveled commercially, but after canceled flights and one incident when state troopers boarded to arrest a passenger, the campaign decided I should fly privately. The first forays into chartered flights were not happy. We had a tiny plane from Los Angeles to Reno in late August. There was no room for everyone's luggage, except for the two pieces I carried with me — a garment bag and a duffle bag, both lime green so Ryan could find them easily — and there was not nearly enough room for the agents. Three agents sat at the rear of the plane on a bench seat on which I might have put Emma Claire and Jack. Hargrave took hear-no-evil-see-no-evil-speak-no-evil photographs of them wedged in there. As we landed, all the oxygen masks on the plane dropped down, which was alarming enough, and in addition they were nasty looking. We had to get back on that plane an hour later to go to Las Vegas, and when we boarded, the pilot was taping the oxygen mask compartment doors shut. Taping them shut! The plan was that we would fly again on this plane from Las Vegas to Washington. "I'm not doing it," I told Ryan. No one would ask anyone else on this campaign to fly on a plane like this. "It's not safe. I have a credit card, I can get my own commercial flight back." The Secret Service started to get fidgety; they don't like changes in plans. "There are no commercial flights to Washington," Ryan said calmly. "Then I'll fly to New York, I'll stay with Cate if she's there, or with my brother. I am not getting back on that plane." We did fly commercially, to Baltimore, an hour from Washington, and Kathleen started pressing the campaign again for a safe plane.

Our next private plane looked like a crop duster. I am five feet two, and I could step directly from the tarmac into the plane, no stairs necessary, it was so low to the ground. Ryan, who had plane envy looking at every Gulfstream or Challenger at the private terminals we used, called it the "Belly Plane." The food Kathleen had ordered for the eight of us — the only meal we would get between 7 A.M. and 10 P.M. — was delivered to a different plane, so we took off hungry. To make matters worse, the edges of Hurricane Ivan were causing terrific turbulence, and the little Belly Plane was getting tossed around. A Secret Service agent threw up — impossible to hide in a cabin about the size of a nine-person passenger van — and I, finding an old granola bar in the tiny galley, bit into it and broke a filling. Most of the disasters associated with the Belly Plane were not its fault, but Ryan vowed not to fly on it again.

Five days later we had the plane we would have for the rest of the campaign. The crew rotated every few days, but after the first few rotations, Brett Karpy, a blonde, outgoing thirty-something pilot, asked to stay on with us. It was Brett who made sure we had meatloaf for dinner, and Brett who handed out campaign buttons to the curious who approached the plane surrounded by Secret Service and police cars. We never got on or off the plane without a big smile and his shouted "Good Luck!" When we got on the plane for the last time, the trip from Des Moines to Boston, he had heard news of the good exit polling and had bought champagne. I wouldn't miss sitting knee to knee with Hargrave for hours on end, with all of our belongings stuffed around us or on the floor behind our legs. Poor tall Karen and maybe poor Ryan, whose seat faced hers, certainly wouldn't miss the cramped accommodations. I wouldn't miss crawling over suitcases and briefcases and passing meals back and trash up on every leg. But I would miss Brett. We all would. On December 28, 2005, Brett Karpy died. He and another pilot were on their way to pick up another customer, to flash that great smile at them and make them comfortable, when their plane crashed in California and they were both killed instantly. He had just turned thirty-four.

There are people, like Brett, open and warm, whom I won't ever forget. I won't forget Brett, and I won't forget Hope Walz. We had a house party in Mankato, Minnesota, at the Walz home. It was a bright house and someone had stenciled a saying on the wall: *Fear less, hope more; whine less, breathe more; talk less, say more; hate less, love more; and all good things are yours.* You could tell that was the way this family lived. Tim had been in the National Guard in a support role near Iraq, and Gwen was left home with a daughter too young to understand why he was gone or how long he was gone. So Gwen filled a candy bowl with jelly beans. Every day Hope could eat one, but only one, and when the bowl was empty, her father would be home. I guess I needed a kid fix, so when Hope took my hand to show me her precious bedroom, the house party was put on hold for a few minutes. We sat on her bed and talked; she asked if I would read her a book, and I did, then I wrote a note to her in it. You can tell a lot about people by watching the way they interact with their children. Hope's warmth was a product of Gwen and Tim's warmth. I would see them several more times during my campaigning. Gwen came to New Hampshire, bringing Hope's hello and a bracelet for me. And I saw them all again at Minnesota State University, back in my hold room, where I greeted all my friends.

Not everything was rosy and perfect, including me. At the Walz house party, one of the mothers was trying to buy body armor for her son who was headed to Iraq. She was trying so to hold in her fear and her grief. Was this what being a mother now meant, looking for body armor? Her fragility haunted me that day and the next, and when another mother sending a son to Iraq approached me after a town hall, instead of conveying the hope and strength I wanted to convey, all of the previous mother's anxiety came out. I left that second mother in worse shape than I'd found her. I turned to Hargrave, *What have I done?* I didn't make that mistake again, and I didn't forget that I had made it once. It wasn't the only mistake I made, but I hope it was the only one where someone other than me was hurt by it.

Not every event was a success. John had visited the Page Belting Company in New Hampshire during the primaries, and his visit was what one political commentator called "A Moment" — people shouting out, "You understand us. I've been waiting for someone like you." All magic. Campaigns being imperfect, we tried what Hollywood tries all the time, the sequel. During the general election I was doing Page Belting 3 or maybe even Page Belting 4, and the topic was to be health insurance. Here was the problem: Mark Coen, the president of Page Belting, made sure his employees had good health insurance. I was talking to a well-covered, well-satisfied audience who had no questions on health care for me. Sylvia Larson, a state senator who was wonderfully supportive during the general election and who appeared with me at every New Hampshire event, just shrugged.

I made another group of friends who also

appeared with me at many events: the Military Moms with a Mission. I first met Lisa at a panel discussion in Pensacola, Florida. Her husband, like my father and grandfather, was a naval aviator, and when she spoke so eloquently about her disappointment with the way the military was treating her family and others, I knew she should be included in the Military Moms tour that was starting. At least twenty-five years my junior and with the long, straight hair of a college girl like my daughter, she would have been one of my closest friends if she lived next door. Gentle, polite Lara, well-spoken Pat, angry and inspiring Nita — our converted Republican — and Maura, full of enough life to motivate the rest of us, filled out the troop. We kept coming together, then splitting apart, coming together, then splitting. Youngstown, Ohio, Morgantown, West Virginia, Laconia, New Hampshire. Nita came to Philadelphia to be in the crowd for one of my events. What I remember most of these women — who were from all parts of the country, from all sorts of lives — is that though their only connection was that they were mothers and wives of men in the military, that was enough to transcend their differences. They were united in a cause, and they had obvious affection for one another. I honestly hated it when they piled into their van headed to the next event without me, laughing and waving goodbye.

There is a familial culture in campaigning, the sense that you can argue among yourselves but no one outside can say anything bad about my brother, my sister, my friend. It was the collective sense of being a part of something, the shared experience of bad food, no sleep, and, for months at a time, the same history. It is easiest to see with the traveling crew. Think about this. You know everything about this person. You know when they're sick. You know when they're tired. You know how they're feeling. You've been there with ups and downs. You eat every meal with them. You spend every hour of the day with them. You're on the plane flying back and forth across the country, sitting there playing Boggle, singing, laughing, and running through the earlier events. When Ryan's pants ripped, Hargrave and I each offered to sew them for him. We were mothers, and we didn't stop because we were a candidate's spouse and her companion.

I know it happens at the staff level, and I have seen the affection these people who meet and work together, campaign after campaign, develop for one another. I am certain it happens in Republican campaigns, just as I saw it happen in Democratic campaigns. In between campaigns they go to each other's weddings, they send baby presents, they meet for weekend vacations. The question for some candidates, though John and I never stopped to pose it ourselves, is whether to be a part of this extended family, and if we became a part of it, how deep that connection would go. We just joined in, and our naiveté really paid off. We didn't know during the Senate campaign that the candidate didn't usually get Christmas gifts for his staff. So we bought them, well, suitcases. A gift and a joke at once. If we didn't join in, they'd be a family and we'd be on the outside. What fun would that be?

At the beginning of October, our family — our big family — moved to Chautauqua, New York, where John prepared for the vice presidential debate. Because it was past the regular season for vacationers, we had this extraordinary place almost to ourselves. Between debate preparation sessions, we would sit on the porches of the Athenaeum, a grand Victorian-era hotel, and look across the expanse of grass, across Lake Chautauqua, looking across to where Grant or

Roosevelt might have looked — so long had the resort been a refuge from politics. And a place of politics, too. And it was both for us. In the morning we would eat breakfast with the children, then head to an auditorium where for hours a mock vice presidential debate would take place, John being John, of course, and Bob Barnett playing Dick Cheney, thick notebooks of Cheney's positions and statements in front of him. As many a consultant suspected, I would undo some of their work during breaks. John would say, "What they are suggesting doesn't feel right to me," and I would support him, *Do what feels right.*

During one of the breaks, several of us remained in the auditorium to talk about the possibility of a question asking John to name three political mistakes he had made. Not a question any politician, any job applicant, anyone for that matter wants to answer. Before the break John had come up with two, but he hadn't come up with a third. When he and Mark Kornblau got up to get some of the lunch laid out in the next room, Ron Klain, Bob Shrum, David Ginsberg, and I stayed on the sofas talking. I had an idea. What about his vote confirming education secretary Rod Paige? John had been really unhappy with Paige's performance, as well as the revelations that had emerged about the Houston school district Paige had headed before his cabinet job. Well, maybe, said Klain. In a minute or two, he and Bob got up to get sandwiches, too. David and I talked until John came bounding back in the auditorium. "Shrum's got a great idea for the third mistake," he said. "Voting for Rod Paige!" David and I looked at each other and laughed. It is, you should know, campaign practice to take credit for other people's ideas. But this, perhaps, was a first: taking credit for an idea of the candidate's spouse. We have ribbed Bob mercilessly since.

It was a good time, a break before the last push, a time to watch football games on television — the area the staff had commandeered had a big TV and tables filled with food. I got a few of them to play Boggle with me, but it was really a young person's space, and I had my own young people to tend to. After the afternoon debate preparations, we would go back to the porches and watch the children play football on the lawn — Emma mostly speeding away from whomever was trying to catch her, whether she had the ball or not, and Jack wanting to be the quarterback and finally losing the job when he threw the football from four feet away directly into Matthew Nelson's groin. But soon the halcyon days were over, and the whole troop packed for Cleveland.

When I traveled with John, we traveled in his larger plane, John and most of his staff at the front, the Secret Service in between, and the press in the rear, everyone a little territorial — this had been their seat for weeks, "See that bag of chips on the floor? That's my bag." So the plane was crowded on the Monday afternoon we left for Cleveland, crowded and giddy with anticipation. The debate was seventeen hours away. Sam, Mary, Marcus, Lexi, Linda, Derek, Mark, Robert, everyone tense and excited and no one in a mood to fight about seats. We got to Cleveland and saw the familiar face of Al Rutherford, who looks more like a diplomat than an advance man. We had worked with Al in the primaries, and Sam knew that John would be completely at ease knowing Al was in charge in Cleveland. Another hotel — entered through the service bays — so I couldn't say which one. Cate arrived, and the next day so did the children, after a couple of days back home at school. John's parents were there somewhere, but I didn't see them until after the debate. There was this sense that there was a tornado all around us, and yet Al created this serene island so John could focus. And then time sped up and suddenly Cate and I were being seated next to Kristen Breitweiser, the beautiful and courageous September 11th widow who traveled with John in much the way the Military Moms with a Mission traveled with me. Cate and I were holding hands, we were in what would be John's line of vision, and Gwen Ifill, the moderator, was giving the audience instructions on clapping, which they usually ignore, although that would not be the case tonight. Tonight all was serious. It was as if there were two Titans clashing. We'd read the press analysis. Experience and judgment on one side of the table and humanity and intelligence on the other. And then the debate began, and John immediately started dismantling the notion that he was looking at a man of judgment.

I watched Dick Cheney's hands. I had taken enough depositions as a lawyer to know to watch his hands, and they were in motion. The man I had seen on television, sitting completely still in a meeting with the President or speaking as his flat hand punctuated his sentences in the air, this man was now holding one hand down with the other. I could have told Dick Cheney that I had been in many an argument with John and that he could, if he chose to, shake you. Cheney made his points about John, undoubtedly scored some points, but he never had what he clearly had expected to have: the upper hand with this whippersnapper. Finally, I think in desperation, though I am certain I will never know — Cheney said something he thought sounded dismissive of John and which was patently false: "The first time I ever met you was when you walked on the stage tonight." I turned to Cate, for I had sat for what seemed like hours next to Lynne Cheney while John sat two seats away next to Dick Cheney at the National Prayer Breakfast. It was untrue. When the debate was over, the families — as they always do — go up to the stage, hug their family, and exchange civilities with the opposition. John picked up Jack, who had run out to him, wanting to know, insisting to know in his deepest, most threatening, four-year-voice, *Which one is Cheney?* I had made my way to Cheney and, poking a finger at his lapel, I said, "You have too met John. We were all together at the National Prayer Breakfast." In the Kerry staff room they were watching on monitors; they couldn't hear me, they could only see me poking my finger. What, they wondered, was she doing now? "Oh, yes," he smiled, "we were."

Within minutes, of course, the entire press corps was poking their fingers in his lapel. Immediately on networks and blogs, the footage and the photographs went up. It was gratifying in one sense, but it changed what people were talking about. They weren't talking about the focus groups who had watched the debate and decided, without knowing about the misstatement, that John had won the debate. Instead they were talking about John and Cheney previously backstage at *Meet the Press,* or John and Cheney at the swearing in of Senator Elizabeth Dole, or. . . . The next day Cate was on CNN's *American Morning* with Bill Hemmer. Liz Cheney, Dick and Lynne's thirty-something daughter, was participating by remote and still backing the line that her father had never met John before. She explained that thousands of people attend the Prayer Breakfast, which they do, but she was looking at the remote camera, not the television monitor, so she could not see that as she spoke these words, CNN was showing John and Dick seated right next to one another on the dais, the "thousands of people" below and in front of them. Cate, who always was composed, was thinking to herself: *Okay, finally a softball.*

We all left Cleveland together, with Charlotte and Greensboro, New York, LaCrosse, and Milwaukee on our schedules. We stayed where the children wanted in Milwaukee: the Hilton with the indoor water park. We would have done it for the children, but it was also fun to see the Secret Service, in their suits, avoiding the cannonballs and water sprays. And then we were off in our different directions. Gone now were off times, walking the property in North Carolina we had purchased accompanied by the Secret Service; B.A., the architect; Tom Hunter, who would help us with the site plan; and Andrew Young, all of us sitting on fallen trees eating the sandwiches Andrew had brought. Gone were times for the parent conferences at the children's school that I had managed to fit in earlier. I would see the children on the weekends and in the evenings, but there was less than a month left before the election.

As we traveled, in a sense we took with us the people we had met, thinking of them and speaking of them. How often I mentioned McKinley Bailey, a beautifully spoken boy, not much older than Cate, who had already served in Afghanistan and in

Iraq. "When I was in Afghanistan," he said, "I knew why I was there. When I was in Iraq, none of us knew why we were there." A woman in her eighties, like Mary, should not be driven to tears because she could not afford her medicine, and I could not, would not drive her from my thoughts. And then there was Beverly. I had spoken to an organizing meeting, a rally really, in Grand Rapids. I gave a speech, which I am not very good at doing, and then I took questions. The last question came from Beverly, who was maybe just shy of forty, her skin so dark I had to focus to see her in the darkened theater. "My son is in Iraq," she got those words out, and then she fell apart. "I can't sleep, he can't sleep," she gasped between sobs. And then she could not speak at all. Her whole body was racked by fear and love. I'd seen this grief, and it would be wrong to say she hadn't earned the right to such debilitating grief. She had. I could only hug her and pray for her son. And take her with me.

The last days felt particularly intense, for we knew that it was our last chance to change minds. I did a town hall in Sandusky, with, as improbable as it sounds, a veteran named Del Sandusky, who had been on John Kerry's Swift boat, and with a woman whose husband had been called up at fifty and had trained to go to Iraq using his finger as a gun and a make-believe transport to practice how to evacuate after a roadside bomb exploded. He practiced without guns and without vehicles, and then he was sent to Iraq. If there was anyone other than a true believer in that town hall, surely they would be convinced, but were there any? From there we went to a union hall in Lima, where I was introduced by a young woman, Christina Lhamon. The next day I heard that her car tires had been slashed that night after we left. I knew from what she'd said when she introduced me that she had no money to replace them. *Get them replaced. We can do that for her.* Ryan agreed.

And I went back to Pittsburgh. First to the Southside Market House, where my Aunt Alba Whitacre, my father's youngest sister, waited for me. She asked not to be identified, so of course I made her do everything but twirl around. I was proud of her: she raised a houseful of children alone, she'd taught school. A few days later I went to Brownsville, south of Pittsburgh. I had asked to go; it was my father's hometown. And it seemed the whole town was there to see his daughter. Certainly every living member of his high school class was there, including Frank Ricco, who was the head of the Sons of Italy lodge where we met and who had been class president when my dad was vice president at Brownsville High School. I had to start the event with an update on Dad, the sad news that the gregarious young man they knew had been silenced and now seated by a stroke. They brought presents and photographs for me and for him, and I met children and grand-children of people I did not know. It was in the rope line that two tiny ladies, twins still dressed alike or nearly so at eighty, told me they were in class behind my father and had always had a crush on him. There was no doubt in my mind I was home.

There was a certain insanity to the sched-ule, but who could say so with so much at stake? Lancaster, Des Moines, Reno, Car-son City — *No, I don't know John Kerry's position on grazing rights,* and I had long ago learned never to try to wing it. Fess up and take the hit; never bluff. Elko, Denver, Grand Junction — of FATSO fame. And then south to Florida before joining Cate, for just the evening, in Kenosha, Wisconsin. It is now twelve days before the election.

Now, unless you're the sort of reader who

skips the first chapter, you know that I discovered the lump in my breast in Kenosha. Hargrave was scheduled to leave for the weekend in a couple of days; her son John's college was having Parents' Weekend. She fretted about what to do, but she told Karen and Ryan and perhaps Kathleen McGlynn, who came to take her place for the weekend, about the lump, and she made them promise to make certain I didn't get too tired. In fact, the next days were wonderful. I know my memory is clouded by the Wallingford's Orchard in Maine. There I answered questions as I stood in a wagon that had been piled with hay and parked in front of the open doors of a barn. It was next to impossible, standing outside as I was, to hear the questions from inside, but there were some helpful boys sitting at my feet, their legs dangling from the side of the wagon, who would repeat them for me. It was a very crisp and entirely luscious day, a perfect setting. And to top it off, the Wallingfords gave me a box of the most delicious apples I had ever eaten. And Ryan gave them all Elizabeth! buttons in thanks. I definitely had the better end of that trade.

As hard as it is to believe, except when I was showering or talking to John — and we talked several times a day, always have when we're apart — I didn't think about the lump. From Auburn, Maine, it was a Michigan rally, then Cincinnati, and finally a town hall in Harrisburg. I had been talking for the past three months, honing what I said and how I said it, stealing good lines from John and from Cate when I would hear them. For example, Cate — speaking on college campuses — would remind students that the 2000 election had been decided by fewer votes than the number of people who resided in the average dorm. But the crowds to whom I had been speaking were not large — several hundred. A thousand would be an excellent crowd. And now I was doing a town hall that would be carried live on C-SPAN. Now, I don't know how many voters who are still undecided a week out watch C-SPAN. My guess would be in the single digits, but I treated all town halls as if they were my chance to convince the entire country. I didn't have a lump on my mind, I had a town hall on my mind.

When it was over and I had done all I could, the lump started to creep into my thoughts, but by then it was only a few days until I would see my doctor in Raleigh, and this would — I assumed — be cleared up. Before going home, though, I would go to Florida. It was there that I met Ann Marie

Mattison. She is beautiful and regal, like a young Adele Graham, the wife of Senator Bob Graham of Florida who once, when John complimented her on a handmade wooden "Graham" button she was wearing during the primaries, said, without the least rancor, "I believe it was made for me before you were born." Anne Marie was lovely in every way. Her assignment in the program was to speak for a few moments and lead us in the Pledge of Allegiance. She used her minutes well. She spoke of her son, tall, handsome, intelligent, tenacious. She talked about how Jeffrey always wanted to do the right thing, serving in the Army, joining the Florida National Guard. He wanted, she said, to be president one day. Jeffrey Mattison Wershow was killed in Iraq on July 6, 2003. I have the bracelet Anne Marie gave me with his name on it, and I will always have it.

I left Florida and went home. Home to see my doctor, Wells. Home to get a mammogram and ultrasound. Home to wait for John. Although I didn't want to burden John with the news that it was likely that I had cancer — I had kept the secret for over a week already — telling him was the medicine I needed. From the moment I told him, I knew what he would do: he would start taking care of me, he always had. And in a very real sense I was, at that moment, unburdened. It all moved to him, all on his shoulders. Though I regret that it must have been such a terrible weight for him, I felt so safe with my care in his hands. I had read his depositions of doctors; he had always learned what he needed to know and often he knew more than the doctors he was questioning. He knew the questions to ask. He seemed intuitively to know when he wasn't being told the whole story. Dr. Hudis later told him he had the mind of a medical researcher, a considerably better compliment than "Mom" telling me I was a born waitress, I think. I knew he understood the medicine better, knew better the questions to ask, and I was right. After news of my cancer became public, people said to me how strong I must have been to keep this secret and continue campaigning, when I hadn't kept the secret at all — Hargrave and then John knew, and they, not I, carried the weight. Hargrave would ask me in the days ahead what I was going to do, and I would tell her, *Whatever John thinks is best.* I wasn't being deferential, I was being smart: he would look after me far better than I would look after myself.

But first we had to vote — an old friend from college, Gerry Cohen, handed us our absentee ballots — and speak at the Bon Jovi concert at the fairgrounds. I spoke to Cate at home, telling her I had another bump, like the one I had had before, and after the campaign I would get it checked out.

Hargrave talked to me about stopping campaigning. We were sitting on the stoop at my house with Peter Scher, who also knew what was going on. She said, "Can you continue campaigning through Tuesday, knowing what you know?" I looked out at my yard, at the driveway where nearly two years before John had talked to the press after announcing he was a candidate. It had been such a long road. I can do it. Hargrave said, "You have every reason in the world not to." No, I can do it. For a hundred reasons, for Beverly and Mary and George and Hope. For us, too, for all the reasons that led John to that spot on the driveway. And I knew, too, what the response would be if I canceled my remaining schedule — speculation that I'd delayed announcing my cancer until the last minute in an effort to garner sympathy votes. I could deal with what I had on my plate, but I didn't know if I could deal with that ugliness. And John was taking care of it. If we couldn't wait, he'd know. We went to vote and we went to the concert.

But that first night, we didn't want to be apart. Our schedules were sending us both west, so we said goodbye to Cate, and I joined John's caravan. I would spend the night with him in West Virginia and drive to our events in Ohio in the morning. Cate and Adam, with whom she had been traveling, set off for another round of college campuses and we took off in John's reconfigured 737. It wasn't the same gleeful we usually were when we were all together. Karen was usually happy, because she had a beau who traveled with John. The Secret Service was happy because there was actual leg room on this plane. Ryan was happy because the food was better and because Reggie Hubbard from John's staff, not he, took care of the luggage. But tonight John and I were tired, beaten down. We rested against each other in the dim cabin.

And then the plane caught fire. No, it's not a joke. If this were a movie, they would have to leave out the cancer or leave out the fire, because no one's luck is this bad. The fire turned out not to be serious. The battery for a large video camera had exploded, setting a seat afire briefly and causing a lot of smoke. There was an alarming degree of disorganization, and it was Ryan who finally grabbed the extinguisher and Ryan who finally insisted that we land the plane to make certain there wasn't unseen damage. We made an emergency landing. Fire trucks surrounded the plane and firemen rushed on board. Jack was ecstatic, as any four-year-old boy would be, asking them questions as they were stuck four and five deep in aisles filled with camera equipment and laptops and duffle bags. The Secret Service was hesitant to take us off the plane, because they had made no alternative arrangements. There were no waiting SUVs here. So we waited for the all-clear in the front of the plane, with the television on, watching CNN's live shot . . . of the plane. Meanwhile, the office was trying to find Cate or Adam before she saw a television screen, to tell her that her family was all right. And everyone was scrambling to figure out where to stay. The winning hotel was the worst of the general campaign. It smelled like smoke and sewage, and there was a dampness to everything. But I was there with John, and I didn't want to be anywhere else.

Having Emma Claire and Jack on the plane changed the dynamic for everyone, I think. The following day the press and crew, afraid that Emma Claire and Jack were going to miss Halloween, decorated the plane and bought candy so they could trick-or-treat down the aisles. I had brought their costumes with me — the only problem was getting Jack not to dress as a red Power Ranger every day — and they happily collected their goodies. Emma Claire is devoted to her father, and when I was not on the plane she claimed the seat next to him. Jack, on the other hand, would get on the plane and head to the press section, high-fiving the Secret Service on his way to see his friends. His friends set up a basketball hoop in the rear of the plane and taught him some sort of simple gambling game that might have worried a mother of a child with an allowance. When we were in hotels, he would come in early — Jack is our early riser — and say, "It's okay if you want to sleep. I'll go see my friends. What room is Dave in?" Dave has no idea how many times we protected his sleep. We had no better ambassador than Jack Edwards.

We left John and the children on Saturday morning and went on with our schedule. Hargrave was continually asking me whether I didn't want to stop altogether or just join John. The night before she had asked again, asking whether we should just join John.

There would be less pressure on me. "No," I said, "and since we have to drive to our event in the morning, we need to leave earlier, don't we?" I couldn't contemplate stopping. She said, "So we're going to do the whole deal? Your schedule as originally planned?" Yep. I found out later she went to Karen and Ryan and said, and I can just hear her mother/teacher tone, "There will be no whining from any of us from here on out. I don't want to hear it from anybody. If she can do this, we are not tired. Whatever she wants to do, we're there." Typical, wonderful Hargrave.

The next days weren't difficult anyway. I thanked people in phone banks and rallied with get-out-the-vote workers. I appeared at a couple of events with the serenely lovely Annie Glenn, John Glenn's wife. An extraordinary high school student, Molly Dickson, spoke at one. I went to two lovely Cleveland churches on Sunday. It was pleasant and easy. It was no longer about convincing; it was about making sure people voted. With forays into Pennsylvania and Wisconsin, I crisscrossed between Iowa and Ohio — two states we apparently lost, I have to point out, in case you are wondering about my effectiveness. Three places stay in my mind, Stephanie Tubb Jones's extraordinarily beautiful and intimate church, Bethany Baptist in Cleveland; the well-loved and well-worn William McKinley Elementary School in Cedar Rapids, where we had a rally with Tipper Gore and Senator Harkin; and the Inn on Coventry in Cleveland Heights. It was there, on October 31st, the last day of Breast Cancer Awareness Month, that I met the two women who, fighting cancer themselves, gave me my pink ribbon pin and asked if I was a survivor and I didn't know how to answer.

We got in the car, and I turned to Hargrave. *Did you see her?* Yes. *She gave me this pin,* I said, fastening the pin on my lapel. *She looked strong, didn't she? I mean except for the hair, she looked strong.* Yes, Hargrave answered, she did. And then we were quiet.

The next day was even less pressure, except for being on Larry King's show opposite Jeb Bush. That night the advance team, Jim McGreevy, Cooper Ray, and Henry Stern, brought champagne and bath soaks for us, and, although I don't drink much, I drank a glass with them and our troop, and I was happy and tired, sitting there reliving the campaign in my flannel pajamas.

Then it was the end. The last day, the final

get-out-the-vote effort in Cedar Rapids, the last television broadcast from Des Moines — after my meltdown in the stylist's chair. The beginnings of a celebration as the first votes came in and we flew to Boston. And then, as soon as I arrived, it was a flurry, police cars with sirens — we never used them — leading us at breakneck speed to the Boston hotel, then straight up to the tiny studio the campaign had set up there. At first, I didn't see Ted Koppel. He stood quietly in the corner until I took a breath, and then he said, "Just want to shake your hand," and he wished me well. He was hearing the same numbers I was hearing.

When I knew it looked bad, I wanted John. I was exhausted from the day, ending as it did with several hours in the remote chair doing radio. No one knew when John would arrive. The Internet connection in our room wasn't working; even the television was on the fritz. The world was changing quickly, and I was in an information-free zone. Ryan fixed everything in the room and then receded. I managed to hug him before he backed out of the room. He'd been there before, in 2000, when things started to fall apart in the Gore campaign. He went to his room, wanting to stay away from everyone, but Jack walked into the room, climbed up beside him, and watched television with him. He just sat there, the way Jack does, his hand on your arm, or his leg thrown across yours. I think Ryan knew then that John and I were going to be all right. Yes, we had to endure this final awful march, and yes, there was the cancer. But we also had this: this boy, these children. We'd be fine.

John finally came, exhausted but not yet empty. He wanted to fight. Hargrave got Nancy and Jay and my niece Laura and brought them to my room — they did not have the identification pins the Secret Service used to determine who was supposed to be on our closed floor. I talked to them and to Cate, who had gotten back to the hotel after representing us all afternoon at Boston events. As John talked on the speakerphone in the main room, I took Cate to the next room, a little dark room we didn't use, but a good place to tell her what would happen the next day. At that point I didn't know yet that there would be a concession speech. I only knew that tomorrow I would certainly be told that I had breast cancer. And then my brother and sister came in, with my niece Laura, and I told them too. I speak to my brother and sister once a week, maybe more — less, certainly, during the campaign — and though we are all in our fifties and live thousands of miles apart, I know when Jay quits smoking and I know when he starts again, I know when Nancy gets her hair cut or what the doctor said in her last visit. We cannot disconnect. And we don't want to. They wanted to come with us to the hospital, to be there with us. I couldn't let them; it would be too much. So we just held each other until we were so blasted tired we couldn't, and Jay and Nancy went back to their rooms, each leaning down to hug John before they did, each whispering to him, *Take care of her.*

CHAPTER 14
WASHINGTON

THE HOSPITAL

"You have breast cancer." Those are the words one in eight women will hear, but, trust me, knowing those odds doesn't make it any easier to hear it. And those words were what Barbara Smith said to me, to us — Cate and John and me — on the afternoon of November 3rd, the day after the election of 2004.

Earlier that day, the three of us had arrived at Faneuil Hall in a motorcade past lines of well-wishers waving and cheering, reaching their hands toward the car, four and five deep on the sidewalks as we passed, just as if it were a victory celebration. As we'd done a hundred times before, we stepped out of the SUV and into a building, into a quiet space — this time a bookstore in a basement, I think — where we were to wait until the event — this time John Kerry's concession speech — was ready to begin. His daughters, Vanessa and

Alex Kerry, came in; it would be our last time with them, probably, certainly like this. On the campaign train ride through the Southwest in August, Emma Claire gave half of her dolphin-shaped best-friend bracelet to Alex, who, sweetly, had worn it, at least for a while. Alex got a lot of points with me for that. And I had grown especially fond of Vanessa — she had a spirit that would serve her well, one she had needed in the past and would need in the months to come. The room broke up into sexes and age groups, like rooms had been doing since junior high school dances. Cate talked to the Kerry girls. The two Johns talked. Then Teresa came in, hobbling toward me, her ankle thickly wrapped. Her shoe had broken and she had fallen, and as sorry as I was that she was hurt, I was just pleased to be able to listen to a conversation about something as trivial as a twisted ankle. It was probably really painful, but it was, after all, a twisted ankle. The election and the two tough years that preceded it. This awful unwanted speech now. The appointment with the breast surgeon to follow. A twisted ankle was actually just what I needed. I let myself concentrate on her every word.

Cate and I sat in the front row with the Kerry women as the men stepped up to the stage. My husband spoke first. We listened as he gave his speech, listened as he never used the words concede or lose or defeat. His defiance was a small gesture, but we had learned about how precious hope could be — and we had more lessons ahead — and somehow saying those words seemed to us the same as relinquishing hope, so even with the concession speech to follow, he would not say them. John finished to warm applause and left the stage, left John Kerry alone to receive the palpably extraordinary love of the people gathered there, left him to say the words that John would not.

He said them. And then it was over. We rode in the same car in which we had arrived, in the same seats, Cate and John and I again, now away from Faneuil Hall, still cheered on by the waiting crowds. No one else knew, but we were driving on to face our next fight.

If there was ever a day and a place where we would be identifiable, it was this day in Boston, so I was glad we had a little special treatment at Mass General. Someone met us at a back door, met us and a pared-down Secret Service group, their faces solemn for the present chore. Through back corridors and empty stairwells, we made our way to a bright examining room. There we first met Barbara Smith, who would later be my surgeon. It was impossible not to have immediate confidence in this serene, intelligent woman. She explained the needle biopsy and the process for getting results, and she asked if John and Cate wanted to stay for the procedure. I could have told her the answer. They hadn't stayed in our bedroom as I gave myself hormone shots before Emma Claire and Jack were born, they weren't likely to stay now.

When they left, she put the needle next to the lump and with a dull click pulled out the tiniest amount of tissue. She did the same thing under my arm, from a lymph node. She left to have the tissue examined, and my family came back in. Cate's face was stained with tears. It was, for me, a worse moment than the moments I knew lay ahead. I so love this child, this young woman who had been through so very much, who had slept on two chairs and an ottoman in our room for two years after her brother's death, who was now drained and exhausted from working for months as hard or harder than anyone else in the campaign, and I had promised myself that I would protect her from any more pain. Yet here we were. Though I knew I hadn't the power to spare any of us this, it did not make it hurt less. Not for her, not for me.

Whatever she'd surmised from her conversations with John and me in Raleigh, on election night she'd heard directly from me that I was pretty sure I had breast cancer. She and I had stood alone in a small dark hotel room, arms resting on each other's shoulders, bands playing below us in Copley Square. She'd already been weakened by the crush of the day, but it could not wait. I'd needed to tell her what would happen the next day, I needed to land the next blow here, alone, so that she would be ready. She hadn't broken. This is the child who did not cry when the end of her finger had been accidentally cut off when she was seven — it regenerated, which can happen at that age — and she did not cry election night at my news. She stiffened then so we could tell my brother and my sister who waited a few steps away. But now she was here in the hospital room, held together only by years of practice at holding herself together. A friend, journalist Meryl Gordon, told me afterward that she wanted to speak to God on our behalf to say, "These people have had enough. Enough already with them. Leave them alone now." And I surely felt that way about Cate.

Barbara Smith came back in the room to a huddled family, but when she said those words, that it was cancer, we rallied. In the next hours, we even laughed and teased one another. We now had a dragon we could slay. At other times it had been different. Wade had had no chance to save himself, and we had had no chance to save him. John had been unable to convince the Kerry campaign to continue to fight. His protestations were ignored. Nothing we could do would fix these things. But we could fight cancer. It was terrible and ominous, and for Cate, for John, and the younger children, I admit that I was afraid to lose this fight. But it wasn't, by a sad and huge distance, the worst news we had ever heard. Wade's death had spared us that and spared us some degree of fear as well.

I don't want to misrepresent this. My reaction was to get ready for battle, but I wasn't always strong. I wasn't even strong all that first day. I had times along this path when I wanted to say I've had enough, I can't keep dealing with the latest side effect, the latest setback, the latest scare. I'd be in great pain or just not be able to do things I'd always done, and I'd say I know I have to kill this dragon, but the killing it is killing me. How easy it would have been along this road to fall back into that fear, but there was always someone waiting to help. John bringing me a soda and a sandwich, my sister calling to cheer me up, Chris Downey coming by with flowers, John Auchard coming by with dinner. A letter from Cedar Rapids or a card from Harrison, New Jersey — I had met them or I hadn't, but they reached out. Connective tissue that wouldn't wither even when I wanted to, that held me up when I could not stand, that would not let go. And so I was nourished by strangers and friends. But at this moment, it was the three of us.

As we followed Barbara Smith on our way to the CAT scan, we teased the Secret Service detail, who were trying to be invisible in their dark suits in the white-walled halls, surrounded by white-coated hospital staff. It was hopeless; they stood out more than we did. They were probably glad to stand outside the room while I went in to be scanned. The CAT scan would look at my torso to determine whether the cancer had spread. We were still jovial, John and Cate perched on stools while the huge machine hovered over me. Jovial until Barbara said there was an "anomaly" in my liver. The news set us back, hard. There was a two-thirds likelihood it was not cancer, she told us — and a one-third likelihood that it was, which she didn't say or have to say. A one-third likelihood of metastasis to the liver. The laughing stopped; even false cheerfulness was out of place. We left Mass General at least as somberly as we had come in.

At midnight, Cinderella's coach turns back into a pumpkin, and on the day after the election, the chartered plane that had carried John, a staff, and a press corps across the country for more than four months was gone, not even a pumpkin left. My smaller jet and my pilot Brett Karpy were carrying someone else where they needed to go, or maybe he was having a long-overdue vacation. And we were in Boston, Cate and John and I were leaving Mass General and stepping into an unknown future . . . with no way to get there. My good friend Gordon Livingston had once told me about a friend who was going helicopter skiing, whatever that is. He added, somewhat embarrassed I think, that he thought it was good to know people of all classes. So now I add that it was our great fortune that someone we knew owned a plane that would get us back to Washington, to the children who had left Boston earlier that morning, so we could contemplate, in our own home, alone, what we had been told that afternoon at Mass General. There was a small staff with us on the plane ride home, a skeleton crew of John's Secret Service detail and mine, Peter Scher, and Miles Lackey. We decided that we would release the news of the breast cancer to the press, that maybe other women would then get the timely mammograms I had missed and would not have to hear the news we had just heard. But we didn't mention the possible metastasis, not to Miles or Peter, not to the public. We needed to deal with this news privately first. In some ways working with the press release was good. It gave us something to talk about, and when it was done, we all fell silent. There was a sad dignity to the silence.

It was dark by the time we got home, and the children were already asleep. We put our suitcases filled with dirty clothes down on top of the suitcases filled with dirty clothes that we had left the last time we had been home, and we went in and kissed the foreheads of our sleeping children. When I came back to our room from loading the first of twenty loads of laundry, John was sitting in the chair next to the bed. Sometime during the campaign he had taken one of the

Elizabeth! buttons that Ryan had had made and clipped it into the upholstery on the back of his chair. Somehow it was too much to come home to such an uncertain tomorrow and see that gay button, the symbol of a time of promise. He had his head in his hands when I walked in. I have always believed that one of the things that makes a marriage work is the teeter-totter of it: when he is down, it is my turn to be up. When one of us is overwhelmed, the other has to tighten up and take the blows. It is never a one-way street. It surely wouldn't be in the months ahead. He just needed a few minutes, and then we were ready for bed, but not, it turned out, ready for sleep.

All of what had happened in the previous twenty-four hours, which included the emotional weight of all that had happened in the last years, was heavy on us, but the heaviest of all was the one-third likelihood that the cancer had metastasized to my liver. John fretted that he hadn't taken care of me, though the blame, if blame had been useful, was mine, not his. When he finally picked up a book from the night table, finally forced his mind to think of something, anything else, I got up and got onto the computer. I typed "metastasis liver cancer prognosis" into Google, and I pressed Search.

"If the surgery is not successful, the disease is often fatal within three to six months." That's what I read. And that's when I decided I wasn't searching for prognosis again.

The next morning we got up, and the first hours were so innocent and familiar: Jack climbing into our bed as soon as the sun came up, the dressing and breakfast making, and the storytelling as if we hadn't seen them the morning before. John told the Secret Service agents, who were still there, that we wanted to take the children to school ourselves. Did they really need to go with us? Did we really need a motorcade? Weren't they going to leave at some point? They said yes, they would be leaving, and John said, "Well, we'd rather just take the children to school without the motorcade, without the fuss." So we all said goodbye. We shook hands and hugged on the street, outside the house with the children coming down the front stairs with their backpacks. Jack's Secret Service agent came over to him.

"Well, Jack, I'm going to be leaving now."

"So when are you coming back?"

"I'm not coming back."

"Why?" said Jack. "We're friends."

"Well, since the campaign is over, I won't be coming back."

I don't know which one was sadder. Jack said, "Oh," and he gave him a hug.

Jack invited him and Joe Casey, who had been with Jack earlier in the campaign until he got a significant promotion to the President's detail, to his fifth-birthday party the following May. After all, they were friends.

When we came home from delivering the children to school, we turned ourselves fully to this next battle. It was now Thursday, November 4th, and we didn't know whether I had cancer somewhere other than my breast. We didn't know who was going to do the testing I obviously needed. We didn't even have a doctor in Washington, D.C. All we knew was that we needed to move on all these fronts right away. At the same time, it was still just two days after the election, one day since the campaign into which we had thrown ourselves for so long had closed its doors, although it was still weeks before the last vote would be counted. I was sapped; I had held on to the secret of the cancer so long that when it came out, almost all my energy went with it. Whatever little was left evaporated when I Googled "metastasis liver cancer prognosis." But John was a cauldron — restless, wanting to fix it all, knowing he

528

was blocked in every direction. In the next days while we waited for a call back from the doctor or while I read to the children or talked to Cate on the phone (she'd finally gone to New York to start the job she had put off for four months), he would slip upstairs and, in whispered phone conversations, continue the campaign battle. He did it until the doing of it was patently useless, trying all the while to protect me from his frustration and disappointment. I needed, he was certain — and he was certainly right — the power of his optimism. He had to turn himself entirely to the battle in which he could have some effect.

He would be there for my fight, as I had been there for his. But it wasn't a fair trade. My fight was one neither one of us wanted; we knew it would drain us in ways we hadn't even yet imagined. We would have to summon reserves that we knew from sad experience were there, but it was nothing to which either of us could look forward. On the other hand, I thrived on his fight; it had fed me to campaign beside him these past two years. I needed it, and in the months ahead, when I would sit so tired and alone or with him beside me, I missed it — Hargrave and Ryan and Karen, the young people around me, the seniors I embraced, the mothers and the waitresses, the sense of purpose that was so much bigger than cancer. But it was over, and all I had to fight was cancer, a fight that would only take from me and from him and would never nourish me, or him. He got the short stick.

We talked to Dr. Cliff Hudis at Memorial Sloan-Kettering Cancer Center in New York on that anxious Thursday. We asked Cliff to oversee my treatment, to make sure we were making wise decisions. Cliff had precisely the no-nonsense way of talking that we needed. He's brilliant in the most accessible of ways, and although he serves nothing with sugar, he's never negative. If it hadn't been for that spot on my liver in the CAT scan, I would have felt great after talking with him. But there was no denying that spot. We also talked to Barbara Smith from Boston about what our next steps should be. She recommended that we see Bob Warren at Georgetown University Hospital. We didn't waste a minute. By early that afternoon, two days after the election, we were in Dr. Warren's office. Friday we were at the hospital again, and again on Monday for more tests. And on the next Tuesday, November 9th, a week after the election, I had my first chemotherapy session.

When we first went to the Lombardi

Center at Georgetown University Hospital, the staff wanted to reassure us, but words were not going to put us at ease. Test results might, so we kept asking about the MRI of my liver. We thought of little else, including the breast cancer, except whether the anomaly the CAT scan had identified was a benign angioma — a collection of blood vessels — or metastasized cancer. Dr. Susan Ascher would do the MRI. Between Susan in Washington and Dr. Barbara Smith in Boston, I felt as if we had walked onto the sets of soap operas peppered with attractive women playing doctors. But these doctors were for real. Knowing how anxious we were about the MRI, Susan arranged for one immediately. I think I was in the MRI scanner within a half hour of meeting her. Although a technician usually watched the MRI images, Susan watched them herself. John sat with me in the room where I was placed into the scanner, and from his chair, he could see Susan studying the images on a monitor in the next room as the dye they had put in me made its way to my liver. If the anomaly, the growth, didn't take up the dye, it was cancer. When it filled up my anomaly, the dye going where the blood would have gone, Susan knew it was an angioma. John said he could see the relief wash over her face. For now we were on the right side of the statistics, but we were still a long way from the end of the testing.

We agreed that I would participate in a clinical study that involved additional testing during the course of chemotherapy — periodic MRIs and something like needle biopsies, where a core sample from the tumor would be drawn and analyzed every few weeks. My doctors knew that the chemotherapy, surgery, and radiation regime they were suggesting was effective, not because they had guessed it might be effective but because this sequence had been honed through trials and studies long before I found my bump in Kenosha. Dr. Warren had an arsenal at his disposal, an arsenal provided to him by doctors and scientists surely, but available only because women before me had said yes when they were asked if they would participate in a trial or a study. And with each trial, each study, each woman, the treatment for breast cancer was improved. I knew I could not repay those women — most much braver than I, many of whom had taken a chance with their own treatment in order to help find the best treatments for all of us — except by helping the women who would come after me. It was, oddly, like cleaning the graves of children buried near Wade after their mothers had died. It is a continuum in which I believe. And in this case, I might be making it better for myself, too. The study meant we would be getting more information, and more information was good, wasn't it?

Well, maybe not. It was 8 P.M. that first Thursday night when I had the last of that long day's tests, a bone scan. We weren't worried; in our mind the real test, the MRI of my liver, was behind us. While I lay on yet another metal table dressed in yet another sheet studying the last film the technician had taken, a scan of the bones in my hand, still glowing on the monitor, the technician read the bone scan film in an outer room. John sat beside the technician, who spoke to himself as he pulled up each image. John listened to his easy patter. "This is fine, this is fine, this is fine," and then he stopped. In a few seconds he said, "You know, this is abnormal." He kept saying it. He turned to John, "I really want to send you home not worried because I know you don't need this right now, but there's something on one of her ribs on the left side." Although it didn't look like cancer, although it could be anything, including something as benign as getting bumped there years before, it could be bone cancer. No odds this time with which to chase away sleep. No Googling "bone cancer prognosis." It lay there as I lay on that table, covered by the thinnest of sheets. And it remained unresolved until the end of the next week when we went up to see Dr. Hudis in New York. Dr. Warren had sent the bone scans with me so that he could have Dr. Hudis' opinion. I don't think Dr. Warren thought it was cancer, but he wanted us to have a second opinion. And we got it in just a few seconds. It might have seemed anticlimactic had it not been the ending for which we had hoped. Cliff looked at the films and said this is absolutely nothing. That's all we needed. We trusted him entirely. And we knew we could now quit worrying about bone cancer.

At the end of the tests on that first Thursday, we sat again with Dr. Warren, to map out a plan of attack. He was organized, attentive, and sweet — and aggressive in his treatment, which was particularly consoling to us. Barbara Smith had already given us the broad strokes: chemotherapy, pause, surgery, pause, radiation. Now we were filling in the line drawing and deciding when to start. He was talking about starting the chemotherapy in a few weeks. No, no, we said, we wanted to start right away. Tomorrow? He couldn't make that work. Monday? No. We wound up starting chemotherapy on Tuesday, November 9th, one week after the election.

So the first weekend after the 2004 election was also the last weekend before chemotherapy started. We had some of the staff over to the house, we watched football, we played basketball with Jack and Ian Moore from next door, Emma Claire played with Patsy's dog in the back alleyway, and I tried to spend the time not thinking about being sick. It was hard, of course, because I was sick, and hard, too, because people who wished us well kept telling us so. Teresa Heinz called me to give advice about what she had learned — she'd sweetly been on the phone doing what we had been doing, trying to find the best place for my treatment.

"There are plenty of good doctors," she said. "Just don't use . . ." and she named one of the doctors on my team. There were real valleys in this process, and sometimes the valleys are precipitated by little pieces of misinformation from which no one can really protect you. And on that first weekend, Teresa's warning — which we concluded was wrong — sent me into a real valley. If you had hit me in the face with a two-by-four, I don't think my expression would have been much different than it was listening to Teresa. I wanted to know why and I didn't want to know why she'd said that, and mostly I wanted the conversation to end. I thanked her for all the work she had done on my behalf, and I meant it. Then I hung up and fell right off the razor blade on which I had been sitting, the one I had been denying for the past days. There was no part of me that did not feel beaten. In the bad-moments department, this was pretty huge. This time it was John's turn to be the upbeat to my downbeat. He reminded me what I, on reflection, might have figured out, if reflection had been possible: people who have bad medical results want to find a reason, and a lot of people blame a doctor. He'd seen it hundreds of times when he practiced law, hundreds of times when he had turned cases away because — despite a bad result — the doctor had done nothing wrong. Not all cancer patients live, even those getting the very best care possible.

When Vicki, Ted Kennedy's wife, called to share with me what she had learned when her daughter had had cancer, I broke apart again and told her about the conversation with Teresa. Vicki suggested we talk to Alan

Rabson, deputy director of the National Cancer Institute, about my team of doctors. Dale, a friend from English graduate school, had also recommended I speak to him. John, seeing how desperately I needed reassurance, moved mountains to get Dr. Rabson on the phone. He assured us that we had made good choices, that we had a fine team of doctors. John ran interference for me from that time on, protecting me from anything that might send me back down. And that evening, after a mild November day, he and the children and I all walked down to Thomas Sweet's and walked home, each with an ice cream cone, as if we hadn't a care in the world.

On the first day of chemotherapy, Anne O'Connor put us in a small room on the clinical trials hall and went to find the nurse technician. She came back in with Mercedes Watson. Mercedes is tall, and dark-skinned with a pretty face, and eight different hairdos — one for each of my eight sessions over the next fifteen weeks. She was strong and cheerful, a perfect match for us or for anyone needing to feel that all good things were still possible. It is said that cancer is a disease that hits the whole family. Well, Mercedes signed on, too; she would be part of our family for this fight.

Throughout the treatments, she was by my side, telling me what she was doing, no matter how obvious it was, and telling me what I could expect to feel. Between her lessons and warnings, she would fill the silence with stories about her family or her house or the weather. As Christmas approached, it was what could she get her son or how much help her daughter had been wrapping presents. I would talk about wrapping presents with Cate — in our hectic lives lately that usually meant staying up till 4 A.M. on Christmas Eve wrapping gifts that would be unwrapped at 7 A.M. — and it turned out Mercedes and her daughter did the same thing. The one thing the conversations would not be about was cancer. It was as if we had both come early to a PTA meeting, and although we didn't know each other well enough to talk of real intimacies, we knew we had something in common, so we talked about life in a general easy way. Just like at PTA.

So here John and I were — a week after the election, a week after private planes and hairstylists, after Secret Service and buttons with our photos on them, a week after stages and television cameras — here we were, the two of us, in the most spartan of hospital rooms. One bed. One chair. A doorway to the corridor, through which we would watch as passing patients or staff would casually look in, then slow or circle back for a second and third walk-by as they tried to figure out if that man in the jeans and sweater really was John Edwards. A side table for my soda and Mercedes' supplies. An IV pole. And a single window out of which we couldn't see much except the weather.

The first four chemotherapy sessions — one every two weeks — would be injections of two drugs. These drugs, I knew, were going to kill all growing cells in my body. I was warned they were going to make my nights uncomfortable and my days unpleasant. I would feel tired and sore. I would bruise and bleed, my skin would change, my nails would yellow, I would feel nauseous, and I would get sores in my mouth. And my hair would fall out. I could not wait to get started. I wanted to be a warrior.

Can you go to war while you are sleeping? Because if you cannot, I was not actually a warrior. The first drug Mercedes gave me each visit was something to stop nausea. It worked — I was never nauseous — but it also made me sleep. If there was an expected side effect, good or bad, of any drug they gave me, I experienced it. Once when I had a day surgery, the doctor, who had warned me that the anesthetic could cause nausea, hadn't listened to his own warning. As he was leaning over to tell me I was fine and could go home, I threw up all over his shoes. My white blood cell count was supposed to go down during chemotherapy, and it did. So I gave myself injections at home to keep the count up, and that worked, too. The Taxol I was later administered could cause an allergic reaction that, if it occurred, would show up at the first dose, turning my torso and face red. And it did. In a few minutes, fortunately, the redness faded. Anemia? I had it. So when Mercedes started whatever medicine made me sleep, I would drift off on cue, while Mercedes told stories about the deer in her neighborhood that had startled her, or some problem she had with her car, and I would sleep through at least half the session. The list of distasteful side effects gets far worse after anemia and sleepiness; it would give me no pleasure to write it, and it would give a reader no pleasure to read it.

I knew that I would lose my hair. In my battle against victimization, I cut it off before it fell out. Kevin, who cut my hair and later went shopping for wigs with me, came over and shaved my head the week before my hair was supposed to fall out. Jack and John volunteered to let Kevin cut theirs off, too, but I convinced them it wouldn't help me to see more bald people in my family. I felt they were a part of this fight without going through this sweet gesture of solidarity.

The loss of hair appeared to be the only part of cancer and cancer treatments that interested the younger children. When I first cut my hair off, I let them watch and then rub their hands on the little fuzz that Kevin had left. They were expecting my bald head, actually anticipating it with eagerness because I had sat them down weeks earlier and talked about my cancer before the news of it was released to the press.

"Mommy has a bump," I said. "And that bump is called cancer. Cancer is very bad, but I will get rid of the bump and the cancer by taking really strong medicine."

They looked bored. Somber, but bored. Or maybe just bored.

"And that medicine is so strong that it will make my hair fall out."

I think it cheered them up. "Your hair's gonna fall out? All of it? When? Can I see?"

The children never acted scared, and we never talked about the fact that some people die of cancer. When, on the news, they were announcing somebody's death from cancer, as when Peter Jennings died or when Dana Reeve lost her fight, we'd switch the channel immediately. Cancer can still kill me, but there's no reason for them to spend their days — or nights — thinking that it will.

I thought — wrongly it turned out — that we had painted a rosy, even funny picture of the upcoming fight with cancer. But they were knocked more off balance by my primary-school rendition of my disease than I had suspected, particularly Emma Claire, who was six years old. It would show up in a letter she would write or in the answer to a teacher's question. There her Christmas wish would be for me to be better, for cancer not to hurt me anymore. But with me, she was always stoic. If we all acted strong with one another, it was easier for each of us to actually be strong. So we did. Even Emma Claire, at age six.

Our trips to the hospital for chemotherapy would start before nine in the morning with bloodwork. Though I was in a major hospital, it was like the scene from a low-budget film, some actors playing multiple parts. The fellow taking my paperwork at the reception desk, Desi Ravonimanantsoa, would clock me in, wait a few minutes, stand up and call my name, and then walk me back to the blood-drawing room, where he would put on gloves and, now the technician and no longer the receptionist, take my blood. There were regulars, too, patients on the same schedule I was on. Each visit, Anne O'Connor would ask whether I had seen my boyfriend that day. My "boyfriend" was a large man about twenty years older than I who would give me a chocolate candy out of his Captain Kangaroo pockets each time I saw him in the blood-drawing room. Nothing like candy with a morning blood draw.

I would see Dr. Warren for an examination before getting to my chemotherapy room and Mercedes by 10 A.M. We would be in that room until 2, or 3, or even 4 P.M. We would have a rare visitor. Cate's boyfriend from college, Trevor, a medical student at Georgetown, came to see us in our little room, and Zam-Zam Murad, the other nurse technician, would stop by to check on us. But mostly it was just us, and it was quiet. The change from our previous intense, high-pressure, busy, people-filled campaign existence to our new intense, high-pressure, slow-paced, lonely disease-fighting existence was at no time more noticeable than when I was lying in bed, connected to my IV, with John reading in a chair at the foot of the bed, and a pleasant woman would come with a little cart and ask, "Want a sandwich? I've got P and J, I've got an egg salad left." And we'd say, "You don't have any tuna salad left?" She'd check and invariably say, "Well, look. I've got one tuna salad right here." And we'd get it. One tuna salad and one P and J, and we'd split them.

Most of what happened during those months of chemotherapy happened at home. I would have my chemotherapy session on Tuesday, and then I would have a couple of good days when I could do just about anything I wanted. I would shop for fresh groceries. I had lunch with friends. After those days, for the next week or longer, I would really try to minimize what I did. The steroids I took made me hungry and achy, but the worst was the Neupogen injections I did daily for a week each cycle to keep my white blood cell count up. They had warned me about Neupogen's side effects, but I was cavalier. The shots weren't hard — I had done this when I was trying to get pregnant. But with each round it got worse. With each round my bones and my joints hurt more, my knees were stiffer, my fingers ached more. And there was no respite in being still: when I would lie down in bed, it was constant pain from head to toe. Walking was difficult — I would plan my trips up or down stairs — and writing was almost impossible. I was trying to answer letters I had received, but after three or four notes, my hands would be in a painful cramp. I had tried so not to be a victim, to be the master in this, but it was hard not to feel the strain of it when the drugs were so debilitating. I didn't like it, but it was undeniable: I was a victim. I suppose we might have learned when Wade died that all control is illusory, but we cling to that, even after all the lessons. And despite the lessons, I cling to it still.

It helped to have Emma Claire and Jack. I could sit and read to them — and they understood that was about all I could handle then and they never complained. It helped to have Randy Galvin and then Heather North, who helped with the children, who would cheerfully run with them when I could not. It helped to have Lexi and Matthew, who managed the schedule of appointments, who made sure I had the medicines I needed and rides when it was difficult to drive. And most of all, it helped to have John. I thought all the time as I was dealing with this, feeling the aches, marking off days of my life in which the only thing I did was fight cancer, that there are women who were doing exactly what I was doing except they were hauling the groceries, taking care of the kids without help, and going to work. I had lots of help, the luxury of no job, and I had John.

On one snowy day that closed the area schools, I passed a woman — her obviously bald head covered by a knit cap — in the halls at Georgetown Hospital. She had two young children and she was carrying snacks for them, taking care of them, while John was carrying everything I might need during my chemotherapy session. It was impossible not to feel lucky . . . and guilty. My empathy increased as we started getting correspondence from the insurance company. It was unintelligible. John was a senator, a presidential candidate, and a vice presidential candidate; we were both lawyers — for decades — and we still had no idea of what most of the insurance company notices meant. Were they rejecting claims for the most basic services? Was only part of an MRI charge covered? Did they not have the right documentation from the doctor or was this procedure never going to be covered? We could not imagine what it would be like for someone like the knit-capped mother of two who depended on her insurance. Where would she even get the time to figure out what these letters say and what she needs to do to satisfy the insurance company? And if nothing is going to satisfy them, where's she going to get the money to pay for what she thought was covered by insurance? I thought about all the meetings on health care policy that had taken place in our family room, young dedicated people who had studied the problems and were suggesting responses and programs to John. To his credit, John was at least as informed by the woman in the knit cap as by the academics. At meetings he would invite the anecdote, the stories of how policies affected real people's lives.

The staff learned, of course. To get John's attention, don't start with how well your idea polls. Start with "I met a young father who . . ." or "I have an aunt who inspects nursing homes and she said . . ." Maybe it was the storyteller in John, the part of him that had been informed about health care first by those whom the system had mistreated, the part of him that had for twenty years told those stories to juries. And it wasn't just staff telling stories to John. John and I would both be talking about what we were hearing. How in the world were people making it? The answer is that some weren't. Some were, of course, but some of those only with the generosity of others.

During the campaign, I had held a panel discussion on women's health care in North Carolina. On the panel was a woman named Pat, whose husband had gotten up one morning and, with his — and her — health insurance, walked out on her. And then she discovered she had breast cancer. Her community stepped up, the doctors and nurses, her friends and neighbors, and she was making it. She gave me a lovely jacket she had made, which I might have worn instead of what Hargrave called my Courage Jacket if we hadn't had to return it because it exceeded the Senate's gift restrictions. After I was diagnosed, Pat sent me a lovely — and considerably less expensive — cap she had made, passing on the generosity she had been shown. At a Silver Lady Fund benefit in Miami, I heard from a woman who had made it through her struggle because the Fund had helped her with transportation and child care, meeting the expenses of the disease that insurance would never reach. John packed away what we saw and heard, packed it away for another day. There was so much to be done, but for now we had our own fight.

For the clinical study I had more tests and more MRIs. The MRIs were a completely leveling experience where — so that a record can be made of changes in the tumor — you lie facedown with your bare chest hanging over the edge of a table. And there were also periodic analyses of core samples of the tumor. A beautiful Greek doctor, Erini Makariou, very polite and very elegant, would apologize as she shot a little needle into my breast — it sounded like a children's cap gun — to take a core sample of the cells in the lump. The first time she had to take a sample, she said it was easy as pie. You've got a huge target there, she said of my tumor. From where do you want to take the cells? By the last core sample collection, she was just beaming, saying, "It's hard for me. I try to put the needle in but there's nothing there. It just goes right through." It was, I imagined, like the wrappings left over from what had been a full package of cancer.

I don't know what the study said about how much doctors can learn from such constant testing during chemotherapy. What I do know was that, as a patient, it was terrific to have constant progress reports, particularly since the tumor was responding to the chemotherapy. And what's more, the clinical study team, like the chemotherapy team, made me feel I had people who were cheering for me the whole time. Ann Gallagher, who monitored the study, held my hand during these sessions, squeezing it with excitement as the good results rolled in, and smiled as if she herself had just gotten the best present imaginable. Honestly, they couldn't have been better cheerleaders if they wore sweaters with Elizabeth written across them. This was their victory, too. I know that people say they are under Dr. So-and-so's care. I didn't think of it that way. I liked my doctors immensely, but I spent more time with Ann and with Mercedes, and I felt I was under their care. It was with them — and John — that I most wanted to celebrate whenever we got good news.

After four sessions of the first drugs, I started my four sessions of Taxol, again once every two weeks. Taxol took longer to administer, and I felt more drained after each session. The truth is, I had just gotten worn down. I had used up all of my reserves. It is like a marathon, in which your body cannot possibly store all you need to finish the race, and you know that what must propel you in the last miles, if you make it, is simply the will to finish. And that's where I was. On the days when my hand wouldn't cramp, I could answer letters. The rest of the days, well, I was pretty useless. The hardest part was the children, for I could hardly be reassuring when I was so sore and tired, so very tired that by the end of chemotherapy I was going to bed before them. In a sad reversal, they would come into my bedroom and kiss me goodnight.

My last chemotherapy session was on February 15, 2005. Mercedes had a friend of hers make me a cake with the UNC logo on it. Mercedes, as usual bragging about someone else, told us how difficult it had been to get the *N* and the *C* just right, and hadn't her friend done a nice job? We brought cookies — for Mercedes and all the nurses who had fed John cookies over the last fifteen weeks, and we brought flowers for Mercedes and Ann. It couldn't be a tearful goodbye because it was such a happy goodbye. We couldn't be sad, and yet, despite the cake and the cookies, we couldn't quite celebrate either the end of a great collaboration.

Beginning right away after Boston, in the

first days after we told the public, we started getting letters and notes. The first mail came to John's Senate office — cards, faxes, letters, e-mails, gifts. It was clear the Senate staff could not add this to their job description, so we released my e-mail address to the public. The first day there were more than a thousand e-mails. By the end of the week there were twenty thousand. I tried reading the e-mails, answering some as I could, but they kept coming too fast for me to have any hope of responding quickly. For much longer than a reasonable person should have, I held on to this pipe dream that it was going to be possible to answer them all as they came in. Among the first I read, to which I responded, was from a woman who, upon hearing that I had breast cancer, had scheduled a mammogram and discovered that she, too, had breast cancer. She started her treatment just weeks after I started mine. That single e-mail was all the reassurance that I needed that we had done the right thing by making a public statement. As I type this today, I am still responding to each one. And the number of e-mails is up to sixty-five thousand.

And then the notes and cards started coming. Tens of thousands. It was daunting, but I started writing notes to people who had sent letters and cards and gifts through the regular mail. The staff worked with me on a form I could send out in response, but it turned out I could not just sign a form letter, not after I read the notes and letters, not after I opened the gifts. Even a card that had been simply purchased and signed was such a tender gesture. As I look over the vast variety of cards, I think of the imagination that went into buying each of them and choosing the exact right one — every one of them as different in their way as people are different — and two or three times there were cards with part of the front cut off, and I think one was a birthday card and I imagined it had been sent by an elderly woman who wanted to reach out right away, so she cut off the "birthday" part of an unused card she had in her desk. I look at the card from the Gilbert family, a get-well card with a teddy bear holding a bouquet of glittery pansies, and it occurs to me that the youngest daughter, Clara, might have picked it out. I recognized some cards, slightly yellowed, as being in the style of the 1930s or 1940s, and I imagined a widower finding a card his wife had saved for all these decades and sending it now to me. Some cards captured all the cards, as Ann Shewcraft's message that *This is the tiny seed of faith that grows into the little act of trust that blossoms into one small and simple prayer then opens into a field of love and healing that completely transforms the landscape of the heart.* That was it, exactly, as described by American Greetings. Each card, each note, was a small gesture, and yet they became — each one and together — transforming. Even if John and Mercedes had left, I wouldn't have been alone in that chemotherapy room. Look at all my company.

So, for as long as I could write — and at one point it became too hard — I signed the letters we had drafted and I wrote a personal note of thanks on the bottom of each. But it was finally too hard, as my hands cramped and my fingers became swollen. A box might have five hundred letters in it, and once I could sign and write notes to two boxes' worth in a day, but I would pay for that. I started on a more sensible regimen of signing, but it was slow, and I was embarrassed that we had printed out all the letters with the same date, in the beginning of February, and then it became April and then May, and I was still writing notes on the bottom of letters dated February 7th. Finally my hand gave out, after about fifteen thousand responses. It was not too long after the surgery when I developed lymphedema, for which I was supposed to avoid repetitive motions — and I had to stop altogether for a time. The only upside was that I didn't worry any longer about that February date. Now I have started again, despite the lymphedema, despite some neuropathy that has dulled the nerves in my right hand, and I will write — as slowly as I need to — for as long as it takes.

Even when I wasn't writing in response to the letters and the e-mails, these strangers who had reached out to me were my companions. I had talked to the press a little. I had early interviews about the breast cancer with Katie Couric and Larry King, trying to encourage women to get the mammogram I had not gotten for too many years and trying to encourage breast cancer patients to participate in these important clinical trials and studies. But after going out once, to the Kennedy Center Honors, in my wig, I pretty much tucked myself into the job of fighting the cancer and being as much of a mother and a wife as I could manage. And answering mail.

It's not that I wanted to crawl in a hole, but it drained me to get dressed up and go out. It was easier to give all of my energy to this fight and my family and not any energy to trying to be a personality or even to being a pulled-together human being. But my companions now were my family, my caregivers at Lombardi Cancer Center, John's devoted staff, the Moores — or, as Jack called them, the Mister Moores — next door, and the tens of thousands of people I did not know whose hands were linked, who were holding me up with letters, cards, candles, and books, with quilts and caps, and with prayer.

I was warmed by the great affection and concern for me in the letters, particularly from cancer survivors. For me as Elizabeth Edwards, yes, but mostly, I think, just for Elizabeth as a woman they would never meet but who now was a sister in something deeply painful and gripping and mysterious. Many — some who wrote in thick black pencil in language plain and fierce on lined paper ripped from notebooks — said they had never written a letter anything like this one before. One woman said she was worn out helping her children with homework and she suddenly just reached for one of their three-hole notebook sheets and began writing to me. I felt graced to have given them the cause or chance to record or transmit what some had held inside for a very long time. It was my fierce and probably stubborn, and definitely naive, ambition to respond to every one. I wrote, and many wrote back. Some people Xeroxed my original handwritten letter and sent a copy with their second note, or third. One man wrote back to say how astonished he was that I even wrote out the envelope, which suggests that the response to him got into the right envelope, for which I am very grateful, since the stacks of letters would sometimes tumble under the weight of a child's hand "helping" me straighten the piles. One woman religiously re-sent a picture of her dog eating a George Bush chew toy. Another sent a different card every week for months. I am overwhelmed with the immensity of the net with which I was provided and overwhelmed with the impossibility of containing it here in a thousand words or two thousand, for it was the seeming endlessness of it that took my breath away, then and now. Henry James wrote in his preface to *Roderick Hudson* that "universally, relations stop nowhere, and the exquisite problem of the artist is eternally but to draw, by a geometry of his own, the circle within which they shall happily appear to" stop. And this will be my problem here. It is impossible to come to terms with the enormity of the net that these people threw out to the floundering me, without reading each line, without imagining each sender. And drawing the circle around those I will share leaves too many who touched me outside it.

There were two kinds of men who wrote, those who treated me as a mother and those who treated me as a daughter, and I was left to guess whether the treatment corresponded to their ages. The women who wrote seemed to convey both an intimacy and a distance. From Montana and New Mexico and Hawaii they wrote "Hello from Montana," "Hello from Hawaii." Some, and this touched me, never even put a return address. Many invited me over to lunch when I was in town, or to use their guest room, and some looked forward to "hearing from you soon," which I think was just an upbeat way of closing and made no demands. Some sweetly apologized for their audacity, as they described it, in writing to me familiarly. The connective tissue of the net they wove for me — and for themselves — was that much stronger because the threads were so different from one another. As they wrote to me, I honestly think they were writing to each other and to all of us.

Their desire to share, which means to give more love, was almost overwhelming. And there was something, too, about the contact that I suspected, and hoped, put their own lives and their own trials onto a larger scale and on a greater stage and helped them understand their dignity and importance and the connected scope of their lives, for they really did share with me, and maybe, knowing that, you can understand how I could not simply sign a form letter in response.

One of the first survivor letters I received was postmarked November 5, 2004, right after my breast cancer was announced. It was addressed to Ms. John Edwards. Washington, D.C. That's all there was on the envelope. Because of a hunch and the special kindness of some unknown person in the United States Post Office, it got to me. Then the letters and e-mails from breast cancer survivors and others — and over 65,000 e-mails — began to pour in. They came from all over my home state of North Carolina, from New York and Los Angeles, from small towns, from farms, from prison inmates, from nuns and rabbis and pastors, from the entire Republican Women's Club of Lake Highland, Texas, from people I had met and people I would never meet, from fathers and brothers and sons, and men like John V., who told my husband what his wife's surgeon had told him, that husbands can become the forgotten patients. Verlene B. was one of the first to write me that breast cancer is a family disease, and she is right. I was soon overwhelmed by the sea of support, or perhaps more literally by the lines cast me when I was still at sea and still coming to terms with what breast cancer might mean to me, to John, and most of all to my children. Five of the many boxes of letters sit across from my desk right now, and every card, note, every line, photograph, drawing, ribbon, and letter, mattered deeply to me and matters still. My gratitude goes to everyone for their tenderness, advice, encouragement, humor, honesty, courage, tears, recipes, and love, and also for the generosity they showed in understanding how right it can sometimes be to be touched by the hand of a stranger. I can only thank a few people and almost at random, but I thank all of you deeply. But for now I send my gratitude to only a few —

 . . . to Joan C. for her recognition that you become a survivor on the day you are diagnosed.

 . . . to Bessie B., who was operated on a few weeks before my own cancer was discovered and who showed her stubborn determination to be a survivor when she placed an exclamation point after her signature.

. . . to Gay Neil W., who said swimming was the best exercise, adding that I probably had a heated pool. I don't, but I'm going to get myself one of those, on Gay Neil's advice.

. . . to Barbara Ann E., who in the midst of her third bout with cancer sent me prayers, and also her sore regrets that her hair loss made her look so much like Dick Cheney.

. . . to Shirley R., who terrified me with warnings about a "cranial prosthesis" until her parenthetic note made it clear she was talking about a wig. (In a letter from Monnie B., I learned that because wigs are indeed considered prosthetic devices and that doctors write prescriptions for them health insurance will cover the cost. Unfortunately I read that one a little too late to do me any good.)

. . . to Sandra W., who at almost sixty continued teaching school when hooked up to an IV, and then, during radiation sessions, made plans to buy a Harley. She had gotten through the surgery fine, but when she made her first visit to the oncologist's office and walked into a room filled with exhausted women in hats or turbans or with their heads bare, she cried for the first time. Bald men, she then announced, listen up. I share your pain and now understand about cold heads and necks.

. . . to Nancy D., who bothered to notice that we shared the same birthday.

. . . to Alan C., who was convinced I had touched lives all across America, and who told John, "I will not go a night without praying for her."

. . . to Pam S., who fought cancer as a single mother of a son with diabetes. In the most grim moments, she believed, as I did, that "the refusal to be a victim matters."

. . . to Sue S., whose mother had breast cancer and who wrote of her concern for Cate.

. . . to Ada C. and Mary C., who each wrote that they could hardly write for crying. I might have taped Mary's closing to John's bathroom mirror — "Your wife is a goddess of knowledge and beauty" — if I wasn't afraid it would get a laugh from a husband of twenty-nine years who has seen a very un-goddess-like me more often than I can count.

. . . to the Bates family, whose note started, "We are not asking for anything."

And then they offered us their thoughts and prayers.

. . . to Jerry H., who had testicular cancer. He wrote that God gives us strength to do the hard things He chooses to lead us through. Personally, I prefer to go around such hard times but I can't always convince Him to see it my way.

. . . to Angela L., whose confidence in a good outcome, was based on the fact that we "military brats safely get through many challenges in our young lives."

. . . to Mark W., who reprised John's campaign call "Hope is on the way." Now I want them to feel the hope we send them.

. . . to Sharon C., whose lump was diagnosed as a ductal carcinoma the size of a peanut M&M — and who now looks at peanut M&Ms in an altogether different light.

. . . to the many who wrote to me as Elizabeth, or Eliz, or even sometimes Liz, and to the many others who with equal kindness addressed me as Mrs. Edwards, and who, some of them women in their eighties and nineties, apologized for having taken the liberty of including me in their prayers.

. . . to Donna R., who sent a fax the day the announcement was made to tell me of a product that had helped her beat long odds. She added, with such perfect honesty, *if someone told me that holding a chicken over my head would cure my cancer, I'd probably try it.*

. . . to Adele C., who gave herself one cry daily and decided it would be in the shower. Although she never allowed herself to cry in front of her children, she admitted that some days she took two showers.

. . . to Margaret D. and the elderly neighbor she had hardly ever spoken to. As Margaret and her husband drove home from the hospital after her surgery and then pulled into their driveway, the neighbor walked up to her and told her that she herself had had a mastectomy forty years before. They hugged each other and they both wept.

. . . to the matter-of-fact and far-stronger-than-she-knows Julie J., who after her own August 2004 diagnosis wrote to say she had just gotten through the chemo, and *I'm a wimp,* she added, *so if I can do it, you certainly can manage.*

. . . to survivor Gina S., who wrote of her friend Rachel, who had been battling a brain tumor, successfully, for fourteen years: "It doesn't define me," said Rachel, "it's just one small part of who I am. I'm not a woman with a brain tumor. I'm Rachel, I'm married to Bill, I'm a counselor, I have green eyes, I like Ethiopian food, and I have a brain tumor."

. . . to Jonell M., a survivor who said that simultaneously it is horrible and it is not that bad.

. . . to Kathy M., who when she numbered the angels along her path named family, friends, doctors, her congregation, prosciutto-and-gruyère pastry pinwheels, and mini-sausage quiche.

. . . to Jan B., who was delighted when her straight hair grew back with an ever so soft lovely curl. But what got her, and it really got her, was that a year later it was back to the same old straight hair. (Jan, at least you got the curls for a year. I got my straight hair back and it was solidly gray to boot.)

. . . to eighty-year-old Shirley H., who called me "dear girl," and to eighty-six-year-old Ival S., who called me "honey."

. . . to thirteen-year-old Jane A., who gave me good advice on how to keep up my spirits. Her mom is a survivor.

. . . to Suzanne K., of my home town of Raleigh, who offered to come play the violin for my children.

. . . to Ray M. and his wife, Courtenay, who was diagnosed with the same cancer as mine on the same day. When he began telling friends about her illness, wonderful people came forward to share their stories of the triumphs against breast cancer. "As I've told my wife since this ordeal began," he wrote, "I feel like I've been going through life under a blanket; breast cancer is so common and I really had no idea."

. . . to Susan M., whose first words to her doctor when she heard her diagnosis were "But my son is five years old!"

. . . to remarkable Robin S., the mother of two disabled children, who when her friends asked, "When does G-d think you've had enough?" after she was diagnosed with breast cancer, answered "that G-d could not prevent my getting cancer but tapped me on the shoulder to find the cancer in time to get treatment and be around to continue to fight for my children."

. . . to Marjorie W., who wrote that when her daughter's fifth-grade teacher was diagnosed with breast cancer, she did not want to tell her students. But then she decided, If Elizabeth Edwards can tell the country that she has breast cancer, I can at least tell my class, and she did, and the children were wonderful.

. . . to Barbara S., who wrote to say we had met at a rally in Ohio on October 24,

2004. She said that she had been wearing a survivor shirt from the Race for the Cure, that I had come up to her and hugged her, and that she had felt a strong special connection.

. . . to an unflappable Mrs. S., who at the time of a bad prognosis thirty-six years before had told her pessimistic doctor point-blank, "I have five children to raise, so forget your prognosis!"

. . . to Jan G., who told her crazy, zany woman friends who all wanted to help to write her letters, which she put in a notebook. "Sometimes at night," she wrote, "when every demon from hell was sitting on my chest telling me I was going to die, I would get up and go read that notebook. Those prayers, scriptures, and heartfelt words brought me comfort and courage. I could hear those women's voices in the words they wrote to me. I will keep that notebook forever." I know just what Jan meant — I have these letters.

. . . to Cheryl S., who has the courage to say that having breast cancer is a good thing, for like so many survivors, her life is better now than it was before.

. . . to Susan N., who wrote to say that when she watched us on television, it pleased her John and I always sat close to each other.

. . . to Kathryn Z., who looked for the bright side when she noted that I would have no shampoo bills for a while (except for John's).

. . . to the high-spirited Cristin C., whose extremely detailed advice about chemotherapy and radiation included "#8: When it comes time for radiation [when they mark the radiation field with permanent blue dots] don't settle for tattoos in an ugly color. I went down to the local tattoo parlor to get some ink the same color as the freckles on my chest and a young woman with enough studs and metal in her face to attract a magnet treated me like I was the most important person on the planet and custom tinted a bottle of tattoo ink for which she refused to accept any payment."

. . . to Krista S., who was right about everything except the most important thing: "I know," she began, "well wishes from total strangers like me can't mean much." And how completely wrong was another well-wisher: "My name is Nancy F. and I'm nobody very important." So many people wrote in the humble and generous spirit of Ginette R.: "I'm pretty sure you won't personally see this e-mail, but I don't care. Prayers travel further than any e-mails."

. . . to Jane R., who seconded what Arthur Ashe believed, that "from what we get, we can make a living; what we give, however, makes a life."

. . . to Marianne J., who encouraged me with her conviction that "if I were a cancer cell and I found myself in YOUR body, I would run like hell for the nearest exit!!!"

. . . to Edward C., who wrote that his late father, who had (but did not die from) throat cancer, used to say that the waiting room at the cancer treatment center was the most spiritual place he had ever been . . . and he'd been to Rome, Assisi, and Canterbury.

. . . to Elysse W. from Manhattan, who wrote that "I did go to St. Patrick's today and light a candle for you. Believe me that's something because I'm Jewish not Catholic. I just felt I needed to do something for you that was more than the norm."

. . . to Lynn L., who had met me years before as an unknown mourner at Oakwood Cemetery, and although a "humanist-agnostic," she promised to pray for Wade whenever she walked by his grave. A promise is a promise, she said, and she followed through and discovered prayer. She wrote to wish me well and to say she had been baptized on May 27, 2001.

. . . to Michael and Christina M., who sent wishes for my recovery, and a picture of their daughter Kaitlin, "because, in our biased opinion, she is simply beautiful."

. . . to Wendy H., who cited Albert Einstein: "There are two ways to live your life," he said. "One is as though nothing is a miracle. The other is as though everything is a miracle."

. . . to Wendy F., whose mother died of breast cancer and who thought it would be a fine idea to have one room in the White House painted pink.

. . . to the Landskroner family, who invoked the healing power of children, and for the blessings understood by Bessie Burke Bennett, who taught first grade for twenty-six years and who, although she and her husband had no children of their own, invited her students — over 1,000 children in all — to spend one grand night each year in a big sleepover at their house.

. . . to Linda S., a former classmate who wrote me as "Mary Beth."

. . . to Steve T., who set a place for me at his family's Thanksgiving dinner. You have no idea how wonderful this made me feel.

. . . to Nancy G., who sent me a glow-in-the-dark rosary that her kids liked when they were little. "I don't know," she wrote, "somehow it's good to have something to hold onto."

. . . to Steve C., who wrote to John and quoted Ralph Waldo Emerson — I do love Emerson — "You can never do a kindness too soon, for you never know how soon it will be too late."

. . . to the so many lovely children who wrote me, seven-year-old Emily F. of Vermont; eight-year-old Brittni L. of Oregon, eleven-year-old Joseph H. of Indiana; eleven-year-old Zoe S. of Texas, who forcefully expressed her dislike of "cookie-cutter politician's wives"; and to three twelve-year-old boys, Gabe H., Taylor P.-A., and Ansel N., in Ms. Fay's class in Madison, Wisconsin, all of whom wrote to say they hoped I would soon feel better.

. . . to Rabbi Hirshel L. Jaffe, who passed on the old Jewish saying that words that come from the heart enter the heart.

. . . to William M. Cox, M.D., who wrote from the Alaskan coast of the Bering Sea, where he was reading mammograms 160 miles from the Russian border.

. . . to Kate P., who wrote eloquently about cancer's double-edged sword of suffering and human connection.

. . . to the undoubtedly glamorous Mary Anne D., who compared chemotherapy's aftermath to a cheap-champagne hangover she once had after a long night in Paris.

. . . to Lawrie C., who sent lines from Proust: "The real voyage of discovery consists not in seeking new landscapes, but in having new eyes, in seeing the universe with the eyes of another, of a hundred others, in seeing the hundred universes that each of them sees."

. . . to Beverly M., who when her radiologist son agreed with the recommendation of a mastectomy, immediately expressed her chief concern: How would she undress in the open dressing rooms at Loehmann's? (Actually, Beverly, I have the answer to that for those with mastectomies or those who are simply shy: instead of underwear, wear a bathing suit.)

. . . to Paula M., whose daughter cut off her own hair and made bangs from it that she placed under her mother's turban.

. . . to Jessica H., whose mother died of breast cancer when she was six, Emma Claire's age.

. . . to Linda T., who answered the question "Why us?" with the hope that everything happens for a reason — and then she gave a good one: "Perhaps our reason is as simple as the fight against breast cancer has been given two new voices."

. . . to well-wishers from London, Rome, Munich, Brussels, from Chartres in France, from Minsk in Belarus, from Mexico City, from American soldiers stationed in Baghdad, from Taiwan, Kuala Lumpur, Mozambique, India, Liberia, Australia, Canada, Senegal, Brazil, Sweden, from Buenos Aires and Patagonia at the tip of South America, from a Maasai warrior in Kenya, from Muslims who offered prayers to Allah for me, and from an Ethiopian who sent me the Lord's Prayer in Amharic. Many thanks to all those who sent good wishes and prayers in Spanish, French, Portuguese, German, and, if I am not mistaken, Chinese.

Among the correspondence I received were special letters from cancer survivors who had also lost a child. I was blessed that they had opened up to me. It broke my heart to hear from Kathy D., who worried so for her ten-year-old son when she was diagnosed. His teachers later told her that he did fine, and she believed Jack and Emma Claire would be fine, too, although she conceded that Cate would probably have a harder time. She spoke of the strength women must have, and how difficult it is to keep some things hidden. Near the end of her warm letter, her heart went out to me for the loss of my son Wade.

Then, as she ministered to me, she added what I knew to be the central fact of her life, "I lost my only son, the real love of my life, on July 31, 2001." Eileen L. survived cancer but had lost her daughter, Elizabeth. Miki G., battling both breast cancer and heart failure, had lost three sons and has no time for anger. Perhaps one's "heart cannot really open until it breaks," she wrote.

Lee, Evelyn F.'s son, died when he was only eight and a half. Survivor Donna Z. lost her son Jeff in a car accident in 1991, and she admitted to what I already knew: "I have bad days, but," she added, "I love to laugh. So did Jeff. What a clown!" How much there was in that simple exclamation point! Josephine G., Ruth D., and Claire K. all won the fight against cancer but lost their sons. Some lost their children to cancer, like survivor Laura P., whose son died at twenty-two. Margaret R. lost her daughter to cancer nine days before I felt the odd shape in my breast; Liz died on October 12, 2004, leaving the sad and beautiful legacy of three daughters of her own. Sandra, the daughter of Walter and Rose S., was almost exactly my age, born six weeks after me. Walter and Rose buried their lovely blonde daughter — they sent me a photograph — after breast cancer took her four months before I found my own. Alex N. died at sixteen from a bone marrow disorder, and Fredi shared this grief at the same time that she offered her good wishes. After the death of her son Quinn, JoAnn K. found the solace I had in the poetry of Edna St. Vincent Millay.

There might have been some who would have quit reading, who would have been overwhelmed by the pain, the grief, the misery. I thought instead of the Chinese parable about the mustard seed. A woman's son dies, and she is inconsolable. She carries his body in her arms to the temple and demands that the priest find a way to restore his life and banish this grief. He will do that, he says, if she will go to all the houses in her village and bring back a mustard seed. She starts to set off, but he stops her. The house in which you find the mustard seed must be a house with no grief. With her son draped across her arms, she goes from house to house. Time and again she finds mustard seeds, but in each house she also finds grief. Finally, exhausted, she returns with her son to the temple. She understands, and she lays his body down. I had already visited these houses, I already knew there was grief. These were not strangers writing me, these were my companions, and

I welcomed their conversation as we walked together.

And there were gifts. I have such a splendid library of books on cancer now. Whenever I got a duplicate book, I would leave one in the waiting room of the clinic with a note that anyone who wanted could take it home. I lived a lifetime believing that the reason the words are in a book is that they be shared, and now I was doing that, because they had been shared with me. When a cap to cover my bald head was too small, I passed it on, and now I have passed on almost all those I wore — and I had a great collection — to the women behind me on this path, saving just a few to remind me of the journey. There were bracelets from Elizabeth and Jenzi, from Donna, Jo, and Helene. There were contributions to breast cancer research groups and clinics. There were contributions to the Wade Edwards Foundation, which runs the learning labs. It is impossible to list them all and impossible to leave any single one out. But the ornaments will hang on my Christmas tree, the quilts will adorn our chairs and beds, the books are on our shelves, and all of those hundreds and hundreds of people who thought to spend a few moments thinking of us will be with us always.

There were two very special gifts. Henry Walentowicz, with whom John and I went to law school, and his beautiful wife, Karina, gave me a rosary they had gotten from Pope John Paul II. I did not know how to accept it, though I wanted to, and I didn't know how to return such a lovely gesture. It sits by my bedside now. The second gift is hardly one gift, but hundreds of gifts — started by a single generous soul. John had a supporter whose screen name on the campaign blog was Lilfroggy. When I was diagnosed, Lilfroggy created a website, PrayersforElizabeth.org, so that people from around the country — around the world, in fact — could have a place to post their best wishes, to send out that thread of support. Those threads made each day easier for me. While I was concentrating on my family and my extended campaign family and the circle of people closest to me, a whole unimaginably large community was forming to hold me up and boost my spirits. Someone told me about the website, and I would visit and read and be cheered. Lilfroggy enlisted Julie Simon, who turned the website into a booklet, which she sent me and that I cherish, a collection of affectionate threads and posts. I read every word. If I felt bad after a restless night, I would find the website, and once I had the book I would read that too, and I would remember how much my success in this battle meant to people I didn't even know. They had seen me briefly on the campaign trail, or, like Ben and Alexander, had seen me on C-SPAN, or had never seen me at all. I think every person who watched me at a town hall in Harrisburg, Pennsylvania, wrote — and mentioned it. I reminded Melody, who wrote of her daughter's second-grade teacher — a compliment I carry with me — and she started her post with the words I would hear throughout: "We are pulling for you."

There were cancer survivors, like Jen and Carol and Pat and Ellen. Maggie is a survivor who wrote, "Cancer has a frightening sound to it but don't let it spook you. It is just a word and words can be changed into other words very quickly. Like 'cancer survivor, cured, no evidence of a recurrence.' " Vickie managed to cheer me up by teasing John, "Hang in there, Elizabeth, and know that people in this country do love, care, and respect you and yeah, your husband, what's-his-name." Shari, Andy, and their two children posted, "You enveloped us and showed us such caring and compassion. Now it's our turn to help you." And Thom reminded me to "lean into the strength you would receive from your family, friends, and thousands of people who have never met you but feel touched by you." And I did. Sherry's confidence would buoy anyone: "The breast cancer is simply another box to check off your list of things you will overcome. Period."

Sonja reminded me just by the act of posting that I was never alone. Marilyn let me know that if I did feel alone, I could call her. Martha told me that she would be asking the Quaker meeting in Columbus, Ohio, to "hold you in the Light," as Quakers say, until you are well again. Brenda sweetly wrote, "May the angels walk with you and keep you safe." They did, and they had names like Sonja and Brenda and Martha and Marilyn.

There was a political bent to some of the postings, but as in the letters, the politics seemed to slip away, but not always. Michelle wrote, "God bless you, Mrs. Edwards. Thoughts and prayers are with you and your family from the blue states and from the red states." Someone with the self-confidence to call himself "Animal" wrote: "I've always liked politics, but John Edwards inspired me to get involved in this year's election. Part of the reason was because of you, Mrs. Edwards. You would always lift us up with your positive message when things were down. We are all here and praying for you." Richard wrote that we need you to get strong again so you can fight for health care for all the women who don't have it. And Kevin wrote that he had voted for Leonard Peltier, the Native American artist and activist, and added, "I wish you a speedy remission of your cancer and may GOD bless you and yours." Casey D. reported that John's message motivated her 103-year-old friend Mammie of Atlanta to vote for the first time in her life. And Caroline L. sweetly wrote that after reading an interview with me in the *New York Times Magazine,* she wanted to make up a bumper sticker that read "Elizabeth Edwards, reason enough!"

Gordon said enough nice things about my campaigning that I felt good before I reached his good wishes on my health: "I have nothing but admiration for you in the way you held yourself during the campaign. You are a down-to-earth, sensible soul. Seeing you on C-SPAN and various talk shows was always a breath of fresh air, never shrill, never partisan, never harsh. Just straightforward, honest, with a quiet dignity and integrity. You have done nothing short of truly elevating political discourse in this society and nation. Thanks for all your service to the country. And may better health and healing find you as you endure this recent setback." If I need a press secretary ever again, I am looking for Gordon.

A lot of people who had not voted for my husband, like Kevin, sent good wishes but also pointed out that we had political differences — and often they wanted to state that right from the start. Dan from Raleigh sent good wishes, but began his e-mail with "I am a Republican." Tommaso and Stacy from Durham started their e-mail to John by announcing, "I did not vote for you," but ended with a prayer that "God heal your bride Elizabeth." I do like being called his bride. Porter described himself as a right-wing blogger and Bush supporter, then said, "When the day is done we all are people and Americans," and sent his warmest wishes. Rachel M. sent a note that wished me well, adding, "I am a diehard Republican — see, we aren't so bad after all."

There were more Democrats, admittedly, who wrote, but despite the fact that most of these people had gotten to know me in a political campaign, there was very little politics, even from those we knew from politics.

Sweet Ashish Patel wrote. Ashish was in high school when I met him, earnest and energetic and smart. Time and again he would reach out to us, with photographs or magazines or something for the children. He made booklets for us with news stories and calendars from the campaign, something the busy staff promised but never had the time to do. He sent a cake once, flowers another time, and he called to tell us when he got into Vanderbilt University. The most important thing Ashish gave us was Ashish himself. It was no surprise to see that he had posted. "Just from meeting you a couple of times," he wrote, "I have no doubt you will get through this. You have become like a part of my family through the campaign trail. All of America is behind you and rooting for you to win this battle."

The theme of family came up over and over. Sapphire wrote, "Your extended family across America is wrapping you up in their arms, hugging you tight, and offering you the strength of millions of well-wishers. All with the same goal in mind . . . to see you beat this easily! Namaste!" Loquatrix wrote what I was feeling, "I became quite fond of you all these last many months.

Quite the extended family you have in this fine country!" And there were people of such naturally good hearts, like Sandy and Joe A., who wrote, "Our thoughts and prayers are with you. I feel like you're part of our family. You have worked so hard this last year. It is now time to rest and take care of yourself. We love you." I was lucky, I knew, to have the loving and supportive family I did, but I was doubly blessed to have this huge circle reaching out and embracing me. And, I hope, my larger "family" made it a little easier on my family at home.

Cate used to call home to check on me and to rib her father that she was the only one in the family with a job. John was devoting a lot of time to caring for me, but I could see he was also restless. We talked about what was next. The people he trusted most called him and talked to him about what was next. He probably tossed and turned at night wondering what in fact was next. And finally we pulled everyone together, and John and I had meetings with the people whose opinions he trusted. At the first meeting, the people who had been so important to John — and to me — in the past, Robert Gordon, who coordinated John's domestic policy agenda; Derek Chollet, who was invaluable on foreign policy; Wendy Button, not just John's speechwriter but a clear thinker; Miles Lackey, who had been John's Senate chief of staff and knew John as well as anyone; David Ginsberg, who was with John longer than anyone; Peter Scher, from the vice presidential campaign, who had been quickly wrapped into our little family; Bruce Reed, the youngest elder statesman and one John trusted completely; and Jennifer Palmieri, who had been John's press secretary in the primary campaign for president and whose wit was matched by her good sense. These people had come into our lives at different times, in different roles, but now we were wrapped up in their lives and, even more so, they were wrapped up in ours.

The meeting was run by Nick Baldick, who had run the primary campaign and who was the most organized no-nonsense person in the room, excluding John. Nick walked through a list of things John might do as John sat and listened to the vocations and avocations he might consider. His expression didn't change. It all sounded too political, too calculating, too mundane, and I could see that he was just as restless in that room as he was when alone thinking about the future. And then Robert Gordon brought up poverty, and it was as if a flame had suddenly been ignited in John. He became so animated, happy, really. To him, all the other ideas had felt like holding patterns that were not so much efforts to accomplish anything real as decent ways of filling the time until he made the decision to run or not to run for office. But the mention of devoting himself to poverty swept away all the other ideas. It felt good and right to him, and to me. It was what he had been talking about in the campaign; it was what he had given time to in the years before he'd had any thought of going into politics. In that moment everyone in the room knew what John would do next. "I want to do something that makes a difference," he said, "and if I never run for office again I will feel great about how I've spent my life." I sat there, my knit cap covering my bald head, and I thought, *This is why I married this man.*

Between the end of chemotherapy in February and the surgery scheduled for March, we went to meet the radiation oncologist at Washington's Sibley Hospital. Since radiation would be five days a week for six or seven weeks, we figured she planned to walk us through the daily routine. But it wasn't what she wanted at all.

Although she was in charge only of the radiation plan, she wanted to change our surgical plan. We had planned for Dr. Smith to do a sentinel node biopsy — testing the most likely lymph node to see if the cancer had migrated. If it was positive for cancer cells, more lymph nodes would be removed; if it was negative, no more would be taken. The radiation oncologist's preference that we initially take more lymph nodes was clearly the most cautious course, but it was caution that came at a very high price. It meant the chance of a lifetime of lymphedema in my right arm, which would limit my activities from then on — and I hadn't missed a side effect yet. For the first time in the process, I felt angry. Admittedly, she was saying something I didn't want to hear, so I am sure that that elevated my reaction. She is a great radiation oncologist, but, I wondered, was she the right one for me? I thought it improper to have tried to undercut the surgeon without at least consulting her, and so I went home and called Dr. Smith. I told her about the conversation, and I made clear to her that I was going to do what she recommended, that I chose her as my surgeon because I trusted her.

The next day, the radiation oncologist called, ostensibly to see how I was doing. I was really frank with her that I didn't think what she had done was right. She said she was just trying to make sure I had the best treatment, which I am certain was her motive, but I explained I didn't like her doing it behind Dr. Smith's back. Our frank conversation allowed us to move on. Honesty and transparency allowed the relationship to find a workable place, where I could have the confidence in her I needed and where she could have the appreciation she deserved for her great skill. In any case, it turned out that the sentinel node biopsy that Dr. Smith performed was positive, and I had to have the lymph nodes out, surgery that I had hoped to avoid.

The procedure was scheduled for March 7th, first thing in the morning, at Massachusetts General Hospital. Lexi Bar, who had worked with us for so many years, made all the arrangements for the trip to Boston, and she even came with us so if there were any problems she could handle them and allow John and Cate, who would both be there, to concentrate on me. I had insisted that John, who had to be in North Carolina that Sunday, stay for the UNC-Duke basketball game at Chapel Hill and fly up to join Cate, Lexi, and me later that night. He demurred, I insisted. Yell for all of us, I said, knowing of course that he wouldn't. He claps, he doesn't yell.

The original plans were for Cate to fly from New York and for me to fly from Washington, and we would meet at Logan Airport in Boston, go to the hotel together, have a late lunch there, and watch the basketball game on television. Everything seemed on track until Cate and I noticed that we were both scheduled to be in the air at tip-off. We called, frantic. No, no, we have to be on the ground, in the room, before The Game starts or we are staying put in New York and Washington until it is over. So the flight schedule was changed, and we arrived before the 4 P.M. tip-off. Cate and Lexi and I sat on a tiny couch in our hotel room and watched the UNC-Duke game.

Here's a secret about the people who work on campaigns: not many of them know much — and way too many know nothing at all — about sports. As much as I love David Ginsberg and Miles Lackey and Matthew Nelson, I don't want to watch basketball with any of them. We are serious fans. Lexi, on the other hand, was great company. A Cornell graduate, she didn't have any uncomfortable basketball allegiances — meaning she didn't cheer for Duke — and she was a sports fan through and through.

The hotel staff had been really sweet — they knew why we were back in Boston — and they left platters of fruit and sodas and water for us, so we wouldn't have to leave the room while we contemplated the upcoming surgery. What it meant for us was that we never had to leave the room during The Game.

Carolina was ahead at halftime, and in the silly way of sports superstitions no one was allowed to change seats. The second-half score was tied when Duke went on a 9–0 tear, and now with 2:45 left in the game, we were down nine points and Duke had all the momentum. The magic of our assigned seating had worn off, so Cate and I changed places. Jawad Williams tipped in a shot, then Raymond Felton caused a turnover and freshman Marvin Williams sank two free throws. Cate and I looked at each other. Not moving again, we said. Sean May converted a three-point play, and suddenly it was 73–71. David Noel stole the ball with thirty seconds to play. We guessed that even John might be yelling. Felton was fouled, and he made his first shot. We were down one. Felton missed his second — but with seconds left, Marvin Williams won the rebound and put it back for the lead. With the free throw he then made, Carolina had scored eleven straight points. Duke's final shots failed, and Carolina won the game. Here we were in a hotel in Boston screaming and yelling. We had a hotel room with a beautiful water view, but the only thing we were looking at was a television screen, and it looked beautiful to us. It was just the surgical preparation I needed, and, we decided, a very good omen.

Early the next morning we went in for the surgery. So much of what I had been through before was private. In the blood testing room, there might have been only one other patient. In the examining rooms I was alone. During my chemotherapy sessions, I rarely saw another patient. Here, however, at this great medical center preparing for surgery, I was getting a lesson too. In the area where I was prepped there were two rows of beds, ten beds at least on each side, with a center aisle. And every bed was occupied. Every bed a story of trial and, we hoped, of triumph. Certainly every bed held the story of a life turned upside down by disease.

After the surgical prep, I was wheeled to another room where the anesthesiologist came in and talked to me. We had a dear friend, Maureen, who is a doctor in Boston, and she knew how persnickety I was about anesthesiologists and how important I thought it was to get the right one. So Maureen got me the anesthesiologist she herself would have used, a warm pillow of a woman who spoke gently and worked her magic. Once she gave me the anesthesia, I was out. Afterward I was asked: Do you remember this about the surgery? Not a bit. Do you remember that about being wheeled in? Not a bit. I remembered none of the surgery. I remembered nothing about the first postoperative hours in recovery either. I awoke in a private room, John reading in a chair, Cate on the small couch.

Barbara came in at some point in my fading in and out of sleep and told us that the margins were clean — she cut enough tissue around the tumor in order to be certain that she had not left cancer cells — and that the sentinel node biopsy had been positive, so she had taken additional lymph nodes, five of which had some minuscule number of cancer cells, and the others were clean. So that was that. We stayed overnight that first night, and we could have stayed the next as well, but there was a 3:00 P.M. flight, and I wanted to be home. Cate flew back to work in New York — although she came to Washington to be with us the next weekend — and almost in a blink, this part of the fight was over.

Heather North had stayed with the children, and I am sure she needed a break by the time we got back, but she didn't really get one. I was wearing a drain so that the waste fluid from the surgery would not collect in my body. It was merely inconvenient, but it did mean that with the surgery and the drain, the children had to keep more distance than they were used to doing, so Heather's work was not done. In a few days, Dr. Warren took out the drain, but apparently I still had some liquid that should have drained. It collected and collected until I was sloshing everywhere I went. Jack, Cate, and I were watching the NCAA basketball tournament on television that weekend, and every time I moved, I would slosh and Cate would look over at me, frowning. "You need to do something about that," she said.

I tried to reach Cliff Hudis in New York; he knew the answer to everything, but he wasn't in, so I did what I had vowed not to do. I got back on to the computer and typed "lumpectomy sloshing" into Google. By the time Cliff called me back, I already knew what it was. I told him I had Googled it. "Googled what?" he asked. "Lumpectomy sloshing." There was a hearty laugh on the other end of the line. He confirmed that the

Internet information was right: it might be uncomfortable and a little embarrassing, but it wasn't a problem. But it was a lot of liquid. By the time Dr. Warren took it out, a few days later, he had to use every syringe in the little examining room, then root through neighboring rooms for more. As side effects go, it was one of the more amusing ones, which only goes to show how cheerless side effects really are.

It was about this point that I put my foot down. Every conceivable test was being scheduled for me. I wanted to be cautious, but I thought I was getting celebrity treatment — more testing, more caution than was reasonable or usual. One day I canceled a series of tests that they were going to do. "I'm just not doing it," I said. "If you give these to everyone, fine. If not, I'm not going to do them." I haven't gotten a thank-you note from my health insurance carrier yet.

The last step in the fight was radiation, every weekday morning at 7:15. If everything went smoothly, I was back home before the children left for school — but that happened only about half the time. Sometimes the machines were slow in warming up, or the card reader that monitors who has come for their radiation was on the fritz. It was always something, but the worst it meant was fifty minutes instead of twenty-five. Who, after all we had been through, could complain about that?

The early-morning radiation sessions gave me the day to do what I needed to do. We had to plan our move back to North Carolina. We had to plan what the days would look like when we got there. Schools. Furniture. Summer camps. Jobs. What were we going to do? We knew John was going to work on poverty and work issues; it was like electricity, powering him, exciting him. He wanted to do three things: something real, something where he could see a policy translated into real terms; something academic, gathering the best minds, some of whom had advised him in the campaign; and something where he could advocate for change, using his skill communicating with people for this cause. I had seen him do this before — when Wade died, and later when he decided to run for the Senate — and I knew that when he set his mind to it, it would happen. He'd done it when I needed this care: he'd moved mountains. I had enough on my plate, but I wanted to be some part of this, even if it was just sitting in on the meetings, watching it unfold.

And that spring, it did unfold. The real program that will make a difference in people's lives is set up. In a rural North Carolina county, a very poor, very black county in the eastern part of the state, where a lot of kids don't go to college, the program College for Everyone has already started providing every high school graduate the chance to go. Those graduates who get into college and agree to work will have their tuition paid for their first year. It will be a demonstration that it can be done. The academic work found an umbrella at a newly created Center on Poverty, Work, and Opportunity at the University of North Carolina. And the advocacy has taken him across the country working on raising the minimum wage and fighting for the rights of workers, particularly service sector workers. This may all seem outside my story, but this is a man who gave me everything he had, just at a time when he had every reason to focus on his own losses. It gives me such pleasure to see him again wrapped up in something positive, something inspiring of his own. So I sat silently — well, mostly silently — and happily through the meetings that took place in our D.C. house. Mornings in radiation, afternoons in meetings on poverty, evenings packing away what we would take to North Carolina. It seemed like life was regaining a cadence.

I would leave the house at 6:30 A.M. and drive over to Sibley Hospital to be there for radiation at 7:00. John stayed home, and while I lay on the radiation table, John was making the children breakfast. At radiation, I saw the same people every morning. A sweet man with a German accent and I were the earliest patients. He'd usually beat me in and be sitting in his black socks, wingtips, and hospital robe by the time I clocked in. We'd talk. If there was a new magazine on my table, I would share it with him, and he would do the same. We didn't have to say many words to feel the connection between us, and we didn't have to name our afflictions or say our names; they were not important. I never knew what kind of cancer he had. I never knew his name. I only knew we were on a journey together, and that was what was important. I finished at the end of May, and his last day, his freedom day as he called it, was to be June 11th.

Toward the end of my treatments, the clinic staff began to suspect that another patient was attempting to get a picture of me for her webpage, a "right-wing blog," they said. I never learned what raised the warning flag and I never knew who the woman was, but as soon as I arrived, a nurse would escort me out of the waiting room

596

into an examining room in the back, and when my radiation session was complete, they would walk me to a side door, avoiding the waiting room. I admit it made me feel good that these people wanted to protect me, even if from nothing more threatening than being photographed during those early hairless mornings. I didn't begrudge her for trying, if she was, to get a photograph, but I was angry that she had cost me the last mornings with my German friend.

I would come in socks, slip-on shoes, sweatpants, and a sweatshirt so that I wouldn't need to change into a robe — the changing time might eat into my get-back-to-the-children time. So I'd go into the radiation room and take off the sweatshirt and the T-shirt bra that since the surgery I had taken to wearing for comfort, and climb up on the table under a radiation machine that looked like the end of a gigantic ballpoint pen. My two technicians were entirely different sizes. Hope Shorter was engaging and warm, and very tall. Barbara Higginbotham was more reserved, but since she was short, she recognized when the height of things was an obstacle, and she always lowered the high table for me. They would circle around me, adjusting the machinery, marking my breasts, taking four times as long for setup as for the actual radiation. We talked some at the beginning and end of my treatments, but while they were working, I left them alone. I sang along to the same piped-in songs every morning. I even took to napping during radiation; they'd have to wake me up to tell me to go home.

Over time, radiation works like the sun, a sun focused on a narrow and tender spot of skin. The doctor had warned of the side effects of burning and blistering, and foolishly I had thought I was finally managing to avoid one. Until the skin on my breast, neck, and underarm started to turn red and blister and pucker. B.A. Farrell, our friend and architect, was driving me back from the beach at night when my first blister broke. In the dark car, I slipped my hand under my shirt and felt the warm liquid. On my fingers was a thin paper of skin. Was that skin? What is the liquid? I couldn't see in the darkness. As close as I am to B.A., I was not going to unbutton my shirt, even in a darkened car. I found a paper napkin and slipped it in over the wet place, while B.A. talked about the new Sunbrella fabrics. It turned out to be a blister, one of a series, where the skin was like the top piece of wet plywood floating above the other layers and ready to peel off at any time. The radiation oncologist with whom I had had such an awkward start was great, giving me the usual topical cream she gave her patients and then even going shopping for a new one she thought might work better. Even with the creams, it was a nuisance and mighty uncomfortable, but the worst, I figured, was over.

Everything had gone well. But, honestly, I think I was prepared for any result. Even an optimist has trouble finding something good in the death of a child. But Wade's death had given me a level of protection: words couldn't hurt, and even the words "You have breast cancer" couldn't hurt so much. Unlike so many women who had to sit stoically and receive the news that their life would not play out as they had planned, I had already had to make that adjustment. Lump in my breast, bump in the road, just things to be dealt with, and we would. It was hard, of course, not so much for me, as for what it meant for my children. It meant the very real chance that I would not be there for them.

As the treatment drew to a close, I was also closing our life in Washington, packing and labeling and throwing out. I packed away some of the gifts I had gotten from strangers and from friends, from supporters of John and supporters of other candidates, from survivors and from the families of those who had lost their fight. One present — one I wear today — encapsulates all of these people, all that I believe about the innumerable, amorphous, wonderful "us." It came from Christine Lavin, a singer-songwriter to whom we had listened for years. I heard her once on NPR — it may have been 1992 — and I did what we all do, I went to the CD store and I said I think they said Christine Lavin. Lavin, could that be right? Can you help me find something by her? From that point she became one of the constants in our family. She is funny and poignant, and she wasn't a stranger to finding grace in an unpretentious gift. I remember reading a liner note somewhere about the pleasure she took when Andrea Marcovicci — whose voice I also love — sang one of her songs. I already liked a woman who would take such pleasure in this.

In the package from Christine was a scarf. I've gotten lots of beautiful scarves, and this is certainly a beautiful scarf, but more wonderful is the story of this scarf. Christine had taken it with her on tour, and she had asked women in her audiences to work on it, to make a little knot tie or knit a little. John and I had seen her sing at the Cat's Cradle in Carrboro once, and as I read her letter, I imagined that scarf making its way through an audience like that Carrboro audience. This scarf was everything I believed in. It was a gesture — not a difficult gesture, but a thoughtful one. It was the counterpart to including the bag boy in the conversation. It was remembering to say hello to the child, not just the adult. It was thanking the referee after the game. It was pulling people in because you believe in the grace a community gives each of us. Anyone who thought to do it, to reach out to others and bring them into this gesture, could have done it, but too few know the blessings a simple gesture actually brings. This scarf is Christine's gift at the same time that it is the gift of all those women whose names I'll never know. And it is, also at the same time, something in which I can literally wrap myself and something in which I can figuratively wrap myself, this huge community of people — spread out among the towns she toured — people who were pulling for me and who believed in the strength of that tiny knot they tied.

CHAPTER 15
HOME

In March, my niece Jordan married her long-time boyfriend Ken. The whole family gathered in Sarasota, and people from the campaign who had known Jordan when she worked in the primaries came as well. Marc Adelman was sitting at one of the tables, and Jack crawled up in the chair next to him. *Hi,* Jack said, maybe a little surprised to see him there. *Are you in my family?* Marc responded, *Well, not exactly.* Almost, but not exactly.

Family is what we make it. The Anania family that includes the Ohio Ananias. The traveling family of the campaign. The young people who shared Thanksgiving with us — the young soldier from Vietnam in 1966 and the campaign workers in 2003. Our closest family includes Wade, who has been dead for more than ten years. Emma Claire, so used to hearing of Wade, lamented once that it was sad that Jack was born too late and never knew Wade. But neither had she. He had just been so much a part of our family that it hadn't occurred to her that she never met him. This Valentine's Day, they released helium balloons to him in heaven. Their idea, not mine. In our family, we talk about Wade and the funny or silly or wonderful things he would do because we have accepted his new place in the family. When I see Emma Claire fly across the yard with grace and speed, I always think how much Wade would have loved to have her acceleration instead of his lumbering gait. When I open Jack's palm and point to the single freckle improbably placed there, we laugh that Wade sent one of the many from his cheeks, just to let us know he was all right. And as Cate watches Emma Claire and Jack cuddle and fight, play and tease, she almost always turns and asks, "Were we like this when we were their ages?" And I almost always say, "Just like that."

Just like that, life has found its cadence again. The cancer seems to be gone. I have yet another set of doctors. We have a new town, well, an old one really, for John and I found land near where we started, near the Chapel Hill church in which we were married. We're back buying flowers at Southern

603

States and ham at Cliff's Meat Market. Back home. The younger children are in school, and in basketball, and soccer, and baseball. Cate is starting law school. The house we are building is nearly done, and I can walk through the shell of it, imagining our lives there, imagining the sounds of the children playing or the *ka-thump ka-thump* of a basketball being dribbled. When I am there alone I can even hear the washer running, so real is the life to which we have been, for a decade, slowly moving.

And I have finished this book. But in the writing of it, so many people came back to me, sat here in this room with me. I know that my father's great gift to me, of reaching out and pulling people toward me, has made this life possible. Because from each one, I have taken something — and I hope that I have also given back — and that something meant that I could weather the next storm. From the first important days with my brother and sister as my constant support, and in each step since. From all of them together I could create a net, a huge safety net that allowed me to climb ahead with the boys on Mt. Fuji, or to protest a war when my father's job was to defend it, or to go out with a fellow in law school who didn't seem to share any of my interests, or to breathe again after Wade died, or to try to have more children with Cate's blessing, or to say, *Yes, you should run* and then to do whatever was asked of me, and finally to keep standing when I heard the words *It's breast cancer.*

It has been easier to do all these things not simply because of my splendid family, not simply because of the Hargraves and Glenns and Sallys in my life, but because everywhere I go, people smile back at me. I am stronger because John Moylan and Ed Smith give me a hug when they see me, but I am also stronger because Edward the mailman smiles, and Sam the bagger at the grocery store smiles. So what this book is, after all, is a shout from up on the tightrope: thank you all. Like the letter my father received forty years later from the crewman aboard the Mercator he flew safely home over the Sea of Japan. I've had a good life, and I just want to thank you for it.

POSTSCRIPT
HOME, FROM
A NEW ANGLE

This was meant to be a very different chapter. The beginning of our new lives, filled with pastures in which the dogs could chase deer before they reached the flower beds, packed with afternoons exploring the woods with the children, and filled with evenings together at our long kitchen table. There would be stories of the next campaign, of course, and of the friends with whom we have reconnected here and across the country. That was what I had hoped to write. And then I broke my rib, and somewhere a snowball fell on an embankment and rolled and rolled until an avalanche took away the thoughts of any truly carefree days for me or for those who love me. And so I write this chapter instead. You have to forgive me that, although so many have reached out to me and deserve to be here, this chapter is a tribute mostly to those closest to me:

606

those with the most to lose from the most recent diagnosis that the breast cancer has spread to my bones and is now classified as incurable.

John and I sat in the car watching Jack's baseball practice. John first sat in the bleachers, but when the sun set, a cold April night had replaced the warm April day, so now we sat together in the semi-warmth of the car facing the field and watching seven- and eight-year-olds practice punching their fists into their gloves and leaning forward onto the toes of their new cleats, their elbows resting on their knees, waiting for the next ground ball. Coach Mitch, the model of the dedicated and serious parent-coach, was throwing the grounders, cheering them on when they handled one, reassuring them when it sped between their legs to the greening grass of the outfield. In one rotation, Jack was playing left field, or rather he was standing at the edge of left field, kicking up dirt and watching the wind carry it. I remembered him doing the same thing last year when Coach Mitch coached Emma Claire and Jack. Jack would be kicking dirt in left field and Emma Claire would be looking for four-leaf clovers in center. I would call out from the bleachers: *Baseball.* Just one word.

Just a reminder about why we were there. I rolled down the window and did it again now for Jack. *Baseball.* Sometimes we all need reminders when we are distracted from the task in front of us.

It was just the previous week that John and I were the ones kicking dirt, trying to put ourselves anywhere except where we were, which was in a small room at UNC Hospital, waiting, huddled, for a bone scan. But that was where we were, waiting for the inevitable crush of bad news from my doctors.

And could it only have been a week before that when John had come home from campaigning and all seemed so well? It had been late when I heard him come in, but I awoke. I lay in bed listening to the sounds to which I have become accustomed over the last thirty years, the sound of his unpacking his bag in the closet, stepping into the shower to rinse off the day, brushing his teeth, padding down the hall to kiss the sleeping children good night. I love those sounds, the comfortable predictability that comes with a long history. Honestly, sometimes I awake as he comes in but fall back asleep before he finishes his ritual. But not tonight. Tonight I turned toward him when he climbed into bed and reached across for me.

Long day? Yes, he answered, how's your

back? I had pulled a muscle in my back the day before, lifting a chest of drawers from behind a row of cardboard boxes in the storage room. I knew better: you lift with your legs not your back, but when you lean to lift — as I had to over the row of boxes in the storage room — you are always using your back. I had felt the pull as soon as I lifted. Stupid me, I had thought. Why had I been so impatient? I should have waited for John to come home, but I had tired of seeing a lamp in the corner on the floor where I planned to have a lamp in the corner on a chest, so I had gone ahead alone. I remember moving into the house last summer. John was traveling, and I had wanted everything to look perfect when he came to the house for the first time. I put away thousands of books, unrolled rugs, made beds, unwrapped and washed dishes. And pulled a muscle in my back. But it was worth it to see his face, get his kiss, when he came in to a house that was the colored-in picture of the house I had carried in my head for months, the picture I had described to him for just as long. The pulled muscle then was uncomfortable but worth it. And now, I suppose, I had done the same thing, on a smaller scale.

It's not too bad, I lied, as he moved toward the warmth on my side of the bed. He laid his head on my shoulder and reached his arm over me to pull me close. As he pulled, I felt a bolt of pain up my back and twisted quickly under his embrace. And then he heard it: a pop, or a crack. A crack, we now know. The next day, Dr. Lee, who had been treating my back, sent me for an X-ray. The rib might be broken. And the following day, he called with the results. A rib on my left side was cracked, he said matter-of-factly. But the X-ray showed something suspicious on the other side, and he wanted me to get a bone scan. I hung up after scheduling the scan, but the thought was already gnawing in my head: what was he looking for? I had promised myself when I was fighting breast cancer two years before that I wouldn't Google any more medical conditions. But I broke that promise to myself. And, again, no good came of it. I called Dr. Lee's frank, smart nurse Ursula and told her what I had found online. They must be looking for cancer. He called right back. I am worried, I told him. He was honest, which I wanted, but his simple words were a dagger: I am worried, too.

John came immediately when I called, even though he was on his way to Indianola, Iowa. I said, "I need you." It was all I had to say. He cancelled an evening campaign event and came back to North Carolina. I have e-mailed with the Iowa family in whose home he was supposed to have had a house party that night, and who had undoubtedly cleaned and prepared snacks for the friends and neighbors who were gathering to listen, preparing to decide — maybe in March — for whom they would caucus for president almost ten months later. The Waltons wouldn't accept my apologies; he was where he should be, they said. I couldn't really disagree. That night, back in North Carolina, John held me sweetly, tenderly, as we each lay awake, each pretending to sleep, each waiting for the morning sun to fill the room, waiting to go to the hospital, waiting to hear the words that were already playing on a loop inside our heads. The cancer is back, the cancer is back, the cancer is back.

Making breakfast for Emma Claire and Jack, packing their lunches, driving them to school, we forced ourselves to stop the loop, to concentrate on the children and the usual morning rituals. *Baseball.* This was the most compelling diversion we could imagine. They had climbed out of the car, loaded their backpacks on their backs and, as they always do, stood together on the sidewalk waving good-bye until we drove around the circle and headed out. As soon as we waved and drove on, the loop started again.

Now we were alone in the small examining room. I'd had an injection that would travel through my bones and illuminate the "hot spots" where cancer might be lurking, and now we sat waiting for the scan itself. A woman on the elevator spoke to me about this book, and I let myself lean into her words about what it had meant to her. I leaned into her words, and into the book and thoughts of all that had happened in the last six months. For a few minutes more, I could be the woman who had won her battle with cancer and lived to write about it. I said hello to *Baseball* and let myself fall into the memory of those halcyon days.

My first book reading was on a warm October night in New York. Could it only have been six months before? Since the end of the 2004 campaign and the end of the breast cancer treatment in Washington, I had been struggling to take off the pounds I had put on during those ordeals. But I had put them on slowly over those two and a half years, and they were coming off only at the same speed. But by the first reading, I had gotten back to a weight where I felt more comfortable. I wasn't through — still am not — but I no longer worried about how I looked. Jennifer Palmieri, whom I had gotten to love in the 2004 primary campaign, and I had gone shopping for some new clothes for the book tour, and the criteria for each purchase was *Is it pretty?* We laughed like teenagers as we stood in stores trying on jackets in the aisle. It wasn't enough for it to fit — when I had weighed more, that was nearly the sole criteria; it wasn't enough that it be stylish. It had to make us feel pretty.

There is a picture of John and me that night that I love because it captures in a frame the thirty years of affection between us. I wore a soft, white, and very pretty new sweater for the first reading, and John sat beside me for a photograph. He was just back from Uganda with the fabulous George Biddle and the International Rescue Committee, and though he was worn out — physically from the travel, emotionally from all George had shared with him about the plight of the Ugandan refugees — he and I had been apart too long, and we couldn't separate. We had talked daily while he was gone, but we needed to touch one another, and the photograph captures that. He was looking at me the way he had thirty years before. For the first time since my hair came back, I felt pretty. Or as pretty as one feels at fifty-seven. Which, if the love of your life is looking at you the way John was looking at me, is very pretty indeed.

Before the reading, I stood in a small back room in the huge bookstore in New York, surrounded by supporters and bookstore managers and student reporters and the young staff who had been with us for so many years. John was by my side. I hadn't done much publicly since the cancer. I had never done a book reading. And this book, as you have seen, exposed me in a way that made me even less certain, naked in a sense. As John and I walked out onto the small stage, I wasn't sure I could do this well, or do it at all. I grabbed for John's hand, and he could feel my anxiety. It has been this way for so long, finding our strength in each other. He leaned over and kissed me. You're going to be great, he whispered. They'll love you. I love you.

We walked out to flashbulbs and applause, back into the light. John sat in the front row and — in a gesture hard for some politicians but not for him — let the light shine entirely on me. I read to the earnest and kind faces in the folding chairs in front of me and in the aisles as far back as I could see. Then there were questions. Questions from breast cancer survivors, from political supporters, and even from Sue Brand Medeiros, who had been a classmate at my high school in Japan almost forty years before, the first of a long list of Zama High School alumni who would show up at readings across the country. At the end of the reading, I started signing books. Most of the people who waited to have their books signed came with their own stories. I didn't stop any of them. Stopping them would have made it seem as if I thought my own story was more important than theirs, and nothing was further from the truth. The line moved slowly as I heard them out, each story tender and heartbreaking in its way.

The line had been crawling forward for about an hour when a slender woman came up, a man beside her; they stood close in that way that only couples stand in relation to one another.

"My name is Fredi," she said. "I was one of the people who wrote you after the breast cancer."

I smiled up at her. "Thank you so much."

"I had breast cancer, too," she continued.

"How are you doing?" I asked, reaching for her hand.

"I am well."

"That's great." I started to look down at the title page, ready to sign her book, but she went on.

"And we have something else in common."

I put down the pen. I knew what it must be. "My son Alex died." She pulled out a picture of a handsome young man dressed in a suit, posed before a row of front-yard bushes.

"I am so sorry." I took the photograph and rubbed my hand across his dark hair and deep smile.

"I picked up your book when we came in," she said, looking over at the man beside her, "and I opened it randomly to page 319. I turned to my husband and noted the page: that's my birthday, March 19." She had scanned down the page and was surprised to see her name. I had mentioned her letter, she told me, on that very page. And I had mentioned Alex. "It was so wonderful to see his name in print, permanently there," she said as her eyes filled with tears. This was exactly why I had included his name, to make his presence among us permanent. We embraced. Ours was the first of many hugs like this on the book tour — and since — and an affirmation that our connections with one another can be slender but important.

Some connections were not slender. I stayed until nearly midnight signing books at Quail Ridge in Raleigh, my bookstore — well, it is not really my bookstore, it is Nancy Olson's, but it is where I shop at home. As the hour got later and later, Nancy stood over me, trying to get me to sign less personally, but as soon as she stepped away, there would be someone in front of me who was dear to me, and I was back to writing a paragraph before signing the book.

It wasn't always that way. In Charlotte, I knew only a few of the people at the signing, but it still took a while to work my way through the line; so many had their heartbreaking stories to share that by the time we left there was a chance we would miss our flight to Atlanta. We asked Mike, the driver of the car the publisher had hired, how long it would take to get to the airport. About an hour at this time of day, he said. And then there will be long security lines. Well, I asked, how long to Atlanta? A few phone calls later, and Mike was driving us to Atlanta. Sam Myers, who had managed advance work for John in 2004, was in the front seat, and Jennifer Palmieri and I spread out in the back. This was, I knew immediately, the best song-singing trio from 2004. We started singing somewhere in South Carolina and didn't stop until Mike pulled in at the hotel in Atlanta sometime after 1 A.M. Periodically as we drove, Mike would check in with his home office in Charlotte. His last call went something like this: "It's raining. It's midnight. We just crossed into Georgia.

And I got three people in the car singing Broadway show tunes."

Everywhere, there were connections. In Washington, D.C., it was a classmate of my aunt's from her 1939 high school class. She had gone to the beauty parlor that day in preparation for my reading and had gathered old photographs of them in Brownsville. A member of my UNC basketball e-mail group — she had joined the group at age sixteen, and although she had been a member for more than ten years, I had never met her — showed up at the Seattle book signing. Wade's English teacher who had retired to the West Coast. Reiko, and Steve, and Freddy, and a half dozen other Zama High School alumni. When I went to Des Moines, Iowa, the hairdresser who thought she had made me cry was there — with her whole family. And we cried again. And it was in Des Moines that a woman leaned over close to me when it was time to sign her book. "I lost my son," she said in a whisper. I thought I might sign the book in his memory, so I asked her his name. She stepped back and paused. A look of panic and grief crossed her face. "I can't say it." I thought of when I could look at the edges of Wade's face in photographs but could not let my eyes rest on his eyes, when the pain was simply too great. This lovely woman before me broke my heart.

As I traveled from city to city, I came to talk about them all, to talk about what they meant to me. We spend our lives weaving a tapestry of sorts. The largest ribbons of color are our family and closest friends. But a tapestry made up of just these people has gaps. The other people we weave into our lives — some only thin threads — are what gives our life its texture and its strength. They fill the gaps in the most amazing ways. Their colors reflect on the ribbons and on us. Weaving them into our tapestry creates for each of us a magnificent, dense, and interesting life. And when life takes a wrong turn — as it will for all of us — that tapestry becomes a blanket that we can wrap around us, or a safety net into which we can fall. As I have so many times.

And as I was again, as John and I sat waiting for the bone scan in March 2007. We sat for what seemed too long a time, and neither one of us wanted to break the silence. All that was on our minds was dark, and conversation about it was impossible, and conversation about anything else was impossible. It was finally time for the bone scan; the infusion had had its time to work its way through my bones. JoAnn Belanger, the nurse who was patient services manager in radiology, came to get us. I got into the obligatory wheelchair and JoAnn pushed me the short distance to the room in which the scan would be performed. John walked beside me, past other patients in the hallway, some with a spouse beside them, some alone, all standing at the edge of the same cliff. We talked to each of them as we passed them. So many recognized John, were happy to see him, hoping, I suspect, that this fortuitous meeting was an auspicious sign. John had already announced a universal health care plan, and — this might only be true in a few places like Chapel Hill where the population pays inordinate attention to politics — several of my fellow patients in that hallway knew about it and spoke of it: we need you, they'd say, we need that plan. They would talk politics to John, and they would all wish me good health. A thread here. A knot there.

The technician in the room where I would get the scan was pregnant; her baby boy was due in July. Maybe that was a good sign, I told myself. As they prepared me — and prepared the giant machine above me — for the scan, she told us about getting into school, about how she had applied late and thought she would have to wait a year, but then at the last minute there was a space for her. A pretty student technician worked at the computer while this young pregnant woman answered our questions about her life. We tried to fall into her story. Tried hard. But it was really *Baseball*. The diversion wasn't really working. Finally it was time for the scan to begin. The room was quiet as the machine started moving over me. A large monitor was in front of the pretty student, and mounted near my head was a small one, on which we could watch a fuzzy outline of my skeleton form as the machine moved down my body. The outline was fuzzy, but the black spots on the skeleton were clear enough. I kept my eyes closed at first, but there was no point. I could hear John pace around the room, I could actually feel his worry. I opened my eyes long enough to see the circle of black on my torso, and I closed them immediately. The machine made several passes over me, and between the passes John would grab for my hand. I opened my eyes again to see the image of my body, the black lines that were the broken rib and the black spots that were cancer. I closed my eyes, slowly this time, and concentrated on John's hand around mine, his pulling my hand up to his mouth, kissing my fingertips. I let my mind drift off, out of this room, out of this hospital, away from this day.

John was holding my hand the same way he had only slightly more than a month ago. With my eyes closed, I could almost pretend it was then, not now. John and I had sat, as we have for so many years, across the table from one another, not cuddling in the way of new lovers, but looking at each other's face in the comfortable way of longtime lovers. The conversation was easy, even the pauses were full — of history and love — after all these years. It was Valentine's Day. I had flown across the country to be with him in California where he was campaigning, and he had made me awfully glad I had. We talked and laughed, and I suppose we must have eaten, too. He'd reach across the table and take my hand and kiss my fingertips in the gentle way he has always had. It seemed, even in this Los Angeles restaurant on a busy night, that we were all alone, and just as in love as on our first Valentine's Day in 1975, when I had been too sick to go out and he brought me hyacinths and sat with me then, too.

But now it was 2007, and we were not really alone. Not in a crowded restaurant on Valentine's Day in Los Angeles, and not at UNC Hospital in Chapel Hill. A young couple came to the table in LA. To see John, I know, but they did not leave before asking about my health. I didn't know I was lying when I said I was fine. And then the couple in the next booth came over. The woman and her friends had been praying for me. The waiter told us about his band. The manager told a story about John Kerry having sat in the same booth a few months before. The circle that had been just the two of us expanded, as it had so many times, to let in those good-hearted people who just wanted to wish us well, just wanted to share a piece of themselves with us. They often apologize: we don't want to bother you, but we wanted to wish you . . . How could we mind that? I am not naïve; not everyone wishes us well, but those people rarely approach us. On that night and again in the hospital, every person was generous. On our way back to our little holding room in the hospital, the faces of the hospital staff, the hands of the patients waiting for their own news, all reached out to us. Anne Lamott writes in *Grace (Eventually)* about her pastor Veronica, who says, brilliantly I think, that people should be able to see Jesus' love in the face of a Christian. I don't know to what god, if any, the people who shared themselves with us prayed, but I was certain that I was seeing God's love as I watched the faces in the hospital hallway as we went back after the bone scan, knowing in our hearts what the black spots on the monitor meant.

It was not long before the radiologist came in. We had never met him before but he had an aura of experience and confidence. There was no sugarcoating in his news. "I have looked at the scan, and we should assume that we are dealing with metastatic disease. The biopsy will confirm it." Not *The biopsy may tell us differently.* He knew better. We knew better.

At some point in the day it seemed that the usual procedure of allowing us a day or two to adjust to each piece of news, after which we'd come back for the next round of tests, was being considered. I admit that the thought of waiting made me panic. I convinced myself I could not make it through a wait. John would have to leave before we knew, I feared. In truth, we had always made it through the things we never thought we could navigate, but to have understood that would have required some distance and I had no distance whatsoever. I told JoAnn, who was sitting in the large room outside the little examining room John and I had commandeered, that I couldn't wait; I wanted Lisa Carey, my oncologist, to come over to radiology — she had clinic in the morning — so that I could make sure that she, too, knew

I couldn't wait. I fell back into the tiny room, back into John's arms, and cried. Between my sobs, I managed to say, "I can't wait. Please tell them it has to be today." He wrapped his arms around me until I calmed down, and then he went out to JoAnn. When he came back, he assured me that we would finish today.

The biopsy that would come next would simply confirm that the cancer was back — well, that the cancer had never really left. I would later describe to our children that the big pieces of breast cancer — in my breast and lymph nodes — were killed by the treatment that I had gotten in Washington but that tiny, almost invisible pieces of the cancer had not been killed. They were so little that we didn't know they were there until they grew a little bigger, and now they had grown, this time in my bones, and now the doctors could see them. On my rib and in my hip. Another primary school explanation — true in its broad outlines and, I hoped, not scary. Not scary the way I was scared. John could not go into the biopsy, so I closed my eyes and my mind again while they drew a sample of the tumor in my bone. Leaving *Baseball,* I thought of Cate instead.

It had only been a couple of weeks since she had come down from Cambridge, where she was in law school. John was gone a lot with the presidential campaign that had started after Christmas, and I missed him even more than I usually did. I got to see him, in an odd way. My brother Jay had a wonderful young man, Peter Cairns, who worked for him, and Peter had begun video-taping the campaign, the events and behind the scenes. We had tried it before, but the process of getting the film from the camera to the Internet — where I, and the public of course, could watch John — took much too long. Peter was a wonder. He was experienced with the camera, which was great, but he was also a wonder with turning it around. John and I had done a health care day in New Hampshire, and Peter came up from New York by train to film it. On the train trip home, Peter had edited the film, creating a tight piece, and then, using his cell phone, forwarded it to my brother. And he was a joy to be around as well — and the perfect silent lens when he was working. But even with Peter's videos going up on the campaign website and on YouTube, I still missed John. Maybe over the past couple of years I had been spoiled by his constant care of me. Whatever it was, Cate could see it, and she came down. She took a few days off from school, and she came to be with me. I urged her to go visit her friends, but she demurred: she could see them later. She had come to be with me. So we shopped and cooked. We watched television and talked about her law school classes. And we played with Emma Claire and Jack, and by the time she left, I was rejuvenated. By her generosity and love. Once during her visit, her boyfriend, Trevor, called when we were cooking. After a minute, I took the phone.

"Hello, Mrs. Edwards," he said, with a trace of nervousness.

"I just hope you know," I told him, "that you are incredibly lucky to have Cate."

"I do know that," he said, and I believe he does know. How could he not?

I had called Trevor the afternoon before John and I went to the hospital. John was not yet back from Iowa, but I knew when he came that we would call Cate. And I knew that after Cate talked to us, she would call Trevor. So I called Trevor in the afternoon to tell him what was happening with the bone scan and the likely recurrence of the cancer. Trevor was a third-year medical student at Georgetown; he had kept John and me company during my chemotherapy there two years before. I had to go to the hospital the next day, and I couldn't take care of Cate the way she had taken care of me when I needed her a couple weeks earlier. But Trevor could take care of her. We were lucky: Trevor could.

The biopsy was over. Banish thoughts of beautiful Cate, of sweet Trevor. Time for *Baseball*. And the biopsy results showed precisely what the radiologist had said they would: the cancer was in my bones.

The time after the biopsy was the worst. It would be followed by a CT scan, which would look at my soft tissue and organs to see where else the cancer had surfaced. What was the likelihood, John and I each wondered silently, that it had reappeared in more than one place in my bones but nowhere in my organs? I couldn't say it aloud; maybe he hadn't thought of it that way. He couldn't say it aloud; maybe I hadn't thought of it that way. While we waited for Lisa Carey to come over from the clinic, we simply held on to each other. John stroked my face, in love and in fear. It was impossible to look right at him and impossible not to try to soak in every bit of his face, his eyes, his hairline — untameable, like Wade's — in the time I had with him. It is hard to describe the test of public life, the way people believe — to some degree correctly — that you belong to them. There are awful examples, of course, of those whose motives are selfish or not admirable, who pry their way into the lives of public people in order to exploit a kindness or a generous gesture. They are to be endured and, to some extent I largely chose to ignore, feared. They remind me of a more malicious version of the people who wandered into our house in Annapolis, walking around our living room, putting their hands on our things. It is a sad fact that these people are a threat to anyone with even the smallest amount of celebrity.

But most of the examples of people to whom you belong are like the nurses around us or the people in the restaurant in LA or the earnest campaign staff. They actually care about us, or they care about the same things we care about, about what we work for and dream for, and they are happy to be a part of making the dream come true. And it was these people who were around us now. Matthew Nelson and John Davis from the campaign, young men with whom we nearly lived every single day, came to the hospital to help. They placed calls, first to Cate — who was as strong as she has always been, a complete joy and marvel to us both as we talked to her about what we were learning — and to our parents so we could let them know what was happening. And we let Matthew and John in, of course, because they are as much a part of our lives as we are of theirs. But first, for a few minutes, it was just John and me.

In perhaps far too many words, I have written about the ways in which my incredible life has been possible only because of the people who have reached out for me along the way. And nothing could be more true. But for a moment, I want also to say a little about this man I was so fortunate to marry nearly thirty years ago. As we sat in that room, he took my hand in his, and his fingers spun the $11.00 wedding ring on my finger. He watched it turn, and I spoke first.

"It's been a long journey."

"It's not over," he answered, but he didn't, couldn't, look at me at first. His fingers just turned the ring around and around. Then he lifted his face, and his eyes found mine. "Will you marry me again?" he asked. "This summer, on our anniversary, will you marry me again?" We had talked about renewing our vows, but this wasn't that same idle conversation. This was urgent, pleading, and full of love. A real proposal.

"Can you take thirty more years?" I asked, knowing it was somewhere beyond reason to say such a thing.

"More than you know," he said.

"Yes," I said, "I will marry you again."

No marriage is perfect because no person is perfect. It is not to be whispered in the political world where all the rough edges of life are sanded away, where every marriage is presented as perfect, flawless, but the exercise of sanding away the edges has always been a waste of time: who really doubts imperfection in the real world? John and I have been married thirty years, and we have argued, we have disagreed about the children and about jobs, about how long it takes to put away the Christmas ornaments, about why he insists on going for a run at dinnertime. Rarely, but from time to time, we have been disappointed in one another, because that is the true nature of real intimacy and mutual dependence. Your ability to be vulnerable to another person is a measure of the degree to which you are truly intertwined. This wasn't meant to be a love story, but it is impossible to be honest without saying how much we needed each other, how much we leaned into a history of being totally intertwined — emotionally, intellectually, physically. The inconsequential bumps that tested us, those little disappointments, when laid next to the harder chasms we faced together, faded away entirely. In the end, and I prayed this was not the end, enduring love, respect, and the decency of a person, the core of who they are in the hardest moments, are what matter. And we had seen the hardest moments together. I had seen his goodness when everything else was stripped away. In the awful times we had survived, when pride and prestige had gone, when there was no mask left at all, I saw the man beside me as honorable and humble and compassionate. I would not have chosen any other companion, not for my lifetime and not for this terrible moment.

I was stronger when he was with me. He had left the room after the biopsy results came back, when the nurses came in to insert the IV that I would need for the CT scan. They talked about how much they admired him, how glad they were that he was running for president. I listened to them talk about how strong he was on health care, and I suppose I started to crumble. I might have held it together if he had been there, but without him my thoughts went dark. He had to keep running, I thought. The nurses might have thought that the IV was painful. It was not. My tears were from panic at the thought that this cancer might take him out of the race; that the patients in the hall who had thanked him for fighting for health care, and the nurses who had for years seen him as their champion, and the people I had met in 2003 and 2004 who cried on my shoulder would not have his strength, his determination. It might have seemed odd to someone who had not spent years in this fight, but this was his life and mine, a life we had purposefully chosen, a life for which we had sacrificed already. It wasn't just the unknown number of my remaining years that hung in the balance here, it was also our life's work.

When the nurses were through, they left and John came back in, thanking them, but his eyes were locked on the panic in my face.

"What do you need?"

"I need to know my children will be protected. I need to know you are going to be happy. And I need to believe that our country will have the chance to be led by you, that those people in the hall will always get what they need."

The CT scan I was about to have could take away all those things. I knew. He knew. So we didn't talk. Matthew and John Davis came back into the room and we talked of politics and the campaign, of the people with whom we would need to meet after the day's testing, and they were the sweetest versions of efficiency imaginable. As John and I held on to each other in front of them, you could almost see their hearts break for both of us — for the years I would surely lose, and for the woman John would surely bury.

John and I were later asked whether we were in denial when we spoke publicly about the cancer. We were not. We are not. I will die much sooner than I want to. I will leave a splendid man and an amazing young daughter with yet another casket to choose, another funeral to attend when they place me in the ground next to Wade, and I will not be able to hold them and comfort them. And I will leave two magical children whom I love with all my being too early. Jack asked me who would be the grandmother of his children. How could I answer? I tried to speak, but the truth was that unless there is a breakthrough or unless I finally draw the long straw, I will not see the birth of his children. I know all these truths. They stomped into the hospital room that day, and they never really left. They are now our constant companions. But I am not letting them sit at the grown-ups' table. Those truths are ill-behaved, they don't know when to speak and when to be silent, and so they have to sit at the children's table in the next room. I go and sit with them periodically; I need to let go periodically. I let them yell at me about death for a few minutes so that I don't yell at me about death all the time.

After the CT scan, we waited for the results. And waited. And waited. I don't know now how long it was; it must have been three hours but it felt like six. JoAnn, strong and warm, kept assuring us that they just wanted to be thorough as they went through the scans. But I didn't believe her. I believed those boisterous truths who had moved in with us. We were sure it was taking so long because the metastasis was so widespread. JoAnn would look me in the face with her hands on my shoulders and say over and over, they are just being careful. I listened, but I didn't hear her, wouldn't hear her. The voices of the truths were too loud.

There was no diversion, there was only mounting fear. We had come to the hospital ten hours earlier, and the news just kept getting worse with each test result. I had to get out.

"I am leaving," I said. "I can't wait for the scans, I can't wait for Lisa. I need to get out of here. It is whatever it is, and my waiting here won't change that. I want to go home. I can't stay here. I can't stand it another minute."

I don't know whether I would have left. John knew we should stay but he didn't want to see me fall apart. And I was falling apart. We cleaned up the little room in which we'd waited, in which John and the boys had had lunch. John moved a little slowly, I suspect to give the doctors a chance to appear. And, as he had hoped, Lisa Carey finally came in.

Lisa is beautiful, like the movie version of an oncologist, and she is measured and precise. She sat before us and spoke slowly and carefully. "We have been through all the scans. There were some small spots in your lung. They could be cancer, but in truth they could be a lot of other things. As you know," she said — because I had had benign spots before — "most people have some spots in their lungs. If I had seen them without this bone scan, I would have told you to come back in six months and we would check your lung again." *That is good,* I thought, *careful Lisa is not alarmed.* But the alarm bell was still going off in my head. I waited for the guillotine to drop, waited for the list of places in my body that were not capable of being swept under the rug. She paused, and our breathing stopped. The pause went on too long. John and I gripped each other's hands. This was where Lisa was supposed to say that the scan had lit up like a Christmas tree with recurrences.

Instead she said, "That's it." That's all there was. There was still no way to know how aggressive the metastasized cancer was; there was still no way to know the length of prognosis. But we felt as if an immediate death sentence had been lifted. In a world that is far too relative, this was perhaps the most relative moment of all: the cancer had metastasized, but not as badly as we had feared, so we were nearly jubilant. I felt like turning to the Noisy Truths that had been screaming at us: "See? You can go home now." Of course, they couldn't. The death sentence was still there. Lisa went over the likely treatments, none of which sounded nearly as difficult as the first treatment I'd had for the breast cancer in 2004 and 2005.

I turned to John. "I want to see the children, and I want you to continue the campaign."

John turned to Lisa. "Can Elizabeth physically handle the campaign? Is there any reason that campaigning would be bad for her?"

"No," Lisa answered right away. Then she looked at me and, with a sly smile, whispered, "Do you want me to say you shouldn't?"

"No," I told her, "I want to continue."

We hugged Lisa and JoAnn. I thought about how hard I had been on them, how I wouldn't listen, couldn't listen, didn't want to wait, didn't want to stay, and how, despite my being impossible, they had hung in with me. And how, undoubtedly, they would do the same thing tomorrow as another woman watched the end of her life slipping out of her grasp. So I hugged them tightly again, and our new family — or our old family with our new reality — went home. We now knew the devil we faced, and, though there was no doubt that the devil held the best hand in the long run, we had not yet lost to it. All things seemed possible.

We called Cate on the way home. She wanted to come down from Cambridge. We'll figure it out, we told her, as we pulled up to the house. The younger children were waiting for us, dressed in cleats for their soccer practice. Could we come to their practice? Not today, we told them, because we have a meeting here in a little bit. There were a few minutes of normalcy — water bottles and folders from school, complaints about what I had packed for their lunches, and reports on a field trip. They left, but the warmth of their presence still filled us up, and we had to remind ourselves: *Baseball.* The task in front of us was telling a nervous, concerned campaign staff and the world what we had found out, and what we had chosen to do.

We gathered those closest to us on the campaign at the house and on the phone. David Bonior, who headed the campaign, sat quietly to one side of me. Harrison Hickman and Jonathan Prince were nearer to John. Jennifer Palmieri and Christina Reynolds were around me. I had known Jennifer for five years and Christina for almost ten, and I loved them both. I could feel their love for me, too. As we waited for the group to gather, the "girls" talked, taking the opportunity to let our hands fall on one another's shoulder or thigh, talking of anything except the topic for which we were gathered. We had material: Christina's shoes — unisex suede slip-ons — clearly did not qualify as pretty. Jennifer and I promised to take her shopping with us.

When the room was full, John told everyone what we had learned and what we had decided to do. It was easier for these people who had worked beside me to look at John as he talked; no one knew exactly what to do with me. I watched John too, because in my peripheral vision I could see people wipe their eyes discreetly. I had had my crying time; they had not.

We would have a press conference, John told them. People should be able to ask questions and see Elizabeth. The decision to continue would seem more logical if people could see that — as they say — you wouldn't know I was sick unless you knew I was sick. The mood changed from grief to purpose when the conversation opened up. Those we had gathered discussed when the press conference could be. As soon as possible, they advised. We needed time to call our extended families, we said. They shouldn't hear this first on television. It would be the next day. Then the conversation moved to where it could be. When it was finally decided that the event would be at the Carolina Inn, it felt just right. That was where John and I had had our wedding reception.

In the intervening hours, what seemed like a reasonable decision — to announce in person, to answer questions — became part of a completely unreasonable media frenzy. We were protected in part because the press has the campaign phone number and not ours. We finally turned off the television and spent a normal evening walking the long driveway, playing catch in the backyard, listening to the children read. We made plans for the younger children and me to go to Cambridge the following day to see Cate. The children would stay the weekend, and I would head with John to California.

This time it was different. This time *Baseball* did not mean getting back to thinking about cancer. This time *Baseball* meant getting back to living our lives. It didn't happen right away. Right away was continued frenzy. The press conference the next day, at which John and I spoke and then Lisa, reluctantly, spoke, was played and replayed endlessly, accompanied by a national debate — can you imagine? — about our decision to continue living our lives. It was, we knew, part of the public-figure bargain we had struck.

The only part of the debate that was troublesome — and I think it must be so for everyone who faces death when they have young children — was Emma Claire and Jack. I came home last night from a one-night, two-day trip away from them. John was still gone. So the children slept with me. There wasn't much sleep for the mother in the middle, but I wouldn't have traded it, Emma Claire's hand on my arm, then her leg across mine, Jack with his head nestled against my neck, periodically waking and giving me a kiss. But our internal debate about Emma Claire and Jack and campaigning did not start with the diagnosis; it started with the decision to run for president. In 2003, we could take the children with us more readily, but by the fall of 2007, they would be in fourth grade and second grade, and missing school would not work for them. Dick and Jane Gephardt and their children basically relocated to Iowa in 1988 when Dick ran, and I suspect it was less a political decision than a personal one, so their dearest relationships would not suffer. We had talked about that in December: Iowa has a great public school system, it could be home base for us for the year. Or we could homeschool them and they could travel with us. But as with so many decisions that don't seem to have urgency, we had talked but not decided. Now it was time to decide. When Wade had died, it had given us great peace that we had no regrets about the way we had raised him, the love we had shown him, the time we spent with him. We hadn't spent every minute with him; few parents can. And in fact, John had tried cases across North Carolina, and he had been gone sometimes for weeks helping families who needed his strong voice against an insurance company that would not accept responsibility or a corporation that had put profit before its employees' or customers' well-being. As we watched our older children grow, we could see them adopt, in subtle — and sometimes not so subtle — ways, the sense that certain people unfairly got the short end of the stick. Wade would stand up for a boy who was being bullied. Cate withdrew from friends who were elitist, and she eventually decided to go to law school so she could practice public interest law. Even in John's absence, they had learned from him what was important. The same way, I think, that the Gephardt children learned the importance of public service: by living with it. And that is what we had decided: that part of parenting is showing by example the things you value and hope they will value. Even if there is some small measure of rationalization in that — and I admit that there could be — there is also a large measure of truth. So John and I settled on taking the children with us beginning in the fall of 2007. I could homeschool them in language arts — which I had expected to teach before I went to law school — and social studies; we would hire someone to tutor them in math and science, for although I know fourth-grade math, I do not know how to teach someone else fourth-grade math. In my spare time at the computer — which is to say when I have insomnia — I am already mapping out museums and caves and aquariums on our expected paths. My own history, played out across continents, has made me understand the wider world in a way that even the books I so loved never could. I have begun to think of this imperative as a gift.

Cancer as a gift is something that I read about, as my cancer community — and we are all connected — struggles to see the silver lining. The gift is an appreciation of our own mortality and therefore an increased appreciation of the days we have. We would trade it all for the peace of good health, but I can watch my husband comb my boy's hair, or I can listen to Emma Claire sing the words on a birthday card she received first to the tune of "O, Christmas Tree" and then in rap, and then listen again and again, and I can see Cate's number come up on the telephone and feel a little explosion of happiness inside me. And maybe I would have felt all the same ways, but I think that at the very least I feel these small joys more keenly. John and I were going our separate ways for a week after the South Carolina Democratic Convention. We walked out from the crowds and the cameras together, and I turned and said, "This is where we split." He wrapped me up in his arms, we kissed, and we each put our hands on our hearts. We have always done it; it just hasn't always meant as much. *How much of my remaining life is that week?* When I turned to go to the waiting car, there was yet another bank of cameras, clicking away. "Give us a break," I pleaded. But by the time I was home, our private moment was on the Internet.

Our children learn something from our

644

choice to live. They will have struggles, I know, struggles from which I cannot protect them, struggles after I am gone. And when they come, our children will remember how their family, how we, chose to handle hardship. I want them to say, "We did not give in to hardship. We did not let it take away our lives or the meaning of our lives." If they learn that lesson, then we will have made the perfect parenting choice. But no one ever knows, do they? We each do our best. And those of us facing diagnoses like mine try even harder to do the right thing, because there is a good chance we are not going to get a do-over.

I have, again, received magnificent letters and e-mails, and again I want to focus on a single gift, a box of paper cranes from D. Sidhe in Washington State. When I was living in Iwakuni, Japan, my mother would take us to the town and to Kikko Park on festival days — and there are many in Japan. To get there we would walk across the spectacular wooden five-hump Kintai Bridge — once used only by samurai. Even at ten, I knew this bridge was special. It was magnificent when there was no one crossing, and it was enchanting on festival days when it would be bright with Japanese girls and women in their traditional dress, and men and boys mostly in Westernized starched white shirts over loose trousers and getas. The park was edged with elaborate temples, but for children like Jay and Nancy and me, the temples were hardly there; we were enchanted by the vendors, some in plain carts with the fantastic aroma of simmering clams or shrimp encircling them, some kneeling beside ornate carts with their wares dangling from pagoda-like roofs, some with their bright merchandise on a yard of silk spread on the ground. My brother would run to find the man squatting behind the collection of fireworks spread out on a swept patch of dirt. Each time Jay would ask Mother for the big rocket-shaped flares standing upright in front of the little man, and each time she would allow Jay to buy only the crackerballs, pea-size balls of powder wrapped in lovely paper that exploded in a small puff with a loud noise when they were thrown to the pavement. They cost five yen — or about one and half cents — for ten, and he could fill his pockets for a quarter. Nancy and I picked out a pretty notebook with an ornamental string tie or a comb case wrapped in hand-made paper, but — like Jay's rocket fireworks — we never got what we really wanted: the thousand cranes, the wonderful origami paper cranes hung on a dozen strings, one crane below another.

Nancy and I knew the story of the thousand cranes, and how if you folded all one thousand you would get your wish. I've read *Sadako and the Thousand Cranes* to my children, but long before it was a book, it was a story that the children of Iwakuni — only thirty miles from Hiroshima — all knew. Sadako was a toddler in Hiroshima when the atomic bomb was dropped, killing a third of the city's population. A decade later the child, who appeared to have been spared, was diagnosed with leukemia, a result of her radiation exposure. She began folding paper cranes and praying for recovery. Although her mother later said she had finished what she began, the story I heard then has stayed with me — and I like it more: she *didn't* finish, but her devoted classmates folded the remainder of Sadako's cranes, and she was buried with one thousand paper cranes, her own and theirs for her. A Children's Monument was placed in Hiroshima's Peace Park in 1958, while we lived nearby. My mother never let us go to the museum in Hiroshima that displayed the horrors of the atomic bomb. It was a symbol of the madness of man. She thought we would never forget it if we did. Instead she took us to the Children's

Monument with Sadako and her crane atop the memorial. It was a symbol of goodness and hope. And we never forgot that. And now, from D. Sidhe, comes a box of one thousand cranes, the ones I wished for at eight, the ones I told my children as I read meant hope and health, the ones D. Sidhe sent me. My thousand cranes.

I wrote earlier that I could not reconcile the death of Wade with a God who would choose to intervene. I have been criticized — perhaps by people who would have criticized any Democratic spouse no matter what — for saying that the wind that swept Wade's car from the road was a metaphor for the hand of God. But any reading of the Book of Job would say the same thing. Satan provokes the Lord to touch His hand against His devoted servant Job and test his devotion. Job learns of the test with these terrible words: "Your sons and daughters were eating and drinking wine in their eldest brother's house; and behold, a great wind came across the wilderness, and struck the four corners of the house, and it fell upon the young people, and they are dead." I don't think God reached out his hand and struck Wade. But I know He did not stop the wind from blowing or the car from flipping or the boy from

dying. And I know that He will not stop me
— or any of us — from dying. He will, however, if we ask Him, give us strength to face
whatever is before us. I have asked for that,
and He has sent me you, all the friends and
strangers, all the people in ropelines and air-
ports and grocery stores who smile when
they see me, or cry when they see me, but always who hug me; Lonnie in Las Vegas and
Bob in Orangeburg; S.C. from my Secret
Service detail in 2004 who came to see me;
Sue Haney who greets me with a smile at
every hospital visit; the young people —
Heather, Jed, Katy, Kat, Kathleen, Matthew,
John, Christina, Jennifer, Pauly — a list too
long of those who make my life then and
particularly now not only easier but possible;
my old friends — Glenn and Sally and Hargrave and Tricia, Tammy and Lynn and
Chris, Gwynn and Ellan — for whom there
is less time and they patiently wait; Theresa,
who lets me pile on my grief and complaints
on her and lets me walk out somehow
stronger; Lisa and Cliff and Eric and Nancy
and Don, who lent me their brilliance and
let me break down when I needed to.

And He sent me my family. My brother
Jay, who has been as strong and steadfast
and loving as any brother could be, and his
special wife, Jackie, who has never be-

grudged a panicked late-night call from me. My sister Nancy, who faced her own struggles and still had more to give to our family, to our parents in particular; it makes me nervous, honestly, that I follow this fine, funny, warm, warm woman as their caretaker, for I know I cannot measure up. My parents and John's, who have to watch from the sidelines with their hearts aching, but never show it. How hard must that be? And Emma Claire and Jack, who make the days or years I have left so full of joy and purpose, who make me smile when I don't want to because they deserve the smile, they deserve the memory of the smile. I was crying the other day — alone, I thought — and Emma Claire and Jack came in. They both came to me and hugged me.

"Why are you sad?" Jack asked.

"I just am," I said. "I'll be fine in a minute."

"Is it us?" Emma Claire asked.

I pushed the tears aside. "No, oh no, my sweetheart." How could I let them ever be left with such thoughts? "I think I just wanted to make some brownies. Anyone want to make brownies?" I doubt the non sequitur worked on them, but they skipped off to the kitchen for brownie-making, and I resolved then that the days I have left with them will be days of joy and laughter and brownie-making. There will be no other kind.

If I said I knew what to do about making this easier for Cate, my precious gift, I would be lying to you, and I have been honest here. Cate, however, has always seemed to know intuitively what to do to make things easier for me. Maybe whatever I had to give to Cate I gave a long time ago. I don't worry about her, because she could not possibly be more splendid. And now I only worry about time. I want God to give us time. Time I want with her, time I think she wants with me. We are fitting it in. I just don't want either of us to feel shortchanged when the last day comes, although as I type those words I realize how ridiculous that wish is: of course we will feel shortchanged. Maybe I should say instead that I want her to survive and thrive when the part of her grapevine that is entwined with mine is pulled apart. I want her to hold on to pieces of my vine, and I know she will.

And John. It is like the letter I wrote to Wade and placed in his casket. *You know.* I could have married several men — an embarrassing number, actually — but I never considered it because I was certain I would know when the right life-mate came along.

Well, I met John and I didn't know. But I came to know, came to love, came to grow with John and beside John and in John, and John in me. And I believe that when I have needed strength, God lent me John. When I need understanding, God lent me John. When I was imperfect and needed to be loved nonetheless, God lent me John. And when I do die, it is John who will keep fighting for all the things about which we have cared so deeply. Will he decide to throw out the carefully marked boxes that go with the Hallmark ornaments? Probably. If he can find them in the attic. Will he decide that there are too many markers in the drawer in the project room? Surely. Will he decide we have too many books? I hope not. But more important, will he stop fighting for equality and opportunity and respect for each of us? That would break my heart. Will he stop caring about the single mothers he saw at the self-help center in Madison, or the children trying to go to school squatting on mats in a dusty market square in Delhi? He can't. It is one of the reasons we cannot stop now, while I live; it would give him permission to stop when I die.

I keep waiting to learn the way this story ends. There is no real end, I suppose, for like each of us, I start each day with the hope that it will be good and full, and I end each day with a prayer for another day like the one I just had, and one day . . . one day for each of us, there simply is not another day. My dear friend Wendy Button, whom I love, sent me *Collected Poems* by Jane Kenyon. She was New Hampshire's poet laureate when she died from leukemia in 1995. One of Jane's poems is — like Nancy Olson's bookstore — my poem now, too.

OTHERWISE

I got out of bed
on two strong legs.
It might have been
otherwise. I ate
cereal, sweet
milk, ripe, flawless
peach. It might
have been otherwise.
I took the dog uphill
to the birch wood.
All morning I did
the work I love.

At noon I lay down
with my mate. It might
have been otherwise.
We ate dinner together

at a table with silver
candlesticks. It might
have been otherwise.
I slept in a bed
in a room with paintings
on the walls, and
planned another day
just like this day.
But one day, I know,
it will be otherwise.

ACKNOWLEDGMENTS

The note I wrote to Wade that I placed in his casket said only You know. And it is the note I send to each of you who helped me and touched me and laughed with me or cried, who climbed or fell with me. You know. The great impossibility of this book has been that I cannot stop thinking of each of you and how much you have meant to me, and how much this life — and certainly this book — would not have been possible without you. It was hard in the writing not to include every one of you and nearly impossible here not to thank you, each of you. But I will reluctantly conform to convention and thank by name those who have made the actual writing of this book possible.

I came to this process a neophyte and was fortunate to find just the professional guidance I needed from Bob Barnett, who placed me in the hands of Doubleday Broadway and an editor, Stacy Creamer, who believed in me and in this story and made the experience as easy as an editor possibly could. This book is clearly better because Stacy read it before you did. And I was lucky that Stacy had such an incredible supporting cast, David Drake and Laura Swerdloff, in particular. I was fortunate in the first days to have the skill and vision of Aimee Molloy and throughout to have the wisdom and kindness of my longtime friend John Auchard, both of whom helped me find a shape for the book. I pressed into service those to whom I so often have turned in the past: Brad Anderson, Alexis Bar, Jan Bolinger, Saundra Daddio, Guy Decker, John Dervin, Dan Doherty, Karen Finney, Randy Galvin, David Ginsberg, Martha Hartmann-Harlan, Eileen Kotecki, Miles Lackey, Hargrave McElroy, Kathleen McGlynn, Ryan Montoya, Sam Myers, Jennifer Palmieri, Jonathan Prince, Christina Reynolds, Kim Rubey, John Schoo, Meghan Scott, Gayle Steele, and Colin van Ostern. They have never once let me down.

There were some without whom this book might never have been written for they made the physical pulling of the pieces together possible, including Heather North, Lisa Carey, Andrew Young, Martina Young, Lori Krause, and Matthew Nelson. There are those, too, whose constant support and love made these pages better, including Glenn Bergenfield and Sally Plyler.

And my family. When I bare my life, I know I bare theirs, too. They haven't just been gracious about that, they have been my best cheerleaders and my most honest critics. My thanks and my love to my brother Jay and my sister Nancy, to Mom and Dad, to my beloved John and my precious Cate. This is your book, too. You know.

ABOUT THE AUTHOR

Elizabeth Edwards, a lawyer, has worked for the North Carolina Attorney General's Office and at the law firm Merriman, Nichols, and Crampton in Raleigh, and she has also taught legal writing as an adjunct instructor at the law school of the University of North Carolina. She lives in Chapel Hill, North Carolina.